ACCESS TO JUSTICE FOR VULNERABLE AND ENERGY-POOR CONSUMERS

How do ordinary people access justice? This book offers a novel socio-legal approach to access to justice, alternative dispute resolution, vulnerability and energy poverty. It poses an access to justice challenge and rethinks it through a lens that accommodates all affected people, especially those who are currently falling through the system. It raises broader questions about alternative dispute resolution, the need for reform to include more collective approaches, a stronger recognition of the needs of vulnerable people, and a stronger emphasis on delivering social justice. The authors use energy poverty as a site of vulnerability and examine the barriers to justice facing this excluded group.

The book assembles the findings of an interdisciplinary research project studying access to justice and its barriers in the UK, Italy, France, Bulgaria and Spain (Catalonia). In-depth interviews with regulators, ombuds, energy companies, third-sector organisations and vulnerable people provide a rich dataset through which to understand the phenomenon.

The book provides theoretical and empirical insights which shed new light on these issues and sets out new directions of inquiry for research, policy and practice. It will be of interest to researchers, students and policymakers working on access to justice, consumer vulnerability, energy poverty, and the complex intersection between these fields.

The book includes contributions by Cosmo Graham (UK), Sarah Supino and Benedetta Voltaggio (Italy), Marine Cornelis (France), Anais Varo and Enric Bartlett (Catalonia) and Teodora Peneva (Bulgaria).

Access to Justice for Vulnerable and Energy-Poor Consumers

Just Energy?

Naomi Creutzfeldt
Chris Gill
Marine Cornelis
and
Rachel McPherson

•HART•
OXFORD • LONDON • NEW YORK • NEW DELHI • SYDNEY

HART PUBLISHING

Bloomsbury Publishing Plc

Kemp House, Chawley Park, Cumnor Hill, Oxford, OX2 9PH, UK

1385 Broadway, New York, NY 10018, USA

29 Earlsfort Terrace, Dublin 2, Ireland

HART PUBLISHING, the Hart/Stag logo, BLOOMSBURY and the Diana logo are trademarks of Bloomsbury Publishing Plc

First published in Great Britain 2021

A catalogue record for this book is available from the British Library.

A catalogue record for this book is available from the Library of Congress.

Library of Congress Control Number: 2021940377

ISBN: HB: 978-1-50993-943-5
ePDF: 978-1-50993-944-2
ePub: 978-1-50993-945-9

Typeset by Compuscript Ltd, Shannon

To find out more about our authors and books visit www.hartpublishing.co.uk. Here you will find extracts, author information, details of forthcoming events and the option to sign up for our newsletters.

We'd like to thank our children and partners, who were patient and understanding while we were stealing time to write this book during lockdown in 2020. Their support was the greatest gift amidst our digital juggling act.

FOREWORD

Questions of access to justice for consumers in and out of courts have been rambling on, still largely unsolved, for many decades. Despite a push for Alternative Dispute Resolution (ADR) methods, meaningful access to justice is still illusory for many but perhaps most of all for those living in energy poverty. In the European energy sector where consumer detriment is high, consumers are largely passive in their market engagement and the pursuit of their rights.

More broadly, we are witnessing the ascendancy of a nuanced conceptualisation of the driving forces of domestic energy injustices and deprivation. Recent scholarship has shown how the social inequalities and risks associated with energy poverty are systemic and interconnected, challenging earlier dominant understandings in which they were treated under relatively separate disciplinary registers, while being interpreted as problems of individual behaviour and choice. All of this is contributing to the emergence of a dynamic and multilayered approach towards energy vulnerability, in which the focus is on the diverse factors and conditions that characterise at-risk households and places, rather than the circumstances that delineate energy poverty as a fixed state existing at a particular time and place.

Of particular significance here is the notion that energy vulnerability includes bottom-up factors as well as wider structural drivers: from the chains of provision involved in delivering energy between producers and consumers, to the capacities for action and power dynamics involved in energy demand. In addition to the more traditional focus on energy access, affordability and efficiency, energy vulnerability thinking also considers a series of factors around how energy is used. These include the ability to switch to a different or more convenient energy provision system as required by the nature of household energy demand, in addition to the social implications of state or corporate-led subsidy and support schemes. Many such contingencies have a pronounced spatial aspect, with dwellers in specific types of urban and rural locations being particularly vulnerable across a wider variety of factors, due to the multiple forces involved in shaping the built fabric of cities and regions.

It is against such a complex and rapidly evolving conceptual and policy terrain that this book explores the barriers that vulnerable and energy-poor consumers encounter in accessing justice. The book's added value resides in the empirical research conducted with policymakers, practitioners and consumers, which provides new insights into the nature of the access to justice gap and how it may be better addressed in future. The book is a welcome addition to the latest debates on energy justice, vulnerability and poverty as well as the developing literature on vulnerable consumers' access to justice. It pushes the envelope of existing knowledge on the topic by introducing a whole new series of questions around the law and policy frameworks that mediate citizens' access to just decision-making and distributional processes.

The focus on ADR is particularly novel, given the lack of evidence and theorisation of this mechanism's ability to address the challenges faced by energy-poor households. Notably the research points to a 'holistic vision' for access to justice. It challenges the status quo that has made ADR a firm favourite with legislators when its adoption has in fact been driven by unproven theoretical concerns and very little by way of underlying empirical evidence. The book recommends making the lived reality of consumers' experiences central to policymaking because it powerfully illustrates the barriers that stand in the way of access to justice. Understanding this experience would lead to the adoption of appropriately designed ADR capable of delivering substantive justice. The book explores the literature on dispute system design (DSD) and unpicks how to implement them to serve the vulnerable by looking at dispute resolution methodologies in their broader social and institutional context. This is notably by acting on supply and demand for ADR and devising collective redress mechanisms that this can be best achieved at EU level.

The book also touches upon legal consciousness studies, which are concerned with the everyday responses of ordinary people to law and the way in which they perceive and understand the law. The book presents evidence of legal alienation and relational distance in the energy market and puts forward the intervention of local actors such as NGOs, charities, volunteers, local hubs and community groups to bridge the access to justice gap.

One of the most rewarding and unique aspects of the book is its attention to the conceptual foundations of current discussions in the energy inequality and justice domain, paralleled by a discernible contribution to socio-legal research and the formulation of tangible policy recommendation. This book promises to be of interest to a wide readership: from scholars working in different social science domains, to students, practitioners and decision-makers grappling with energy justice challenges on a day-to-day basis.

Learning from its findings ought to help reflect on how and why energy poor consumers still get a rough deal, from paying more to not being able to defend and claim their right. It is hoped that the practical solutions the book proposes can help unlock *JustEnergy* for all in the EU and beyond.

Stefan Bouzarovski[1] and Christine Riefa[+]
11 December 2020

[1] Professor of Human Geography at the University of Manchester, author of *Energy Poverty: (Dis)Assembling Europe's Infrastructural Divide* (Palgrave Macmillan, 2018).

[+] Reader in Consumer Law at Brunel University, editor of C Riefa and S Saintier (eds), *Vulnerable Consumers and the Law: Consumer Protection and Access to Justice* (Routledge, 2021).

ACKNOWLEDGEMENTS

We would like to thank the Economic and Social Research Council for funding our *JUSTENERGY* project (grant number ES/P010237/1). It enabled us to explore access to justice and vulnerability in the energy sector from 2017 to 2020 in the UK, Catalonia, France, Italy and Bulgaria. We are extremely grateful to all the individuals and organisations who made themselves available for interviews, provided information and helped us understand better what is happening on the ground. Our special thanks to Lewis Shand-Smith and Matt Vickers (Ombusdman Services); Nataliya Aleksandrova; Marina Varvesi (AISFOR); Marta Garcia Paris (ECOSERVEIS); Franck Billeau (Reseau Eco Habitat). The team conducted interviews in Bulgaria, France, Italy, Catalonia and the UK. We were overwhelmed by the stories we heard and admire the amazing work that is being done to help fight energy poverty. We especially thank those people who let us into their homes and those who met up with us to share their stories. We will never forget the experience and hope that telling some of their stories will help open eyes and translate into actions to help improve access to justice for the most vulnerable in our society.

We are very grateful to Stefan Bouzarovski and the researchers contributing to the COST ENGAGER initiative for having opened doors to research on energy poverty for us and for discussing many issues along the way. We would also like to thank the members of NEON – the European Network of Energy Ombudsmen – for the stimulating discussions and exchange of experience that have encouraged us to explore this topic.

Our project team is made up of Naomi Creutzfeldt and Chris Gill as academic leads, Rachel McPherson (a fellow academic) and Marine Cornelis (expert energy consultant). The project benefited greatly from the lively engagement, discussions and complementary areas of expertise of the team. This book is a hybrid in the sense that part one was co-written by the project team and part two is an edited collection of country case studies. We are grateful to the authors of these chapters for their insightful contributions. Marine Cornelis (France); Cosmo Graham (the UK); Teodora Peneva (Bulgaria); Sarah Supino and Benedetta Voltaggio (Italy); and Anaïs Varo and Enric R Bartlett Castellà (Catalonia). Also huge thanks to the stellar team at Hart Publishing: Kate Whetter, Roberta Bassi and Rosemarie Mearns, who supported our hybrid approach to this book and were very patient.

Huge thanks to Marie Selwood for editing chapters of this volume and for being so incredibly efficient and flexible. We would also like to express our appreciation to Carol Anderson, who provided interview transcription services, and Carolyn Hirst who we commissioned to conduct a series of literature reviews that have supported delivery of our project. We also thank Mike Leach, Samuel Banda and Jude for their remote collaboration in the design and artwork to create the book cover for us. We love it.

TABLE OF CONTENTS

PART II
ACCESS TO JUSTICE, ADR
AND ENERGY POVERTY IN FIVE COUNTRIES

LIST OF CONTRIBUTORS

Enric R Bartlett Castellà is Lecturer in Public Law at Universitat Ramon Llull, Esade, in Barcelona, Spain, where he has served as the Law School's Dean. He has a PhD in law and is secretary-controller of local administration. He has been Deputy Ombudsman of Catalonia (1993–2004). His most recent studies deal with the regulation of the economy to achieve a just energy transition, in issues such as energy communities, fighting energy poverty, investment protection, or to promote innovation.

Marine Cornelis is the Executive Director and founder of Next Energy Consumer, a Turin-based policy consultancy focused on consumer protection and empowerment issues, and acting at European and international levels. Before this, Marine was managing NEON, the network of energy ombudsmen, from Brussels. Marine is a French national with a background in political sciences and economics.

Naomi Creutzfeldt is Professor of Socio-Legal Studies at the University of Westminster. Her interests in administrative and civil justice systems and ADR (as pathways of informal dispute resolution) have a broader scope, addressing questions of access to justice, vulnerability and consumer protection.

Chris Gill is Senior Lecturer in Public Law at the University of Glasgow. His research interests include access to justice, administrative justice, alternative dispute resolution and street-level bureaucracy. Chris has published widely in these fields, as well as having carried out a range of consultancy projects for organisations including the Council of Europe, Citizens Advice and the Parliamentary and Health Services Ombudsman. He is currently writing a book on the relationship between redress mechanisms and public administration. Ongoing projects include researching the relationship between legislatures and individual grievances (as part of a Scottish Parliament Academic Fellowship), and the development of more therapeutic approaches to handling conflict in public administration settings.

Cosmo Graham is a Professor at the Leicester Law School, University of Leicester, United Kingdom.

Rachel McPherson is Lecturer in Criminal Law at the University of Glasgow. She is particularly interested in socio-legal methodologies. Her research considers how vulnerability is conceptualised and the lived experiences of those facing inequality before the law.

Teodora Peneva is Assistant Professor at the Economic Research Institute of the Bulgarian Academy of Science. She has been exploring energy poverty in Bulgaria since 2010 when she worked as a market analysis expert at an electricity supplier. Teodora wrote her PhD thesis on the topic in 2013 and continued her professional career as an academic in 2017. Teodora has published widely on energy poverty. Her critical view is based on analysis of datasets from the statistical institute and interviews with experts and market players in the sector.

Sarah Supino is a lawyer at Salvini e Soci – studio legale tributario fondato da F Gallo, an Italian tax law firm. She has a PhD in law and business from LUISS Guido Carli University in Rome with focus on business, finance and taxation. She is author of several publications on energy poverty in specialised journals, and is co-author, with Benedetta Voltaggio, of the book *La povertà energetica. Strumenti per affrontare un problema sociale* (*Energy Poverty: Tools to Address a Social Problem*) published in 2019.

Anaïs Varo is a PhD candidate and Lecturer in Political Science at the University of Girona. She is also a board member of the UNESCO International Chair/Network for a Sustainable Human Development. Her research focuses on energy precarity, energy vulnerability and energy poverty policies through an intersectionality lens.

Benedetta Voltaggio is an Italian lawyer, specialising in tax law. Now, she is working in the tax department of one of the most prestigious banks in Europe. She is co-author, with Sarah Supino, of the book *La povertà energetica. Strumenti per affrontare un problema sociale* (*Energy Poverty: Tools to Address a Social Issue)* published in 2019.

LIST OF TABLES AND FIGURES

Part I

Part II

Introduction

I. Introduction

A long-standing concern of socio-legal scholarship has been to investigate how ordinary people do (and do not) access justice. Analyses of legal systems across the world have overwhelmingly concluded that access to justice is highly constrained for ordinary people and even more so for those who might be considered vulnerable.[1] This book argues that vulnerable and energy-poor consumers in the European Union (EU) face significant barriers in accessing justice.[2] Among the solutions offered to remedy the failings of existing systems of justice, alternative dispute resolution (ADR) has featured prominently. With promises of cost-savings, increased party satisfaction and longer-lasting conflict resolution,[3] policymakers in Europe are increasingly pursuing policies to boost ADR provision, at the same time as reducing access to courts.[4] This has been particularly evident in relation to consumer-to-business disputes in Europe, where a large-scale shift has occurred towards resolving disputes out of court through the implementation of the consumer ADR Directive (2013/11/EU). While the development of ADR has been welcomed in some quarters, there is a lack of empirical evidence regarding the access to justice benefits that have accrued from it,[5] especially for those who are most vulnerable. This book begins to fill this gap.

The main questions this book addresses are:

- What are the current barriers to access to justice for vulnerable and energy-poor consumers?
- How should we define and conceptualise access to justice?

[1] L Ervo and A Nylund (eds), *The Future of Civil Litigation: Access to Courts and Court-annexed Mediation in the Nordic Countries* (Springer, 2014); M Galanter, 'Reading the Landscape of Disputes: What We Know and Don't Know (and Think We Know) about our Allegedly Contentious and Litigious Society' (1983) 31 *UCLA Law Review* 4; H Genn, 'What is Civil Justice For? Reform, ADR, and Access to Justice' (2012) 24 *Yale Journal of Law & the Humanities* 397; S Wrbka, *European Consumer Access to Justice Revisited* (CUP, 2014).

[2] This book is based on our ESRC *Just Energy* research project (2017–20) on Alternative Dispute Resolution and access to justice for vulnerable and energy-poor consumers: esrcjustenergy.wordpress.com.

[3] S Blake, J Browne and S Sime, *The Jackson ADR Handbook* (OUP, 2013).

[4] eg, Ministry of Justice, 'Alternative Dispute Resolution for Consumers' (Department for Business Innovation and Skills 2015), available at: www.gov.uk/government/publications/alternative-dispute-resolution-for-consumers/alternative-dispute-resolution-for-consumers.

[5] C Albiston and R Sandefur, 'Expanding the Empirical Study of Access To Justice' [2013] *Wisconsin Law Review* 101 (UC Berkeley Public Law Research Paper No 2282498).

- How effective are the current law and policy frameworks for addressing access to justice for vulnerable and energy-poor consumers?
- How effective has ADR been in providing access to justice for vulnerable and energy-poor consumers?
- How can access to justice for vulnerable and energy-poor consumers be enhanced in future?

Our research sheds light on timeless questions of socio-legal interest at the same time as addressing the urgent question of whether the current, radical shift towards ADR in European consumer dispute resolution is serving the interests of consumers. We chose to look at the European energy sector because questions about access to justice, ADR and consumer vulnerability intersect prominently here. This sector features significant levels of consumer vulnerability and energy poverty,[6] and addressing this is a growing concern of policymakers.[7] A recent study found significant levels of consumer vulnerability in the European energy sector, with drivers of vulnerability including: personal characteristics; behavioural issues; market-related factors; access issues; and situational drivers.[8] The energy sector is also an area that features long-standing EU-mandated ADR, providing elements of comparability between countries, while also featuring significant national variations.[9]

This book sets out, therefore, to explore the barriers which vulnerable and energy-poor consumers encounter in accessing justice. In relation to laws and policies seeking to enhance access to justice for vulnerable and energy-poor consumers, the book analyses the extent to which their implementation is effective for those most in need. Thus, the book seeks to understand the access to justice gap for vulnerable and energy-poor consumers through an analysis of top-down laws and policies and in relation to the bottom-up reality of their implementation. While the complexity and limitations of top-down law and policy are well understood, the barriers to implementation and the needs of those experiencing vulnerability and energy poverty on the ground have been much less closely examined. The book addresses this through our empirical research with policymakers, practitioners and consumers, in order to generate

[6] M Bartl, 'The Affordability of Energy: How Much Protection for the Vulnerable Consumers?' (2010) 33 *Journal of Consumer Policy* 225; M George, C Graham and L Lennard, 'The Energy Penalty: Disabled People and Fuel Poverty' (Centre for Consumers and Essential Services, University of Leicester, 2013), available at: www.energypoverty.eu/publication/energy-penalty-disabled-people-and-fuel-poverty.

[7] eg: S Pye, A Dobbins and C Baffert et al, 'Energy Poverty and Vulnerable Consumers in the Energy Sector across the EU: Analysis of Policies and Measures' (INSIGHT_E, 2015), available at: ec.europa.eu/energy/sites/ener/files/documents/INSIGHT_E_Energy%20Poverty%20-%20Main%20Report_FINAL.pdf; Ofgem, 'Vulnerable Consumers in the Energy Market: 2019' (Ofgem, 2019), available at: www.ofgem.gov.uk/publications-and-updates/vulnerable-consumers-energy-market-2019.

[8] Pye, Dobbins and Baffert et al, 'Energy Poverty' (n 7).

[9] N Creutzfeldt, 'What do we Expect from an Ombudsman? Narratives of Everyday Engagement with the Informal Justice System in Germany and the UK' (2016) 12 *International Journal of Law in Context* Special Issue (Comparative Socio-Legal Studies) 437.

new insights into the nature of the access to justice gap and how it may be better addressed in future.

In this introduction, we begin in section II by providing an orientation to the key concepts explored in this book. Section III outlines the intended contribution of the book to socio-legal scholarship, highlighting the theoretical and empirical debates that we will address. Section IV provides an outline of the arguments that will be presented throughout book. Section V discusses the methodology used for our underpinning empirical research. Section VI describes the structure of the book.

II. An Orientation to Key Concepts

To assist readers approaching this book from a range of disciplines, this section provides a brief orientation to key concepts that we go on to explore in the book. More detailed accounts of each concept are provided as the book progresses (Access to Justice in chapters one and two; ADR in chapters three and four; Consumer Vulnerability and Energy Poverty in chapters one and three).

A. Access to Justice

There is no single definition of access to justice. The concept of 'access' is relatively straightforward, although accessibility can be a matter of degree – it includes both the ability to engage a remedial mechanism in the first place, and the ability to make effective use of it once it is engaged.[10] Questions of access also raise issues with regard to what is being accessed. For instance, access to justice should not be seen as restricted to accessing remedial mechanisms, but should also include access to advice and advocacy. A greater difficulty comes in defining what justice means. This has of course been the subject of significant philosophical and jurisprudential enquiry, but for our purposes the debate has centred in whether access to justice is restricted to 'legal justice' or a broader conception of 'social justice'.[11] Access to justice, particularly in the consumer context, is not simply a matter of the pursuit of individual rights through private enforcement. Instead, access to justice should be seen as having a collective dimension and as involving approaches that consider injustice on a systemic rather than purely individual level. Access to justice must also be interested in the achievement of substantive justice as well as the availability of procedural remedies. While we go on to elaborate these points

[10] Wrbka (n 1).

[11] T Cornford, 'The Meaning of Access to Justice' in E Palmer, T Cornford, Y Marique and A Guinchard (eds), *Access to Justice: Beyond the Policies and Politics of Austerity* (Hart Publishing, 2016).

in greater detail in chapter two, for now, Garth and Cappelletti's classic definition provides a suitable starting point:

> The words 'access to justice' … serve to focus on two basic purposes of the legal system by which people may vindicate their rights and/or resolve their disputes under the general auspices of the state. First, the system must be equally accessible to all; second, it must lead to results that are individually and socially just.[12]

B. ADR

ADR is an umbrella term for a wide range of dispute resolution processes. The common feature of these processes is that they are not courts and are distinct from court adjudication. Gill et al[13] highlight key forms of ADR as including negotiation, mediation, conciliation, arbitration, adjudication, complaint boards, expert evaluation, neutral evaluation and ombuds.[14] There are various important distinctions between types of ADR, including the extent to which they seek to generate agreement between the parties or impose a decision, and the degree to which their processes are formal or informal.[15] Some processes such as negotiation and mediation offer open and unstructured processes, and emphasise the pursuit of interest-based agreements that work for both parties. Others, such as arbitration and adjudication schemes are more similar to courts in that they produce binding win-lose outcomes, albeit with streamlined processes.[16] In European consumer settings, commonly used forms of ADR include arbitration, conciliation, complaint boards and ombuds.[17] Across the world, the prevalence of ADR within justice systems has grown massively in the last 50 years, with ADR seen as a means of cutting costs associated with courts and enhancing access to justice for consumers.

C. Consumer Vulnerability

A growing consumer vulnerability literature has been concerned with the way in which vulnerability should be defined.[18] A consumer is vulnerable when personal

[12] B Garth and M Cappelletti, 'Access to Justice: The Newest Wave in the Worldwide Movement to Make Rights Effective' (1978) *Articles by Maurer Faculty* 1142L 181, 182.

[13] C Gill, J Williams, C Brennan and C Hirst, *Models of Alternative Dispute Resolution (ADR): A Report for the Legal Ombudsman* (Legal Ombudsman, 2014).

[14] In this book we use the term 'ombudsman' if that is the organisation's name, and we choose to use the terms 'ombud/ombuds' as gender neutral terms.

[15] Scottish Mediation, *Bringing Mediation into the Mainstream in Civil Justice in Scotland* (Scottish Mediation, 2019) 12.

[16] M Palmer and S Roberts, *Dispute Processes: ADR and the Primary Forms of Decision Making*, 3rd edn (CUP, 2020).

[17] C Hodges, I Benöehr and N Creutzfeldt-Banda, *Consumer ADR in Europe* (Hart Publishing, 2012).

[18] C Schultz and MB Holbrook, 'The Paradoxical Relationships between Marketing and Vulnerability' (2009) 28 *Journal of Public Policy & Marketing* 124.

circumstances and characteristics combine with aspects of the market to create situations where the consumer is significantly less able than a typical consumer to protect or represent his/her interests in the energy market; and/or significantly more likely than a typical consumer to suffer detriment, or that detriment is likely to be more substantial.[19] The multidimensional nature of vulnerability is demonstrated in the European Commission's recently issued definition, which argues that vulnerability refers to those consumers who are at higher risk of detriment as a result of their socio-demographic characteristics, behavioural characteristics, personal situation, or market environment.[20] The large spectrum between a short-term passing state (situational) and a permanent feature of someone's daily life (structural/systemic) makes vulnerability a challenging element to identify and act upon.[21] Increasingly, the concept of vulnerability is enshrined in law and regulation,[22] although it remains unclear to what extent the concept is leading to additional protections in practice for certain individuals and groups. There have also been inadequate connections made to policies on access to justice and ADR.

D. Energy Poverty

Vulnerability is closely linked to energy poverty, and the latter can be seen as an extreme form of vulnerability. Energy poverty 'occurs when a household experiences inadequate levels of essential energy services in the home, such as heating, cooling, lighting and use of appliances'.[23] Understood as a type of vulnerability, energy poverty is a 'culturally sensitive and private condition, which is temporally and spatially dynamic'.[24] Energy poverty in Europe is caused and reinforced by: high-energy prices; low incomes; inefficient buildings and appliances;[25] and individual household energy needs (for example, illness). According to Brunner et al: 'A relationship between poor mental health – and well-being more generally – on the one hand, and cold housing and living in energy poverty on the other, is now evident'.[26] The concept of energy poverty is still emerging and

[19] See: www.ofgem.gov.uk/ofgem-publications/75550/consumer-vulnerability-strategy-pdf.

[20] Directive (EU) 2019/944 of the European Parliament and of the Council of 5 June 2019 on common rules for the internal market for electricity and amending Directive 2012/27/EU (Electricity Market Design Directive).

[21] The multidimensional nature of vulnerability is demonstrated in the European Commission's (2016) recently issued definition, which argues that vulnerability refers to those consumers who are at higher risk of detriment as a result of their socio-demographic characteristics, behavioural characteristics, personal situation, or market environment. See K Rademaekers et al, *Selecting Indicators to Measure Energy Poverty* (European Commission 2016), available at: ec.europa.eu/energy/sites/ener/files/documents/Selecting%20Indicators%20to%20Measure%20Energy%20Poverty.pdf.

[22] eg, Ofgem, Consumer Vulnerability Strategy; Electricity Market Design Directive.

[23] S Bouzarovski and S Petrova, 'A Global Perspective on Domestic Energy Deprivation: Overcoming the Energy Poverty–Fuel Poverty Binary' (2015) 10 *Energy Research & Social Science* 31.

[24] H Thomson, S Bouzarovski and C Snell, 'Rethinking the Measurement of Energy Poverty in Europe: a Critical Analysis of Indicators and Data' (2017) 26(7) *Indoor and Built Environment* 879.

[25] B Boardman, *Fixing Fuel Poverty: Challenges and Solutions* (Earthscan, 2010).

[26] KM Brunner, M Spitzer and A Christanell, 'Experiencing Fuel Poverty: Coping Strategies of Low-income Households in Vienna/Austria' (2011) 49 *Energy Policy* 53; L Middlemiss and R Gillard,

has only been recognised explicitly (and to a limited degree) in recent European legislation.[27]

III. Contribution to Socio-Legal Scholarship

This book seeks to contribute to a number of strands of socio-legal enquiry on access to justice. One of these relates to empirical work that has sought to understand the prevalence and extent of access to justice problems[28] and the nature of the barriers facing people seeking justice. Empirical enquiries have been conducted in a range of contexts, but there have been no detailed studies of access to justice in relation to the European energy market. And although there have been a number of works investigating access to justice for consumers these have generally adopted theoretical rather than empirical perspectives.[29] A further contribution of our approach relates to the emphasis we have on vulnerable individuals and groups, rather than taking a 'generalist' approach to access to justice.[30] In line with the notion of 'recognition justice',[31] we place a special emphasis on recognising the distinct needs of certain individuals and groups and assessing access to justice accordingly. Our approach, which seeks to provide a qualitative understanding of the lived experiences of key actors both providing and seeking access to justice, therefore, aims to enrich the existing empirical literature.

Another strand of enquiry is more theoretical and relates to the conceptualisation of access to justice. A limitation of some access to justice literature relates to the fact that access to justice remains undefined or that assumptions are made that there is a shared understanding of what access to justice means. This has resulted in criticism that access to justice can be 'all things, to all people' and that there is a lack of precision and, therefore, utility to the concept.[32] Where attempts have been made to tackle the thorny issue of definition, significant debate has ensued about the proper limits of access to justice. This has included questions about whether access to justice should have a procedural or substantive focus, whether it should not only include the pursuit of individual interests but also the realisation

'Fuel Poverty from the Bottom-up: Characterising Household Energy Vulnerability through the Lived Experience of the Fuel Poor' (2015) 6 *Energy Research & Social Science* 146.

[27] A Dobbins and S Pye, 'Member State Level Regulation Related to Energy Poverty and Vulnerable Consumers' in K Csiba, A Bajomi and A Gosztonyi (eds), *Energy Poverty Handbook* (The Greens/EFA Group of the European Parliament, 2016), available at: bpie.eu/wp-content/uploads/2016/11/energypovertyhandbook-online.pdf.

[28] H Genn, *Paths to Justice: What People Do and Think about Going to Law* (Hart Publishing, 1999).

[29] C Riefa and S Saitier (eds), *Vulnerable Consumers and the Law: Consumer Protection and Access to Justice* (Routledge, 2020); Wrbka (n 1).

[30] P Hughes, 'Advancing Access to Justice through Generic Solutions: The Risk of Perpetuating Exclusion' (2013) 31 *Windsor Yearbook of Access to Justice* 1.

[31] K Jenkins, D McCauley and R Heffron et al, 'Energy Justice: A Conceptual Review' (2016) 11 *Energy Research and Social Science* 174.

[32] Cornford (n 11).

of collective goals, and whether its emphasis should be on legal justice or broader ideas around social justice. Here we seek to contribute through what we have described as our 'holistic vision' for access to justice (see below).

An increasingly voluminous literature that we seek to address is on the role of ADR in access to justice. This literature tends to be firmly divided between proponents and critics of ADR, with major ideological fault lines separating the two. One of the major criticisms of the literature is that it is driven by unproven theoretical concerns and that insufficient attention has been paid to exploring the underlying empirical reality.[33] We seek to add to the literature here not only by enhancing the empirical research base, but by addressing some of the key claims of critical literature on ADR. For example, we argue that ADR (if it is appropriately designed) is capable of delivering substantive justice and that many of the criticisms of ADR can be addressed through good dispute system design (DSD). At the same time, we caution against accepting many of the claims in the ADR literature in the absence of further empirical enquiry.

In the specific context of European consumer disputing,[34] the literature has tended to focus on mapping the variety of approaches across Europe, with an underlying assumption that the features of ADR will naturally promote accessibility and a concern for vulnerability. There is, therefore, a need to begin to test these assumptions[35] and to investigate whether, how, and to what degree – in the context of the increasing dominance of ADR as a primary form of consumer dispute resolution in many contexts[36] – access to justice for the vulnerable is being delivered. This literature also features an ideological rift between ADR enthusiasts and those who maintain the value of traditional court-based systems. Again, the literature here has tended to be either theoretical or descriptive, with studies often relying on published and organisationally produced data rather than involving in-depth primary empirical research.

Thus, one of the contributions we seek to make is to turn scholarly attention away from the rather unhelpful battle of ideologies that still dominates the literature and towards the adoption of DSD perspectives. The literature on DSD proposes and evaluates approaches to the design of dispute resolution systems and a considerable body of research now exists which can be drawn on in seeking to improve access to justice. At the same time, the DSD literature has not tended to emphasise access to justice concerns, with the focus having been mostly on the nature of dispute resolution processes. There has also been less concern with questions around the institutionalisation of dispute resolution methods and broader,

[33] N Creutzfeldt, 'Ombudsman Schemes' in P Cortes (ed), *The Transformation of Consumer Dispute Resolution in the European Union: A Renewed Approach to Consumer Protection* (OUP, 2016).

[34] Hodges, Benöhr and Creutzfeldt (n 17); P Cortes, *The New Regulatory Framework for Consumer Dispute Resolution* (OUP, 2016).

[35] C Gill and C Hirst, *Being Complained about: Good Practice Principles and Guidelines* (2019), available at: www.gla.ac.uk/media/Media_636618_smxx.pdf.

[36] C Hodges, 'Consumer Ombudsman: Better Regulation and Dispute Resolution' (2015) 15 *ERA Forum* 593.

systemic approaches that emphasise collective aspects of dispute resolution. We seek to contribute here through the adoption of more holistic, therapeutic and preventative approaches to DSD, which look at dispute resolution methodologies in their broader social and institutional context.

A further strand of literature to which we wish to contribute relates to legal consciousness studies. These studies are concerned with the everyday responses of ordinary people to law and the way in which they perceive and understand the law. A particular strand of this literature has focused on legal alienation and the idea that people are increasingly alienated from law and distrustful of public institutions. We seek to add to the literature here by presenting evidence of legal alienation in the energy market, as well as by drawing on the concept of relational distance to describe the nature of the gap between consumers and formal, law-based institutions.

Our approach in this book, therefore, is firmly situated in the tradition of socio-legal studies and socio-legal methodology.[37] At the same time, we hope that the book will contribute to other disciplines. The concept of access to justice is, for example, beginning to gain some traction among scholars studying energy poverty and vulnerability from a range of social science perspectives. Developing work on energy justice, although often rooted in more global perspectives, share elements of our agenda. The cross-cutting nature of access to justice means that the particular approach we adopt here has the potential to address parallel themes explored in disciplines including social policy, geography and economics. An access to justice perspective, underpinned by a socio-legal approach to the subject, therefore, has the potential to contribute to existing multidisciplinary work on energy markets and consumers.

IV. Outline of the Book's Content and Argument

Chapter one introduces what we call 'the access to justice challenge', exploring the gap between the ideal and reality of access to justice. Meaningful access to justice is illusory for billions of people around the world. In the European energy sector, consumer detriment is high, consumers are largely passive in their market engagement and in the pursuit of their rights, and vulnerable and energy-poor consumers face particularly acute barriers to accessing justice. Structural social conditions (race, class, demographic characteristics, etc), cultural and social norms, individual cognitive processing, and practical features of institutional design (such as the availability of advice or the complexity of procedures) add up to significant challenges. The nature of the liberalised energy market, and its reliance on the existence of active consumers, creates further problems for individuals

[37] N Creutzfeldt, K McConachie and M Mason (eds), *Routledge Handbook of Socio-Legal Theory and Methods* (Routledge, 2019).

and groups who are unable to engage fully with energy services or seek solutions when things go wrong. Drawing on our data, we argue that the lived reality of consumers' experiences powerfully illustrates the barriers that stand in the way of access to justice. We argue that these experiences represent the key starting point for thinking about access to justice, how it should be defined, and how it might be achieved.

In chapter two, we set out our proposal for a holistic vision of access to justice. The chapter claims that, despite early accounts of access to justice taking a broad view of the concept, there has been a reversion – driven partly by ideological preference and partly by pragmatism – towards narrow definitions of access to justice. We argue for a broader view, with non-legal advice provision, alternative forms of dispute resolution, internal complaint handling arrangements within firms, and a broader range of social and community actors being recognised as important to the delivery of access to justice in practice. We also argue that an emphasis on narrow procedural justice is inadequate. Instead, consideration needs to be given to questions around the achievement of substantive justice. Overall, chapter two argues for a holistic vision of access to justice that involves recognition of: the (often non-legal) reality of people's everyday justice problems and the need as a result to take a broad view of the actors and institutions that might deliver access to justice; the importance of collective interests in relation to people's justice problems and the need to see access to justice as facilitating the achievement of social justice, remedying the substantive conditions that leave people vulnerable and energy-poor; and finally, the need for policy and institutional design processes to recognise, involve and engage those who are excluded from justice.

Chapter three considers the EU's law and policy framework, with a particular emphasis on the extent to which it recognises, and seeks to protect, vulnerable and energy-poor consumers and the development of ADR as part of the possible solution to the access to justice challenge. We argue that EU law currently provides only limited protection of the needs and interests of vulnerable and energy-poor consumers. While there is increasing rhetorical recognition of the needs of vulnerable and energy-poor consumers, major stumbling blocks currently exist in terms of how the concepts should be defined and operationalised. The development of ADR for energy consumer disputes has been presented in part as a measure addressing access to justice. At the same time, however, cost-reduction has been an important driver, with the obvious potential for conflict with the aim of bringing about greater access to justice. There has also been limited attention paid to how ADR should take account of the needs of vulnerable and energy-poor consumers and a failure to join up policymaking in these areas. Collective approaches to redress remain underdeveloped at EU level, and subject to much national variation. These approaches are argued to be essential to delivering justice for vulnerable and energy-poor consumers who are unlikely – even with better designed systems – ever to be able to trigger private enforcement mechanisms. Overall, we argue that despite a range of interventions, there remain widespread and acute problems for vulnerable and energy-poor consumers in accessing justice.

Chapter four considers the problems and potential associated with ADR as an access to justice measure. Given the scale of the challenges we outline in chapter one, we argue that a sanguine approach to the potential for ADR to provide access to justice needs to be adopted. The claims made for ADR (similarly to the counter-claims made for courts) are often hyperbolic and ideologically driven. The reality is that ADR, even before considering how it operates empirically, is not currently designed to overcome the barriers to dispute emergence that occur at each of the naming, blaming and claiming stages of dispute emergence.[38] We argue that the starting point for considering the contribution of ADR to access to justice has to be one of realism, which resists the overly enthusiastic accounts presented in some policy and scholarly narratives. In considering these issues, chapter four addresses two sets of arguments in the literature on access to justice and ADR. One set of arguments questions the effectiveness of ADR and its ability, inter alia, to reduce costs, simplify processes for parties, and lead to the kind of more flexible and creative conclusions that are assumed to form part of ADR. The other set of arguments revolves around ADR and settlement, and the extent to which ADR provides access to substantive justice. Overall, we argue that ADR can contribute to access to justice, including in its substantive dimension, and can perhaps do so more effectively than courts, as a result of its ability to look beyond legal justice and the flexibility of its processes. However, given the diversity of ADR arrangements, much depends on the form and design of the ADR body.

Chapter five is empirically focused, and our findings confirm existing data that suggest that ADR has a limited reach in relation to delivering access to justice beyond a white, middle class, male and wealthy demographic of users. We found that consumers faced a range of barriers to accessing justice in the energy sector, including: lack of awareness of rights and ADR; the poor practices of energy suppliers; regulatory and technological barriers; and psychological barriers. ADR providers were uncertain about the limits of their role, particularly in terms of providing the kind of extra support that vulnerable and energy-poor consumers might need and in being able to address fundamental, substantive issues in relation to consumers' problems. Important themes in terms of the effectiveness of ADR included a need to work in partnership and in a more systemic way, with closer relationships particularly required with the third sector and energy suppliers.

Chapter six introduces two important frameworks to help conceptualise the access to justice problem: legal alienation and relational distance. Legal alienation provides an important framework for understanding situations where people have limited understanding of their rights and limited identification with the laws

[38] W Felstiner, R Abel and A Sarat, 'The Emergence and Transformation of Disputes: Naming, Blaming, Claiming …' (1981) 15 *Law & Society Review* 631.

and state-provided systems to assist in realising them. Relational distance meanwhile is posited as a way of describing the large gap that exists between the lived experiences of vulnerable and energy-poor consumers and the world inhabited by lawyers, bureaucrats, regulators and ADR bodies. Together, a lack of mutual understanding and identification between consumers, energy suppliers and the institutions that regulate the market are argued to represent an important barrier to accessing justice. Our data shows how apathy, cynicism and alienation arise in consumer experiences. A lack of trust in public institutions, a general passivity in response to unfair systems, and a perception that the law supports the interests of the powerful, all contribute to alienation. We argue that one of the ways in which alienation and relational distance might be overcome is through the intervention of local actors such as NGOs, charities, volunteers, local hubs and community groups. These actors are able to provide a bridge between formal institutions and vulnerable and energy-poor consumers. We argue, however, that local groups should be seen as more than intermediaries when it comes to access to justice. Our data show the important problem-solving work carried out by local actors, who are able to deal with people's problems holistically and provide the kind of immediate support and help they need. Local actors should be seen not only as a source of referrals into formal justice systems, therefore, but as a key part of access to justice systems and as having an important role in the development of a more preventative, grass roots and integrated model of access to justice.

Chapter seven weaves these threads of argument together in order to set out proposals for the achievement of a more holistic vision to access to justice. This chapter draws on DSD, therapeutic jurisprudence and preventative law approaches in order to argue for a reformed system of access to justice. Our particular focus is on how ADR could be developed as an access to justice institution, as well as on how partnerships and systemic work among a range of actors could be developed. We argue that the ombud should be recognised as having significant benefits, among other forms of ADR, when it comes to increasing access to justice. However, existing ombuds models do not go far enough. While they have the potential to deliver added value, they are not designed in a way that is genuinely inclusive. We propose three broad sets of design options to address the current limitations of ADR in delivering access to justice. The first set involves changes to the 'supply' of ADR. This would involve making processes more adapted to the needs of vulnerable and energy-poor users and thus more attractive to them. The second set involves trying to increase 'demand' for ADR. This would involve greater promotion of ADR and working with stakeholders to ensure referrals. The third set involves, counterintuitively, reducing demand for ADR by seeking to help resolve issues at an earlier stage. The proposals we make here draw inspiration from the way in which some ombuds operate in the public sector, and suggest a role for ADR that involves: advocacy; the regulation of internal complaint procedures; systemic investigations; and greater integration of services and partnerships with other access to justice actors.

V. A Note on Case Study Selection and Methodology

We chose Bulgaria, Catalonia, France, Italy and the UK as case studies. We did this for the following reasons: they feature different historical, legal and political approaches to ADR and access to justice;[39] and they all agreed to take part in the project and facilitate access to their own data and to introduce us to other stakeholders. In addition, the countries feature different policy approaches to consumer vulnerability and energy poverty and fit within a different area of the European Commission's matrix for assessing the extent to which countries employ strategic and sector-specific measures to tackle vulnerability and energy poverty.[40] Given the qualitative nature of this project, we did not aim to select representative cases, but we did wish to include a range of relevant settings. In this book, we present our overall findings on the state of access to justice for vulnerable and energy-poor consumers, rather than presenting detailed country-specific data. We will provide more detailed comparative accounts in future publications to support the general findings and arguments presented here.

We adopted a qualitative methodology involving desk research and semi-structured interviews. We started off with a desk-based mapping exercise. This provided an initial account of access to justice policies, ADR bodies and the extent to which consumer vulnerability and energy poverty were recognised in each jurisdiction. We collected data and produced country reports about policy frameworks and the institutional context for consumer protection in the energy market.[41] Then, we conducted 80 in-depth, semi-structured interviews. First, we interviewed stakeholders and spoke with ADR providers, practitioners, regulators, energy companies, non-governmental organisations (NGOs) and policymakers. We also held a workshop in London in early 2019 with NGOs that are actively fighting energy poverty on the ground, and this generated helpful data which we draw on here. The next step was to conduct in-depth interviews with vulnerable and energy-poor consumers. The identification of consumers as research participants was done through third-party facilitators (ADR providers and NGOs). These third parties were asked to invite consumers with whom they were in contact to take part in the research if they felt they met certain pre-set participation criteria. All interview data collected were subject to thematic qualitative analysis using Nvivo.[42] For this purpose, the interviews were translated into English.

[39] Creutzfeldt, 'What do we Expect from an Ombudsman?' (n 9); Cortes, *The New Regulatory Framework* (n 34).

[40] European Commission, *Consumer Vulnerability across Key Markets in the European* Union (European Commission, 2016).

[41] See project website for reports: esrcjustenergy.wordpress.com.

[42] MB Miles, AM Huberman and J Saldaña, *Qualitative Data Analysis: A Methods Sourcebook and the Coding Manual for Qualitative Researchers* (Sage, 2014).

VI. The Structure of this Book

This book is organised into two parts. The first part, as outlined above, is about our *Just Energy* project and details our theoretical and empirical findings. The second part includes contributions from experts (academics, policy experts, and practitioners) in the jurisdictions we studied as part of our project. The aim of part II is to consider the core themes explored in our project from a range of different jurisdictional perspectives, as well as from the perspectives of practitioners and policymakers. Parts I and II are connected but distinct. The authors in part II adopt their own approaches to the issues and bring their own insights to the debate around access to justice for vulnerable and energy-poor consumers. Their accounts provide a repository of more detailed jurisdiction-specific insights, as well as enriching the book by considering the key themes of access to justice, ADR, vulnerability and energy poverty, from a range of perspectives.

PART I

Access to Justice for Vulnerable and Energy-Poor Consumers

1

The Access to Justice Challenge

I. Introduction

This chapter is about access to justice and the barriers facing its realisation. The chapter begins by setting out what we have described as 'the access to justice challenge': the fact that meaningful access to justice is illusory for billions of people around the world. Despite access to justice being recognised as a fundamental right in international law,[1] a very significant gap exists between the ideal and the reality. Indeed, access to justice is perhaps the paradigmatic example of the need for a law-in-context approach; the gulf between 'law in the books' and 'law in action' is as far apart here as it is anywhere. The vast scale of the access to justice gap globally, measured in billions of people suffering exclusion, is reflected in the narrower concern of this book; namely, energy consumers suffering very substantial unremedied detriment and being highly unlikely to seek help for their problems. Having defined the scale of the problem, the chapter turns to consider the factors that underlie the gap between people's problems and their effective resolution. The research literature on access to justice suggests a number of important factors, including the cost and complexity of accessing remedial procedures, demographic characteristics, individual cognitive processing, and ideological and socially produced preferences, all of which provide some pieces of the puzzle that help explain the access to justice gap. The chapter reviews all of these factors, using Fesltiner et al's classic 'naming, blaming and claiming' model as a basic organising framework for discussing the multidimensional and clustered factors that explain limitations on access to justice.[2] Having done so, the chapter considers the particular issues facing energy consumers and the kinds of problems they encounter. The chapter argues that there are a number of distinctive features of the consumer relationship which present particular and additional barriers to accessing justice. The chapter then considers the concepts of vulnerability and energy poverty and the acute challenges that are faced by individuals and groups who fall

[1] I Benöhr, 'Consumer Dispute Resolution after the Lisbon Treaty' (2013) 36 *Journal of Consumer Policy* 87; I 'Benöhr, *The Impact of Competition Law on the Private Law Concepts of Nullity and Damages: Primary EU Law and Private Law Concepts* (Intersentia, 2017).

[2] W Felstiner, R Abel and A Sarat, 'The Emergence and Transformation of Disputes: Naming, Blaming, Claiming …' (1981) 15 *Law & Society Review* 631.

within these definitions. Here we present some highlights from our data, which provide insights into the lived experiences of consumers and the barriers they face in accessing justice.

II. The Scale and Nature of the Access to Justice Challenge

There is a vast and growing literature on access to justice and chapter two will consider the theoretical dimensions of the concept. Here, the focus is on defining the scale of the access to justice challenge and the barriers to access to justice that have been identified in research. A recent global survey of 101 countries found that:

- 49 per cent of people surveyed had experienced a legal problem in the previous two years;
- only 29 per cent of people who had experienced a legal problem sought any form of advice to help them better understand or resolve their problem, and those who did seek assistance preferred to turn to family members or friends;
- 1.4 billion people have unmet civil and administrative justice needs.[3]

A report by the World Bank concluded that the figure was even higher and that around 5.1 billion people – two-thirds of the world's population – lack meaningful access to justice.[4] Interestingly, the World Justice Project found that the most common problems relate to consumer issues, housing, money and debt. Ramsay, surveying the research literature, confirms that in the Global North, money, debt and consumer issues are the most common types of justice problems faced by individuals.[5]

As will be argued below, most literature on access to justice is, in fact, concerned with access to lawyers and access to courts. However, the likelihood of people seeking any kind of external help when they experience a problem is low across the board: only 17 per cent of people surveyed by the World Justice Project took their problem to an authority or third party to mediate or adjudicate.[6] In the specific context of the consumer sector, there is evidence of a similar lack of propensity to pursue justiciable matters. The Consumer Conditions Scoreboard for 2019, for example, found that while one in five European consumers experienced

[3] World Justice Project, *Global Insights on Access to Justice* (WLP, 2019) 6–7, available at: worldjusticeproject.org/sites/default/files/documents/WJP-A2J-2019.pdf.

[4] World Bank Group, 'A Toolkit for Justice: A Cost–Benefit Analysis of Legal Aid'(2019), available at: click.mailings-intbar.org/?qs=55ecf83a2236e21ee23216a4d3dd1f956ba659a298cfc2116d6cffc71a50c4f570339adfd6f090891995b51ec3082552.

[5] I Ramsay, 'Consumer Redress and Access to Justice' in CEF Rickett and TGW Telfer (eds), *International Perspectives on Consumers' Access to Justice* (CUP, 2003).

[6] World Justice Project, *Global Insights* (n 3).

a consumer problem, only 5 per cent of those had recourse to an alternative dispute resolution (ADR) body.[7] And, despite some of the wilder claims about the value of ADR in expanding access to justice, empirical reality suggests that the reach of ADR is limited to a narrow and privileged demographic: in a survey of 3,190 European consumers who had used ADR, Creutzfeldt found that the typical respondent was male, over 50, educated and employed.[8] Another recent survey found strikingly similar demographics of consumers using ADR and small claims courts in the UK:

> Our survey indicated that the characteristics of consumers that took a dispute to ADR or the court are very different to the general consumer population. Of the consumers who had used ADR, 69% were male, 69% were over 50 years old, 66% held a degree level qualification or higher, and 42% had a household income of over £50,000 … Consumers who had used courts reported similar characteristics.[9]

Overall, empirical data confirms that access to justice is uneven and typically reserved for the few, not the masses. Sandefur,[10] for example, reviewing empirical enquiries about unmet legal needs,[11] argues that there is a vast amount of the population with unmet legal needs. These people typically have clusters of problems rather than one isolated problem, and the vast majority of justiciable problems are resolved outside the formal justice system. Further, studies show that there is an important connection between unresolved legal problems and broader issues of health, social welfare and economic wellbeing.[12] People who are disadvantaged and living in energy poverty, for example, suffer the consequences of a lack of access to justice in their everyday lives. This results in a vicious cycle of poverty, inequality and marginalisation. The burden of this justice gap falls disproportionally on the most vulnerable, including women, children, minorities and people with disabilities.[13] As noted in the introduction, therefore, there is in practice a very sizeable gulf between aspirations around access to justice and

[7] European Commission, *Consumer Conditions Scoreboard: Consumers at Home in the Single Market* (European Commission, 2019), available at: ec.europa.eu/info/sites/info/files/consumers-conditions-scoreboard-2019_pdf_en.pdf.

[8] N Creutzfeldt, *Ombudsmen and ADR: A Comparative Study of Informal Justice in Europe* (Palgrave Macmillan, 2018).

[9] Department for Business, Energy & Industrial Strategy (BEIS), *Resolving Consumer Disputes: Alternative Dispute Resolution and the Court System* (BEIS, 2018), available at: assets.publishing.service.gov.uk/government/uploads/system/uploads/attachment_data/file/698442/Final_report_-_Resolving_consumer_disputes.pdf.

[10] R Sandefur, 'Access to What?' (2019) 148 *Daedalus* 49.

[11] P Pleasence and N Balmer, *How to Resolve 'Legal' Problems* (Legal Services Board, 2014), available at: www.legalservicesboard.org.uk/wp-content/media/How-People-Resolve-Legal-Problems.pdf; H Genn, *Paths to Justice: What People Do and Think about Going to Law* (Hart Publishing, 1999).

[12] M Buckley, 'Evolving Legal Services: Review of Current Literature' (2013), available at: cleoconnect.ca/wp-content/uploads/2015/01/Appendix-A-Evolving-Legal-Services-Literarture-Review.pdf; P Pleasence, N Balmer and T Tam et al, *Civil Justice in England and Wales: Report of the 2007 English and Welsh Legal Needs Study* (Legal Services Commission, 2008).

[13] Jim Yong Kim, 'Energy Access is a Social Justice Issue' (*World Bank Blogs*, 4 November 2015), available at: blogs.worldbank.org/voices/energy-access-is-a-social-justice-issue.

the realisation of those aspirations. As Benöehr has noted,[14] access to justice is recognised as a fundamental right in various international instruments, including the International Covenant on Civil and Political Rights (Articles 2 and 14), the UN Guiding Principles on Business and Human Rights, the European Convention on Human Rights (Articles 6 and 13) and the European Union (EU) Charter of Fundamental Rights (Article 47). However, this formal recognition has done little to change things on the ground for individuals, so that 'consumers still face major barriers to enforcing their rights in practice'.[15]

Energy consumers are among those that are most likely to be excluded from accessing justice. The energy market, referred to by some as an 'inherently flawed market',[16] features high levels of consumer dissatisfaction and a failure to meet consumers' needs.[17] The energy sector regularly comes out at the bottom of league tables rating customer experiences in various industry sectors.[18] Indeed, in a recent European Commission Survey, 58 per cent of European consumers agreed that the electricity market in their country did not work well. The European Consumer Organisation (BEUC) has argued that: 'Even after the adoption of several EU legislative packages, European consumers have often difficulties to effectively exercise their rights and therefore essential characteristics of a well-functioning retail energy market are still missing'.[19] And, although available mechanisms of redress provide some level of remedy to the detriment estimated to be borne by energy consumers, there remains a considerable level of unremedied detriment in the European energy market: the total post-redress financial detriment in 2017 in the EU-28 was between €1.9 billion and €6.4 billion, as compared with between €2.4 billion and €7.2 billion pre-redress.[20]

III. Understanding the Barriers to Access to Justice

The scale of the access to justice gap is therefore significant. As we will see, there is a range of factors that are linked to particular individuals' and groups' proclivity to access justice. Generally, however, it is important to understand the process through which justice is accessed in order to understand the factors which present barriers at various stage of that process. The foundational approach is

[14] Benöhr, 'Consumer Dispute Resolution after the Lisbon Treaty' (n 1); I Benöhr, *EU Consumer Law and Human Rights* (OUP, 2014).

[15] Benöhr, *EU Consumer Law and Human Rights* (n 14) 178.

[16] M Ioannidou, 'Effective Paths for Consumer Empowerment and Protection in Retail Energy Markets' (2018) 41 *Journal of Consumer Policy* 135, 137.

[17] Accenture. *The New Energy Consumer* (Accenture 2013).

[18] BEUC, *Consumer Rights in Energy Markets*, BEUC Position Paper (BEUC, October 2013).

[19] ibid 3.

[20] European Commission, *Study on Measuring Consumer Detriment in the European Union* (European Commission, 2017), available at: ec.europa.eu/info/sites/info/files/consumer-detriment-study-final-report_en.pdf.

Felstiner et al's work.[21] Their naming, blaming and claiming framework emphasises the social dimensions of disputing and seeks to provide a way of explaining how the problems individuals experience emerge (or, more commonly, do not emerge) as legal problems. The distance that lies between someone experiencing a problem and finding a remedy to it is considerable, and the general emphasis of the access to justice literature is on the multiple and complex overlapping factors that prevent the realisation of access to justice in practice. These factors have been summarised in various ways. For instance, Crawford and Maldano talk of epistemological inequality, socio-economic inequality, and legal market inequality as ways of explaining differential access to justice between individuals and social groups.[22] In this chapter, we use Fesltiner et al's framework as the basis for classifying the different factors.

The decision to follow this approach is not merely one of preference or convenience. Instead, we agree with Palmer and Roberts[23] that a failure to recognise and follow through on Felstiner et al's insights about the processes through which disputes emerge is responsible for the often narrow focus on redress mechanisms that is displayed in access to justice literature and policy. Such a focus tends only to recognise barriers to 'claiming' and ignores the social, cognitive and cultural factors that often prevent disputes getting anywhere near a redress mechanism, regardless of its features. Indeed, as we shall see, many access to justice policies start from an opposite point of view: the problem is not that most disputes do not emerge, but that there are too many disputes and that they represent an unreasonable burden on the public purse. The policy problem is, therefore, conceptualised as being about managing demand and often focused on 'sorting out' the court system, whereas Felstiner et al's framework suggests that the broader reality of access to justice problems (and the possible solutions to them) is to be found elsewhere. Of course, we do not suggest that questions around institutional design are irrelevant – clearly the types of mechanism (and their features) made available by the state to deal with people's problems will have some effect on whether they are used or not in practice. We merely suggest that this is not the only consideration. Albiston and Sandefur refer to 'bottom-up' and 'top-down' approaches to access to justice, which consider both the demand and supply sides of the problem.[24] This is the approach we follow here, considering both the bottom-up views of potential justice seekers and the top-down perspective of the state seeking to respond through the provision of appropriate mechanisms of redress.

In the paragraphs below, we begin by highlighting some general issues that arise from the access to justice literature in relation to each of the naming,

[21] Felstiner, Abel and Sarat (n 2).

[22] C Crawford and D Moldonado, 'Access to Justice: Theory and Practice from a Comparative Perspective' (2020) 27 *Indiana Journal of Global Legal Studies* 1.

[23] M Palmer and S Roberts, *Dispute Processes: ADR and the Primary Forms of Decision-Making* (CUP, 2014).

[24] C Albiston and RL Sandefur, 'Expanding the Empirical Study of Access to Justice' [2013] *Wisconsin Law Review* 101 (UC Berkeley Public Law Research Paper No 2282498).

blaming and claiming stages. We then move on to look at the specific issues affecting vulnerable and energy-poor consumers.

A. Factors that Impact on People's Ability to Name a Problem

The factors here relate largely to what Crawford and Maldano describe as epistemological inequality.[25] People are often unaware of their rights due to a lack of legal education. Unsurprisingly, marginalised and excluded sections of society are much less likely to have access either to direct knowledge of legal rights and processes or to sources of informed help and advice.[26] Indeed, a criticism of current policies that seek to address the access to justice gap is that they are overly generic and do not sufficiently recognise the need to target disadvantaged groups that face the most acute barriers to access: for instance, demographic characteristics such as class, race, ethnicity, gender, disability and other health conditions, sexuality, age (youth or old age), income level, education level and geography (urban/rural/remote). While membership of a group that might generally be considered to be suffering some level of social marginalisation does not mean that all members of such groups will be excluded from accessing justice, group membership presents particular hurdles, especially given the propensity for specific problems to exist in clusters:

> We should not underestimate the extent to which legal and other problems reinforce each other or how, in general, they prevent resolution of problems for many people who do not experience the traditional grounds of disadvantage. However, we also cannot ignore that, for those who have suffered and are suffering traditional forms of disadvantage, this reinforcement effect of myriad problems looms large indeed.[27]

Many of these factors represent fundamental barriers to accessing justice because they prevent individuals from recognising a problem as such in the first place. Of course, many of these barriers are also likely to affect behaviour throughout the dispute emergence process.

B. Factors that Impact on People's Ability to Blame Someone for a Problem

Having identified that a problem exists, people must then be in a position to ascertain who is to blame for that problem. This may seem straightforward, but

[25] ibid.

[26] P Hughes, 'Advancing Access to Justice through Generic Solutions: The Risk of Perpetuating Exclusion' (2013) 31 *Windsor Yearbook of Access to Justice* 1.

[27] ibid 8.

research shows that rather than people being over-litigious and overly keen to blame others for their problems, many people in fact adopt a fatalistic approach which involves accepting problems rather than seeking to resolve them. Sandefur, for instance, in reviewing empirical evidence on access to justice, notes that when people are asked to characterise a problem they have experienced, 56 per cent talked about the problem being 'bad luck/part of life' or 'part of God's plan'.[28] The World Justice Project survey meanwhile found that only 29 per cent of those surveyed understood their problem to be legal in nature as opposed to 'bad luck'.[29] Another factor discussed by Sandefur relates to people's limited advice-seeking behaviour: seeking informed advice might help individuals see that a problem is not simply bad luck, but that someone is to blame and a remedy is available. Where advice was not sought, 46 per cent of people said they had no need for advice, with the second most common reason being that advice 'wouldn't make any difference'. This suggests both a degree of fatalism and a lack of trust in professional and outside sources of advice. In this situation, membership of social networks is likely to be important in determining people's ability to understand the source of their problems – having strong social and community bonds can give people access to help and resources that assist them in conceptualising their problems differently and can affect their disputing behaviour (we return to this issue below).

C. Factors that Impact on People's Ability to Make a Claim in Relation to their Problem

The key factors in relation to claiming relate to: the availability of sources of legal/informed advice; limited financial resources and the high costs of accessing professional advice; the availability of legal aid to support legal claims; the complexity of the law in the particular area of dispute; and the complexity and length of the procedures that are required to raise a claim. For those who are aware of having suffered an injustice and whose conceptualisation of the issue has allowed them to blame another party and frame the matter as one that is capable of some kind of formal resolution, the major barrier to claiming is cost.[30] The cost of legal advice is high and out of reach, not only for people on low incomes, but increasingly for people on middle incomes. Similarly, the cost to government of either subsidising legal advice or providing direct advice (through advice and advocacy agencies) is considerable and, therefore, there are limits on what is available to those with a potential claim. Greene found that members of poor and

[28] RL Sandefur, 'What We Know and Need to Know about the Legal Needs of the Public' (2015) 67 *South Carolina Law Review* 443, 449.

[29] World Justice Project, *Global Insights* (n 3).

[30] DL Rhode, 'Access to Justice: A Roadmap for Reform' (2013) 41 *Fordham Urban Law Journal* 1227.

minority groups are less likely than their higher-income counterparts to seek help when they experience a civil legal problem.[31] She concludes that there are two sets of barriers to accessing justice for poor and minority ethnic people:

1. structural barriers to access – focusing on funding, lawyer availability and the number of legal aid offices and their locations;
2. cultural and cognitive barriers to access – focusing on barriers to access stemming from life experiences that result in help not being sought in the first place.[32]

Newman argues that the accessibility of legal systems has traditionally been conceived in terms of economic barriers and, to a lesser degree, cultural or psychological barriers, but very rarely has access to justice been considered along spatial grounds.[33] He discusses concerns about 'advice deserts' and 'justice deserts' in rural areas, as austerity results in the institutions of justice consolidating in the larger towns and cities of England and Wales. The ability to lodge a claim may therefore not only be limited by resources but also by geographical issues in relation to the availability of advice.

IV. Particular Barriers Facing Energy Consumers

A. The Nature of the Energy Market

Energy consumers are potentially subject to all of the barriers discussed so far; however, the kinds of problems they experience and their relationships with liberalised energy markets present distinct issues. As noted above, the energy market has been described as one that is 'inherently flawed'.[34] The progressive liberalisation of European energy markets has been underpinned by the assumption of traditional economics that energy consumers would behave as classically rational economic actors. In other words, when faced with a choice of suppliers in a liberalised market, consumers would be able to assess rationally the offers made by competing energy suppliers and choose the tariffs and services that would maximise their economic wellbeing. Energy suppliers would then respond to this consumer behaviour by competing with each other on price and service quality, creating an efficient market. As Poudineh has pointed out:

> [T]he key objectives of a regulator with respect to the retail business is to create a market with low barriers to entry for suppliers and low barriers to switching for consumers.

[31] S Sternberg Greene, 'Race, Class, and Access to Civil Justice' (2015) 101 *Iowa Law Review* 1263.
[32] ibid 1317.
[33] D Newman, 'Attitudes to Justice in a Rural Community' (2016) 36 *Legal Studies* 591.
[34] Ioannidou (n 16).

> There is almost consensus among economists that realising these two objectives will result in efficient electricity prices, innovations, and improved service quality.[35]

The problem, however, is that the assumptions around consumer behaviour that underpin the design of liberalised markets have not materialised and have generally failed to respond to interventions aimed at triggering rational behaviour, such as switching.[36] A major barrier to access to justice, therefore, is the fact that the energy market expects consumers to behave in a way that most of them do not. The expectations of active consumption are not only unrealistic in relation to the average consumers, but also may have particularly exclusionary consequences for vulnerable individuals:

> An important feature of existing retail electricity markets is that they are designed such that a potentially active consumer would benefit most. An active consumer in this context means a user who is receptive to information provided by suppliers or who has the ability to search and find relevant information, can analyse available choices and react accordingly, or who can bargain for a better deal. Not all small consumers … would fit this definition.[37]

Instead, the reality for energy consumers is mostly one of passive consumption, albeit with a small core of active consumers (some 'prosumers' are now even able to generate electricity through micro-generation and sell this back to the grid). Ioannidou points to different categories of energy consumer: active engaged consumers, passive engaged consumers, and disengaged consumers.[38] Active engaged consumers are those who meet Poudineh's definition above. Passive engaged consumers are those who have the ability to access and assess market information but choose not to do so. Disengaged consumers are those who are likely to be vulnerable in some way and face the steepest barriers to market participation. Waddams Price has referred to the problem that energy regulators and competition authorities have to deal with as 'customer inertia'.[39] This inertia can be seen in low levels of switching activity. In 2018, only 8.1 per cent of European energy consumers switched suppliers,[40] with the highest switching rate in Norway (18.8 per cent) and the lowest in Bulgaria (0.002 per cent). A number of particular barriers have been identified as standing in the way of increased switching

[35] R Poudineh, *Liberalized Retail Electricity Markets: What We Have Learned after Two Decades of Experience?* (2019), available at: www.oxfordenergy.org/wpcms/wp-content/uploads/2019/12/Liberalized-retail-electricity-markets-EL-38.pdf.

[36] C Waddams Price, 'Back to the Future? Regulating Residential Energy Markets' (2018) 25 *International Journal of the Economics of Business* 147.

[37] Poudineh (n 35) 12.

[38] Ioannidou (n 16).

[39] D Deller and C Waddams Price, 'Energy Affordability and Old Age: Expenditure versus Self-reported Perceptions' (2018) 35 *CCP Research Bulletin* 14–16, available at: competitionpolicy.ac.uk/documents/8158338/8193544/UEA+CCP+Research+Bulletin+Issue+3 5+Spring+2018+UPDATED.pdf/cc9c68e5-fb3c-dc85-3395-6a8ccb8961a0.

[40] Council of European Energy Regulators, *Annual Report 2018* (CEER, 2018) 32.

behaviour, such as the complexity of the market, difficulties in understanding energy tariffs and the differences between them, the homogeneous and insubstantial nature of energy as a product, transaction costs when switching, uncertainty about service quality with new suppliers, perceived barriers to switching, and behavioural biases.[41]

In summary, there are two particular challenges for access to justice arising from the liberalised energy market: the dominance of rational theories of consumer behaviour which assume active participation and, as a result, penalise those who cannot participate; and the reality of largely passive energy consumers, with inertia seeming to result from a rational choice for passive engaged consumers and from vulnerability factors for disengaged consumers. This generalised inertia in relation to switching behaviour in the energy sector is echoed in the literature on consumer disputing. Here, however, rather than rational economic models being largely disconfirmed by consumers' actual behaviour, they have been applied as the central way of explaining why people who experience problems do not complain.

B. Cost and Rational Apathy

Consumer problems, such as those experienced in the energy sector, are often seen as a paradigmatic example of what Cappelletti and Garth call problems that affect 'diffuse interests'.[42] These problems do not arise so much out of individual issues in bi-party relationships, but affect collective interests:

> The problem can be formulated like this. An individual consumer complaint or grievance may be the result of an individual experience but, in these days of mass production and consumption, it is likely that the experience is shared by other consumers. Contractual arrangements are often common to groups of consumers.[43]

A particular issue for consumers is that, while the potential detriment suffered is large in the aggregate, losses for individuals are typically small.[44] The 2011 European Commission Consumer Scoreboard showed that the mean losses suffered by consumers amount to €375, with median losses of €18.70.[45] Similarly, Hodges et al found that consumer disputes tend to involve comparatively low-value claims.[46] In France, for example, the average award of the energy ombuds was €73, while

[41] Poudineh (n 35).

[42] BG Garth and M Cappelletti, 'Access to Justice: The Newest Wave in the Worldwide Movement to Make Rights Effective' (1978) 27 *Buffalo Law Review* 181, 182.

[43] C Graham 'Consumer ADR and Collective Redress' in P Cortes (ed), *The New Regulatory Framework for Consumer Dispute Resolution* (OUP, 2016) 429.

[44] Y Sutatip, *Access to Justice in Transnational B2C e-Commerce: A Multidimensional Analysis of Consumer Protection* (Springer, 2015).

[45] European Commission, *Consumer Conditions Scoreboard* (n 7).

[46] C Hodges, I Benöhr and N Creutzfeldt-Banda, *Consumer ADR in Europe* (Hart Publishing, 2012).

the average amount in dispute with the EDF ombuds was €1,120.[47] A particular problem for consumers, therefore, as groups of individuals with diffuse interests, is that the cost of a problem to any individual consumer is often too small to warrant them taking on the cost and risk of seeking redress.[48] The European Commission's Consumer Scoreboard for 2019 found that 39.7 per cent of consumers who had experienced a problem did not complain because they considered the amount of detriment to be too small.[49] This was the second highest reason for not taking action, behind thinking that it would take too long (42.4 per cent). Benöhr argues that cost and inefficient procedures are the main barriers to consumers accessing justice in Europe.[50]

While much has been made of the importance of the low value of consumer claims in explaining the barriers facing consumers, these should not be overstated. For low-income households and those at risk of fuel poverty, what professional elites consider to be small sums can be a significant portion of their weekly or monthly budget. In an age of increasing energy prices, where energy costs are taking up a larger share of people's incomes,[51] even relatively small amounts of detriment can be very significant for people and their families. Apathy may be rational for those on middle and high incomes, but is less so for those on lower incomes. In these cases, barriers beyond cost are likely to be significant.

C. 'Behavioural Consumers'

Indeed, just as assumptions of energy market liberalisation about consumer behaviour in the market have turned out to be wrong, so explaining claiming behaviour in the consumer context purely in terms of rational cost–benefit analysis is incomplete. A rational assessment of the value of a potential claim against the costs of redressing it must play a part in individual claiming behaviour. However, Stürner has pointed out that the barriers which consumers experience are not purely related to cost, despite sometimes being conceived as such in consumer policy narratives: 'The psychological barrier seems to be too high to overcome. Consequently, the courts' doors remain shut'.[52] This is supported by Ramsay who has argued that while simply removing cost barriers might work for purely rational actors, such measures would not overcome how people feel about the law and whether they want to use it.[53]

[47] ibid 381.
[48] Garth and Cappelletti (n 42).
[49] European Commission, *Consumer Conditions Scoreboard* (n 7) 9.
[50] Benöhr, *EU Consumer Law and Human Rights* (n 14).
[51] Deller and Waddams Price, 'Energy Affordability and Old Age' (n 39).
[52] M Stürner, 'ADR and Adjudication by State Courts: Competitors or Complements?' in M Stürner, F Gascón Inchausti and R Caponi (eds), *The Role of Consumer ADR in the Administration of Justice* (Dr Otto Schmidt, 2014) 13.
[53] Ramsay (n 5).

Insights from Ewick and Silbey's work on the ways in which individuals in the United States experience legal problems and conceptualise their relationship with law are important here.[54] Their study concluded that people's understanding of law is socially constituted and strongly connected to ideology, with individuals developing differing conceptions of the law (with law being variously majestic, a game to be played, or capricious and oppressive). As Ramsay points out, many of the issues raised in Ewick and Silbey's research were consumer issues.[55] Their insights are particularly important in the consumer context because they emphasise the social constituents of people's understandings of law in everyday life and, therefore, limit the emphasis on purely cost-driven and rational behaviour. As noted above, a particular feature of liberalised energy markets – and the policies that have been developed to regulate them by policymakers – has been the dominance of economic theories that make problematic assumptions about the rationality of consumer behaviour. Such assumptions can both exclude consideration of structural social factors and the individual and social cognitive processes that are responsible for shaping people's understandings of the law and how their problems might relate to it. According to Ramsay:

> The findings of Ewick and Silbey are significant in emphasising the importance of social norms and the complex way in which ideas about legality and law are constructed and reproduced by individuals. It suggests that measures intended to affect social norms may be as important a strategy as reducing the financial costs of consumer action.[56]

Indeed, there are numerous issues that have been identified as important in driving the claiming behaviour of consumers beyond cost. The European Commission's survey of European consumers reported them providing the following reasons for not complaining: perceived length of time to resolve issues; the low likelihood of a satisfactory response; a desire to avoid confrontation; previous failures to resolve consumer problems; a lack of certainty about rights; and a lack of knowledge about how to complain.[57] As will be evident, many of these relate to the way in which individuals perceive situations, their past experiences, and their cognitive orientation to complaining and conflict. Recent research with UK energy consumers has also emphasised consumer passivity in relation to complaining behaviour, with 47 per cent of consumers suffering in silence (the figure rises to 70 per cent for consumers categorised as vulnerable). Millennials were particularly likely to avoid formal complaining behaviour, instead expressing dissatisfaction on social media or to friends and family: 62 per cent of millennials agreed with the statement 'complaining fills me with dread'.[58] Cognitive and emotional processing is, therefore, important in understanding complaining behaviour and the extent to which individuals might be

[54] P Ewick and S Silbey, *The Common Place of Law: Stories from Everyday Life* (Chicago University Press, 1998).

[55] Ramsay (n 5).

[56] ibid 32.

[57] European Commission, *Consumer Conditions Scoreboard* (n 7) 9.

[58] *Consumer Action Monitor* (Ombudsman Services, 2019).

'emotionally deterred' from acting. Recent research has also stressed the role that emotions play in relation to energy consumption. While we see an overall picture of passive consumption in terms of switching and complaint behaviour, vulnerable consumers are often highly emotionally involved with their energy use.[59] Some consumers prefer expensive pre-payment meters, for example, because these allow them to stay in control of expenditure and avoid anxiety around keeping their family and pets warm, ending up in debt, or having to rely on friends and family for help.

D. Unrealistic Expectations of Energy Consumers

The suggestion here is that many interventions to increase access to justice for consumers, largely concerned with reducing cost barriers to claiming, are misdirected because they do not sufficiently address the way in which consumers actually experience problems and the way they understand them. Not only will many of those interventions be ineffective, but Laster and Kornhauser have pointed out that policymakers' narratives about consumers and their ideological framing of how they should behave in consumer markets causes problems that re-enforce disadvantage for those who are most in need.[60] Referring to policy expectations that consumers will be active participants in markets – namely, individuals who are engaged, knowledgeable and confident – they argue that this has led to a 'self-help' approach to the resolution of many legal problems. Ideological preferences have combined with the increased availability of information online to normalise the idea that consumers should be ever more involved in resolving their own problems. Consumers are increasingly expected to 'co-produce' services, and narratives of consumer empowerment, while often well intentioned, have in fact exacerbated problems faced by people who have already been excluded from full market participation before the development of unrealistic policy aspirations in relation to consumer behaviour. Laster and Kornhauser argue that those who cannot meet these aspirations become increasingly marginalised:

> In the information age, DIY problem-solving approaches abound, including for the resolution of legal issues. Unfortunately, the individuals who do not make the grade have become the marginalised … The wonders of technology have seemingly turned us (or the 'capable' majority) into 'gifted amateurs'. The bar of social competence has been raised unnaturally high. Those unable to meet these standards have become the undeserving poor of the technological age.[61]

[59] D Deller and C Waddams Price (eds), *Fairness in Retail Energy Markets? Evidence from the UK* (CCP, 2018), available at: competitionpolicy.ac.uk/documents/8158338/18232983/CCP+%26+UKERC+-+Fairness+in+Retail+Energy+Markets+Report.pdf/6499c409-10c9-8f5a-73a3-0290b5ab022f.

[60] K Laster and R Kornhauser, 'The Rise of "DIY" Law: Implications for Legal Aid' in A Flynn and J Hodgson (eds), *Access to Justice and Legal Aid: Comparative Perspectives on Unmet Legal Need* (Hart Publishing, 2017).

[61] ibid 136.

This shift towards self-help and narratives around empowered consumers is particularly problematic in the context of consumers with small individual claims finding themselves in dispute with large bureaucracies. This results in an inherent power and resource imbalance between parties. And while consumers are typically 'one-shotters', with limited experience of law and claiming, businesses are 'repeat players' and therefore likely to have significant advantages in the event of a dispute being raised.[62] Assumptions about consumers' degree of engagement in relation to legal services (and problem-solving generally) appear therefore to be as flawed as the assumptions made about their behaviour in energy markets.

V. Consumer Vulnerability and Energy Poverty as Barriers to Accessing Justice

A. Moving Beyond 'Generalist' Approaches to Access to Justice

Our concern in this book is not only with 'generalist' policies on access to justice (ie, approaches that make access to justice better for everyone);[63] we are also concerned, specifically, with the realisation of access to justice for individuals and groups who are vulnerable or energy poor. In other words, given the scale of the access to justice challenge we have identified above, we follow Hughes in arguing that access to justice needs to be particularly concerned with the exclusion of the most disadvantaged in society.[64] These socially produced inequalities cannot be ignored. In the context of achieving access to justice in European energy markets, the concepts of vulnerability and energy poverty are useful as a means of focusing attention and prioritising those individuals and groups who are most in need and most likely to suffer injustice without remedy. We argue that the advantage of adopting vulnerability (with energy poverty as a subset of vulnerability) as a complement to understanding barriers to accessing justice is that it takes a multidimensional approach, which includes structural factors and inequalities (race, class, gender, income etc) but at the same time highlights the importance of other factors, such as personal factors, life circumstances, and the particular characteristics of the market. Indeed, the particular advantage of adopting vulnerability as a way to frame access to justice issues is that it calls attention to the fluidity of people's life circumstances. A vulnerability approach allows us therefore to encompass a much broader range of access to justice barriers, which include both static

[62] M Galanter, 'Why the "Haves" Come out Ahead: Speculations on the Limits of Legal Change (1974) 9 *Law & Society Review* 95.

[63] Hughes (n 26).

[64] ibid.

variables and those that are affected by changes in people's circumstances. This is particularly important since changes in circumstances (job losses, illness, family breakup, housing changes) can often be root causes or triggers of people's problems. Given the importance of vulnerability in this book, we look now at key definitions of the concept and its relationship to energy poverty and access to justice.

B. Defining Vulnerability and Energy Poverty

What does it mean to be vulnerable? Over the last 40 years this question has been asked by many researchers, commentators and policymakers in the context of consumer protection and access to justice. A variety of definitions have been offered in relation to what it means to be a 'vulnerable consumer', with there being no single, settled definition of 'vulnerability'. Despite this lack of uniformity, however, central themes and areas of concurrence are apparent. Underpinning many of the concepts of consumer vulnerability which have emerged is the work of Andreasen. In his 1975 work *The Disadvantaged Consumer* Andreasen posits that disadvantaged consumers are those who are particularly prevented in achieving adequate value for their 'consumer dollar' in the urban marketplace because of limited incomes, status within a minority racial group, age and language difficulties.[65]

Later work on vulnerability has moved beyond class-based categorisation. Baker et al's work, for example, interrogates the dominant themes within consumer vulnerability literature, offering an alternative multidimensional and context-specific model which is focused on the experience of the consumer:

> Consumer vulnerability is a state of powerlessness that arises from an imbalance in marketplace interactions or from the consumption of marketing messages and products. It occurs when control is not in an individual's hands, creating a dependence on external factors (eg, marketers) to create fairness in the marketplace. The actual vulnerability arises from the *interaction* of individual states, individual characteristics, and external conditions within a context where consumption goals may be hindered and the experience affects personal and social perceptions of self.[66]

This conceptualisation differs from Andreasen's class perspective in three ways: (i) it shifts focus away from a whole class of people to the individual and the self; (ii) it introduces the idea of vulnerability in the face of 'marketing messages' and thus includes consumers' information-processing abilities; and (iii) it introduces the idea that vulnerability is situation dependent, for example that it results from 'an imbalance in marketplace interactions' and that consumers are often vulnerable because of factors outwith their control. Such a 'multidimensional' model of

[65] AR Andreasen, *The Disadvantaged Consumer* (The Free Press, 1975).

[66] SM Baker, JW Gentry and TL Rittenburg, 'Building Understanding of the Domain of Consumer Vulnerability' (2005) 25 *Journal of Macromarketing* 128.

vulnerability has been particularly influential in how vulnerability is now conceptualised across all consumer sectors.[67]

Indeed, Ioannidou notes that vulnerability includes both personal and market characteristics. Personal characteristics include age, low incomes and disabilities, while market characteristics refer to the features of particular markets that might be especially challenging for people.[68] The market for household goods presents few inherent challenges for consumers, while financial services or energy markets can be extremely challenging in terms of their complexity and technical nature. In the energy market, few consumers understand the units of measurement used (for example, kilowatt/hour) and the way in which tariffs are presented and structured.[69] A particularly salient issue in relation to vulnerability is energy poverty, which results from a mixture of personal circumstances and market characteristics. A household is energy poor when it is 'unable to secure a level and quality of domestic energy services … sufficient for its social and material needs'.[70] Various factors can contribute to an individual or household becoming energy poor, depending on their circumstances and situation. Similarly, most consumers can become vulnerable at some point in their lives and there are many dimensions to vulnerability. These dimensions can stretch from situational and transient to systemic and permanent. A report on consumer vulnerability across key markets in the EU[71] found a vulnerable consumer to be someone who, as a result of socio-demographic characteristics, behavioural characteristics, personal situation, or market environment:

- Is at higher risk of experiencing negative outcomes in the market.
- Has limited ability to maximise their wellbeing.
- Has difficulty in obtaining or assimilating information.
- Is less able to buy, choose or access suitable products.
- Is more susceptible to certain marketing practices.

The report goes on to describe vulnerability drivers in each of these areas. *Market-related drivers* include being unable to read contract terms and conditions and being disengaged from markets (for example, in terms of not knowing contract conditions, or not reading communications). *Behavioural drivers*

[67] C Shultz and M Holbrook, 'The Paradoxical Relationships between Marketing and Vulnerability' (2009) 28 *Journal of Public Policy & Marketing* 124; TM Pavia and MJ Mason, 'Vulnerability and Physical, Cognitive, and Behavioral Impairment: Model Extensions and Open Questions' (2014) 34 *Journal of Macromarketing* 471.

[68] Ioannidou (n 16).

[69] ibid.

[70] S Bouzarovski, *Energy Poverty: (Dis)assembling Europe's Infrastructural Divide* (Palgrave, 2018).

[71] London Economics, VVA Consulting and Ipsos Mori, *Consumer Vulnerability across Key Markets in the European Union* (2016), available at: ec.europa.eu/info/sites/info/files/consumers-approved-report_en.pdf.

concern consumers' basic orientations: more impulsive consumers are, on the whole, more likely to be vulnerable on several dimensions, while consumers who are unwilling to take risks are generally less vulnerable. Among the *situational drivers*, finding it difficult to make ends meet and having friends who cannot make ends meet, are found to be especially important. Among the *access-related drivers*, using the internet less frequently than once a month is linked to consumer vulnerability on several dimensions. And, finally, some *demographic characteristics*, such as both young and old age, and having a mother tongue different from the official language, are linked to consumer vulnerability.

The European Commission found that acute vulnerability issues in the energy sector tended to include older consumers (65+), economically inactive consumers, and those with lower educational attainment.[72] Consumers in these groups were found to have more difficulties in understanding and acting upon marketing information, as well as having lower rates of switching. Meanwhile, in its 2019 *Consumer Scoreboard*, the European Commission examined the proportion of consumers experiencing different types of vulnerability. The results show relatively widespread problems, particularly in relation to experiencing financial difficulties and having trouble engaging with complex markets. The proportion of consumers who felt vulnerable for various reasons was reported as follows:

- offers, terms, or conditions are too complex (34.2 per cent);
- poor financial circumstances (24.2 per cent);
- current employment situation (17.3 per cent);
- age (14.6 per cent);
- health problems (13.8 per cent);
- personal issues (12.1 per cent);
- belonging to a minority group (8.7 per cent).[73]

As Noone and Ojelabi have argued, the success of access to justice policies depends on whether disadvantaged individuals are able to access remedies and, if they are able to access them, how they fare thereafter.[74] As a result, we will be particularly concerned in this book and the chapters that follow to prioritise vulnerable individuals and groups in our discussions of access to justice.

[72] European Commission, *Second Consumer Market Study on the Functioning of the Retail Electricity Markets for Consumers in the EU* (European Commission, 2017), available at: ec.europa.eu/newsroom/just/item-detail.cfm?item_id=53331.

[73] European Commission, *Consumer Conditions Scoreboard* (n 7) 56.

[74] M Noone and L Ojelabi, 'Alternative Dispute Resolution and Access to Justice in Australia' (2020) 16 *International Journal of Law in Context* 108.

VI. Barriers Experienced by Vulnerable and Energy-Poor Consumers: Highlights from Our Data

Our interviews with vulnerable consumers, third-sector actors, and ADR bodies revealed in stark terms the reality of people's everyday experiences of energy poverty and vulnerability. As we argue at various points throughout this book, attending to and understanding these experiences is crucial both in elucidating the scale of the access to justice challenge, but also in designing solutions to overcome it. In this part of the chapter we highlight: lived experiences of energy poverty and vulnerability; stretched public services and community support; and the effects of changes in the energy market and technology.

A. Lived Experiences of Energy Poverty and Vulnerability

As we will argue in chapter six, the reality of vulnerable consumers' lives are very remote from the formal laws and institutions that seek to help them. Here we provide some examples of these situations. In Bulgaria, where poverty levels were high (and there exists limited state assistance) it was reported that people would stay in one room in order to limit heating costs. In France, two homes were visited by members of the research team. Such home visits fully exposed the conditions that people were living in. One of these visits was to a 48-year-old man who lived alone in a house with dangerous electrical wiring and a wood-burning stove which emitted unhealthy high levels of carbon monoxide. Reliant on an electric heater, the man reported that he only turned on his heater at night in order to save costs. The house was notably cold to the members of the research team.[75] His living room windows had gaps which let cold air in. The house contained damp and mould. The man's conditions were those of acute poverty. The poor condition of the property he lived in impacted on his ability to heat his home, and his lack of money prevented him for remedying the condition of his property. This cycle would only continue to be perpetuated without third-party assistance.

Also visited in France were a couple whose home was likewise in very poor condition: they had experienced rat and mice infestations and a local social worker had cautioned against their grandchildren visiting the property. The couple relayed an experience whereby a fire took hold in their home on Christmas Eve and they were reliant on a neighbour to call the fire department given that they themselves were not in possession of a telephone. Even seeking basic emergency help was beyond their immediate capacity. French Third Sector 12,[76] who worked for a local

[75] An extended discussion of this visit, including photographs of the man's home, are available on our research website: esrcjustenergy.wordpress.com/author/esrcjustenergy/.

[76] All data are reported anonymously.

NGO, meanwhile, noted the extent of the problems that might be faced; problems that will often remain hidden to the wider community:

> Misery is hiding. When you see [a] house, you don't think that behind the facade this situation is much worse. Houses are judged by their facades, some people make hasty judgements and feel that to get out of their situation, the poorest should simply sell their house. But the reality is often quite different, much more miserable and unimaginable (French Third Sector 12).

In Britain, poverty was also widely experienced by participants in the research. One research participant highlighted the plight of a family who could no longer afford to pay for their gas:

> Last winter, it was cold, and we had families sat in the dark, in the cold, because if you can't afford to put your gas on, your boiler goes off, too. So, when you can't afford to put gas on, your boiler goes off. So that affects, obviously, your heating, your radiators, and things like that. So, we had a family, and it was seven, half seven at night, and they were sat in the dark, with no electric, and no gas (UK Third Sector 8).

Other British participants commented on extreme poverty becoming normalised, with a situation of ongoing crisis becoming standard for many people:

> As volunteers, we're going into situations that are life and death for people, it's crisis situations, it's people on the verge of suicide … it's deteriorating, I think. Before, people were … struggling, but managing. And now, it's completely changed (UK Third Sector 8).

Such extreme poverty had impacts not only on people's ability to access any kind of services and help, but on all aspects of their lives. It goes without saying that living in conditions of extreme poverty has a significant impact on someone's physical and mental health.

> We have had an incident in the last 12 months where someone was threatening to attempt suicide while we were there … That was purely because she'd run up a debt on a prepayment meter and she couldn't get any gas on and it was through the cold snap, you know, where it was freezing and snowing like it felt forever and she just couldn't get warm (UK Third Sector 1).

B. Stretched Public Services and Community Support

For NGOs involved in community work, issues pertaining to energy were experienced as part of a wider picture of poverty and deprivation. This poverty was often linked explicitly to state support and the (reduced) welfare provision available to those most in need within society. The poverty in question overlapped with issues relating to crime, education and employment. It encapsulated the responsibilities of landlords and the availability of adequate housing. Energy poverty was understood as an expression of poverty more widely. The complexities surrounding many energy consumers' vulnerabilities are such that they require assistance: state assistance, help from NGOs and support from family and friends, if available. However, communities and the support available to them were also increasingly stretched as a result of funding shortages. In chapters two and six, we highlight the important role that intermediaries and local actors can play in overcoming the alienation and distance that vulnerable consumers experience in relation to the energy market and formal laws and institutions that are designed to help them. However, while they play a key role, underfunding creates a clear barrier to accessing justice.

Research participants told us that many third-sector organisations are having to do more, with less. Staff are having to deal with more complex problems, with less funding, fewer resources and less financial security. For NGOs, identifying those most in need is often not the problem. Instead, the problem is responding to those in need adequately.

> [T]here is a limited amount of help that's out there … everybody is competing for a limited number of spaces on the bus … there isn't enough help to go around. And, you know, we're finding that households are being turned away, even though they are desperately in need (UK Third Sector 4).

Similarly, an organisation working on support funds for energy management projects in a rural area in France since 2002 noted the critical lack of funding. For them, when staff enter a dwelling, they are not an 'energy label'; their job is more than thermal renovation: it is social action, health, housing and energy. In their view, public health as a whole is being insufficiently addressed. An Italian think tank also emphasised energy poverty as a social problem, noting that the solution lies in tackling the associated problems of crime, city infrastructure, mobility, green spaces and improving the civil relationship holistically. However, with limited resources addressing demands for help and the multifaceted nature of people's energy problems was inherently limited.

C. The Energy Market and Technology

In recent years, the liberalisation of the energy market has resulted in significant changes in many European jurisdictions, with more suppliers competing in the marketplace. It was recognised that some new companies had introduced innovative models which were well suited to the needs of consumers, including those with vulnerabilities, but it was also cautioned that emerging companies were likely to have less experience of dealing with vulnerability and as such this changing market could have a detrimental effect on the most vulnerable. In discussing concerns about engagement from smaller suppliers, one participant noted:

> So, we have one, which has got about 500, 600 customers, and we were having problems … consumers off supply couldn't get through on the phone because they'd all left for the day, at like, lunchtime, because it was a nice day (UK Complaint Handling Organisation 1).

As well as more companies entering the energy market, market liberalisation is founded upon the notion of active consumers creating market discipline, and consumers are therefore increasingly encouraged to routinely change suppliers and 'shop around' for the best deals. This is facilitated through a number of online companies who offer price comparison services. While such services can estimate potential savings, they do not indicate customer service levels or the experience of staff working at that organisation. Where a consumer has additional support needs, the customer service provision offered by their energy supplier may be invaluable, not only to their satisfaction as a customer, but to their health and well-being. In this regard, the current landscape of the energy market may exacerbate consumers' vulnerabilities making it more important than ever that consumers are able to access the correct support.

Both energy suppliers and those involved in complaint resolution have increasingly looked to technology to streamline processes, and some of our research participants spoke at length about the technological developments which were taking place at this time as well as those planned for the future. UK Ombuds 5 discussed the 'real drive to go digital' in complaint handling, linking this to efficiency measures more generally. He also spoke about the increasing digitalisation of the complaint handling in their service, noting that a key objective for them in moving forward was to ensure that their digital service would be customer focused. Specifically, he spoke about the use of speech analytics. This technology offers analysis of telephone calls, identifying key phrases as well as those subtle phrases which can help to identify vulnerability. He discussed his hope for the development of a 'vulnerability algorithm' which could offer personalised service. At the same time, it was recognised that technology could present a barrier for many people and that a drive towards digital services was likely to exclude the most vulnerable. As noted above, some families do not have a telephone to call the fire brigade, let along access to online services.

Among energy suppliers generally, an increase in using online services was reported: emails, online complaint submissions, online meter readings, paperless bills and terms and conditions of contracts being available through their websites. In Italy, the introduction of optic meters was discussed by a local consumer organisation. It was hoped that these meters will target the problem of reading estimates. Wrong estimates can have a big impact on families since expected outgoings can increase suddenly, resulting in an unaffordable bill. This organisation noted experiences of people crying with shame because they could not afford their energy bills. They noted the need in Italy for basic education in order to understand the differences between estimates and meter readings. Similarly, within the UK there has also been the introduction of smart meters which show consumers exactly how much gas and electricity has been used in pounds and pence. Although generally viewed as a tool to help consumers budget for their energy bills, some concerns were raised by a UK NGO, on the basis that such a visual indicator of energy consumption may lead some vulnerable individuals to spend less time cooking (healthier) food from scratch if it becomes obvious that this is more expensive than using a microwave to heat a pre-packaged meal. In this way, there may be a risk of unintended consequences for those who adopt the use of smart meters. While the direction of travel in the energy market was distinctly digital, the experiences of vulnerable consumers we spoke to show the challenges this presents.

For older participants in the study, this increased use of technology as part of energy suppliers' routine customer service was an issue of concern:

> Now I haven't got a computer and I haven't got an email address. I'm 77 years of age now and it goes over my head (Catalan Consumer 6).

Similarly, where family members were dealing with the energy complaints on behalf of elderly relatives, worries surrounding computer access were voiced:

> I tell my nana to download the app, because I don't like her going out the house early on a morning, or late on a night, for gas or electric. And I'm like, nana, just go on your card, and she's like, oh no, I like to go to the shop and pay like that, I don't trust them things. And I'm like, but I don't like you going out on a night, so just do it like that, and she's like, no (UK Consumers 11–17).

The demand for complaints to be made online could be seen to directly impact consumers' ability to engage with the complaints process, thereby impacting access to justice directly:

> It's all done either online, which I can't do it with my hand condition. The only thing was by telephone and telephone doesn't go direct to complaint department, it goes to the general account queries and then you have to sort out yourself from there and how to do it and where to do … I told them I can't go online because of my hand condition. That's the only way (UK Consumer 4).

In addition to concerns relating to the use of computers, some participants emphasised a simple desire to have human interaction in complaint resolution; they wanted their complaint to be heard – literally:

> I'll be 59 next month … So, I've never grown up with computers, so I've never been interested, so I'm quite happy, I would rather speak to people, I would, I think you just get a better, well usually you get on better result sometimes I think just by talking to somebody (UK Consumer 10).

VII. Conclusion

This chapter has shown the significant gap that exists between the ideal of access to justice and the realisation of that ideal in contemporary society. We live in a world characterised by injustice, and remedies are all too often outwith the reach of ordinary people. The factors that are responsible for limiting access to justice are well understood, and there is considerable research evidence to draw on which can help policymakers tackle the challenge. Similarly, the multidimensional challenges posed by vulnerability and energy poverty are increasingly clear and well known. Our data highlight these challenges in stark terms and give a real sense of the lived experiences of vulnerability and energy poverty on the ground. The reality, however, is that access to justice policies rarely take the kind of multifactorial and holistic approaches that would be required to tackle these challenges and the barriers at each of the naming, blaming and claiming phases. There are several reasons for this, including ignorance of the research base, a perception that the scale of the challenge makes it very difficult to surmount, and the framing of access to justice primarily as a matter of court reform and reform of the legal sector. In our view, a narrow framing of access to justice is a major factor behind the continued existence of large access to justice gaps across justice contexts and the significant amount of unremedied detriment in the European energy market. In the next chapter, therefore, we turn to examine different approaches to access to justice and argue that, in order to meaningfully address the barriers to access to justice identified here and to tackle the issues that face vulnerable and energy-poor consumers in particular, a more holistic vision is required.

2

A Holistic Vision of Access to Justice

I. Introduction

This chapter sets out what we refer to as a holistic vision of access to justice. The chapter begins in section II by claiming that, despite early accounts of access to justice taking a broad view of the concept, there has been a reversion – driven partly by ideological preference and partly by pragmatism – towards narrow definitions of access to justice. Such narrow approaches to access to justice equate justice with the concept of 'legal justice', involving access to legal assistance in the form of legal advice and access to resolution in the form of legal institutions. Here, the chapter argues for a broader view, with non-legal advice provision, alternative forms of dispute resolution, internal complaint-handling arrangements within firms, and a broader range of social and community actors being recognised as important to the delivery of access to justice in practice.

In section III, the chapter addresses the tendency for access to justice scholarship and policy to emphasise the procedural dimension of access to justice and the extent to which remedial procedures are available and accessible, to the exclusion of considering matters of substance. Here, the chapter argues that substantive justice concerns cannot be separated from access to justice discussions. While substantive justice is contentious to define and all but impossible to measure, emphasising access to procedures without considering outcomes represents a partial and inadequate approach. Instead, the chapter argues for substantive justice to be foregrounded in access to justice models and, particularly, for substantive justice to draw on ideas derived from social justice, rather than only considering the realisation of legal justice. The argument here is that individualistic and legalistic approaches do not reflect the reality of people's 'justice problems', and that, instead, collective approaches which recognise the social context of individual disputes are required. Moreover, the relationship between access to justice and social justice is argued to be inextricable, existing both as a necessary precondition of access to justice and as the ultimate prize of an effective and accessible system of justice. This part of the chapter concludes that the energy justice framework[1] provides a helpful integrative approach, which incorporates the broader vision of access to justice that we argue for here and which is particularly useful for application in the energy setting.

[1] K Jenkins, D McCauley and R Heffron et al, 'Energy Justice: A Conceptual Review' (2016) 11 *Energy Research & Social Science* 174.

Finally, in section IV, drawing on two of the dimensions of the energy justice framework (around recognition and participation), we argue for a particular need to recognise those who are suffering most from a lack of access to justice and to engage them meaningfully in policy processes around access to justice. Drawing on the 'all-affected principle', we suggest a need for greater participation of vulnerable and energy-poor consumers, in order to counterbalance the traditional domination of legal and policy elites. The lived experiences of vulnerable and energy-poor consumers need to be at the heart of policy agendas and are crucial to the design of policies and institutions for accessing justice. Altogether, the chapter calls for a holistic approach that looks beyond a law-centric, individualistic, procedurally focused, top-down model. That approach and the holistic vision we call for is summarised in Figure 2.1. The rest of this chapter will explain the various elements of that vision.

II. Access to Justice Beyond Lawyers and Courts

A. Narrow, Court-Centric Approaches to Access to Justice

Most accounts of access to justice begin by recognising the foundational work of the Florence Project,[2] but few go on to adopt the broad approach to access to justice it developed. Cappelletti and Garth famously discuss three 'waves' of access

Figure 2.1 A holistic vision of access to justice

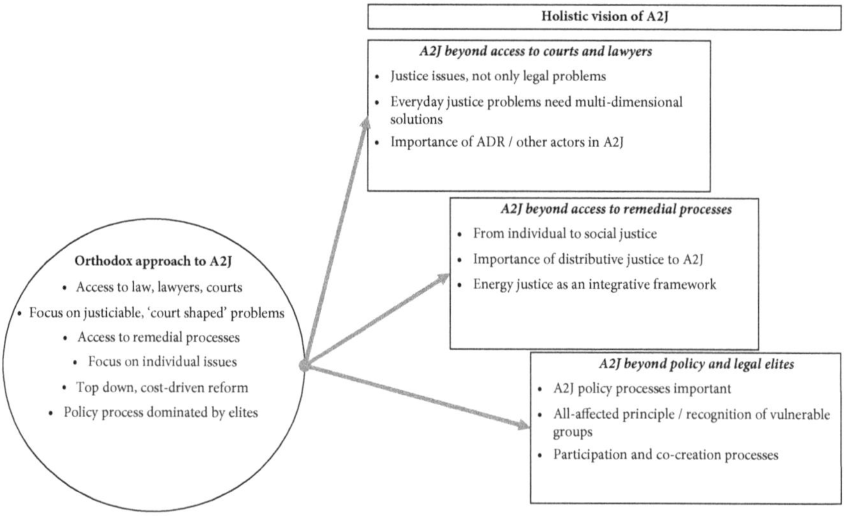

[2] M Cappelletti and B Garth, 'Access to Justice: The Newest Wave in the Worldwide Movement to Make Rights Effective' (1978) 27 *Buffalo Law Review* 181.

to justice concerns, each of which explores an element of how access to justice should be understood and the means through which it should be addressed. The first wave was concerned primarily with access to courts and the emphasis was on the problems faced by poor and marginalised groups in accessing expensive legal services and complex legal systems. The second wave, referred to briefly in chapter one in our discussion of consumer problems, related to access to justice gaps that arise not predominantly because of demographic factors but as a result of the nature of the problems people experience in particular contexts. So-called 'diffuse interests' include, for example, consumer problems, where large groups are affected by similar issues, but there are difficulties in launching individual claims and, as a result, a significant access to justice gap. The third wave, while continuing to incorporate the concerns of the first and second waves, broadened out the concern of access to justice even further so that a host of procedural innovations that might allow access to justice began to be discussed. This included, of course, alternative dispute resolution (ADR) and other means by which people might resolve their problems without accessing courts. Cappelletti and Garth's account is one that takes a broad view of 'justice' that includes a range of mechanisms beyond courts and that sees a role for a range of actors in the provision of justice beyond lawyers.[3]

Since these foundational insights were laid down, however, there has been – in some quarters at least – a retrenchment in the scope and a narrowing in the focus of access to justice as a concept. This has been driven by two arguments: a concern that access to justice has become a meaningless phrase that is insufficiently precise to be of utility;[4] and a critical seam of scholarship which questions the growing role of ADR and other procedural innovations and argues that they could not be considered as vehicles for accessing justice.[5] A more detailed account of critiques of ADR and how it relates to access to justice will be provided in chapter four. Two important contributions have been made by Fiss[6] and more recently Genn.[7] Fiss, in his famous article 'Against Settlement', argued that ADR could not provide justice in the same way that courts could, that it encouraged individuals to bargain away their rights, and could not adequately redress power imbalances between disputing parties.[8] Genn has reprised the argument more recently and contended that ADR is not about justice but, instead, 'just about settlement'.[9] This view of ADR, as undermining the public interest and social

[3] ibid.

[4] T Cornford, 'The Meaning of Access to Justice' in E Palmer, T Cornford, A Guinchard and Y Marique (eds), *Access to Justice: Beyond the Politics of Austerity* (Hart Publishing, 2016).

[5] O Fiss, 'Against Settlement' (1984) 78 *Fordham Law Review* 1265.

[6] ibid.

[7] H Genn, *Judging Civil Justice* (CUP, 2009); H Genn, 'What is Civil Justice for? Reform, ADR, and Access to Justice' (2012) 24 *Yale Journal of Law & the Humanities* 397.

[8] Fiss (n 5).

[9] H Genn, 'Why Privatisation of Civil Justice is Rule of Law Issue', 36th FA Mann Lecture (19 November 2012) 16, available at: www.ucl.ac.uk/laws/sites/laws/files/36th-f-a-mann-lecture-19.11.12-professor-hazel-genn.pdf.

value of adjudication[10] has been important in the development of narrower accounts of access to justice which equate justice only with legal justice.

This approach is epitomised by Cornford who argues that 'because access to justice is access to legal justice it is not to be confused with justice in a more general sense'.[11] His concern is to bring analytical clarity to a concept that in his view has become too diffuse and, as a result, he seeks to identify the 'true meaning of access to justice'.[12] He defines this as follows: 'Properly understood, access to justice entails a right of equal access to legal assistance for every citizen'.[13] Other definitions have adopted a similarly legalistic definition of access to justice. Mullen for example considers that

> access to justice concerns the availability of legal remedies to address wrongs. A person has access to justice where there are effective remedies available to that person to vindicate her legal rights and advance his or her legally recognised interests.[14]

And Wrbka, writing specifically on access to justice for consumers, develops a similar definition:

> We can thus say that the concept of access to justice embodies the ideal that everybody, regardless of his or her capabilities, should have the chance to enjoy the protection and enforcement of his or her rights by the use of law and the legal system.[15]

Each of these approaches to a definition share common features. They emphasise that access to justice should be narrowly concerned with problems that are capable of legal definition, either as 'legal rights' or 'legally recognised interests'. They emphasise that access to justice should be equated to access to 'legal assistance', 'legal remedies', or 'law and the legal system'. And finally, they emphasise that the system should be characterised by equality so that 'everybody' should be 'equally able to protect her legal rights'.

Maranlou argues that the traditional Western approach to access to justice, often misunderstood as an 'international' approach despite limited engagement with different legal, social and cultural traditions, has focused overly on questions of legality. She is critical of the tendency to elide justice with legal justice, which she sees as both limiting and reflective of certain cultural assumptions that are inaccurate in a global context:

> [L]aw and justice are synonymous in the Western debate on access to justice. Thus the term 'access to justice' often refers to access to the legal system to obtain legal redress for

[10] L Mulcahy, 'The Collective Interest in Private Dispute Resolution' (2013) 33 *Oxford Journal of Legal Studies* 59.

[11] Cornford (n 4) 34.

[12] ibid.

[13] ibid 39.

[14] T Mullen, 'Access to Justice in Administrative Law and Administrative Justice' in E Palmer, T Cornford, A Guinchard and Y Marique, *Access to Justice: Beyond the Politics of Austerity* (Hart Publishing, 2016) 70.

[15] S Wrbka, S Van Uytsel and M Siems (eds), *Collective Actions: Enhancing Access to Justice and Reconciling Multilayer Interests?* (CUP, 2012) 2.

> a legal problem. The term 'legal' here appears to identify as 'justice' in addressing many problems encountered in people's everyday lives.[16]

It is perhaps not surprising, particularly in considering the 'core' or foundational aspects of access to justice, that the protection of legally recognised rights and interests through access to legal representation and courts are considered important. However, the extent to which a court and law-centric model has resurfaced is instructive. A recent report by the Legal Education Foundation, for example, considering the topic of 'digital justice', adopts a definition, based on minimum standards of access to justice required by law, that includes four 'irreducible minimum standards' for access to justice:

i. access to the formal legal system;
ii. access to an effective hearing;
iii. access to a decision in accordance with substantive law;
iv. access to remedy.[17]

While there is clearly value in a definition based on minimum legal standards that is capable of being easily operationalised as a means of evaluating access to justice in the context of court systems, this approach must seem reductive in light of the issues raised in chapter one about how people actually experience problems and what they do (and don't do) as a result. Indeed, these principles seem to refer more to questions around the fair and effective functioning of court systems than to the broader question (as we would see it) of access to justice.

B. A More Holistic Approach

For those who choose to define access to justice predominantly as access to legal justice, the development of ADR and a focus on sources of support beyond formal legal advice presents a potential problem. There are perhaps three ways in which such developments can be seen to relate to access to justice.

- ***An aberration***. Some who subscribe to the legal justice view of access to justice may see ADR and attempts to deflect people from legal assistance as undermining the legal system and the values and rights it protects. As such, these approaches cannot be considered as promoting access to justice.
- ***A pragmatic solution***. Cornford notes that some writers accept ADR as a pragmatic response to an imperfect world in which genuine equality of access to lawyers and courts is not possible.[18] Here, alternative approaches do not

[16] S Maranlou, *Access to Justice in Iran* (CUP, 2014) 46.
[17] Legal Education Foundation, *Digital Justice: HMCTS Data Strategy and Delivering Access to Justice* (Legal Education Foundation, 2019) 17.
[18] Cornford (n 4).

provide access to justice but, to the extent that they provide individuals with some kind of remedy, are preferable to nothing. This view sees approaches such as ADR being a potentially helpful means of accessing redress, while maintaining that they do not provide access to justice.

- ***A powerful complement, and addition, to legal justice.*** This view takes a broader definition of justice that goes beyond the law. It accepts that legal justice is important but adopts a legal pluralist approach that problematises the idea of a single, objective paradigm of justice. It also accepts that ADR, by going beyond law, is able to better, potentially at least, reflect the way in which people experience problems and to consider resolutions that may be longer lasting and more creative than ones that are reduced to legal problems.

We will leave the detailed discussion of these perspectives to chapter four. Here, we seek to make a prima facie case for looking beyond courts as the only, or even principal, site of access to justice. We do so by considering four themes: the nature of people's problems and the extent to which they constitute strictly legal needs; the importance of culture and context in determining understandings of access to justice; the need for cost-avoidance strategies in the consumer context and the importance of internal complaint handling; and non-legal advisers and intermediaries as access to justice actors.

C. Everyday Justice Problems

Even where one prefers the 'legal justice' approach on a normative basis, it is difficult to sustain once we examine the types of problems that people, particularly those who are vulnerable and energy poor, experience in everyday life. As shown in chapter one, these problems typically present as complex and intersecting clusters of issues, only some of which are likely to have justiciable solutions yet which can be characterised as constituting injustices. The problem with equating access to justice with legal remedies has been highlighted by Nylund, who argues that this approach does not meet people's needs and that, in fact, the emphasis on legal rights makes people more vulnerable by forcing them to rely on professional legal advice to resolve their problems:

> Going to court often means reducing the conflict to the legally relevant parts of it … lawyers define what the parties need and want, and 'squeeze' the parties to the sideline of the dispute resolution process. In a polycentric, principle-based, teleological legal system, only lawyers understand what the law is and can predict the outcome of the case. Therefore, the citizens are increasingly dependent on lawyers in navigating the legal system, and more vulnerable.[19]

[19] A Nylund, 'Access to Justice: Is ADR a Help or Hindrance?' in L Ervo and A Nylund (eds), *The Future of Civil Litigation: Access to Courts and Court-annexed Mediation in the Nordic Countries* (Springer, 2014) 327.

Sandefur helpfully adds to this discussion by making a distinction between a justice problem and a legal need.[20] When exploring the general question of what assistance people need, she argues that unmet legal needs can be addressed by increasing access to legal services. However, such an approach can only be partial and leaves out a range of unresolved justice problems. Sandefur states that:

> [T]he access-to-justice crisis is bigger than law and lawyers. It is a crisis of exclusion and inequality. Today, access to justice is restricted: only some people, and only some kinds of justice problems, receive lawful resolution. Access is also systematically unequal: some groups – wealthy people and white people, for example – get more access than other groups, like poor people and racial minorities … justice is about just resolution, not legal services.[21]

We will return below to the idea that access to justice should include a substantive element, but Sandefur's point is helpful in focusing attention on the types of problems that we think are important when we discuss access to justice. In Australia, the concept of 'everyday justice' has been advanced to shift the focus away not only from courts, but from dispute resolution altogether. This involves considering not only access to redress mechanisms, but the 'justice quality of people's social, civic, and economic relations … facilitating a culture in which fewer disputes need to be resolved'.[22] Everyday justice, therefore, is interested in the extent to which justice features in people's routine encounters with other people, government, business and institutions. In this sense it is similar to approaches to administrative justice, which define administrative justice as not only referring to redress mechanisms, but as the justice inherent in routine administrative decision-making by government agencies.[23] The result of this kind of more wide-ranging approach is that one must look to a wider range of potential interventions for the provision of access to justice than simply looking to courts and lawyers.[24] Albiston and Sandefur state that empirical studies of access to justice show that the diversity of legal concerns cannot be matched with one solution for all.[25] Instead, improving access to justice will require a complex web of systems working together, rather than a narrowly focused legal solution.

Context is also likely to be important in determining the breadth or narrowness of one's approach to access to justice. Mullen, for example, while adopting

[20] R Sandefur, 'Access to What?' (2019) 148 *Daedalus: The Journal of the American Academy of Arts and Sciences* 49.

[21] ibid 51.

[22] Australian Government Attorney General's Department, *A Strategic Framework for Access to Justice in the Federal Civil Justice System* (Australian Government, 2009).

[23] JL Mashaw, *Bureaucratic Justice: Managing Social Security Disability Claims* (Yale University Press, 1983); M Adler, *Administrative Justice in Context* (Hart Publishing, 2010).

[24] Cristian Farias, 'Everyone Needs Legal Help. That Doesn't Mean Everyone Needs a Lawyer' *New York Times* (13 February 2019), available at: www.nytimes.com/2019/02/13/opinion/legal-issues.html.

[25] C Albiston and R Sandefur, 'Expanding the Empirical Study of Access to Justice' [2013] *Wisconsin Law Review* 101, 119.

a definition focused on legal rights and interests, makes the point that in the context of administrative justice a wider range of remedies exists than ordinary courts (including public inquiries, tribunals, ombuds and internal redress mechanisms).[26] Some of these, such as ombuds, go beyond a notion of legal justice as we have defined it here and provide additional protections that are deemed important in the context of citizen–state relationships. In the consumer context, as Ramsay points out, research has shown that consumers' problems are not 'court-shaped', and the law often 'defines the problems of ordinary people in a manner that may have little meaning for them and that does not offer them the remedies they desire'.[27] One of the problems with a legal justice approach to access to justice, therefore, is that it is top-down in character and begins by thinking about what the legal system provides and then considers how it can meet people's needs. Part of the holistic vision of access to justice we argue for in this book does the opposite, taking a bottom-up approach which starts with people's problems and considers the access to justice question from that vantage point.

D. Culture, Context and Dispute Resolution

Another limitation of the law-centric model of access to justice is its lack of sensitivity to different social and cultural contexts. This limitation exists most obviously when taking a global perspective but is also important in recognising and valuing different cultural and social expectations within communities. Olteanu points out that the vision of access to justice which dominates Western discourses is reflective of the fact that Western states feature well-developed legal systems.[28] This also perhaps reflects the Western development of a court-centric view of justice,[29] with courts and hierarchical forms of legal ordering being seen as principal means of social ordering. Olteanu points out that in developing countries and countries with different legal traditions access to justice needs to be defined in broader ways.[30] This also reflects the growing importance of legal pluralism as a field of study that recognises the value of different legal traditions and the competing claims of different approaches to dispute settlement.[31] Thus, the equation of access to justice with a strictly 'legal' justice needs to be broadened out, and Olteanu cites as an example the definition adopted by the UN Development Programme:[32] '[access to justice is] the ability of people to seek and obtain a remedy through formal or

[26] Mullen (n 14).

[27] I Ramsay, 'Consumer Redress and Access to Justice' in CEF Rickett and TGW Telfer (eds), *International Perspectives on Consumers' Access to Justice* (CUP, 2003) 37.

[28] Y Olteanu, *Access to Justice in Microfinance* (Springer, 2018).

[29] M Palmer and S Roberts, *Disputes Processes: ADR and the Primary Forms of Decision-Making*, 3rd edn (CUP, 2020).

[30] Olteanu (n 28).

[31] ibid.

[32] ibid.

informal institutions of justice, and in conformity with human rights standards'.[33] Maranlou, concerned with access to justice in Iran, stresses the importance of informal and traditional justice systems in considering access to justice: 'Many examples, from sub-Saharan Africa to South Asia, Middle East to North America, value the rise of traditional justice and customary law in providing access to justice for poor and marginalised populations'.[34] While our concern in this book is with European jurisdictions with well-developed legal systems, the point that understandings of justice and how it may be achieved are culturally produced rather than universalist is important in stepping beyond the narrow approaches we have criticised above.

E. ADR and Internal Complaint Mechanisms

The question then becomes which actors and institutions have a legitimate role in access to justice beyond legal advisers and courts. Duggan, in the context of consumer disputes, provides a helpful way of conceptualising the access to justice interventions that are possible, discussing 'cost-spreading' measures and 'cost-avoiding measures'.[35] Cost-spreading measures are those that seek to spread the cost of taking legal action across a range of affected individuals or wider society as a whole and include options such as legal aid and class actions. The key aim of cost-spreading approaches is to allow access to the courts for the consumer to 'fight the case up at [the firm's] level'. Cost-avoidance techniques meanwhile seek to avoid the costs of using courts altogether by providing alternatives to court litigation, including tribunals, ombuds, or compensation funds. Cost-avoidance measures seek to reduce the advantages of firms in litigation and make them fight cases 'down at [the consumer's] level'.[36] One set of approaches that we include within our broader view of access to justice, therefore, is cost-avoiding alternative approaches and this allows us to return to Cappelletti and Garth's original acceptance of ADR providing a pathway for access to justice.[37] As we saw above, questions around cost are particularly important in the context of consumer disputes (although by no means the only barriers to consumer issues being raised). As a result, providing mechanisms that can be accessed at low cost is likely to be beneficial if such mechanisms are combined with interventions that address barriers to accessing justice holistically.

[33] United Nations Development Programme, *Access to Justice Practice Note* (United Nations Development Programme, 2005) 6.

[34] Maranlou (n 16) 12.

[35] A Duggan, 'Consumer Access to Justice in Common Law Countries: A Survey of the Issues from a Law and Economics Perspective' in CEF Rickett and TGW Telfer (eds), *International Perspectives on Consumers' Access to Justice* (CUP, 2003) 46–67.

[36] ibid 50.

[37] Cappelletti and Garth (n 2).

Also important in the consumer context is the internal complaint handling conducted by firms. As already noted in chapter one, most consumer disputes are not referred to external sources of assistance such as ADR. Instead, the great majority of complaints are made to the firm and either resolved or not resolved there. As Ramsay has pointed out 'much consumer disputing takes place at the level of two-party negotiation'.[38] In Genn's landmark *Paths to Justice* report, the role of courts and ombuds in relation to consumer disputes has been described as 'minimal'.[39] As a result, internal complaint systems are a major potential site of access to justice in the consumer context. In the European energy sector, people are significantly more likely to refer a complaint to an energy company compared with ADR. In a recent survey, 35 per cent of European consumers who experienced a problem complained to their energy company, while only 5 per cent complained to an ADR scheme.[40] Of those who complained to their energy company, many were dissatisfied but took their complaint no further. The insight here, therefore, is that, while it is important to broaden the focus beyond courts to consider the potential contribution of ADR to access to justice, that is not the end of the story. External forms of ADR in the consumer context are likely to be as peripheral as the courts are to the resolution of consumers' everyday problems with businesses. If we want to influence the quality of 'everyday justice' experienced by consumers, therefore, an important way of doing so is to seek to improve the way in which businesses handle complaints.

Indeed, proactive and preventative approaches are particularly important in consumer disputing. In some contexts, such as energy, the sector is subject to statutory regulation and the sectoral regulator is potentially a key player in access to justice debates by taking *ex ante* measures that can help prevent justice problems from arising or seek to ensure that they are minimised. Friedman refers to *ex ante* approaches as involving 'routinisation', where measures that favour consumers and avoid problems are embedded in advance, and compares these to 'individualisation', where there is a reliance on *ex post* action on the part of the consumer to sort problems out.[41] As we will argue in chapters four and seven, current approaches to access to justice place too much emphasis on *ex post* mechanisms and insufficiently consider the collective and systemic implications of individual disputes. However, if we take seriously the idea that access to justice is about achieving 'everyday justice' rather than access to remedies, there is potential to think creatively and radically about how current systems of justice operate. Approaches to justice-system design which stress prevention and seek

[38] Ramsay (n 27) 28.

[39] H Genn, *Paths to Justice: What People Do and Think about Going to Law* (Hart Publishing, 1999).

[40] K Rademaekers et al, *Selecting Indicators to Measure Energy Poverty* (European Commission 2016), available at: ec.europa.eu/energy/sites/ener/files/documents/Selecting%20Indicators%20to%20Measure%20Energy%20Poverty.pdf.

[41] LM Friedman, 'Access to Justice – Social and Historical Context' in M Cappelletti and J Weisner, *Access to Justice*, vol 2 (Giuffrè Editore, 1978).

to address the causes of disputes are increasingly gaining salience,[42] and this is a strand of thinking to which this book seeks to contribute.

F. Advice and Non-Legal Sources of Help

Other approaches that are particularly important in the consumer context include sources of non-legal advice (for example, third-sector advice provision). Ramsay calls these 'intermediaries' and notes that, along with lawyers, they include social workers, debt counsellors and consumer advisers.[43] Less formally still, family members, social networks and community groups are potentially important in providing support and advice that can help problems to be defined and pursued towards a solution. Seeing issues people face as 'justice problems' calls for looking beyond lawyers to identify the sources of help that vulnerable individuals need. As we noted above, their problems are often more fundamental than a search for legal solutions and, instead, involve a clustering of problems.

As a result, there is a need to think about how people can be helped more holistically, such as through the integration of advice on justice matters with advice on health, finances, housing and so on. It is also important to build capacity within communities. Support groups that exist at a local level within communities and friendship groups are crucial in building individual capacity and overcoming social isolation. A lack of social networks and group identification can have serious consequences for individuals,[44] while strong social networks provide information, resources, help and support. This fits with our findings (chapter six) that key actors in providing a route to access to justice are not lawyers but grass-roots groups, community actors, charities, local organisers and social networks. Thus, we argue that, in moving beyond a narrow conception of access to justice and paying particular attention to the consumer context, we should not only be concerned with access to courts and lawyers, but we should also adopt an access to justice perspective that includes: access to a range of alternative remedies (including internal remedies within firms); access to non-legal advice and problem-solving; and the potential contribution of *ex ante* approaches such as regulation.

The discussion so far has largely focused on access to justice in procedural terms and the availability, in theory and in practice, of sources of help and remedy. The main argument up to now has been that we must look beyond legal help and remedies in order to better reflect the problems that people actually experience on the ground. The next section turns to a broader question: should access to justice deliver anything more than equal access to procedures (advice,

[42] C Hodges, 'Delivering Justice' (2019) 9 *International Journal of Procedural Law* 149.
[43] Ramsay (n 27).
[44] N Longhurst and T Hargreaves, 'Emotions and Fuel Poverty: The Lived Experience of Social Housing Tenants in the United Kingdom' (2019) 56 *Energy Research & Social Science* 1.

remedy) that provide an *opportunity* for the resolution of their justice problems? Or should access to justice be concerned also with the *realisation* of substantively just outcomes?

III. Beyond Procedural Access to Justice

When thinking about access to justice and seeking to move beyond consideration of access to remedial procedures, what type of justice are we talking about? We have argued above that justice should not be equated only with 'legal justice'. In what follows we discuss three themes: the justification for access to justice having a substantive as well as procedural concern; the need to move from a legalistic and individual perspective to a social justice perspective;[45] and the value of the energy justice framework as an integrative model.[46]

A. Access to Justice as Access to Substantively Just Outcomes

There are good reasons for considering the question of access to justice in a way that restricts the concept to having access to a procedural remedy. This is because, while the concept of 'access' is relatively easy to define, the concept of 'justice', particularly substantive justice, is much more difficult and contentious.[47] In defining access to justice as having a substantive dimension, there is also a particular difficulty in assessing whether access to justice has been achieved. And this is exacerbated when one's conception of substantive justice moves beyond the achievement of narrowly defined legal justice to include broader substantive outcomes such as social justice (see below). The effect of these difficulties is that even where access to justice definitions recognise that the concept must include a substantive element, evaluation and analysis tends to focus on the extent to which remedies are accessed rather than the outcomes of those remedies. A further pragmatic justification for such an approach is that the question of procedural and substantive access to justice could be seen as being first and second order issues. Procedural access is a first-order issue because without access to a remedial procedure in the first place the achievement of substantive justice is not possible. As we saw in the discussion of the barriers to accessing justice above, the significant barriers to accessing procedural remedies and the huge access to justice gap that currently exists explain why a principal concern has been with the procedural dimensions of the concept.

Mullen, for example, notes that there is a 'narrow' and 'broad' view of access to justice, but in each of these views the emphasis remains on access to procedural

[45] D Miller, 'Recent Theories of Social Justice' (1991) 21 *British Journal of Political Science* 371.
[46] Jenkins, McCauley and Heffron et al, 'Energy Justice' (n 1).
[47] S Wrbka, *European Consumer Access to Justice Revisited* (CUP, 2015).

remedies.[48] The narrow view of access to justice considers whether remedies exist; the broader view is interested in whether those remedies can be used by individuals without undue difficulty. While defining access to justice in procedural terms may be a pragmatic response to the definitional and evaluation issues that arise otherwise, the emphasis on procedural justice has been criticised. Ramsay, for example, suggests that one view of access to justice equates it with 'access to legal institutions', whereas the better view 'is concerned with the general conditions of justice in society'.[49] This is the 'everyday justice' perspective we discussed above. Maranlou meanwhile argues that the avoidance of substantive questions has allowed procedural reforms to be used to advance other agendas.[50] For instance, she argues that a procedural approach to access to justice has been co-opted by neoliberal agendas, dominated by cost-cutting and efficiency issues, rather than the achievement of a substantively 'just social and political context'.[51]

Indeed, a risk in failing to articulate access to justice in substantive terms, is that the social values that access to justice ought to protect are lost from sight, allowing the creation of more accessible remedies rather than the realisation of a just society to become the primary focus of attention. The potential for the access to justice agenda to be co-opted by other agendas (efficiency, cost, a means of creating better functioning markets) clearly presents issues for the kind of substantive justice we imagine access to justice will deliver. There is also an implicit assumption in many accounts that access to a remedial procedure will automatically deliver just outcomes; in our view the question of procedural access should be the start rather than the end point of discussions on access to justice. That approach, despite becoming less prominent over time, is uncontroversial in the sense that it returns to early perspectives on access to justice, which adopted the kind of broad view that this chapter argues for. Cappelletti and Garth, for instance, show a concern with both procedural and substantive aspects in their definition:

> The words 'access to justice' are admittedly not easily defined, but they serve to focus on two basic purposes of the legal system by which people may vindicate their rights and/or resolve their disputes under the general auspices of the state. First, the system must be equally accessible to all; second, it must lead to results that are individually and socially just.[52]

Indeed, the emphasis on the achievement of just outcomes has been stressed in recent literature on ADR and access to justice. Critical accounts have suggested that, in the rush to incorporate ADR into civil justice systems around the world, the emphasis has been on making new procedures available rather than 'the quality of justice that results from a given mediation program'.[53] This has also been

[48] Mullen (n 14).
[49] Ramsay (n 27) 19.
[50] Maranlou (n 16).
[51] ibid 46.
[52] Cappelletti and Garth (n 2) 182.
[53] J Nolan-Haley, 'Mediation, Self-Represented Parties, and Access to Justice: Getting There from Here' (2018–19) 87 *Fordham Law Review Online* 1–11, 11.

emphasised by Noone and Ojelabi, who point out that ADR approaches should not only be seen in terms of 'equality of access' but also in terms of 'equitable outcomes'.[54]

B. From Individual to Social Justice: Access to Justice as a Collective Problem

There are two ways of connecting access to justice with social justice according to Cornford.[55] The first is that those, such as Cappelletti and Garth, whose primary interest is in the achievement of social justice, see access to justice as a vehicle for delivering societal change and greater equality.[56] The second is that those, such as Roger Smith, whose primary concern is with access to justice, see social justice as important because social inequality – regardless of how accessible a legal system is made – is an impediment to people realising their legal rights.[57] Whichever approach is taken, our view is that social justice is an important element in conceptualising access to justice. Access to justice will remain elusive without social justice; social justice cannot be achieved in the absence of access to justice. Limiting our focus to legal justice and the realisation of legal rights – that may or may not contribute to social justice – is problematic. This is particularly the case given the ability of powerful sectors of society to use courts[58] and ombuds[59] to preserve and expand their advantage, at the expense of those who are already weaker and marginalised. The use of law and the realisation of legal rights in practice is, as we have seen, strongly influenced by social, psychological and relational dynamics, which means that focusing on legal justice ignores a host of factors that will determine whether outcomes for individuals and particular social groups are just. Social justice is, therefore, inherently connected to any consideration of access to justice: the only real question is whether we see it as the goal and substantive outcome of access to justice or as the necessary precondition for achieving access to justice in the first place.

At this stage in our argument, we must define social justice. Since social justice as a normative goal can have an element of utopian vagueness to it, it is perhaps more sensible to begin by considering what we mean by social injustice. Social injustice can be understood as maldistribution, exclusion and disempowerment. These factors are interdependent and can lead to marginalisation of groups and

[54] L Ojelabi and M Noone, 'Jurisdictional Perspectives on Alternative Dispute Resolution and Access to Justice: Introduction.' (2020) 16 *International Journal of Law in Context* 103, 103.

[55] Cornford (n 4).

[56] Cappelletti and Garth (n 2).

[57] R Smith. *Justice: Redressing the Balance.* (Legal Action Group, 1997).

[58] M Galanter, 'Why the "Haves" Come Out Ahead: Speculations on the Limits of Social Change' (1974) 9 *Law & Society Review* 95.

[59] B Hubeau, 'The Profile of Complainants: How to Overcome the "Matthew Effect"?' in M Hertogh and R Kirkham (eds), *Research Handbook on the Ombudsman* (Edward Elgar, 2018).

individuals.[60] Social injustice is observable through various appearances of social settings such as poverty, class, race, ethnicity, gender, sexual orientation, environment and law.[61] Social justice can be defined as the conditions that exist once such injustices have been remedied. This might include: preventing poverty; the necessity of education; inclusion in the labour market; sustained social security standards; fair distribution of wealth and income; the pursuit of generational justice; and greater gender equality for all citizens of the world.[62] There are two important ways in which social justice has been further defined. One relates simply to the creation of a society that is based on a fair distribution of various social goods; the other foregrounds the implicit tension between the achievement of individual goals and social justice:

> Some students of social justice consider its meaning in terms of the tensions between individual liberty and common social good, arguing that social justice is promoted to the degree that we can promote collective goods without infringing upon basic individual freedoms. Some argue that social justice reflects a concept of fairness in the assignment of fundamental rights and duties, economic opportunities, and social conditions.[63]

Justice understood in terms of the distribution of wealth, opportunities and freedom within a society has a focus on collective justice. Here, 'individuality gives way to the struggle for social justice'.[64] Put differently, social justice helps us reframe issues that are thought of as individual in origin to include broader social, political, economic and cultural understandings. Social justice is a contextually bound and historically driven concept.[65] This produces a tension between abstract conceptions of justice and what is right, good and moral. Social justice then embraces equality and advocates equal rights for all (distribution of basic needs, life chances and opportunities) with the end goal of elimination of inequalities.

Emphasising the collective nature of social justice helps us to recognise that approaches to access to justice have tended to focus on individual remedies and the achievement of individual rights. The focus on individual wrongs and models that see justice as the realisation of rational self-interest arguably distracts attention from larger structural imbalances and inequalities in society. Giving people an accessible remedy for a consumer problem, for example, does not meaningfully redress the detriment that arises from the domination by powerful corporate interests of political, social and economic discourses and the subsequent

[60] V Bufacchi, *Social Injustice* (Springer, 2012).

[61] ibid; K Carragee and L Frey, 'Communication Activism Research: Engages Communications Scholarships for Social Justice' (2016) 10 *International Journal of Communication Forum* 3975.

[62] O Cramme and P Diamond, *Social Justice in a Global Age* (Polity Press, 2009).

[63] Janet L Finn and Maxine Jacobson, 'What is Social Justice?' (*OUP Blog*, 2017), available at: blog.oup.com/2017/03/what-is-social-justice/.

[64] HM Government, 'Social Justice Transforming Lives' (2012), available at: assets.publishing.service.gov.uk/government/uploads/system/uploads/attachment_data/file/49515/social-justice-transforming-lives.pdf.

[65] D Miller, *The Principles of Social Justice* (Harvard University Press, 1999).

widespread detriment faced by consumers. As noted above, there is a danger that individual approaches merely exacerbate disadvantage, with only the wealthy and powerful using legal remedies, leaving the marginalised even further behind. In this context, we can see access to justice not as a means of changing society and achieving social justice, but as a mechanism which largely preserves the *status quo* and is designed to militate against social change. Nader, for example, has criticised the provision of ADR for consumer disputes as a form of second-class justice and means of pacification.[66] Rather than driving social change, therefore, the individualisation of disputes and their containment within particular procedural remedies diffuse broader political demands for change. People are given just enough justice to prevent social disorder, while powerful interests and fundamental inequalities remain unchallenged. Unless access to justice narratives are linked to narratives that recognise and address the inequalities that currently prevent the realisation of a just society, then the concept will have limited bite and be subject to potential co-option as discussed above. This, in our view, is a major justification for considering social justice as a substantive goal in the context of the access to justice debate.

The extent to which social justice should be a goal in the context of ADR has been subject to recent debate in the literature. Ojelabi points to growing levels of inequality around the world, with a declining middle class and a growing gap between super-rich elites and those on low incomes. The question is how ADR responds to this context and the extent to which it challenges or is co-opted by those who benefit from social inequality.[67] This limited approach may be pragmatic given the scale of the challenge. However, there is an increasing focus by some on the need to ensure that dispute resolution systems contribute to some broader, positive vision of fairness in society. Hodges, for example, talks about the potential contribution of ADR in Europe to the realisation of core European values such as solidarity and the creation of a society with compromise and consensus at its heart. In this view, providing ADR for consumers 'seeks to support not just a society based on law and market exchange but also a fair and cohesive society'.[68] A similar approach is suggested by Cortes, who argues that ADR fulfils public functions which should bring about benefits not only for individual parties but society as a whole. He draws a parallel with corporate social responsibility and argues that ADR needs to think about its contribution to the achievement of social values beyond the resolution of cases.[69]

[66] L Nader, *The Life of the Law: Anthropological Projects* (University of California Press, 2005).

[67] E Waldman and L Ojelabi, 'Mediators and Substantive Justice: A View from Rawls' Original Position' (2016) 30 *Ohio State Journal on Dispute Resolution* 391.

[68] C Hodges 'Consumer Redress: Implementing the Vision' in P Cortes (ed), *The New Regulatory Framework for Consumer Dispute Resolution* (OUP, 2016) 368.

[69] P Cortes, *The Law of Consumer Redress in an Evolving Digital Market: Upgrading from Alternative to Online Dispute Resolution* (CUP, 2017).

Writing in the context of public services ombuds, O'Brien has argued that approaches which emphasise individual redress are beset by 'legal pathologies' that prevent the contribution of the ombuds to a more collective, democratic, 'demosprudential' discourse around citizen–state disputes.[70] The failure to connect individual issues with wider collective interests and, indeed, the public interest is problematic. Mechanisms that consider injustices primarily as matters for individual resolution, rather than seeing them in their broader social context, tend to atomise issues and shift the focus away from addressing issues that are collective in origin. For instance, many legal systems are reluctant to allow collective redress approaches or public interest litigation, albeit these approaches are growing in some jurisdictions.[71] Systems that overly focus on individual wrongs, therefore, are in danger not only of being used in ways that simply replicate and reproduce existing social conditions but also in ways that prevent collective approaches. An individual justice orientation also takes insufficient account of the broader public interest. A narrow focus on individual redress tends to minimise the public interest in access to justice and dispute resolution.[72] Very few justice problems, as we have defined them above, are simply disputes between two parties. Particularly in the consumer context where diffuse interests tend to be widely affected by market practices, each dispute is likely to also engage the interests of others who are suffering similar detriment at a collective level and the general public, whose general interest is in the achievement of fair market practices.[73] The point is that there is more to many justice problems than individual interests, and that the resolution of individual disputes cannot automatically be equated with the realisation of a just society. Concepts of social justice that bridge individual, collective and public interests are important in ensuring that we move beyond mere procedural access and beyond the achievement of narrowly defined and individual legal rights.

The adoption of such an approach is, of course, not without its problems. A likely criticism is that it places too much weight on the shoulders of access to justice and adopts an unrealistically utopian vision. This is perhaps why we have seen a retrenchment in the access to justice scholarship from the progressive and emancipatory position adopted by early proponents such as Cappelletti and Garth.[74] Can any system of justice realise the aims of social justice? There is, of course, also a danger that the apparently neutral notion of access to justice (which numerous commentators have suggested is hard to disagree with) becomes seen as politicised. Not all political traditions adopt the same approach in relation to the undesirability of social inequality, and a broad view of access to justice could

[70] M Doyle and N O'Brien, *Reimagining Administrative Justice: Human Rights in Small Places* (Palgrave Pivot, 2020).

[71] C Hodges, 'The Private Sector Ombudsman' in M Hertogh and R Kirkham (eds), *Research Handbook on the Ombudsman* (Edward Elgar, 2018).

[72] Mulcahy (n 10).

[73] Wrbka, Van Uytsel and Siems (n 15).

[74] Cappelletti and Garth (n 2).

be seen as inappropriate or contentious as a result. More pragmatically, we have already noted above that substantive issues could be considered second-order issues in the absence of widespread procedural access to justice. Emphasising the need for potentially divisive and contentious debates on substantive goals could stand in the way of finding more practical solutions in the short term. While we note these potential criticisms, we believe it is important to maintain a focus on social justice in discussions of access to justice. To do otherwise risks taking an unduly narrow procedural approach which fails to meaningfully evaluate the relationship between remedial procedures and fundamental social conditions. Rather than being 'objective' or 'neutral', such narrow approaches may in fact preserve the status quo and militate against the achievement of social justice in practice. Avoiding politicisation cuts both ways. Indeed, a particular concern is that narrow takes on access to justice can be co-opted by neoliberal and managerial agendas whose emphasis on cost-cutting, efficiency and individualism pushes out other important values. Access to justice should therefore, in our view, be legitimately seen as a collective enterprise that ultimately seeks to challenge, rather than maintain, social injustice.

C. Energy Justice as an Integrative Framework

In this section, we discuss energy justice as a possible means of integrating various of the strands that we have introduced so far as part of our holistic vision for access to justice. Energy justice has emerged as a cross-cutting social science research agenda which seeks to apply justice principles to energy policy, energy production and systems, energy consumption, energy activism, energy security and climate change.[75] The energy justice approach involves 'the examination of global problems from the viewpoint of proximity, widening social inclusion, and ensuring fair process'.[76] The framework helps explore major inequalities of global energy systems, identifies who the victims are, and how these people can be empowered to solve these inequalities. While the framework examines energy justice in its global context, the parallels with the matters discussed in this chapter so far should be obvious: an emphasis on distributive and procedural justice alongside a need to recognise social injustice and the needs of the most vulnerable.

To help identify where injustice occurs, the energy justice framework involves three dimensions which reflect different conceptions of justice,[77] as shown in Figure 2.2.

[75] Jenkins, McCauley and Heffron et al, 'Energy Justice' (n 1).

[76] D McCauley, *Energy Justice* (Palgrave, 2018) 13.

[77] D McCauley, K Jenkins, R Heffron and H Stephen, 'Energy Justice: A Whole Systems Approach' (2013), available at: cris.brighton.ac.uk/ws/files/484893/Energy%20justice%20a%20whole%20systems%20approach%20-%2010.08.2014.pdf; Jenkins, McCauley and Heffron et al, 'Energy Justice' (n 1); B Sovacool, M Lipson and R Charf, 'Temporality, Vulnerability, and Energy Justice in Household Low Carbon Innovations' (2016) 138 *Energy Policy* 495–504.

Figure 2.2 Fuel poverty as three types of interrelations in energy justice

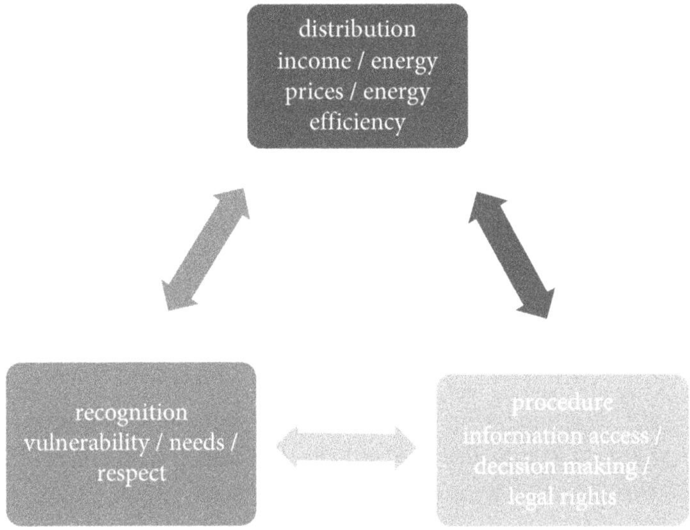

These dimensions aim to provide a complete approach to the identification of injustice and the achievement of energy justice.[78] Looking at each dimension in turn: first, procedural justice puts an emphasis on people being part of the decision-making process, understands justice as public participation,[79] and explores the ways to achieve 'just' outcomes through local knowledge mobilisation, greater information disclosure, and better institutional representation.[80] Second is distributional justice: this considers who gets what and understands energy as a social good, addresses harms of energy provision as a social ill, and uncovers injustices. Third is recognition justice. It calls for better recognition of groups that are ignored by society, to reduce social inequalities.[81] The procedural and distributive aspects of the framework reflect the discussion above and our conclusion that there is a need for both procedural and substantive accounts of justice in considering access to justice. The third dimension, relating to 'recognition', is more novel and perhaps fits best with Hughes's notion that access

[78] G Walker, N Simcock and R Day, 'Necessary Energy Uses and a Minimum Standard of Living in the United Kingdom: Energy Justice or Escalating Expectations?' (2016) *Energy Research and Social Science* 18 10.1016/j.erss.2016.02.007; Jenkins, McCauley and Heffron et al, 'Energy Justice' (n 1); B Sovacool and M Dworkin, 'Energy Justice: Conceptual Insights and Practical Applications' (2015) 142(C) *Applied Energy* 435.

[79] N Adger, J Paavola and S Huq, *Towards Justice in Adaptation to Climate Change* (MIT Press, 2006); BK Sovacool, 'How Long Will it Take? Conceptualizing the Temporal Dynamics of Energy Transitions' (2016) 13 *Energy Research & Social Science* 202.

[80] Jenkins, McCauley and Heffron et al, 'Energy Justice' (n 1).

[81] S Mazan, E Voyvoda and M Lacey-Barnacle et al, *Energy Justice – A Social Sciences and Humanities Cross-Cutting Theme Report* (Shape Energy, 2017).

to justice strategies must not only seek generalist solutions, but instead identify and remedy particular sources of social disadvantage.[82] Recognition therefore calls for an approach to justice where those who suffer most from injustice are identified, and their needs and interests are recognised within political and legal processes. We are interested in recognition justice as a critical part of the puzzle which speaks to vulnerability and differentiated needs, calling attention not only to economic drivers but cultural and symbolic ones.[83] This understanding of justice moves away from the individual and can help us to conceptualise access to justice as a shared problem facing particular individuals, groups and communities. Each aspect of the energy justice framework is important, and the achievement of the ultimate goals of substantive justice is reliant, for example, on the delivery of procedural justice and recognition. The interconnection between each aspect of the energy justice framework and the need to approach justice from a holistic perspective is shown in Figure 2.3.

This adds a very helpful insight to discussions of justice which focus on the procedural/substantive divide and fits well with our focus in this book on vulnerable and energy-poor consumers. We therefore consider energy justice to provide a helpful and integrative approach that is well suited to deal with the particular access to justice issues that arise in the energy context.

Figure 2.3 The relationship between dimensions of the energy justice framework

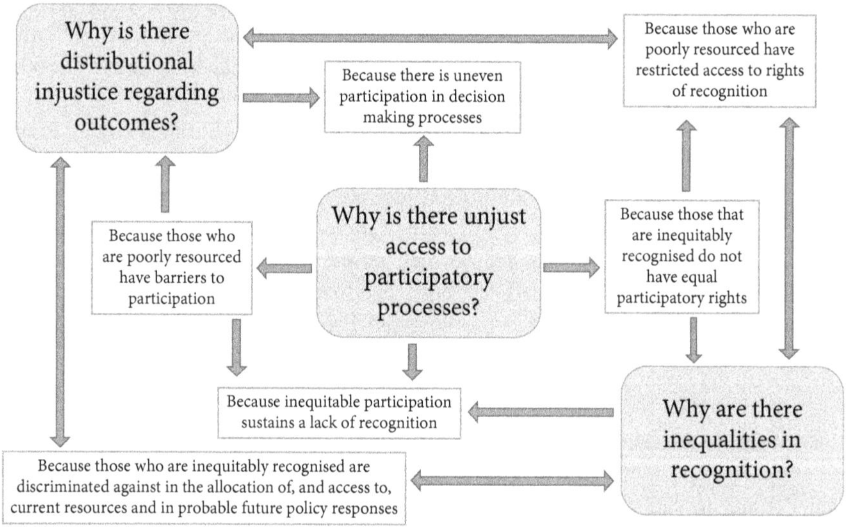

[82] P Hughes, 'Advancing Access to Justice through Generic Solutions: The Risk of Perpetuating Exclusion' (2013) 31 *Windsor Yearbook of Access to Justice* 1.

[83] N Fraser, 'From Redistribution to Recognition? Dilemmas of Justice in a "Post-Socialist" Age' (1995) 212 *New Left Review* 69.

In addition, as we go on to discuss below, the way in which issues around recognition and procedural justice are framed as part of the energy framework provides important insights for the development of access to justice policies and reforms.

IV. Reforming Access to Justice

Access to justice is just the beginning of a long list of unmet needs, especially for those who are vulnerable and living in energy poverty. Policy measures tend to provide a fire-fighting approach towards extinguishing urgent problems, rather than finding long-term solutions. What is the balance to strike and how can people that live in challenging and desperate situations be helped out of their mounting difficulties (their cluster of problems)? We suggest a solution would be to rethink the access question through the all-affected principle. This would accommodate all people and their individual complex needs that are currently failing to be dealt with by the system. One of the reasons for this is that access to justice discourses are often dominated by legal and policy elites, so that issues are framed in narrow, top-down ways that fail to address the reality of people's everyday 'justice problems'. The lived experience of vulnerability, energy poverty and a lack of access to justice is rarely the starting point for reforming justice systems. The interests of the most vulnerable members of society are rarely 'recognised', as called for by the energy justice framework, nor is there meaningful participation by such individuals and groups in processes of change and reform.

In addition to adopting a broader definition of access to justice as a field of enquiry, therefore, we propose that the policy processes underpinning access to justice reforms need to be rethought. We propose to consider access to justice policy processes through the all-affected principle, aligned to the needs of people in vulnerable situations. The all-affected principle claims that people have a right to participate in (political) decision-making that affects them.[84] As an extension of procedural access to justice, this principle goes further to suggest that access to information, advice and support is important (before even thinking of solving a problem). In our context, this principle translates to allowing people who are affected by the lack of access to justice to be part of the conversation about how to remedy this. For example, energy companies and ombuds could benefit from user engagement and feedback to explore how they can help vulnerable and energy-poor consumers before they have to engage with their energy company, approach an ombuds or, most likely, do nothing. The questions we ask here about how to

[84] J Schaeffer, 'The Boundaries of Transnational Democracy: Alternatives to the All-affected Principle' (2012) 38 *Review of International Studies* 321; C Gould, *Globalizing Democracy and Human Rights* (CUP, 2004).

include vulnerable people in the *access* and the *justice* debate are paralleled in the questions being asked about implementing a *just* energy transition:

> How do climate policies affect energy affordability for low-income households, how do they affect the well-being of energy producing communities, and what approaches might help reduce the unwanted side effects of reducing greenhouse gas emissions from the energy sector?[85]

These questions, focusing on vulnerable and energy-poor consumers, need to be asked of the current system and a social dialogue has to emerge. This debate is tied up in layers of complex policy design. For example, Longhurst and Hargreaves' research on the role of emotions also extends to public policy.[86] They argue that measures to tackle energy poverty are not usually able to address energy deprivation on their own.[87] Therefore, it is essential to document lived experience of energy vulnerability and make it part of the policy design: to address both its causes and symptoms.[88] A focus on emotional and individual experiences of living in energy poverty can help inform practical interventions and their delivery (chapter six). Here, we propose not only that research evidence on lived experiences feed into policy processes but also that meaningful dialogue and engagement is created. Given some of the challenges that stand in the way of consumer engagement and participation considered earlier, this is a difficult task. As well as direct consumer participation, therefore, we place particular emphasis on the role of intermediaries, both in terms of helping individuals in particular cases and in representing the views and interests of vulnerable people. While there is significant potential to draw more on the views of those actors and organisations that operate at grass-roots level, there are often barriers to their participation in policy processes which need to be overcome.[89] We return to this issue in chapter six when we consider the role of local organisations.

V. Conclusion

This chapter has argued for a holistic approach to access to justice in order to tackle the significant access to justice challenges and barriers facing vulnerable individuals and groups highlighted in chapter one. We do not claim novelty in relation to our holistic vision. We do, however, argue that it is important to restate

[85] S Carey, D Raimi and K Petersen, 'Community Vulnerability in a "Just" Energy Transition' (*Resources*, 2019), available at: www.resourcesmag.org/resources-radio/community-vulnerability-just-energy-transition-sanya-carley.

[86] Longhurst and Hargreaves (n 44) 8.

[87] R Mould and KJ Baker, 'Documenting Fuel Poverty from the Householders' Perspective' (2017) 31 *Energy Research and Social Science* 21.

[88] Longhurst and Hargreaves (n 44) 8.

[89] D Deller and C Waddams Price (eds), *Fairness in Retail Energy Markets? Evidence form the UK* (CCP, 2018).

that vision in the face of a gradual retrenchment and narrowing of the concept and in the face of neoliberal managerial agendas that have sought to co-opt aspects of access to justice for other purposes. It is also important because access to justice discussions often do not clearly define the concept and, therefore, miss important aspects of it. In setting out our vision we have emphasised the importance of empirical data: the experiences of those who cannot access justice must be the basis for addressing problems and designing justice systems. That idea is at the heart of this book and also responsible for our suggestions about greater involvement of vulnerable individuals and groups in policy processes. This holistic vision and the need for empirical data lays the groundwork for the rest of the book. It underlies and facilitates the arguments that we build through each of the subsequent chapters. Next, we turn to consider the EU's law and policy framework.

3

European Union Law and Policy on Access to Justice

I. Introduction

Our focus in this chapter is on two sets of policies: those that seek to identify and provide particular protection for vulnerable and energy-poor consumers; and those that seek to provide mechanisms for the redress of consumer problems (both individual and collective). We argue that, despite giving increasing attention to these issues both as a component of energy policy and consumer protection policy, these measures have largely failed to reach vulnerable energy consumers. As Riefa and Saintier have argued, in relation to vulnerable consumers generally, 'access to justice is still severely lacking for the vulnerable'.[1] One reason for this is that those who are most in need of justice in the energy sector are exactly those who are least engaged and proactive, both in the market and in seeking redress when things go wrong. As we shall see, the European Commission's routine monitoring of consumer conditions indicates that there remains a significant gap between the rights and protections available to vulnerable and energy-poor consumers and their realisation in practice.

The chapter is divided into five sections. Section II considers attempts to provide specific recognition of, and additional protections for, vulnerable and energy-poor consumers. Section III then considers the development of alternative dispute resolution (ADR) in the European energy sector, as the major access to justice policy with which this book is concerned. Section IV provides some broader context, by discussing European Union (EU) consumer protection measures more generally and the substantive protections of consumer rights in EU law. This section also discusses collective redress and the recently adopted Directive on Representative Actions ((EU) 2020/1828). Finally, section V provides an overview of the results of the European Commission's energy market and consumer conditions monitoring.

[1] C Riefa and S Saintier (eds), *Vulnerable Consumers and the Law: Consumer Protection and Access to Justice* (Routledge, 2020).

II. Recognition of Vulnerability and Energy Poverty in EU Law and Policy

European law and policy increasingly seek to recognise the particular needs of vulnerable and energy-poor consumers. While many aspects of policy remain predicated on assumptions that active consumers will eventually create a competitive and efficient market, there is nonetheless growing recognition of the need to protect those who are unable to engage with the market effectively. This part of the chapter charts these developments and argues that progress to date has been slow and resulted in significant variation across Member States.

A. The Concept of Vulnerability in Consumer Protection Law

Waddington notes that EU consumer protection law takes as its starting point the concept of the average consumer, who is defined as 'reasonably well informed, observant and circumspect'.[2] There are also, however, some 'scarce references to, and limited specific protection provided for, 'vulnerable' consumers under EU law'.[3] For example, the Unfair Commercial Practices Directive (UCPD) (2005/29/EC) provides additional protection to 'particularly vulnerable' consumers in certain circumstances. Article 5(3) provides protection for vulnerable consumers defined as a clearly identifiable group of people who are vulnerable 'by virtue of mental or physical infirmity, age or credulity, where that vulnerability is reasonably foreseeable to the trader'. Where commercial practices affect this group, assessing whether a commercial practice is unfair, involves reference to the average member of this group. The Consumer Rights Directive (2011/83/EU) also mentions the need to protect particularly vulnerable consumers in the preamble at recital 34:

> [T]raders should take into account the specific needs of consumers who are particularly vulnerable because of their mental, physical or psychological infirmity, age or credulity in a way which the trader could reasonably be expected to foresee.

The General Product Safety Directive (2001/95/EC) makes brief reference to the concept of vulnerability in recital 8 of the Preamble and in Article 2, which highlights the particular needs of children and elderly people. Waddington points out that in addition to explicit references to vulnerability, some instruments appear to make implicit references to the need to provide additional protection to certain consumers based on their circumstances.[4] An example is the Credit Agreements

[2] L Waddington, 'Reflections on the Protection of 'Vulnerable' Consumers under EU Law' (2014) Working Paper No 2013-2 (Maastricht Faculty of Law) SSRN: available at: ssrn.com/abstract=2532904 or http://dx.doi.org/10.2139/ssrn.2532904.

[3] ibid 2.

[4] ibid.

for Consumers Directive (2008/48/EC), which requires pre-contractual information to be explained to consumers in a personalised manner so that the consumer can understand the effect of entering into a contract in terms of their particular economic situation. In terms of the case law of the Court of Justice of the European Union, Waddington's survey concludes that the emphasis has very much remained on the concept of the average consumer:

> [N]o definition or elaboration of the concept of 'vulnerability' is found in EU legislation, and the scarce case law of the Court on this issue is almost equally obtuse. In general, the Court has not been willing to allow Member States to require additional levels of protection for certain groups of consumers or to oblige producers or suppliers to adapt their marketing techniques to take account of the needs of 'vulnerable' consumers. It seems that the Court, and indeed the EU legislator, generally regards such requirements as barriers to market access and market integration … any additional level of protection offered to 'vulnerable' consumers under EU law is limited, there is no clarity as to which groups of consumers fall within this category and there is little differentiation regarding the kinds of additional protection which should be offered to the various groups of consumers who are 'vulnerable'.[5]

As Kaprou argues, the lack of a clear definition of vulnerable consumers in EU law is problematic, since the 'image' of consumers defined in law are key to determining who is granted protection and under what circumstances.[6] In relation to the UCPD, which contains the key reference to vulnerability in EU law, Kaprou criticises the arbitrary nature of those included as vulnerable and notes that the approach does not match the broader-based, situational approach to vulnerability which has become widely accepted in academic discourses. As we saw in chapter one, EU policy documents have adopted a broader approach to vulnerability that chimes with modern understandings of the concept, however, EU law has not caught up: 'this highlights a clear disparity between the vision of vulnerability in contemporary EU policy reports and the more rigid class-based definition adopted in the UCPD'.[7] Despite problems arising from poor definition and lack of implementing measures in relation to consumer vulnerability being highlighted in the European Commission's Fitness Check for EU Consumer and Marketing Law in 2017, the subsequent package of measures – the New Deal for Consumers – made few references to vulnerability. Kaprou concludes in relation to the New Deal for Consumers that: 'The wave of reforms in EU consumer law have not had an effect on the vulnerable consumer standard and that is a great missed opportunity to address this issue'.[8] At the same time, however, the EU's policy interest in the issue continues to be evident and it is possible that this will

[5] ibid 14–15.

[6] E Kaprou, 'The Current Legal Definition of Vulnerable Consumers in the UCPD: Benefits and Limitations of a Focus on Personal Attributes' in C Riefa and S Saintier (eds), *Vulnerable Consumers and the Law* (Routledge, 2020) 51.

[7] ibid 55.

[8] ibid 64.

eventually turn into measures that are reflected in law. The recently published New Consumer Agenda, the European Commission's strategic agenda for consumers for the period 2020 to 2025, makes consumer vulnerability one of its five priority areas.[9] At present, however, additional protection for vulnerable consumers remains an underdeveloped issue in EU consumer law, with it being addressed to different extents in Member States' national law and policy frameworks (see below).

B. Vulnerability and Energy Poverty in Energy Law

In comparison to the EU's general consumer protection measures, the concept of vulnerability has loomed larger in relation to energy consumers. Protecting vulnerable consumers is a recurring topic in the Third Energy Package (2009) Directives.[10] Member States are responsible for ensuring that vulnerable consumers can benefit from the opening of markets as much as any other consumer. Acknowledging that 'Energy poverty is a growing problem' (Recital 53 of the Electricity Directive 2009/72/EC), the Directive asks Member States to take special protective measures, such as those in Article 3(7) and (8):

> 7. Member States shall take appropriate measures to protect final customers, and shall, in particular, ensure that there are adequate safeguards to protect vulnerable customers. In this context, each Member State shall define the concept of vulnerable customers which may refer to energy poverty and, inter alia, to the prohibition of disconnection of electricity to such customers in critical times. Member States shall ensure that rights and obligations linked to vulnerable customers are applied. In particular, they shall take measures to protect final customers in remote areas. They shall ensure high levels of consumer protection, particularly with respect to transparency regarding contractual terms and conditions, general information and dispute settlement mechanisms. Member States shall ensure that the eligible customer is in fact able easily to switch to a new supplier.
>
> 8. Member States shall take appropriate measures, such as formulating national energy action plans, providing benefits in social security systems to ensure the necessary electricity supply to vulnerable customers, or providing for support for energy efficiency improvements, to address energy poverty where identified, including in the broader context of poverty. Such measures shall not impede the effective opening of the market set out in Article 33 or market functioning and shall be notified to the Commission, where relevant, in accordance with the provisions of paragraph 15 of this Article. Such notification may also include measures taken within the general social security system.

However, having the principle of subsidiarity at their core, the 2009 Directives failed to make Member States adopt particular definitions of energy poverty and

[9] See: eur-lex.europa.eu/legal-content/EN/TXT/PDF/?uri=CELEX:52020DC0696&from=EN.
[10] See: ec.europa.eu/energy/topics/markets-and-consumers/market-legislation/third-energy-package_en.

vulnerable consumers and left the adoption of protective measures as matters largely for national Member States.[11] The Vulnerable Consumer Working Group (2012–16), formed by the European Commission's Citizens Energy Forum, was critical of this approach and the fact that the definition, identification and strategies to address vulnerability and energy poverty were not prescribed.[12] Subsequently, the Clean Energy for All Package (2019) has continued to require Member States to delineate the concept of vulnerable consumers, which may refer to energy poverty. The definition of vulnerability 'may include income levels, the share of energy expenditure of disposable income, the energy efficiency of homes, critical dependence on electrical equipment for health reasons, age or other criteria' (Article 28 on Vulnerable Customers, Directive (EU) 2019/944). The Directive also requires Member States to ensure that 'rights and obligations linked to vulnerable customers are applied' (Article 28). Energy poverty meanwhile should be defined at the national level using 'a set of criteria, which may include low income, high expenditure of disposable income on energy and poor energy efficiency' (Article 29 on Energy Poverty, Directive (EU) 2019/944).

Dobbins et al argue that these measures provide a welcome focus on energy poverty and vulnerability, but also fail to go far enough and are unlikely to be effective without further EU-level action.[13] Indeed, the problems in relation to the implementation of protections around consumer vulnerability and energy poverty highlighted in Pye et al's[14] study have not been substantially addressed. This report found significant variation across the EU in definitions of consumer vulnerability and associated actions to mitigate it, while less than a third of countries recognised energy poverty as a discrete issue. The report found a need to develop a range of measures for addressing vulnerability and energy poverty, distinguishing between the measures required to deal with each concept:

> Measures focused on vulnerable consumers offer protection within regulated markets, and facilitate access and participation. They are often short-term in nature, providing relief or ensuring ongoing supply in the face of indebtedness. Energy poverty measures on the other hand are explicitly focused on lower income households, and seek to address longer term structural problems of building energy efficiency.[15]

Dobbins et al argue that while there are good reasons for subsidiarity in relation to action taken to alleviate energy poverty (for example, different housing

[11] S Pye, A Dobbins and C Baffert et al, 'Energy Poverty and Vulnerable Consumers in the Energy Sector across the EU: Analysis of Policies and Measures' (2015 INSIGHT_E), available at: ec.europa.eu/energy/sites/ener/files/documents/INSIGHT_E_Energy%20Poverty%20-%20Main%20Report_FINAL.pdf.

[12] See: ec.europa.eu/energy/content/meetings-and-documents-related-vulnerable-consumer-working-group-2012---2016_en?redir=1.

[13] A Dobbins, F Nerini and P Deane et al, 'Strengthening the EUs Response to Energy Poverty' (2019), available at: discovery.ucl.ac.uk/id/eprint/10067578/1/NENERGY-18071320B_Dobbins%20et%20al_STRENGTHENING%20THE%20EU_Final.pdf.

[14] Pye, Dobbins and Baffert et al, 'Energy Poverty' (n 11).

[15] ibid vi.

stock, climate, etc) more direct action is possible in relation to vulnerability. The current situation in terms of action on energy poverty is that only six EU countries have legislated definitions of energy poverty.[16] Meanwhile, all countries have adopted definitions of vulnerable energy consumers, but these definitions vary widely. Dobbins et al highlight four main categories of vulnerability definitions: those that define vulnerability in relation to particular socio-economic groups; those that categorise vulnerability as the receipt of certain types of social welfare; those that tie vulnerability to disability and/or health; and those that tie vulnerability to energy affordability. Their survey of European practice reveals that two-thirds of EU Member States currently adopt measures that seek to address vulnerability and energy poverty. The four main measures include financial support to relieve acute financial problems, safeguards against disconnection, measures to engage consumers, and energy efficiency measures. However, the comprehensiveness and nature of these measures differ widely.

C. Summary

The overall position in the European energy market, therefore, is that vulnerability and energy poverty are subject to no single definition and action to address these issues varies significantly according to national priorities. The concept of consumer vulnerability is more prominent in relation to the protection of energy consumers than in relation to consumers in general. Overall, we can conclude that relatively timid and hesitant steps are being taken at EU level. And almost entirely absent from discussion of consumer vulnerability and energy poverty has been the connection between these issues and access to justice, particularly ADR. The Working Group on Consumer Vulnerability has highlighted the connection, arguing that:

> Regular analysis of the complaints gathered by third party bodies (such as local administration and advice bodies, independent ombudsmen and consumer organisations) can help provide an assessment of market performance in the interest of vulnerable consumers … Member States should ensure that there are channels by which consumers, including people in vulnerable circumstances or their representatives and advisers, can raise general concerns about company practices.

Furthermore, the Working Group argued that independent energy ombuds constitute 'stakeholders [that] can influence and improve the situation for vulnerable consumers in the energy sector'. However, in practice, the particular role of ADR in responding to issues faced by vulnerable and energy-poor consumers in the energy market has not been addressed to any great extent. The chapter now turns to consider the way in which ADR has developed as a strand of EU law and policy.

[16] Dobbins, Nerini and Deane et al, 'Strengthening the EUs Response to Energy Poverty' (n 13).

III. The Development of ADR for Consumer Disputes in the Energy Sector

A. The Growth of ADR in Civil Justice Systems

Before examining ADR in the European consumer and energy sectors, it is important to explain the broader context for developments there. Indeed, the provision of ADR in these settings can be seen as part of a global growth of interest in ADR as a means of improving the functioning of court-based systems of justice. An exhaustive discussion of that context is not possible here, but we can touch on some of its key milestones. Palmer and Roberts identify a number of stages in the modern development of ADR. The first of these began in the 1960s and 1970s as part of the access to justice movement and was driven by concerns about the costs, delays and inaccessibility of the courts. They argued in favour of quicker, cheaper and less formal dispute resolution. The second emerged in the 1970s and consisted of an attack on adjudication itself as a form of dispute resolution, while setting out the potential wider benefits that could be derived from settling disputes. The third, in the mid-1970s, began to discuss the possibility of alternative or complementary forms of dispute resolution (the term 'alternative dispute resolution' was first used by Frank Sander in 1976).[17] Towards the end of that decade, discussions about ADR and procedural innovation began to be translated into institutional form. There were three major development here: the entrance of 'new professionals' in dispute resolution (mediators, arbitrators, adjudicators, ombuds); the remodelling of legal practice, towards settlement approaches and to include mediation; and the emphasis placed by the courts themselves on encouraging settlement. The effect of these changes has been a near ubiquitous transformation of justice systems around the world:

> Over three or so short decades, what appeared in the 1980s as marginal novelties have become established features of the disputing scene. ADR, with its objective in 'settlement' and its principal institutional realisation in 'mediation', is now a virtually unremarkable feature of disputing cultures almost anywhere we look.[18]

The extent to which ADR has grown to become a feature of modern justice systems is particularly evident in the European consumer context, where Hodges has claimed that ADR 'is not an alternative to courts – it is the mainstream method of resolving consumer disputes, and has replaced lawyers and courts'.[19] While the consumer setting is a notable example of the European approach to ADR, broader

[17] M Palmer and S Roberts, *Disputes Processes: ADR and the Primary Forms of Decision-Making*, 3rd edn (CUP 2020).

[18] ibid 323.

[19] C Hodges, 'Consumer Redress: Ideology and Empiricism' in K Purnhagen and P Rott (eds), *Varieties of European Economic Law and Regulation* (Springer, 2014).

attempts to introduce ADR into civil justice systems have been an important feature of EU policy (and that of a number of Member States).[20]

Although the introduction and mainstreaming of ADR into civil justice systems has included discussion of access to justice and ideas around the social benefits of conflict resolution, there is little doubt that government policy in this area has been driven primarily by concerns around cost.[21] The drive to decrease the direct costs of public justice through courts, along with the pressure to reduce legal aid bills and a need to better manage judicial caseloads, were ultimately the most telling factors in the ready adoption by government of ADR as a means of reform. These primary drivers sit in some tension with access to justice, since they concentrate on ways of managing existing demand and reducing costs, rather than opening up justice to a broader range of participants. Transferring litigants from one dispute resolution forum (courts) to another (ADR) may, of course, have some access to justice benefits, but the chances of realising access to justice on a cost-cutting agenda seen slim. As we saw in chapter one, Felstiner et al, in their classic article on the emergence of disputes, showed that access to justice is impeded by social factors that affect the ability of individuals to identify and pursue their problems.[22] Overcoming the barriers to naming, blaming and claiming would involve significant investment in reaching out and including vulnerable, disadvantaged and socially excluded individuals and groups. The growth of ADR in civil justice systems generally can be seen as a move which imperfectly cuts across agendas of social justice, access to justice, court reform and cost reduction. There is, however, an imbalance between these drivers, with the rhetoric of access to justice often providing cover for narrower concerns.[23] As Nylund has argued, the result has been 'a system where ADR often reduces access to justice rather than enhances it. In other words, ADR has often been misunderstood and misused as a tool for enhancing access to justice'.[24] Indeed, as we shall see further in chapter four, concerns about the neoliberal usurpation of access to justice narratives,[25] and the use of ADR to further the interests of powerful actors

[20] Directive 2008/52/EC of the European Parliament and of the Council of 21 May 2008 on certain aspects of mediation in civil and commercial matters.

[21] A Nylund, 'Access to Justice: Is ADR a Help or Hindrance?' in L Ervo and A Nylund (eds), *The Future of Civil Litigation: Access to Courts and Court-annexed Mediation in the Nordic Countries* (Springer, 2014).

[22] W Felstiner, R Abel and A Sarat, 'The Emergence and Transformation of Disputes: Naming, Blaming, Claiming …' (1981) 15 *Law & Society Review* 631.

[23] M Palmer, 'Formalisation of Alternative Dispute Resolution Processes: Some Socio-legal Thoughts' in J Zekoll, M Bälz and I Amelung (eds), *Formalisation and Flexibilisation in Dispute Resolution* (Brill Nijhoff, 2014).

[24] Nylund (n 21) 342.

[25] K Laster and R Kornhauser, 'The Rise of "DIY" Law: Implications for Legal Aid' in A Flynn and J Hodgson (eds), *Access to Justice and Legal Aid: Comparative Perspectives on Unmet Legal Need* (Hart Publishing, 2017).

'interested in trimming budgets and dumping minor disputes out of the court system',[26] are commonplace in the ADR literature.

B. The EU Legislative Framework for Consumer Energy Disputes

We will consider general consumer protection measures that can be seen as having an access to justice dimension in section IV below. Here, we focus on ADR as the major procedural mechanism provided for consumers to access justice and realise their rights in the EU energy market.[27] Two European Commission (EC) Recommendations, in 1998 (98/257/EC) and 2001 (2001/310/EC), set out principles for ADR mechanisms concerned with the settlement and consensual resolution of consumer disputes. These recommendations were aimed at all consumer disputes and were not specific to the energy sector. EU level action in relation to the energy market initially gave little consideration to consumer redress. The 2003 Electricity Directive (2003/54/EC), for example, simply provided that high levels of consumer protection should be delivered through dispute resolution mechanisms, among other measures. A major development came about in 2009 with the Third Energy Package, which included the Electricity Directive (2009/72/EC) and the Natural Gas Directive (2009/73/EC). In Article 3(13) and Article 3(9), respectively, these Directives required that, 'Member States shall ensure that an independent mechanism such as an energy ombudsman or a consumer body is in place in order to ensure efficient treatment of complaints and out-of-court dispute settlements'. The Natural Gas Directive remains in force, while the Electricity Directive was replaced at the end of 2020 by provisions included in the Clean Energy for All Europeans package which apply to the electricity market. Article 26(1) of the Directive on Common Rules for the Internal Market for Electricity (EU 2019/944) provides that:

> Member States shall ensure that final customers have access to simple, fair, transparent, independent, effective and efficient out-of-court mechanisms for the settlement of disputes concerning rights and obligations established under this Directive, through an independent mechanism such as an energy ombudsman or a consumer body, or through a regulatory authority.

Meanwhile, in 2013, the Directive on Alternative Dispute Resolution for Consumer Disputes (2013/11/EU) (the ADR Directive) introduced a new framework for the provision of out-of-court dispute resolution in relation to consumer

[26] I Ramsay, 'Consumer Redress and Access to Justice' in CEF Rickett and TGW Telfer (eds), *International Perspectives on Consumers' Access to Justice* (CUP, 2003).

[27] The EU's predominant focus has been on ADR, with some exceptions, eg, Regulation (EC) No 861/2007 of the European Parliament and of the Council of 11 July 2007 establishing a European Small Claims Procedure.

disputes. Among other things, the Directive provides a set of requirements and standards in Articles 5 to 10 which seek to enhance the consistency and quality of ADR. Article 26(1) of the Directive on Common Rules for the Internal Market for Electricity makes clear that, where a complaint is made by a consumer, the quality requirements of the ADR Directive apply to ADR provided for the settlement of consumer energy disputes:

> Where the final customer is a consumer within the meaning of Directive 2013/11/EU of the European Parliament and of the Council (23), such out-of-court dispute settlement mechanisms shall comply with the quality requirements of Directive 2013/11/EU and shall provide, where warranted, for systems of reimbursement and compensation.

C. Drivers for the Development of ADR Provisions for Consumers in the EU Legislative Framework

In summary, therefore, the effect of the EU legislative framework on ADR is that Member States are required to provide an independent, out-of-court means of resolving consumer disputes in the energy sector, with the vehicle for delivering this suggested as being an energy ombuds, a consumer body, or a regulatory authority. Moreover, ADR mechanisms are expected to meet a series of quality requirements around, inter alia, fairness, independence, expertise and transparency. The specific drivers towards the out-of-court settlement of disputes and the sponsoring of ADR for consumer disputes at EU level can be seen through analysis of the preambles to some the legislative instruments noted above.

The Electricity Directive, for example, introduces ADR as part of a package of measures to strengthen consumer interests, which 'should be at the heart of this Directive' (paragraph 51). This includes strengthening and enforcing consumer rights (paragraph 51); providing consumers with clear information about their rights (paragraph 52); making an action plan to tackle energy poverty, developing national policies to assist vulnerable consumers (paragraph 53); and the provision of effective dispute settlement (paragraph 54). In relation to dispute settlement, the preamble states: 'Greater consumer protection is guaranteed by the availability of effective means of dispute settlement for all consumers. Member States should introduce speedy and effective complaint handling procedures' (paragraph 54). The Directive on Common Rules for the Internal Market for Electricity, meanwhile, places a similar emphasis on consumer rights and interests, but even more so on the ideal of creating a market in which there is full consumer participation and consumers are active rather than passive. Thus, the discussion of ADR in paragraph 36 of the Preamble is in the context of describing a range of measures for improving the ease of switching between providers and the importance of consumer participation for a well-functioning energy market (paragraphs 31–37). Finally, the ADR Directive sees ADR as a means of ensuring the effective functioning of the internal market by promoting high levels of consumer protection (paragraph 2) and enhancing citizens' trust in the market (paragraph 3). ADR in this context is portrayed as providing a 'simple, fast and low cost' solution to disputes (paragraph 5). The development of ADR is seen as crucial to the effective functioning of consumer markets: 'any holistic approach to the single market which delivers results for its citizens should as a priority develop simple, affordable, expedient and accessible system of redress' (paragraph 8). ADR is also seen as 'one of the twelve levers to boost growth, strengthen confidence and make progress towards completing the Single Market' (paragraph 9). Enhancing consumer confidence through effective ADR in turn should 'fulfil the potential for and opportunities of cross-border and online trade' (paragraph 15). The drivers for the development of ADR for energy consumers, therefore, include: providing an accessible means of enforcing consumer rights and protecting consumer interests; delivering dispute resolution at speed and at low cost; enhancing trust and confidence in the internal market generally and the energy market in particular; and ensuring the effective functioning of markets and ultimately boosting trade. In each of these areas, ADR is only one of a number of options with the potential to address these drivers; yet even so, we can see there are great, and potentially contradictory, expectations placed on ADR at EU level. As Cortes has commented, policy aims associated with the introduction of ADR in the consumer context are often 'over stated' and include consumer protection, access to justice and boosting trust in e-commerce.[28] Particularly clear is the emphasis in EU policymaking in this area on unremedied consumer detriment and consumer passivity being barriers to effective functioning of markets and the primary linking of ADR as a means of facilitating market-related goals.

A further issue is that interest in consumer ADR in government has been driven by departments of business or those overseeing particular industrial sectors, rather than departments of justice.[29] As a result, although ADR can be seen as a vehicle for access to justice, that is perhaps not the primary driver. If that is the case, then the question naturally arises as to the extent to which the interests of businesses and regulators in promoting ADR overlap with the interests of access to justice. In some ways, this interest helps to complement the holistic view of access to justice discussed in chapter two, in the sense that it looks well beyond courts and seeks to link dispute resolution to broader social goods (mostly around market efficiencies). The flipside, however, is that industry-based ADR can be a means of extending the power of industries, rather than reducing it, and regulators themselves may struggle to avoid regulatory capture by the industries they oversee. There is also perhaps a question of expertise with potential concerns around the extent to which non-justice system actors understand the issues around ADR from a justice perspective. As Noone and Ojelabi have argued,

[28] P Cortes, *The Law of Consumer Redress in an Evolving Digital Market: Upgrading from Alternative to Online Dispute Resolution* (CUP, 2017).

[29] Hodges, 'Consumer Redress' (n 19).

policy debates have a tendency to focus on the positive features of ADR, while the disadvantages 'have been relegated to the background in most jurisdictions'.[30]

D. Diversity of ADR in the European Energy Sector

The lack of prescription in EU Directives about the particular form of ADR that is required to be provided in the energy sector has resulted in a landscape marked by significant diversity across Europe.[31] In a European survey, Creutzfeldt found that there were five independent energy ADR bodies (that is, independent ADR bodies with an energy-specific jurisdiction solely for energy, which were not part of a national regulatory authority or a government body);[32] 14 ADR bodies established within national regulatory authorities;[33] and 11 ADR schemes as part of a body with a larger ADR remit (for example, complaint boards).[34] In some jurisdictions, the public ombuds also has a role in relation to fundamental rights and access to energy. The diversity of approaches in the energy sector is reflective of the wider diversity of approaches to ADR in the European consumer context.[35]

Cortes refers to the most common forms of ADR in the consumer context as being: ombuds, arbitration, conciliation, mediation and complaints boards. Complexity is increased by the fact that terminology is often used differently in different jurisdictions, so that the meaning of mediation may vary in different contexts, and ombuds may have divergent powers and approaches.[36] The position in relation to ADR in the UK has been summarised as one of 'confusion, gaps, and overlaps',[37] while across the EU there is 'a confusing maze of basic models, names, mixtures of techniques deployed, and variations in national

[30] L Ojelabi and M Noone, 'Jurisdictional Perspectives on Alternative Dispute Resolution and Access to Justice: Introduction' (2020) 16 *International Journal of Law in Context* 103, 105.

[31] C Hodges, I Benöehr and N Creutzfeldt-Banda, *Consumer ADR in Europe* (Hart Publishing, 2012); Cortes (n 28); C Gill, J Williams, C Brennan and C Hirst. 'Designing Consumer Redress: A Dispute System Design (DSD) Model for Consumer-to-Business Disputes' (2016) 36 *Legal Studies* 438.

[32] N Creutzfeldt, *ADR in the Energy Sector in Europe* (National Energy Ombudsman Network 2015), available at: www.neon-ombudsman.org/2015/03/12/independent-ombudsmen-and-adr-providers-building-bridges-in-the-energy-market; Belgium, Bulgaria, France, Germany and the United Kingdom.

[33] Austria, Hungary, Italy, Lithuania, Luxembourg, Malta, Poland, Romania, Slovakia, Slovenia, Norway, Switzerland, Iceland, Ireland.

[34] Cyprus, Czech Republic, Denmark, Estonia, Finland, Greece, Latvia, The Netherlands, Portugal, Spain, Sweden.

[35] C Hodges, *Delivering Dispute Resolution: A Holistic Review of Models in England and Wales* (Hart Publishing, 2019).

[36] Cortes (n 28).

[37] C Gill, N Creutzfeldt and J Williams et al, *Confusion, Gaps, and Overlaps: A Consumer Perspective on Alternative Dispute Resolution between Consumers and Businesses* (QMUL, University of Westminster, Citizens Advice, 2017), available at: www.citizensadvice.org.uk/Global/CitizensAdvice/Consumer%20publications/Confusiongapsandoverlaps-Original1.docx.pdf.

landscapes'.[38] While the ADR Directive could have provided an opportunity for rationalising and bringing coherence to this landscape, few governments have done this to date and, as a result, 'significant opportunities for improvement of consumer dispute resolution – and of markets – remain unrealised'.[39] Indeed, according to Hodges, there is a significant gulf between EU states with well-developed ADR systems for consumers and those that have 'very undeveloped' approaches.[40]

A particular issue in the energy sector relates to the widespread provision of ADR within regulatory agencies. The European Union's Agency for the Cooperation of Energy Regulators' Market Monitoring Report for 2019[41] highlights that, in relation to the electricity market, ADR is currently implemented as follows across Member States: 14 Member States provide ADR through the national energy regulator; nine provide ADR through a third party that is not specific to the energy sector; five provide ADR through a national energy ombud; and two provide ADR through an energy sector specific third party. As the Market Monitoring Report notes: '[Member states] have frequently shied away from designing energy sector-specific third parties as ADR mechanism. Ombudsman also remains a minority choice when it comes to alternative dispute settlement'. Creutzfeldt[42] and Hodges[43] have noted that the provision of complaint-handling services within regulatory agencies has the potential to raise questions of independence for consumers and that there is evidence that consumers feel more confident in approaching an ADR body that is separate both from the industry and the energy regulator. A further issue, which we return to in chapter seven, is that an ADR mechanism that is separate from the regulator allows for the introduction of checks and balances within the system. That being said, as we will explore further below, a certain closeness to the regulator is important in order to allow ADR to influence and change practices within the energy industry.

The chapters in part II of this book provide detailed accounts of the approaches to ADR in our selected jurisdictions. A brief summary is provided in Table 3.1, in order to situate the discussion presented in chapters four and five.

[38] C Hodges, 'The Private Sector Ombudsman' in M Hertogh and R Kirkham (eds), *Research Handbook on the Ombudsman* (Edward Elgar, 2018) 56.

[39] C Hodges, N Creutzfeldt, F Steffek and E Verhage. 'ADR and Justice in Consumer Disputes in the EU' (Foundation for Law, Justice and Society Policy Brief, 2016) 1.

[40] C Hodges, 'Developments and Issues in Consumer ADR and Consumer Ombudsmen in Europe' (Foundation for Law, Justice and Society Policy Brief, 2019).

[41] See: www.acer.europa.eu/Official_documents/Acts_of_the_Agency/Publication/ACER%20Market%20Monitoring%20Report%202019%20-%20Energy%20Retail%20and%20Consumer%20Protection%20Volume.pdf.

[42] Creutzfeldt, *ADR in the Energy Sector in Europe* (n 32).

[43] Hodges, Benöehr and Creutzfeldt-Banda et al (n 31).

A major point of distinction between the different approaches to ADR shown in Table 3.1 relates to the extent to which they focus purely on ADR or perform certain added-value functions. Conciliation and arbitration schemes focus on dispute resolution.[44] Conciliation schemes tend to seek to reach consensual outcomes and only propose solutions if such outcomes are not forthcoming. Arbitration schemes are more straightforwardly adjudicative in nature and involve the imposition of a decision by the third-party arbitrator. Consumer ombuds, on the other hand, tend to combine various forms of dispute resolution within their internal processes and also provide additional functions such as advice, information and support for complainants, along with feedback to industry and regulators in relation to good practice.[45] National public ombuds, meanwhile, may have additional responsibilities in relation to advocacy with regard to fundamental rights and powers to conduct public interest investigations even where a complaint has not been received.[46]

An important point here, therefore, is that the form of ADR being used is crucial for considering the question of access to justice. As we will argue in

Table 3.1 Forms of ADR operating in the energy sector in selected jurisdictions

Jurisdiction	Forms of ADR
Bulgaria (see chapter 9)	Commission for consumer protection Energy regulator Company ombuds (in one company) National public ombuds[47]
Catalonia (see chapter 10)	Consumer arbitration schemes National public ombuds
France (see chapter 11)	National energy ombuds Company ombuds in some companies
Italy (see chapter12)	Conciliation services offered by consumer organisations National Energy Customer Conciliation Service Energy regulator can be asked by the parties to intervene if conciliation has failed
UK (see chapter 13)	National energy ombuds

[44] C Gill, J Williams, C Brennan and C Hirst, *Models of Alternative Dispute Resolution (ADR): A Report for the Legal Ombudsman* (Legal Ombudsman 2014).
[45] C Gill and C Hirst, *Defining Consumer Ombudsmen Schemes* (Ombudsman Services, 2016).
[46] L Reif, The Ombudsman, *Good Governance and the International Human Rights System* (Martinus Nijhoff, 2004).
[47] National public ombudsman schemes are only mentioned here where they have an active remit to consider complaints against energy suppliers.

chapters four and five, narrow approaches to ADR which focus only on providing an out-of-court dispute resolution service are less likely to be able to address the multiple barriers to access to justice identified in chapter one. Instead, to tackle access to justice barriers at each of the naming, blaming and claiming stages of dispute emergence, ADR needs to go beyond dispute resolution and include a much broader toolkit of powers and strategies.

IV. Access to Justice, Collective Redress and Consumer Protection Measures

In this section, we look beyond ADR to other measures that have a bearing on access to justice. The most important measures in this respect relate to collective redress, with the newly adopted Directive on Representative Actions representing an important development. We also provide a brief overview of the broader consumer protection landscape, including the substantive rights and institutions that contribute to the realisation of justice for consumers. The latter have been extensively considered by others,[48] and are largely beyond the scope of this book, but nonetheless provide important reference points for our holistic vision of access to justice and the expanded role we recommend for ADR in chapters five and seven.

A. Collective Redress

The role of ADR in relation to collective redress is currently unclear, although Hodges and Voet have argued that well-designed ADR, in conjunction with regulators, can provide collective redress for consumer problems.[49] In general, however, the perception has been that consumer ADR currently facilitates private enforcement of consumer rights by aggrieved individuals.[50] Given the difficulties surrounding the private enforcement of rights for vulnerable and energy-poor consumers (see chapter one), the potential for taking collective action is clearly important. The matter of collective interests had been partially addressed by the now repealed Injunctions Directive (2009/22/EC), although this only provided for the raising of injunctions to prevent collective harms to consumers and did not address the question of collective redress. A major recent development has been the adoption of the Directive on Representative Actions ((EU) 2020/1828).[51]

[48] S Wrbka, *European Consumer Access to Justice Revisited* (CUP 2015); P Siciliani, C Riefa and H Gamper, *Consumer Theories of Harm* (Hart Publishing, 2020); Riefa and Saintier (eds) (n 1).

[49] C Hodges and S Voet, *Delivering Collective Redress: New Technologies* (Hart Publishing, 2018).

[50] C Graham, 'Consumer ADR and Collective Redress' in P Cortes (ed), *The New Regulatory Framework for Consumer Dispute Resolution* (OUP, 2016).

[51] Adopted on 24 November 2020.

This now includes both the injunction of harmful action and the provision of redress. The scope of the Directive extends to 'a variety of areas such as data protection, financial services, travel and tourism, energy, telecommunications and environment'.[52] However, the approach adopted by the Directive has been subject to significant criticism. Hodges and Voet are critical of the general approach of the Directive, which encourages representative litigation (otherwise known as 'class actions') rather than using other mechanism to secure collective redress.[53] They identify the problems with class actions as follows:

> Almost without exception, class action mechanisms take time, involve cost (which can act as a significant barrier to claimants and those who wish to initiate an action), reduce sums paid to claimants through funders' costs, and deliver limited outcomes.[54]

Hodges refers to this approach to collective redress as 'old technology', with 'new technologies' involving instead the deployment of collective redress by regulators (regulatory redress) and ADR schemes which are able to process mass claims.[55] While it will take many years to witness and evaluate the effect of the new Directive, it has some potential to enhance access to justice if cases are raised that address the collective interests of vulnerable and energy-poor consumers. The need for collective action to address consumer problems in general and those of vulnerable consumers in particular will be returned to in later chapters, where the focus will be on examining the extent to which ADR mechanisms can deliver collective redress.

B. Substantive Rights and Consumer Protection Mechanisms

EU law provides a range of protections for consumers through the creation of rights in both consumer and energy law. These rights are an important part of considering access to justice, since they delineate the extent to which a legal solution will exist to the problems that energy consumers experience. In addition to cross-cutting consumer rights and protections,[56] energy consumers are afforded a range of protections as a result of energy specific legislation,[57] such as: all households

[52] Recital 6 of the Preamble to the draft Directive on Representative Actions for the protection of the collective interests of consumers, available at: eur-lex.europa.eu/resource.html?uri=cellar:adba9e47-3e34-11e8-b5fe-01aa75ed71a1.0001.02/DOC_1&format=PDF.

[53] Hodges and Voet, *Delivering Collective Redress* (n 48). The European approach is distinguished from US-style class actions, however. Under the Directive, representative actions can only be launched with qualified entities, subject to legislative criteria.

[54] C Hodges and S Voet, 'Delivering Collective Redress in Markets: New Technologies' (Foundation for Law, Justice and Society Policy Brief, 2017) 3.

[55] C Hodges, 'Collective Redress: The Need for New Technologies' (2019) 42 *Journal of Consumer Policy* 59.

[56] eg, Consumer Rights Directive (2011/83/EU).

[57] Directive on Common Rules for the Internal Market for Electricity EU 2019/944; Directive 2009/73/EC concerning common rules for the internal market in natural gas addresses (Natural Gas Directive).

should have the right to an electricity connection with the supplier of their choice and with the type of energy they want to use; a national contact point for energy should assist consumers in finding out about their options; certified price comparison tools designed to help them choose the best offers on the market should enable consumers to switch quickly from one supplier to another; when consumers sign a new contract, they should receive clear and transparent information; consumers should have the right to terminate the contract and to turn to an out-of-court body, such as an ombuds, a regulatory authority or a consumer protection body, to help them resolve any dispute; bills should be clear and based on reliable data; all energy consumers, in particular energy-poor and vulnerable consumers, should be protected and benefit from adequate safeguards through national laws.

There have been arguments for the expansion of current protections for energy consumers and, in particular, the creation of a 'right to energy' to overcome injustice in energy markets.[58] Others have focused their access to justice discussions on the design of substantive laws.[59] The scope of these laws and their design have a fundamental effect on individuals' ability to secure justice. Indeed, Siciliani et al have argued that more needs to be done to create a system of consumer law that incorporates 'fairness by design'.[60] This is the idea that fairness should be mainstreamed as an objective of consumer law, and that this should be an integral part of the design of consumer protection systems. In particular, fairness by design involves a positive duty on firms to treat consumers fairly, rather than the emphasis of consumer protection being on *ex post* mechanisms of enforcement and redress. Considering such matters clearly chimes with the holistic approach we have argued for in chapter two, albeit the most pressing issue in terms of the protections offered by EU law relate to awareness and enforcement of current laws rather than the nature and design of the substantive rights afforded to individuals.[61] Indeed, while rights could be strengthened in some areas, we consider the access to justice challenge for vulnerable and energy-poor consumers to be primarily an issue concerning the realisation of existing rights.

In terms of the institutional framework, delineating the boundary between consumer protection policies and policies seeking to deliver access to justice for consumers is not an easy task. There are of course strong connections between the nature of the rights afforded to consumers, the mechanisms available to inform and advise them of those rights, and consumer enforcement agencies.[62] As Gill and Hirst[63] and Creutzfeldt[64] have argued, there is also an overlap

[58] See: www.eapn.eu/wp-content/uploads/2017/05/EAPN-2017-EAPN-EPSU-energypoverty-leaflet-1138.pdf

[59] Wrbka (n 47).

[60] Siciliani, Riefa and Gamper (n 47).

[61] European Commission, *Results of the Fitness Check of Consumer and Marketing Law and of the Evaluation of the Consumer Rights Directive* (European Commission, 2017).

[62] Wrbka (n 47).

[63] Gill and Hirst (n 45).

[64] N Creutzfeldt, 'Ombudsman Schemes' in P Cortes (ed), *The Transformation of Consumer Dispute Resolution in the European Union: A Renewed Approach to Consumer Protection* (OUP, 2016).

Table 3.2 Four Pillars of Consumer Protection (Scottish Government 2013, cited in Creutzfeldt 2016)

Advocacy	Advice	Info & education	Enforcement & redress
• rights of consumers can be represented to Parliament or regulators, so that new policies can be pursued or refined • collected data can be used to highlight systemic issues	• individual consumers can be made aware of their rights and become more empowered, making it easier to avoid unscrupulous businesses, or to take action when they suffer harm	• empower consumers, making it easier for them to avoid harm in the future • signpost consumers to other avenues of help • make consumers aware of their rights	• traders who flout consumer protection or competition laws can be held accountable • consumer detriment can be remedied and consumers gain access to justice

between ADR and various of the institutional actors involved in consumer protection. Understanding access to justice, therefore, and the particular contribution of ADR, requires that we briefly overview the consumer protection landscape. While this landscape varies across national boundaries, the Scottish government's description of the consumer landscape as involving four pillars of advocacy, advice, information and education, and redress and enforcement, covers common elements. We do not have the space to consider in detail the way in which these elements manifest themselves. Here we simply seek to define in broad terms the different elements of the landscape. Table 3.2 below provides a summary based on the Scottish government's four pillars.

Each of the pillars described in Table 3.2 plays an important role in the delivery of access to justice. While our predominant focus in this book is on the contribution of ADR, therefore, our analysis and argument for a reformed system of ADR and access to justice (see chapter seven) are fundamentally grounded in an understanding of the roles of other system actors. We will return to this idea later in the book.

V. Ongoing Problems for Vulnerable and Energy-Poor Consumers in the European Energy Market

This section provides a brief overview of the outcomes of the European Commission's routine monitoring of energy market and consumer conditions. The European Commission's latest *Consumer Conditions Scoreboard* (2019),[65]

[65] See: ec.europa.eu/info/policies/consumers/consumer-protection/evidence-based-consumer-policy/consumer-scoreboards.

showed that less than 45 per cent of consumers were aware of their rights (in general) and that, although one in five had experienced a problem with a trader over the previous year, only one in 20 would turn to an ADR body. The energy sector displays similar problems, with studies suggesting low levels of trust and poor performance. Indeed, energy-specific studies show significant problems for consumers in obtaining information about their rights and in the clarity of energy bills and suggest that there are few energy consumers who lodge a complaint with the relevant third party.[66] Regarding 'consumer detriment', in 2017 the Commission presented a study on consumer detriment in the EU electricity sector.[67] The total post-redress financial detriment over the last 12 months in the EU-28 was between €1.9 billion and €6.4 billion, against between €2.4 billion and €7.2 billion pre-redress. The European Commission also initiated several sector-specific studies on consumer rights in the energy sector, namely the *Consumer Study on Pre-contractual Information and Billing in the Energy Market – Improved Clarity and Comparability* (the 2018 study)[68] and the *Consumer Market Study on the Functioning of the Retail Electricity Markets for Consumers in the EU* (the 2017 study).[69] These studies focus on consumer behaviours and look at how consumers react to the information available to them, starting with the choices they make and the details of their energy bills.

The 2018 study found that vulnerable consumers compare fewer energy offers and find comparison rather difficult, as compared with other consumers.[70] Overall, consumers usually do not spend much time reviewing their bills, either because it is paid by direct debit or, at the other end of the spectrum, because it is too hard to understand.[71] The 2017 study focused more on consumer behaviour, motivations and decision-making patterns, and their evolution over the previous five years. It made specific recommendations on vulnerable and energy-poor consumers and on redress, without, however, linking the two concepts together. The study concluded that about two-thirds of consumers surveyed believed the retail electricity market in their country was not functioning very well. People appear to know how much they spend on their bills but not how much they consume. The study recommended providing targeted information to vulnerable consumers to close the gap between different categories of users.

The 2017 study found vulnerable consumers to be 'older consumers (65+), economically inactive and those with lower educational attainment', while the energy poor are those who have 'difficulties with paying their

[66] European Commission, *Consumer Study on Pre-contractual Information and Billing in the Energy Market – Improved Clarity and Comparability* (European Commission, 2018).

[67] See: ec.europa.eu/info/publications/study-measuring-consumer-detriment-european-union_en

[68] ibid.

[69] European Commission, *Second Consumer Market Study on the Functioning of the Retail Electricity Markets for Consumers in the EU* (European Commission 2017), available at: ec.europa.eu/newsroom/just/item-detail.cfm?item_id=53331.

[70] European Commission, *Consumer Study on Pre-contractual Information* (n 65) 35.

[71] ibid 125.

electricity bills'. Vulnerability was assessed on the basis of behavioural patterns, such as consumers' reactions to information and their desire to compare and switch between offers.[72] The study found a need for companies specifically to target vulnerable consumers to increase the accessibility of the relevant information, for instance on their websites. The incidence of late payment was higher in Bulgaria, Greece, Hungary and Romania, suggesting higher rates of energy poverty. The study recommended going beyond affordability criteria to 'establish methodologies that can be used at EU level to measure energy poverty in both quantitative and qualitative ways'. A wide range of policy measures to address energy poverty and vulnerability were required to consider local conditions and the variety of drivers to 'reflect the differing needs of certain consumers'.

The 2017 study found that in relation to complaint handling, awareness of complaint-handling procedures, and the quality of information received by consumers varies greatly between countries.[73] The study, therefore, recommended that companies improve the communication of information on websites and bills. The study also noted that, in general, electricity companies are the first point of contact, and few consumers lodge a complaint to the relevant third party (ie, ADR bodies, consumer organisations, ombuds or regulators).[74] Almost a third of consumers had experienced a problem during the previous three years,[75] but only one in 10 had complained to their supplier. Consumers were quite dissatisfied with the complaint-handling process. Problems with pricing, consumption and billing were common: 11 per cent of consumers (who had experienced a problem) referred to problems with prices (for example, too high or incorrect); 11 per cent to estimates of electricity consumption (for example, incorrect estimates); and 8 per cent to billing problems (for example, non-transparent or incorrect billing). In recent years, the Consumer Conditions Scoreboard has reported that consumers trust traders more than public authorities and consumer organisations to protect consumer rights.[76] This might explain why, when encountering a problem when buying goods or services (as reported by more than one in five consumers) for which they felt there was a legitimate reason to complain, two-thirds of consumers turned to the retailer. Fear of long delays, lack of financial redress, and

[72] 'Switching rates were lower among over 65-year-olds, economically inactive respondents and respondents with lower education attainment. For example, while 15% of over 65-year-olds had switched provider or tariff in the past three years, this figure was 30% for younger respondents'.

[73] 'A large variation was observed in mystery shoppers' evaluations of electricity companies' websites: while 88% of shoppers in the UK had found information about how to file a complaint on the website, this figure decreased to 26% in Poland. 27% of mystery shoppers reported that a complaint could be submitted on the electricity company's website, 22% found a link to the national body in charge of energy regulation and 19% a link to an ADR body or found information on how to contact an ADR body'.

[74] 'Consumers who had complained to their electricity company largely outnumbered those who had contacted a third party – eg a consumer organisation, ombudsman or regulator (35% vs 5%)'.

[75] 'from 17% in Germany to 60% in Romania'.

[76] European Commission, *Consumer Conditions Scoreboard: Consumers at Home in the Single Market* (European Commission, 2019), available at: ec.europa.eu/info/sites/info/files/consumers-conditions-scoreboard-2019_pdf_en.pdf.

fear of not getting the desired results prevented more than 22 per cent of consumers from filing a complaint at all. Only 5 per cent brought their complaint to an ADR body.

VI. Conclusion

This chapter has provided an overview of EU access to justice law and policy, with a particular emphasis on ADR and the protection of vulnerable and energy-poor consumers. Despite some efforts to ensure access to justice for vulnerable and energy-poor consumers, the reality on the ground is that it is lacking. Definitions of vulnerability and energy poverty remain underdeveloped and, therefore, lack effectiveness as a mechanism for targeting effort and resources. In the context of ADR, there has been little attempt to connect developments here with the wider agendas around vulnerability and energy poverty. Collective redress measures seem to offer significant potential to deliver more holistic access to justice – targeting those most in need and most excluded from justice – but they are currently not used to any great extent and significant doubts have also been expressed about the model of collective redress ultimately legislated for by the EU.[77] And while EU law provides a range of rights for consumers, the predominant concern remains that consumers do not know about them or how to enforce them. Indeed, evidence from the European Commission's routine monitoring work reveals that consumers remain subject to significant detriment and have low awareness of their rights and how to complain. Having outlined the broad context for EU law and policy, chapter four turns to consider the potential for ADR to deliver solutions to the access to justice challenge outlined in chapter one and further developed in the present chapter.

[77] Hodges and Voet, *Delivering Collective Redress* (n 48).

4

ADR and Access to Justice

I. Introduction

This chapter turns to consider the relationship between access to justice for vulnerable and energy-poor consumers and alternative dispute resolution (ADR). The relationship between access to justice and ADR is a contested one which has been subject to much scholarly debate. On the one hand, ADR is the great hope for reforming inaccessible, slow and costly court systems. On the other, ADR is the antithesis of justice, cheap and quick, yes, but resulting in inferior outcomes for individuals and undermining the social value of court adjudication.[1] This argument has largely been conducted on ideological grounds, with little empirical evidence brought to bear on the issues.[2]

Much of the debate has also focused on mediation as a paradigm for ADR, but scant attention has been paid to other forms of ADR, particularly in the consumer sector. Consumer ADR can be seen as having its own 'unique architecture',[3] and, in Europe, consumer ADR in the energy context is now regulated by a series of European Directives and their concomitant national implementation measures (see chapter three). As a result of these measures, while consumers retain access to the courts if they wish, it is expected that ADR mechanisms should be the central mechanisms through which aggrieved energy consumers seek access to justice. The development of ADR mechanisms recognises the barriers to accessing court-based dispute resolution and is a measure (among others) that seeks to ensure the fair and effective functioning of energy markets by ensuring that redress is accessible to consumers facing potential detriment.[4] However, to date, there has been limited research on the extent to which access to justice has been enhanced as a result of the development of consumer ADR generally, and in the energy sector in particular. This is reflected in a broader lack of research on the

[1] H Genn, 'What is Civil Justice for? Reform, ADR, and Access to Justice' (2012) 24 *Yale Journal of Law & the Humanities* 397; L Mulcahy, 'The Collective Interest in Private Dispute Resolution' (2013) 33 *Oxford Journal of Legal Studies* 59.

[2] A Ojelabi and T Sourdin, 'Using a Values-Based Approach in Mediation' (2011), available at: ssrn.com/abstract=2721546; or: dx.doi.org/10.2139/ssrn.2721546.

[3] C Hodges, I Benöhr and N Creutzfeldt-Banda, *Consumer ADR in Europe* (Hart Publishing, 2012).

[4] P Cortes, *The Law of Consumer Redress in an Evolving Digital Market* (CUP, 2017).

effects of introducing ADR on access to justice. As Noone and Ojelabi point out in relation to groups that are traditionally disadvantaged in accessing and using courts: 'it is unclear how these groups fare in accessing ADR institutions and participating in ADR processes'.[5] This is one of the questions that this book seeks to address and which this chapter and the next are specifically concerned with: namely, to what extent does ADR enhance access to justice, particularly for the most vulnerable consumers?

In section II below, we begin to sketch out an answer to this question by reflecting on the significance of the empirical studies considered in chapter one. Section III then examines the critical literature on access to justice and ADR. A key question here is to what extent this generic literature applies to the specific context of consumer disputes and whether there are additional or different access to justice issues that arise. This is dealt with in section IV, which will argue that much depends on the way in which ADR schemes are designed and operate in practice and that, without further empirical knowledge, we cannot dismiss the concerns that have been expressed about ADR. The arguments made here set the scene for the empirical insights and specific design proposals detailed in chapters 5, 6 and 7.

II. Initial Observations Based on the Access to Justice Literature

Chapter one provided an overview of the empirical literature on access to justice and the multiple intersecting barriers facing individuals. Here we provide some initial observations about what the research evidence on barriers to justice tells us about the potential of ADR to improve access to justice. The first is that the low cost of ADR, its relative lack of procedural complexity compared with courts, and the fact that independent advice is not generally considered to be required should reduce barriers to claiming. It may also be that ADR is able to contribute to overcoming naming and blaming barriers. For example, some ADR schemes conduct outreach programmes aimed at helping to ensure they receive complaints from particular demographic groups and have a general mission to improve citizens' awareness of their right to complain. If they can show themselves to be effective, ADR schemes may also reduce barriers to people seeing their problems as matters for fatalism and helplessness and help provide them with agency in relation to the issues they face. At the same time, the scale of the access to justice gap and the multiple and clustering nature of the barriers likely to be faced by most individuals, let alone those who are for various reasons more vulnerable, means we should perhaps be sanguine about the potential contribution of ADR. Simply providing

[5] M Noone and L Ojelabi, 'Alternative Dispute Resolution and Access to Justice in Australia' (2020) 16 *International Journal of Law in Context* 108.

ADR does not seem likely to overcome the passive behaviour of many energy consumers, which requires long-term and strategic action.[6]

This is particularly the case since most ADR bodies are focused on simplifying the process of claiming rather than addressing other barriers that people experience during the dispute-emergence process described above. Identifying these various barriers to accessing justice therefore helps us to begin to tease out the potential nature and extent of the contribution that ADR might make to enhancing access to justice. There have traditionally been three broad approaches to addressing the issue of access to justice for consumers: reducing the cost of resolving disputes in the traditional court-based legal system; moving away from traditional court-based legal systems; and providing education and legal advisory services which target the barriers to access caused by consumers' ignorance of their legal rights. ADR therefore is generally one of a package of potential access to justice measures (we will return to this point below). First, however, we will consider the theoretical debate that has raged over the growth of ADR within justice systems and the extent to which this might enhance access to justice. Perhaps the best way to summarise this debate is that ADR (particularly mediation) has been argued to have both potential advantages and disadvantages for access to justice. Minow has suggested that ADR is a 'frenemy' of access to justice and this encapsulates the ambivalence found in some quarters about the growth of ADR within modern justice systems.[7] On the one hand, ADR appears to open up access but, on the other, it brings challenging questions with it. There also remains little real evidence to inform the debate about whether ADR has opened up the justice system for vulnerable individuals and groups and whether it is producing acceptable outcomes for them.[8] Certainly, developments in ADR have not closed the access to justice gap we sketched out in chapter one, and it seems that many people are reluctant to seek outside help with their problems regardless of whether that help comes in the form of courts and lawyers or ADR.

III. The Critical Debate on Access to Justice and ADR

There are two major strands to the debate about whether ADR helps secure access to justice. The first is concerned with effectiveness and considers whether ADR actually works in practice and delivers fair, quick, informal, cheap, and accessible dispute resolution. This strand is generally more concerned about the process of ADR. The second considers whether, even if ADR does fulfil some policy goals

[6] M Ioannidou, 'Effective Paths for Consumer Empowerment and Protection in Retail Energy Markets' (2018) 41 *Journal of Consumer Policy* 135.

[7] Comment by Martha Minow cited in E Deason, M Green and D Shestowsky et al, 'ADR and Access to Justice: Current Perspectives' (2018) 33 *Ohio State Journal of Dispute Resolution* 303.

[8] Noone and Ojelabi (n 5).

around speed and reduced cost, its emphasis on settlement militates against the achievement of justice. This strand is more concerned with fundamental outcomes. Waldman and Ojelabi helpfully highlight two types of critical discourse in relation to ADR and access to justice.[9] The first came from 'left leaning social justice activists' who were concerned that ADR was being promoted not only as a way of extending state power into private relations, reducing complaints to individual issues and taking attention away from structural injustice, but also as a means of dampening down dissatisfaction and diffusing conflicts that might otherwise lead to social change. Thus: 'Informal justice was viewed as a method for securing the quiescence of the poor and marginalized and maintaining the power base of social and political elites'.[10] The second strand of criticism had a more benevolent view of the state and its potential to use power to redress social inequalities. The main concern here was that ADR took away the ability of courts to pronounce and affirm social and moral values and to publicly give life to society's commonly agreed and authoritative moral commitments. Using ADR deprived the courts of an important social function and encouraged people to resolve issues without reference to legal principles which help to structure and render social relations coherent.

A. The Effectiveness Debate

As outlined in chapter three, a number of potential advantages have underpinned the growth of ADR within justice systems. Herman notes, for example, that at its best, ADR can offer, custom-made, flexible and expeditious processes that are capable of meeting the needs of parties both with regard to method and results.[11] Responding to consumer preferences is often cited as an argument in favour of ADR; research by the Scottish Civil Justice Council found, for example, that three out of 10 consumers who had their case heard in court would have preferred an alternative approach.[12] Indeed, Bush and Folger argue that one of the 'stories' advanced by proponents of mediation is the 'satisfaction story' that ADR is quick, cheap, less stressful, more creative, and capable of offering the possibility of reconciliation.[13] At a theoretical level, ADR (in its consensual guise at least) is supported by Deutsch's theory of cooperative and competitive dispute resolution processes, which posits that cooperative processes are more likely to lead to constructive outcomes while competitive processes are more likely to lead

[9] E Waldman and L Ojelabi, 'Mediators and Substantive Justice: A View from Rawls' Original Position' (2016) 30 *Ohio State Journal on Dispute Resolution* 391.

[10] ibid 402.

[11] M Hermann, 'The Dangers of ADR: A Three-Tiered System of Justice' (1989) 3 *Journal of Contemporary Legal Issues* 117.

[12] Scottish Civil Justice Council, *Access to Justice Literature Review: Alternative Dispute Resolution in Scotland and Other Jurisdictions* (Scottish Civil Justice Council, 2014).

[13] R Bush and J Folger, *The Promise of Mediation: Responding to Conflict through Empowerment and Recognition* (Jossey-Bass, 2005).

to destructive ones.[14] This general theory has been used to support the typically consensual and non-adversarial nature of ADR.

Indeed, ADR advocates greater efficiency (lower cost, less risk) as well as much broader benefits of ADR, including empowering disputants, building community and achieving peace. Advocates of ADR, especially of mediation, believe that adhering to strict notions of legal rights or entitlement and the adversarial nature of the formal legal process often lead to outcomes that harm relationships and even harm society generally. At a fundamental level, Palmer and Roberts argue that legal hegemony and the centrality of courts in Western conceptions of justice are historically contingent and that ADR has in fact existed in many long-standing forms across the world.[15] Taking this view, ADR does not simply constitute a set of alternatives to courts, but a separate value system emphasising horizontal social relationships, the value of community and the importance of enduring and relational settlements of conflict. Perhaps the most important statement on the structuring potential of ADR has been advanced by Bush and Folger.[16] They argue that mediation can not only resolve disputes but, more fundamentally, has the potential to transform broader social relations by changing the way in which people view each other in society and by profoundly reorienting society away from competitive and towards more cooperative processes for resolving social conflict.

To its proponents, therefore, ADR offers both a set of practical advantages that can overcome policy problems associated with courts (cost, lengthy time-scales, lack of accessibility) as well as provide an alternative value system which is ideologically committed to more cooperative processes. ADR sceptics, on the other hand, point to a range of disadvantages. Genn is particularly concerned by the potential for ADR to allow powerful actors to dominate less powerful ones.[17] Delgado et al suggest that this places minorities at risk and means that ADR should only be used for disputes in which parties of comparable status and power confront each other.[18] In later work, discussing the inadequacies of both court and ADR processes in delivering fair processes and outcomes for marginalised groups, Delgado has suggested that, in the context of courts being out of reach to all but the most privileged, attention should turn to understanding in more detail how the risk of prejudice inherent in ADR can be minimised.[19] Hoffmann's research

[14] M Deutsch, 'Cooperation, Competition, and Conflict' in PT Coleman, M Deutsch and EC Marcus (eds), *The Handbook of Conflict Resolution: Theory and Practice* (Jossey-Bass/Wiley, 2014).

[15] M Palmer and S Roberts, *Disputes Processes: ADR and the Primary Forms of Decision-Making*, 3rd edn (CUP, 2020).

[16] J Folger and RAB Bush, 'A Response to Gaynier's "Transformative Mediation: In Search of a Theory of Practice"' (2005) 23 *Conflict Resolution Quarterly* 123.

[17] H Genn, *Judging Civil Justice* (CUP, 2009) 116.

[18] R Delgado, C Dunn and P Brown et al, 'Fairness and Formality: Minimizing the Risk of Prejudice in Alternative Dispute Resolution' [1985] *Wisconsin Law Review* 1359.

[19] R Delgado, 'Alternative Dispute Resolution: A Critical Reconsideration' (2017) 70 *SMU Law Review* 595, University of Alabama Legal Studies Research Paper No 3417808, available at: ssrn.com/abstract=3417808.

showed that a relationship could exist between dispute processes and the social status and power of dispute actors. Examining workplace conflicts, she found men were more likely to use informal processes to resolve their workplace conflicts, while women – who were underrepresented and lacked informal networks – were more likely to use formal grievance procedures.[20] Indeed, feminist scholars have argued that ADR is inherently unfair in failing to recognise that unequal power relations in society will be replicated within dispute resolution processes.[21] Ojelabi, researching the views of community legal advisers on ADR, found that they thought that ADR could enhance access to justice but only if it addressed power imbalances and addressed unfair treatment of disadvantaged groups.[22]

Other concerns about ADR, as we have seen, include claims that it extends the reach of the state and involves it in previously private matters; it privatises disputes, which prevents marginalised groups from operating in solidarity; and the mediator's own power is unrecognised and therefore unaccountable.[23] A further concern in practice is that many of the theoretical claims about the value of ADR have rested on ideas about party self-determination and agency, as well as facilitative approaches that encourage dialogue and cooperative approaches to conflict. The reality, however, is that, with the institutionalisation of ADR within justice systems, these features have been eroded so that models of mediation are more evaluative and settlement-focused.[24] In many cases, consent – the fundamental principle of voluntariness – has been eroded by giving people very little effective choice about whether or not to participate in ADR.[25]

B. The Settlement Debate

Fiss's article in which he lays out the arguments 'Against Settlement' remains in many ways at the heart of criticisms of ADR.[26] Fiss rejected the 'dispute-resolution story' of ADR on the grounds that it could not substitute for the public value of adjudication, which could not be reduced simply to a question of 'dispute resolution'. He argued against the use of settlement in relation to accessing justice due to concerns about power differentials, the individualisation of disputes, and the

[20] E Hoffmann, 'Dispute Resolution in a Worker Cooperative: Formal Procedures and Procedural Justice' (2005) 39 *Law & Society Review* 51.

[21] T Grillo, 'The Mediation Alternative: Process Dangers for Women' (1991) 100 *Yale Law Journal* 1545.

[22] L Ojelabi, 'Community Legal Centres' Views on ADR as a Means of Accessing Justice' (2011) 22 *Australasian Journal of Dispute Resolution* 103.

[23] R Abel, 'The Contradictions in Informal Justice' in R Abel (ed), *The Politics of Informal Justice* (Academic Press, 1982).

[24] M Palmer, 'Formalisation of Alternative Dispute Resolution Processes: Some Socio-legal Thoughts' in J Zekoll, M Bälz and I Amelung (eds), *Formalisation and Flexibilisation in Dispute Resolution* (Brill Nijhoff, 2014).

[25] J Nolan-Haley, 'Does ADR's "Access to Justice" Come at the Expense of Meaningful Consent?' (2018) 33 *Ohio State Journal of Dispute Resolution* 373.

[26] O Fiss, 'Against Settlement' (1984) 78 *Fordham Law Review* 1265.

emphasis on dispute resolution rather than the achievement of justice. As Palmer has suggested, this critique held up the search for truth over the search for reconciliation and as a result 'informal processes represent a danger to this core value'.[27] This argument has been reprised many times since the early 1980s. Genn has provided a particularly important voice in this debate. She refers, for example, to the influence of resources and incentive on outcome, the dangers of losing the influence of the courts in articulating and developing public norms of justice, and the loss of public knowledge about the law.[28] She considers that private justice has other weaknesses, with one being the creation of a suspicion that 'in addition to purchasing a process, the content of the decision can also be bought'.[29] In her Hamlyn Lectures on Judging Civil Justice, Genn states that:

> Policy makers may be interested in promoting ADR in order to clear court lists, reduce the legal aid bill, reduce enforcement problems, reduce court expenditure on judges or reduce expenditure on court administration. In which case, when it is asserted that mediation improves 'access to justice', what does that mean?[30]

She argues in response that mediation does not contribute to access to justice and that mediators are not concerned about substantive justice, saying that: 'The outcome of mediation is not about just settlement, it is just about settlement'.[31] Genn also notes that:

> Only a small minority of settlements are in any way creative or provide something different from what would be available in court. It also seems clear that claimants significantly discount their claims in reaching mediated settlements. There is a price to pay in terms of substantive justice for early settlement.[32]

Many of these views are shared by Blochnar who argues that ADR cannot replace the wider role of courts in developing and applying authoritative legal norms, nor can it address fundamental power imbalances in society that produce social disadvantage. She concludes that 'mediation does not provide justice. It provides access to a process that allows parties to resolve disputes on a pragmatic and cost-effective basis, regardless of the justice of the case'.[33] Nylund is also sceptical about the potential for ADR to deliver justice. While she notes that ADR is often presented as a consensual, open-ended and more relational process, in practice she argues that ADR often becomes simply about reaching a settlement as quickly as possible, with parties often unduly pressured into compromise. As a result, neither the underlying aims of ADR nor access to justice are achieved in practice: 'The more ADR resembles tossing a coin, or an abbreviated trial with (indirect) mediator

[27] Palmer (n 24) 19.
[28] H Genn, 'Understanding Civil Justice' (1997) 50 *Current Legal Problems* 155.
[29] ibid 186.
[30] Genn, *Judging Civil Justice* (n 17) 116.
[31] ibid 117.
[32] Hodges, Benöhr and Creutzfeldt-Banda (n 3) 405.
[33] K Blochnar, 'Alternative Dispute Resolution and Access to Justice in the 21st Century' (2019) 40 *Adelaide Law Review* 343.

pressure to settle, the less it fulfils the ideas and goals of both the Access to Justice and the ADR movements'.[34]

Even among proponents of ADR the question of whether it can or should provide access to substantive justice is unsettled. Some have taken a 'post-modern' view, emphasising the relative nature of justice, the lack of fundamental objective truth, and the importance of cultural and social conditioning in views about justice.[35] Here, the value of ADR is not that it can deliver substantive justice but the opposite: by leaving parties to reach their own view on how a matter should be decided, subjectivity and the possibility of multiple truths is celebrated rather than denigrated. Hyman and Love offer a partial defence of the contribution of ADR to justice on procedural grounds and argue the practice of mediation is deeply attuned to issues of justice. However, they consider that justice in mediation differs from justice in adjudication. They note that:

> In its procedural aspect, justice involves notions of equal access, equal treatment, impartiality of the neutral, giving 'voice' to each side, disputing costs that are appropriate to the amount in dispute, timeliness of the process, and access to necessary resources by both sides. Any process, be it adjudicative or collaborative, that ignores these procedural dimensions will be perceived as unjust by participants.[36]

Hyman and Love stop short of making a case for ADR providing 'substantive justice' because it involves the parties in no longer focusing on their legal rights. Instead, they talk of ADR as the search for a solution to a problem, therefore, a more pragmatic take is suggested in relation to substantive justice which foregrounds the preferences of the parties and their individual interests over (perhaps) wider questions of public interest. Others have suggested that substantive justice is possible, particularly with certain forms of ADR which are norm-generating or norm-advocating.[37] Forms of ADR other than mediation (such as ombuds and adjudication processes) which involve the settlement of disputes through impartial investigation processes may also be better placed to counter arguments that the settlements produced by ADR are without norms. Irvine has also recently argued that we should pay more attention to lay people's constructions of substantive justice and that courts and lawyers do not have a monopoly of knowledge on the subject. Drawing on the interim findings of a pioneering doctoral study, he concludes that mediation offers 'an opportunity for justice to be co-constructed between disputing parties, advisors, mediators, the courts and wider society'.[38]

[34] A Nylund, 'Access to Justice: Is ADR a Help or Hindrance?' in L Ervo and A Nylund (eds), *The Future of Civil Litigation: Access to Courts and Court-annexed Mediation in the Nordic Countries* (Springer, 2014).

[35] See L Ojelabi, 'An Access to Justice Approach to Mediation and the Construction of Positive Legal Professional Identity' (2016) 23 *International Journal of the Legal Profession* 321.

[36] J Hyman and L Love, 'If Portia Were a Mediator: An Inquiry into Justice in Mediation' (2002) 9 *Clinical Law Review* 157.

[37] C Irvine, 'Mediation and Social Norms: A Response to Dame Hazel Genn' (2009) 39 *Family Law* 352.

[38] C Irvine, 'What Do "Lay" People Know about Justice? An Empirical Enquiry' (2020) 16 *International Journal of Law in Context* 146, 159.

Those who are more favourable to ADR also point out that settlement is the norm through the legal and dispute resolution system, with lawyers heavily engaged in settlement practices in the shadow of the court, and courts themselves increasingly pressuring parties to settle their disputes before a hearing is reached. Menkel-Meadow, for instance, considers that:

> The question is not 'for or against' settlement (since settlement has become the 'norm' for our system), but *when, how, and under what circumstances* should cases be settled? When do our legal system, our citizenry, and the parties in particular disputes need formal legal adjudication, and when are their respective interests served by settlement, *whether public or private*.[39]

Menkel-Meadow argues that discussions about settlement tend to assume that the public are more interested in the creation of precedent through litigation than they are about the interests of the parties. While she accepts that the public resolution of a dispute through adjudication could assist in resolving future disputes, she considers that the objectives, needs and values of the parties might often be better served through settlement. There is here a criticism about whether high-minded conceptions of justice and romantic notions of court-based dispute resolution in fact impede access to justice by denying people access to quicker and more pragmatic solutions to their problems.

IV. Specific Issues in the Consumer-Disputing Context

A. The Persistence of the Access to Justice Gap

Consumer ADR in Europe has been described as a distinctive 'galaxy'[40] in the dispute resolution universe and as having a 'unique architecture'.[41] In some jurisdictions (and within particular industrial sectors) ADR has eclipsed courts and lawyers as the primary means of resolving disputes. Further developments in this direction are seen by some as inevitable and as a natural progression.[42] At the same time, even the most enthusiastic proponents of ADR for consumer disputes recognise limitations in the current design and reach of ADR. Coverage of ADR is inadequate in some jurisdictions and industrial sectors,[43] with only 51.4 per cent of European retailers reporting an awareness of ADR and

[39] C Menkel-Meadow, 'Whose Dispute is it Anyway? A Philosophical and Democratic Defense of Settlement (In Some Cases) (1995) 83 *Georgetown Law Journal* 2663, 2664 (original emphasis).

[40] C Hodges, 'Consumer Redress: Implementing the Vision' in P Cortes (ed), *The New Regulatory Framework for Consumer Dispute Resolution* (OUP, 2016).

[41] Hodges, Benöhr and Creutzfeldt-Banda (n 3).

[42] Hodges, 'Consumer Redress' (n 40).

[43] Cortes (n 4).

only 31 per cent willing to participate in it.[44] And there is considerable variation between sophisticated and well-developed forms of consumer ADR and those which are more basic.[45] Perhaps most importantly, despite all the claims that ADR will be preferred by consumers looking for speed, informality and low cost, European consumers are not – generally – making extensive use of ADR. Indeed, only 5.2 per cent of European consumers who have experienced a problem complain to an ADR mechanism and, while this is more than those who complain to courts, the margin between the two is not perhaps as significant as one would assume: 1.9 per cent of consumers having made use of courts to settle their consumer disputes.[46] These figures are very similar to the figures for ADR use in the energy sector. Here, 35 per cent of European consumers in 2016 complained to an energy supplier and only 5 per cent complained to an ADR scheme.[47] As Kirkham has pointed out in the UK, while use of ADR is growing, awareness among the public of most ADR schemes remains very low.[48] Meanwhile, Graham points out that 66 million people took no action to resolve a consumer problem in 2015, while a significant proportion took some action but then gave up.[49] In the context of the energy sector, only 5 per cent of consumers made a complaint to the ombuds service in the UK. There is also clear evidence that courts and ADR not only reach few consumers, but those that they do reach are not representative of the wider population. Multiple surveys examining the demographics of users of consumer ADR schemes conclude that they are used by white, older, educated and wealthier men.[50] And despite claims of user-friendliness, consumers appear to consider that the differences between ADR and courts are, in fact, marginal: '43 per cent of European consumers think it is easy to settle a dispute through an out-of-court process compared with 32 per cent who think it is easy to settle a dispute through a court'.[51]

The argument here does not seek to deny the potential advantages of ADR; instead, the suggestion is that, looked at from an access to justice perspective, we need something of a reality check. Few consumers use either ADR or courts, and the types of people who use them (along with the types of problems they

[44] European Commission, *Consumer Conditions Scoreboard* (European Commission, 2019) 10.

[45] C Hodges, 'Developments and Issues in Consumer ADR and Consumer Ombudsmen in Europe' (Foundation for Law, Justice and Society Policy Brief, 2019).

[46] European Commission, *Consumer Conditions Scoreboard* (n 44) 10.

[47] K Rademaekers et al, *Selecting Indicators to Measure Energy Poverty* (European Commission, 2016), available at: ec.europa.eu/energy/sites/ener/files/documents/Selecting%20Indicators%20to%20Measure%20Energy%20Poverty.pdf.

[48] RM Kirkham, 'Regulating ADR: Lessons from the UK' in P Cortes (ed), *The New Regulatory Framework for Consumer Dispute Resolution* (OUP, 2016).

[49] C Graham, 'Consumer ADR and Collective Redress' in P Cortes (ed), *The New Regulatory Framework for Consumer Dispute Resolution* (OUP, 2016).

[50] N Creutzfeldt, *Ombudsmen and ADR: A Comparative Study of Informal Justice in Europe* (Palgrave Macmillan, 2018); Department for Business, Energy & and Industrial Strategy (BEIS), *Resolving Consumer Disputes: Alternative Dispute Resolution and the Court System* (BEIS, 2018).

[51] European Commission, *Consumer Conditions Scoreboard* (n 44) 28.

experience) are far from representative of the wider population. ADR has not therefore solved the access to justice problem in the consumer context, and serious questions remain about the extent to which it can do so. That is the current empirical reality. As to testing the wider claims of ADR in relation to accessibility, speed, quality of outcomes and consumer-friendliness, Creutzfeldt has pointed out that there remains a dearth of empirical studies on these issues.[52] Indeed, most of the literature relies on published statistics and the accounts of ADR producers, rather than primary empirical research. The lack of a significant evidence base for assessing the claims of ADR in relation to access to justice in the consumer setting are matched by a similar situation in the broader ADR literature. Noone and Ojelabi comment as follows:

> To assess the connection between the variety of ADR institutions/processes and access to justice, there is a critical need for ongoing empirical and in-depth research that not only provides data, but looks at the justice quality of ADR processes and access to justice.[53]

Many of the assumptions that are made about ADR (and indeed about the courts) might be challenged, were such research to be carried out. A recent example from the UK is instructive. Research carried out by the Department for Business, Energy & Industrial Strategy (BEIS) compared the experiences of consumers who had complained to ADR schemes and to courts. The findings are summarised as follows.

- There was no difference in the demographic characteristics of ADR and court users: 'Of the consumers who had used ADR, 69% were male, 69% were over 50 years old, 66% held a degree level qualification or higher, and 42% reported a household income about £50,000 (of those that reported an income). Consumers who had used the courts reported similar characteristics'.[54]
- Consumers were less likely to say they would use ADR again compared to courts, particularly if the result was adverse: '76% of consumers who used the courts and 69% of consumers who used ADR said they were likely to do so again if they experienced a similar problem in future. Where the outcome of the case was in favour of the trader or a compromise these figures dropped to 66% and 43% respectively'.[55]
- Consumers were less likely to consider that ADR processes were fair compared with courts, particularly if the result was adverse: 'In cases where the ADR provider decided in favour of the consumer 83% of consumers perceived the process to be fair. This dropped to 17% in cases where the decision was in

[52] N Creutzfeldt, 'Ombudsman Schemes' in P Cortes (ed), *The Transformation of Consumer Dispute Resolution in the European Union: A Renewed Approach to Consumer Protection* (OUP, 2016).

[53] Noone and Ojelabi (n 5).

[54] BEIS, *Resolving Consumer Disputes* (n 50) 4.

[55] ibid 2.

favour of the trader or a compromise. A similar, but less extreme, variation was seen for consumers who had used the courts (90% v. 53%)'.[56]

- Perhaps most worryingly for the traditional ADR narrative, more consumers experienced problems in the course of using ADR processes than in the course of using courts: 'Most consumers and traders did not experience any problems in using ADR or the courts, although a larger proportion of consumers who used ADR (46%) reported a problem than consumers who used the courts (16%)'.[57]
- In relation to speed and cost, however, the advantages of ADR appeared to be confirmed in this particular data set: '44% of ADR cases lasted less than three months, compared to 34% of court cases. In addition, 81% of consumers who used ADR reported a direct cost of under £50, whereas 59% of consumers who used the courts reported a cost of over £100'.[58]

We should not overstate the significance of this data. The sample size and methodological limitations mean that the findings are not generalisable. But they provide food for thought and should lead us to be cautious about the claims made for consumer ADR, as well as the failings often attributed to courts. It is possible that experiences with ADR reflect the fact that it is 'new technology',[59] and there is evidence that people do not know what to expect from ADR and that this creates problems for them in assessing the quality of their experiences.[60] These are issues that need to be followed up in future research. In the meantime, the access to justice gap remains. While it is likely that ADR in the consumer context has been 'rights generating'[61] in the sense that some people are using ADR and obtaining results who would not have used courts, the evidence we have today is that significant work remains to be done. Many of the putative benefits of ADR remain theoretical and the barriers to access to justice have not suddenly fallen away with the introduction of ADR. Nylund's conclusion about ADR and access to justice has significant resonance in the consumer context:

> Although the use of ADR has so far not resulted in increased access to justice, it still has unleashed potential as a tool to provide access to justice. This requires political will to extend dispute resolution services to new types of cases and populations, not just trying to save money in the judiciary.[62]

[56] ibid 3.
[57] ibid.
[58] ibid.
[59] C Hodges, 'Collective Redress: The Need for New Technologies' (2019) 42 *Journal of Consumer Policy* 59.
[60] Creutzfeldt, *Ombudsmen and ADR* (n 50); S Gilad, 'Accountability or Expectations Management? The Role of the Ombudsman in Financial Regulation' (2008) 30 *Law & Policy* 227.
[61] Cortes (n 4).
[62] Nylund (n 34).

The current story is one of significant potential but where the emphasis needs to be placed much more firmly on reaching new groups and individuals, rather than simply transferring potential court users into ADR systems.

B. Settlement-Focused Critiques and the Enduring Value of Courts

How far do the criticisms discussed above in section III, most of which are advanced against mediation as the emblematic form of ADR, apply to the specific forms of ADR that operate in the European consumer context? As noted above, a range of ADR mechanisms operate in the consumer context, including mediation, conciliation, adjudication, arbitration and ombuds schemes.[63] Mediation-related critiques are, therefore, likely to be most applicable to schemes using more consensual methods such as mediation and conciliation, although the diversity of processes that exist and the lack of clarity and transparency around ADR practices[64] means that it is difficult to say for sure where such critiques do bite in the consumer context and where they miss the mark. A prominent example of the broader settlement critique being applied in the consumer setting has been advanced by Eidenmüller and Engel who claim that the expansion of ADR under the Directive on Alternative Dispute Resolution for Consumer Disputes (2013/11/EU) (ADR Directive) represents a move towards the 'false settlement' of consumer disputes.[65] They are concerned about the privatisation of disputes and the potential weakening of consumer rights that they see as ensuing if enforcement is left to miscellaneous ADR entities rather than courts. Wagner meanwhile has argued that ADR in the consumer context amounts to 'snake oil' rather than being a 'wonder drug', and that it is not appropriate in rights-based settings.[66] The whole point of ADR, according to this critique, is that it should look beyond the law for solutions, and that, to the extent to which ADR is a means of enforcing the law, there are questions about

[63] C Gill, N Creutzfeldt and J Williams et al, *Confusion, Gaps, and Overlaps: A Consumer Perspective on Alternative Dispute Resolution between Consumers And Businesses* (QMUL, University of Westminster, Citizens Advice, 2017), (2017), available at: www.citizensadvice.org.uk/Global/CitizensAdvice/Consumer%20publications/Confusiongapsandoverlaps-Original1.docx.pdf.

[64] M Doyle, V Bondy and C Hirst, 'The Use of Informal Resolution Approaches by Ombudsmen in the UK and Ireland: A Mapping Study' (Ombudsman Research, 2014), available at: ombudsmanresearch.files.wordpress.com/2014/10/the-use-of-informal-resolution-approaches-by-ombudsmen-in-the-uk-and-ireland-a-mapping-study-1.pdf.

[65] H Eidenmüller and M Engel, 'Against False Settlement: Designing Efficient Consumer Rights Enforcement Systems in Europe' (2014) 29 *Ohio State Journal on Dispute Resolution* 261.

[66] G Wagner, 'Private Law Enforcement through ADR: Wonder Drug or Snake Oil?' (2014) 51 *Common Market Law Review* 165.

why it would be appropriate for that role to be given to individuals other than judges. Loos argues that, while the current regulation of ADR may further the individual enforcement of EU consumer rights, it may also hinder the development of EU consumer law[67] (an argument made about the way in which ADR may lead, more generally, to a 'loss of law').[68]

There have been several schools of thought responding to this critique. One is that it is misdirected because it fails to understand the nature of consumer ADR in Europe. As we have seen, mediation is only one aspect of consumer ADR, and one that is not always present in the way disputes are processed.[69] While mediation is increasingly being used as a stage within consumer ADR processes,[70] there is usually the option of a decision being provided by the independent third party if mediation fails. The form that mediation takes is also evaluative rather than facilitative, and it is claimed that this involves providing parties with information about their possible chances of success to encourage settlement.[71] Thus, rather than abandoning norms, to the extent that mediation is used, it takes place in the context of a normative framework and with adjudication by the third party following from efforts to conciliate. While this may be the case, the only systematic study of informal resolution approaches conducted to date has identified a range of concerns around lack of clarity, divergent practices and lack of transparency.[72] There are also potential concerns over structural issues in consumer ADR, such as the fact that individuals are less familiar with ADR processes than businesses and that, as repeat players, businesses may develop close relationships with ADR providers. Despite these concerns, which may well be exacerbated as mediation-based approaches continue to grow in popularity for settling consumer disputes,[73] it is the case that many ADR processes involve third-party adjudication (whether binding or not) and that under the ADR Directive there is a requirement that such adjudications take account of the requirements of substantive law. Nonetheless, there would undoubtedly be benefit in conducting further research to examine what is happening when consumer claims are mediated and whether there is pressure on consumers to accept sub-standard offers in return for closing matters down quickly. This has been a concern in other contexts,[74] and a range of

[67] Marco Loos, 'Consumer ADR after Implementation of the ADR Directive: Enforcing European Consumer Rights at the Detriment of European Consumer Law' (28 October 2015) (2016) 1 *European Review of Private Law* 61, Amsterdam Law School Research Paper No 2015-42, Centre for the Study of European Contract Law Working Paper Series No 2015-11, available at: ssrn.com/abstract=2685651 or: dx.doi.org/10.2139/ssrn.2685651.

[68] Mulcahy (n 1).

[69] Hodges, 'Consumer Redress'.

[70] C Hodges, *Delivering Dispute Resolution: A Holistic Review of Models in England and Wales* (Hart Publishing, 2019).

[71] Cortes (n 4).

[72] Doyle, Bondy and Hirst (n 64).

[73] Hodges, *Delivering Dispute Resolution* (n 70).

[74] Nylund (n 34).

bureaucratic, regulatory and cost pressures may exist which might lead to ADR bodies pressuring consumers to settle their claims.

In relation to the arguments around the privatisation of dispute resolution, the question is whether – in addition to ensuring dispute resolution in individual cases is based on law – ADR entities are able to perform a declaratory function and contribute to public understanding and debates. Courts clearly perform a broader role than simple dispute resolution and, if they are indeed to be replaced by consumer ADR bodies, there is a question about whether they have the capacity, and whether it would be constitutionally appropriate, for them to fulfil these tasks. Here, particularly ombuds schemes have been argued to be effective in publishing the details of cases they adjudicate and providing feedback to regulators and industries on issues emerging from cases. As a result, there is the possibility of ADR performing a public norm-setting role and affecting the future behaviour of parties through publishing data. For some,[75] this represents one of the advantages of ADR, while for others this is part of the potential criticism: namely, the development of a parallel system of justice that operates on a less clear normative basis than the traditional courts.[76] Stürner puts the issues rather starkly:

> A parallel system of 'adjudication' will emerge – the term 'ombudsprudence' has already been coined for that 'case law' … If you don't manage to reform your court system, just forget about it and provide some kind of consider ADR instead.[77]

Indeed, for some the case for moving towards a system of ADR rather than seeking to improve the court system has not been made. This is in part a matter of disputing cultures. It is no surprise that most critiques of consumer ADR have emerged from Germany where the court system is seen as comparatively accessible and efficient. At the same time, the fundamental question of what values are being protected by ADR compared with court adjudication does seem more fundamental and not entirely culturally contingent. As Hodges has pointed out, we are at an early stage in investigating the relationship between justice and consumer ADR.[78] Two arguments appear to underpin the current debate. First, justice is imperfect, and resources are finite: therefore, proportionality is a required element in any system of justice. Second, justice may not be the only thing that consumers want when they have experienced a problem:

> The principles of due process and upholding the law have to be balanced against the principle of proportionality, and the reality of what people want … People who have a simple dispute want it to be resolved quickly and cheaply. They do not want to wait

[75] Hodges, Benöhr and Creutzfeldt-Banda (n 3); Cortes (n 4).

[76] Eidenmüller and Engel (n 65).

[77] M Stürner, 'ADR and Adjudication by State Courts: Competitors or Complements?' in M Stürner, F Gascón Inchausti and R Caponi (eds), *The Role of Consumer ADR in the Administration of Justice* (Dr Otto Schmidt, 2014) 29.

[78] Hodges, 'Consumer Redress' (n 40).

> months or years over a simple issue of whether they have been overcharged or not received what they paid for … They want arrangements to be user-friendly, and to deliver results.[79]

This pragmatic view does not necessarily make claims about the justice value of ADR and instead considers that some justice may be better than none, and that absolute justice may be less important to consumers than speed and cost concerns. A lowering of standards may thus be a necessary accommodation with reality. To the extent that this argument is advanced, it has been criticised as equating to 'poor justice for the poor'.[80] Those whose disputes are not considered important enough for the court system are fobbed off with second-class justice.

The other argument is that ADR does provide substantive justice. Again, Hodges provides an important point of reference and argues not only that substantive justice is delivered by ADR, but that the standard of substantive justice allegedly provided by courts is not well articulated:

> Criticisms of almost all CDR [consumer dispute resolution] schemes as they currently exist in Europe on grounds of failure to deliver justice are misguided. CDR in Europe inherently delivers substantive access to justice (in some Member States to a far greater extent than courts are capable of) and fair and consistent outcomes. There is in fact no official or comprehensive statement of constitutional values or quality criteria for litigation, courts, or judicial decisions, merely reference to some individual principles, such as 'justice' and 'due process'.[81]

While it may be unclear what type of justice ADR provides, the suggestion is that this is not limited to ADR and that similar points might apply if we were to take a more critical approach to courts. One possible way of understanding the substantive justice of ADR in the consumer setting is as a form of equitable justice. Rather than consumer ADR adopting the normative neutrality of traditionally conceived facilitative mediation, this argument suggests that the law is central to consumer ADR, with the added bonus of a broader equitable jurisdiction that can allow for justice to be personalised. As Kirkham has pointed out, the claim here is that ADR provides 'for more justice to be delivered'.[82] Not all ADR schemes have such a jurisdiction, but where they do, this might enhance their claims to the provision of justice. Thus, this argument is not that proportionality necessarily requires a compromise in the justice available in relation to certain kinds of claims, but that ADR in fact provides an additional form of justice by incorporating equitable norms. The downside of this claim to justice, however, is that 'this mandate exposes the ombuds to the critique that its decision-making lacks rigour and is unpredictable to all sides'.[83] To the extent that mediation is

[79] ibid 360.
[80] Nylund (n 34).
[81] C Hodges, N Creutzfeldt, F Steffek and E Verhage, 'ADR and Justice in Consumer Disputes in the EU' (Foundation for Law, Justice and Society Policy Brief, 2016) 5.
[82] Kirkham (n 48).
[83] ibid.

deployed in a way that is indeed norm-sensitive and appropriate in a rights-based context, there are perhaps also arguments to be made that justice is achieved by seeking consensus and avoiding the need for paternalistic and divisive adjudication. As noted in chapter two, Hodges has claimed that ADR fits with, and seeks to realise, a view of European society based on compromise and consensus. While this provides an alternative way of conceptualising the substantive justice of ADR, it is of course in potential conflict with the claims that ADR fundamentally involves the application of legal rules in a norm-based framework.

Thus, the appropriateness of applying settlement critiques to the consumer ADR context remains a contested issue. The lack of clarity over the extent to which mediation-based approaches are being deployed and the form those approaches take in practice is problematic. This question can only be resolved through empirical enquiry and seeking to look into the black box of consumer ADR processes. Where mediation is used, it may be possible to address concerns about transparency and fairness through mechanisms such as publishing decisions.[84] More broadly, the question of what kind of justice is being delivered by consumer ADR is yet to be settled. Does it aim (and perhaps increasingly so given the recent emphasis on settlement) to achieve compromise and to contribute to a society based on ideals of compromise and consensus-building? Is it in fact a straightforward normative model where the law is applied, with the added bonus of equitable approaches in some contexts? Does it prioritise individual preferences for speed and simplicity over notions of justice? Or does it seek to provide proportionate justice, recognising the limits imposed on the achievement of absolute justice?

That the answers to these questions have yet to emerge clearly is perhaps not surprising. And yet, if the holistic vision of access to justice that we set out in chapter two is to be realised, then ADR needs to do more to demonstrate how it seeks to contribute to substantive justice. The focus on procedural simplicity and accessibility needs to be combined with a clearer normative framework for judging outcomes. Is the aim to achieve legally correct decisions? Is it party satisfaction? Is it the reduction of social conflict? In our view, the value of ADR in contributing to a holistic vision of access to justice is the potential to go beyond the application of strict legal rules, to consider people's concerns more holistically, and to seek to achieve socially just outcomes. The current approach to consumer ADR seems some way off this vision, although, as we shall see, there is significant potential for future developments.

C. The Quality and Effectiveness of ADR

Due to the variety of mechanisms in operation, an assessment of the overall quality and effectiveness of ADR in consumer settings is difficult. At a macro level,

[84] Cortes (n 4).

the diversity of models of ADR discussed in chapter three, and the fact that there is imperfect ADR coverage in some industrial sectors, is not ideal. Although coverage in the energy sector is not generally an issue, the fact that a mixture of models operate has been criticised.[85] One of the issues with multiple models operating in different ways is that evaluating and comparing their quality is problematic. Going back for a moment to the discussion about justice above, multiple potentially conflicting claims about the justice of ADR can make it difficult to understand what justice is actually being delivered in practice. While standards may well be different from those we would use to assess courts, there remains a lack of a commonly agreed approach to what constitutes 'fair procedure' in ADR. According to Hodges et al:

> The very plurality of forms of dispute resolution challenges traditional conceptions of what constitutes justice, or fair procedure, in dispute resolution. Constitutional principles that are applied to the courts may or may not be relevant for other types of dispute resolution.[86]

Petrauskas and Gasiunaite refer to a range of potential concerns over the operation of ADR in the European energy sector, including the financing of ADR, lack of information provided to consumers, and the inconsistent quality of ADR.[87] Jeritina and Uzelac, meanwhile, consider that the ADR Directive leaves many questions unanswered, in particular about supervision and financing of ADR schemes.[88] Hodges points out that common criticisms of ADR in the consumer sector in terms of its quality relate to: lack of expertise in law; lack of clear certification and training for ADR staff; decisions that are not transparent, reasoned or subject to appeal; inadequate oversight of operations; and unclear procedures.[89] The ADR Directive addresses some of these issues by providing quality requirements such as: independence, expertise and impartiality (Article 6); transparency (Article 7); effectiveness (Article 8); and fairness (Article 9). However, it remains unclear to what extent these worthy principles are delivered in practice. Kirkham, considering the example of the UK, concludes that 'the regulation of the sector looks deficient. As a result, there is a heightened risk that sub-optimal standards in the sector will go undetected which may in turn undermine user confidence'.[90]

[85] N Creutzfeldt, 'Independent Ombudsmen and ADR Providers', available at: www.neon-ombudsman.org/2015/03/12/independent-ombudsmen-and-adr-providers-building-bridges-in-the-energy-market/.

[86] Hodges, Creutzfeldt, Steffek and Verhage (n 81) 1.

[87] F Petrauskas and A Gasiunaite, 'Alternative Dispute Resolution in the Field of Consumer Energy Services in the EU' (2013) 20 *Jurisprudencija: Mokslo darbu žurnalas* 119.

[88] U Jeretina and A Uzelac. 'Alternative Dispute Resolution for Consumer Cases: Are Divergences an Obstacle to Effective Access to Justice?' (2014) XII(4) *Mednarodna revija za javno upravo* 39.

[89] Hodges, 'Consumer Redress' (n 40); C Hodges, 'The Consumer as Regulator' in D Leczykiewicz and S Weatherill, *The Images of the Consumer in EU Law: Legislation, Free Movement and Competition Law* (Hart Publishing, 2016).

[90] Kirkham (n 48).

His main concern relates to the 'passive' nature of competent authorities set up to approve ADR entities under the ADR Directive and check that quality requirements are being fulfilled. In Kirkham's view, competent authorities are falling short of being a 'standard bearer'. While academic assessment is generally that the ombuds is the leading and preferred model of consumer ADR,[91] other groups have been more critical. In the UK (a jurisdiction often highlighted as having a well-developed consumer ombuds model) the All Party Parliamentary Group on Consumer Protection has produced several critical reports on UK ombuds, including issues relating to low customer satisfaction, poor regulation and problems arising from a confusing landscape.[92] Similarly, consumer activists have highlighted problems with the UK ombudsmen, such as perceived lack of impartiality, poor quality decisions and problems achieving remedies.[93] The extent to which these criticisms are widespread or relate to all forms of ADR is unclear.

D. Added-Value Functions

The picture we have painted so far has emphasised some of the problems, or at least unsettled questions, in relation to access to justice for consumers. We now turn to an area where ADR has the greatest potential for delivering access to justice. This is in relation to added-value functions that consumer ADR schemes may perform in addition to their core role of resolving disputes. These added-value functions are most closely associated with ombuds schemes and are the reason for the general preference among commentators for the ombuds as the leading form of ADR.[94] The two main added-value functions performed by ombuds are the provision of advice to consumers and the provision of aggregate feedback to businesses and regulators. This allows ombuds to provide assistance to consumers (for example, informing them of their rights and how to complain) and to seek to influence the future behaviour of businesses by providing data showing where problems are occurring for consumers:

> [A] strong case can be made that the consumer ombuds model is the more advanced form, as it offers a number of advantages, notably the ability to offer advice and assistance to consumers, to aggregate individual claims (collective redress), to aggregate data on case types and incidence, and to provide feedback that drives behaviour change.[95]

[91] Cortes (n 4); Hodges, Benöhr and Creutzfeldt-Banda (n 3); C Gill and C Hirst, *Defining Consumer Ombudsman Schemes* (Ombudsman Services, 2016).

[92] See: images6.moneysavingexpert.com/images/documents/Ombudsman%20report.pdf

[93] See: images6.moneysavingexpert.com/images/documents/MSE-Sharper_teeth_interactive.pdf; ceoemail.com/ombudsman-omnishambles.pdf. The methodology for these reports has been criticised but they demonstrate that influential consumer activists in the UK take a quite different view of the quality and effectiveness of current ADR systems.

[94] A view espoused by: Cortes (n 4); C Hodges, 'The Private Sector Ombudsman' in M Hertogh and R Kirkham (eds), *The Research Handbook on the Ombudsman* (Edward Elgar, 2018); Creutzfeldt, 'Ombudsman Schemes' (n 52); and Gill and Hirst (n 91).

[95] Hodges, 'The Private Sector Ombudsman' (n 94) 56.

These approaches are valuable from an access to justice perspective because they go further in addressing naming, blaming and claiming barriers to accessing justice than simply providing a mechanism for dispute resolution. The fact that ombuds field enquiries from consumers means they can access a free source of advice about how to pursue their claims with businesses. As Tyndall et al point out, in a recent review of the Parliamentary and Health Services Ombudsman in the UK, the value of the thousands of enquiries dealt with by ombuds schemes is often ignored as a result of a narrow focus on dispute resolution.[96] The attempt to influence prospective business behaviour and prevent problems arising in future is also a very important approach given what we know about consumer passivity and the limited likelihood of direct claims being raised with ADR bodies. Potentially, through influencing better business practice, ombuds can expand the reach of access to justice by ensuing that consumers achieve 'everyday justice' and never need to complain in the first place. As Kirkham has pointed out, an ability to deliver collective justice is potentially very powerful:

> This quasi-regulatory role establishes a capacity for advancing justice that is potentially far-reaching in terms of: delivering for individuals that are otherwise unlikely to complain; preventing multiple injustices occurring in the first place; and improving the reputation of businesses. It is also a role that can be enhanced through the regular interchange of intelligence between an ombudsman and its partner regulator.[97]

Gill and Hirst sought to define consumer ombuds as they operate in the UK and to distinguish them from other forms of consumer ADR. They identify a range of other features which also give them potential advantages from an access to justice perspective. These include: more use of inquisitorial methods; greater accessibility and concern for vulnerable groups; and higher public visibility.[98]

Questions have, however, been raised about the extent to which ombuds fulfil a standard-raising role in practice. Gill, referring to public ombuds, points out that there are numerous challenges that lie in the way of ombuds changing the behaviour of the organisations they oversee, and many of those challenges apply equally in a private-sector context.[99] Graham has also pointed out in relation to the UK energy ombuds that there have been criticisms of the extent to which it has used data to seek to improve industry practice.[100] An independent review of the energy ombuds, for example, concluded that the ombuds had not always reported information back to the regulator in cases where systemic issues, for example around back-billing, had been identified. Kirkham has also questioned

[96] P Tyndall, C Mitchell and C Gill, *Independent Peer Review of the Parliamentary and Health Services Ombudsman* (PHSO, 2018).

[97] Kirkham (n 48) 314.

[98] Gill and Hirst (n 91).

[99] C Gill, 'What Can Government Learn from the Ombudsman?' in M Hertogh and R Kirkham (eds), *The Research Handbook on the Ombudsman* (Edward Elgar, 2018).

[100] Graham, 'Consumer ADR and Collective Redress' (n 49) 427.

the extent to which the potential inherent in adopting preventative approaches to prospectively shape industry behaviour is occurring. He argues:

> Critics of the ombuds, however, point to the lack of evidence that such gains are achieved in practice and express concern about over-regulation. [Footnote omitted] Indeed, far from being a constructive service, the process of attempting to feedback information might be a costly distraction, often delivered too far after the event to make a meaningful impact with providers who, if they are minded to, probably already possess sufficient information with which to change their practices.[101]

Generally, the fact that consumer detriment continues to be high in industries overseen by ombuds suggests, at the very least, that there is further work that ombuds could be doing to develop the preventative aspect of their role. Similarly, the exact nature of the ombuds' advice function is not currently clear. In the UK, many 'enquiries' received by ombudsmen are in fact attempts to complain 'prematurely' (ie, before the business has been given a full opportunity to respond to a complaint, a requirement of most schemes). In such cases the nature of the advice provided to consumers is uncertain and may constitute little more than a referral back to the business complained about. It is not evident whether such advice involves much more than signposting or whether it adds further value by informing consumers about substantive rights, effective ways to present their complaints, and so on.

V. Conclusions

The tale of ADR and its relationship to access to justice is one of problems and potential. The problems include a diverse landscape, featuring multiple forms of dispute resolution, not all of which provide the same breadth of functions or quality of service. Many of the potential problems in relation to access to justice and ADR are obscured by a lack of empirical data. This means that issues around quality and effectiveness, as well as the way in which settlement operates in practice, remain largely matters for speculation. Conceptually, long-standing debates in the literature around how ADR works for disadvantaged groups and whether approaches that emphasise settlement can be reconciled with substantive justice remain unsettled. Perhaps the strongest empirical data relate to the extent of ADR use and the demographic characteristics of those who use it. The reality is that, at present, ADR is little used by consumers and that those who are using it are from an extremely narrow demographic. This represents a major problem for access to justice, since barriers to claiming do not appear to be significantly weakened as a result of ADR and, worse, the narrow demographic making use of ADR schemes may be replicating disadvantage rather than contributing to

[101] Kirkham (n 48) 314.

broader social justice. It is in light of this rather damning assessment that the added-value functions of ADR appear to have so much potential. Even if ADR is perfected to deliver the cheapest, fairest, quickest and most accurate dispute resolution possible, this may not overcome the barriers we have identified in chapter one to the emergence of disputes. More proactive and preventative approaches, combined with a pedagogic and advisory function, offer ADR the potential to address barriers at each stage of the naming, blaming and claiming process in ways that far outstrip what courts might be capable of. Even here, however, we have advised caution since current evidence is very limited in relation to whether such functions are capable of being carried out effectively. These are the issues we will turn to in the next chapter, which turns to setting out empirical insights.

5

ADR and Access to Justice: Empirical Insights

I. Introduction

This chapter focuses on qualitative data collected as part of our *Just Energy* project. We identify four key themes in the course of our interviews with ADR providers and stakeholders:[1] (1) the extent to which access to justice for vulnerable people is currently delivered by ADR and the barriers that exist in this context; (2) the potential and limits around the role of ADR in providing access to justice; (3) the need for systemic and partnership working; and (4) the changes that could make ADR more effective as a remedy for vulnerable and energy-poor consumers. These empirical insights provide the launching point for the discussion in the next section of the chapter, which seeks to draw some conclusions about the current contribution of ADR in helping energy consumers access justice and to take a forward look at how that contribution could be enhanced. Overall, the argument in this chapter builds on the insight in chapter four that ADR has both potential and problems when it comes to access to justice; in the words of one commentator it can be seen as a 'frenemy' to access to justice.[2] However, while the current potential of ADR is unrealised and the access to justice gap remains unbridged, our data show a number of ways in which ADR could be enhanced to fulfil its potential. We begin to discuss these approaches in this chapter, laying the ground for a set of proposals around the effective design of ADR bodies in chapter seven.

[1] This chapter only reports data from interviews with ADR providers and stakeholders such as third-sector actors, energy companies and policymakers. It does not present data we collected in interviews with consumers who had used ADR; we plan to publish this data separately at a later date.

[2] Comment by Martha Minow cited in E Deason, M Green and D Shestowsky et al, 'ADR and Access to Justice: Current Perspectives' (2018) 33 *Ohio State Journal of Dispute Resolution* 303.

II. Empirical Insights

A. Current Levels of Access to Justice

One respondent, UK Third Sector 2, highlighted that a major problem with ADR remained that, however good it might be, most people were still unlikely to use it:

> If you can get to the ombudsman stage, it's fantastic. But like I said, it's just that the people that we're talking about [vulnerable people] would struggle to do that, to go through that process (UK Third Sector 2).

UK Ombuds 2 noted that users of the ombuds service tend to be 'people like me … white, male, university educated, middle class'. The narrow demographic using the ombuds service was a concern for Catalan Policy 3:

> Mostly people that go to ombudsmen are like well educated, middle aged, et cetera, and it's like, are those vulnerable customers? … [Vulnerable consumers might] go to the town hall to see the social worker. But, many of them don't even knock [on] that door, so I don't imagine these people going to the ombudsman … They are not knocking [on] any door (Catalan Policy 3).

Interviewees working in the third sector commented on the fact that there was limited public awareness of ombuds. French Third Sector 3 commented that the national energy ombuds is never mentioned by anyone in his local area. Remedies such as the ombuds and the underpinning laws were seen as too complicated:

> [W]e speak French but we don't understand anything (French Third Sector 3).

The limited reach of ADR in relation to vulnerable people was an issue that spoke to the ethical mission of ADR, according to UK Ombuds 5:

> [W]e know there's only a fraction of people that actually come to us … There's a moral obligation that you want to try to help people that are in a different situation (UK Ombuds 5).

Indeed, interviewees noted that there was a general issue with people – vulnerable or not – failing to pursue complaints all the way to ADR. Bulgarian Policy 2 said that many unresolved complaints were not escalated to ADR:

> The problem in Bulgaria is also not just knowing the rights, but quite widespread apathy and this giving up, thinking that nothing can be changed, that the state institutions cannot really be trusted, that they don't care about people (Bulgarian Policy 2).

UK Third Sector 2 commented that the role of ADR was peripheral and not considered to be a particularly powerful way of resolving people's immediate problems:

> You have to try and solve as many problems as you can before you get to ombudsman, usually. I've never … really thought about them as sort of having a leading role … it's hard to get complaints through, [in a] sort of timely [way] (UK Third Sector 2).

For consumers who were in extremely vulnerable circumstances, ADR had even more limited reach. UK Ombuds 1 gave the example of people who were either not on the grid at all or people who were living in fuel poverty, but whose issues did not end up constituting a consumer problem that was amenable to resolution by ADR:

> [S]ome of the most vulnerable of all you might not be able to identify because, either they've fallen off the grid or … [because of] fuel poverty … that's really hard to pick up, because you might have someone who is paying their energy bill … But what they're doing is, they're using too little energy, because they can't afford to. They're vulnerable but I'll never pick them up (UK Ombuds 1).

Interestingly, there was a strong view that while the overall demographic of people accessing ombuds' services was narrow, a noticeable trend had been that certain types of consumers were becoming more demanding and, potentially, unreasonable in pursuing their claims. French Policy 5, for example, noted that consumer behaviour was changing, in that, 10 years ago, people were almost apologising for filing claims. Today, the approach is more 'take care of me; I can't take it anymore, I want more, I have more demands'. People are losing patience and expressing their anger more than before. There was, therefore, an increasing disconnect between a majority of passive consumers, reluctant or unable to pursue their rights, and a small group of vocal and increasingly pushy consumers seeking to assert their rights in ways that were not always reasonable.

B. Barriers to Accessing ADR

i. Lack of Awareness and Reach of ADR

Catalan Policy 1 referred to the distance that existed between ADR and vulnerable energy consumers, as well as a lack of understanding of the situations of vulnerable people:

> I mean, the problem with the national Ombudsman, company Ombudsman, is that we are closed [up] in [our] offices … I don't know if we are getting to the vulnerable consumers … Because, perhaps these vulnerable consumers, they're not going to enter our website, they are not going to call our phone. They don't really understand a letter or they don't understand the bill (Catalan Policy 1).

Fundamentally, a lack of awareness about rights and the mechanisms available for accessing justice was seen as a problem. Consumers were described as 'illiterate' when it came to dispute resolution and people did not understand terms such as 'ombudsman':

> I think that what our movement is fighting for is just empowerment of the population, because in the end it's just a thing of knowing which are your rights and then using them in order to have a dignifying life … in terms of access to justice and dispute resolution we are illiterate consumers in general. And the systems make us illiterate and we have to fight (Catalan Third Sector 1 and 2).

> What does the word ombudsman actually mean? A lot of people can't even say the word … It's an old, ancient way of working, but actually the ombudsman is there to help you (UK Ombuds 5).

ii. The Practices of Energy Suppliers

Interviewees commented on problems when complaining to energy companies and poor practice among suppliers. For example, UK Ombuds 5 said poor practice included information about the ombuds service being provided in small print on statements, while Catalan Third Sector 1 and 2 commented that complaining could be technical and difficult, even for those who were not in vulnerable circumstances:

> I had to complain once and it was difficult for me. It's not logical … it's not easy … It shouldn't be so juridical or so legal in terms of language … They [consumers] don't know what is a kilowatt hour, they don't know how to understand their energy bills (Catalan Third Sector 1 and 2).

Catalan Policy 5 also commented on the practices of energy companies. She noted the huge power imbalance between companies and individuals and suggested ADR was limited in what it could do about this:

> Oh, justice does really not protect the vulnerable. So, the real power of utilities are really high, and they have hundreds of lawyers to make things as they want … And about ombudsmen and these organisations … they're doing their best … but I'm not sure if it's very useful in practical terms (Catalan Policy 5).

UK Complaint Handling Organisation 1 agreed that poor customer service on the part of energy suppliers was a major access to justice issue. Poorly run call centres, long queues to speak with someone, and poor complaint processes could all put people off taking a concern further. Interviewees' comments about poor practices among energy suppliers and lack of balance and fairness in the complaint-handling system are reflected in survey data. The European Commission found in 2016 that few customers reported being given correct information about complaint-handling processes and ADR by energy suppliers and that only 22 per cent of consumers who complained to energy companies were satisfied with the outcome.

iii. Regulatory Barriers and ADR Processes

Regulations and regulatory barriers could also pose problems. In the UK, there is a regulatory bar on consumers making complaints to the ombuds prior to having received a final decision from an energy company or, failing that, before eight weeks has passed since making their complaint. If complainants tried to bring cases before then, they would be given advice to go back to the energy company:

> We do signpost them … 'You need to call the company back, keep notes about all the evidence ….' If your clued up, that's what you do. If you're somebody who's struggling,

> will you take that in? … there will be a group of people who will just give up because it's too complicated (UK Ombuds 5).

In Italy, Italian Third Sector 2 was highly critical of regulatory and ADR systems. The energy regulator was perceived as favouring the interests of energy suppliers rather than consumers. For example, the regulator had set a very low level of compensation which meant that, even where individuals were able to access ADR, they did not receive adequate redress.

Interviewees also suggested that the most basic requirements of ADR processes can present barriers for vulnerable people that could, in practice, be insurmountable: for example, a requirement that complainants provide evidence to support their cases:

> So, if we're an evidence-based organisation, to get your complaint resolved, you need to send us your evidence. But a lot of people out there, they don't understand: what does that mean? (UK Ombuds 5).

Indeed, some commented that the fact that ADR needed to be impartial and ultimately adjudicate a complaint meant that there was an inevitable formality to the process:

> I do think it [ADR] is a process that's not necessarily going to work for everyone … where it's going to take time to investigate an issue and, you know, if they can't articulate or understand exactly what the problem is, I don't know, necessarily, whether it's the right option (UK Complaint Handling Organisation 1).

This was echoed by UK Third Sector 6 who also questioned whether the outcomes provided by an ombud were always meaningful:

> By the time you've been dealing with an energy company for eight weeks to resolve an issue and then you go to the Ombudsman and you have to get all of your evidence in order to submit that, it's a lengthy process … Sometimes they've asked for an energy company to provide an apology. What's that solving? (UK Third Sector 6).

iv. Technological Barriers

For those without access to the internet, technology issues also presented a barrier. Indeed, providing the opportunity for consumers to speak to a human contact was seen as important. French Policy 5, for example, noted that providing a non-judgemental, human, empathetic point of contact for people was a crucial part of ombuds' work. People often turned to the ombuds saying 'I want to talk to a human'. The growth of digital approaches was recognised as a potential problem in this respect:

> If you're not digitally savvy … we are going to become more digital. And that's going to be, I think, a block to some people (UK Ombuds 5).

Ultimately, however, some of the most vulnerable consumers were seen as unlikely to use either online or telephone means of communication. One interviewee noted that some attempts had been made by the ombuds service to do face-to-face outreach, but this had not been particularly effective:

> We would look at particularly deprived postcodes … where we don't appear to be getting a big enough share of complaints … Then go and turn up at the local, you know, Poundstretcher, or whatever … we used like Emmerdale and Coronations Street actors … and went and did … local radio … Have we seen a particular upturn [in complaints] from that? No we haven't (UK Ombuds 2).

v. Other Barriers

A further issue here was that barriers to accessing justice were not always practical, but instead were emotional or cognitive. Catalan Policy 5, for example, noted that people's personal feelings could cause them to be reluctant to ask for help:

> It is very stigmatising … it is very, it is a big shame to say in front of other people, I cannot pay my bills (Catalan Policy 5).

Indeed, the nature of ADR services was not necessarily a prime factor in explaining who would end up using ADR. The reality for many vulnerable people was that their lives were chaotic, they had pressing problems to deal with, and the idea of approaching any formal institution would not even occur to them:

> Most of the clients that I'm thinking about that we would visit … it's not something that they'd want to do. Their lives are usually pretty hectic and crazy, and actually keeping appointments with ourselves is hard enough without sort of progressing it on. I wouldn't have said that it was something that anybody that I can think of would engage with (UK Third Sector 2).

C. The Role and Limits of ADR

i. Consumer Expectations of ADR

Interviewees noted that the role of ADR as an impartial dispute resolution service was sometimes misunderstood:

> People that contact us, they think we can help them there and then. They think we're here as a quick fix service, and we can deal with it that day. We simply can't. It's not the way we work … I think that sometimes customers think we are a consumer champion so that we're here specifically to help them. And, obviously, we're not, that's not our role (UK Ombuds 6–10).

Others similarly commented on the gap that could exist between what consumers expect ADR to do and what is possible in practice. French Policy 5 for example said that there was a need to raise awareness about what ombuds are and are not. People come to an ombuds with a lot of hope: they entrust their case to the ombuds and believe the solution can only be positive. In reality, the result will not necessarily meet 100 per cent of their expectations.

Ultimately, unless the ombuds service was able to find a flaw in the way an individual had been treated by an energy company, there was nothing that could be done directly to help such a person:

> We can signpost them elsewhere, and there's obviously charities, and there's, you know, different heat charities, or Fuel Direct, or any of these sorts of things and Step Change and stuff like that. But, you know that, without just wiping off the balance, really, you're not giving them what they want. But unless that's the right thing to do, we can't do that (UK Ombuds 6–10).

At the same time, providing support and a listening approach was seen as part of the ombuds' role. French Policy 5, for example, commented that the ombuds' role was about supporting people who were making 'a cry for help', so that they would not be left behind. This involved carefully trying to understand people's needs and spending time listening and being empathetic. Interviewees described how consumers envisage getting more support from the ombuds service and feel let down when these expectations are not met:

> They'll say, you're supposed to be supporting me. Like, you're supposed to be acting on my behalf, but you're trying to explain to them that we are an impartial body, and we're here for both you and the company, to try and resolve the issue … But you do know that they do need some support (UK Ombuds 6–10).

In the UK, vulnerable consumers can access an advocacy service which involves active representation of the consumer and negotiation with the energy supplier. This service has no formal power to impose a solution but, instead, represents the consumer's interests and pushes for positive solutions.

> We're very much advocating on their behalf. So, there will be occasions where, frankly, we're pushing a case because the consumer is vulnerable and concerned, rather than, necessarily, we maybe think it's a legitimate case (UK Complaint Handling Organisation 1).

The fact that this organisation does not need to maintain impartiality was seen as being more in keeping with what consumers were often looking for in approaching an external source of help: namely, an ally and an advocate rather than an impartial, quasi-legal body. This echoes Creutzfeldt's findings that people have mixed expectations of ADR and ombuds, as either an advocate, an ally, an interpreter, or an instrument.[3]

[3] N Creutzfeldt, *Ombudsmen and ADR: A Comparative Study of Informal Justice in Europe* (Palgrave Macmillan, 2018).

ii. Limits in the Support ADR can Provide to Consumers

UK Ombuds 6–10 mentioned their own uncertainty surrounding how far they could go in helping vulnerable consumers and providing them with advice and additional support:

> [W]e were told, if advice is needed and it will help the complainant, or person on the phone, just give it to them, because it could help in the long run. But, again, I don't know if that's standard practice, that we should be helping and advising people. I don't know (UK Ombuds 6–10).

Some interviewees pointed out that, while doing more on vulnerability was a priority, they could not infinitely expand the service provided. ADR was constrained not only by fundamental ideas of what ADR service should be, but also by the realities of a consumer energy market with tight margins and expectations that ADR would operate efficiently and at low cost:

> We have to make sure that we're efficient. You get all of this stuff that says, oh, energy companies make vast amounts of money … They don't tend to make it out of energy retail … So, when you start looking at … why aren't we doing that? Why don't we just put our prices up? Why don't we …? … The reality is, well, I'm not sure it would in the end do any favours. Firstly, you've got that challenge of, well, everyone come to the Ombudsman, and are we the right people to be doing that? Maybe not … And then you've got the question of, well, ultimately, who pays for that, and what's the most effective way of doing it? And it's unlikely to be by us just expanding our remit over and over again to provide general, kind of, you know social support, when we're not there to do that (UK Ombuds 2).

Another interviewee similarly commented that more support ought to be provided to vulnerable consumers, but at the same time ADR bodies needed to avoid a perception that they were ambulance chasing by encouraging consumers to complain. In relation to helping consumers before the eight-week timescale had elapsed for the company to deal with a complaint, UK Ombuds 5 commented:

> We have to be quite careful, because we can be seen to be ambulance chasing, that type of work, because that's not what we do. But we do signpost and say, this is what you should do now (UK Ombuds 5).

As we will see further below, there was a sense therefore that simply having more people come to ADR bodies and having an expanded system of support would not be the most effective way of helping consumers in vulnerable circumstances. There were limits to how many people could and should access ADR and a view that ADR – in an efficient system of consumer dispute resolution – needed to remain a last resort rather than one that is widely used:

> If you think about what an ombudsman's here to do, an Ombudsman, by definition, should almost be an exceptional [remedy] … we don't want to start building customer journeys where the Ombudsman is an integral part of a customer journey … That would tell you there's something more fundamentally wrong with the journey and the

> system. So, there'd be a bit in here, well, philosophically, I'd be a bit worried … I don't get the sense of, you know, that it is being seen as well, the answer is just the Ombudsman will pick all that up (UK Ombuds 2).

> My personal view is that it should be very much a backstop; it shouldn't be, like, something that everyone … like, large numbers of people need to go through and get that support … The onus really should be on suppliers to make sure that they're providing the right customer service initially (UK Complaint Handling Organisation 1).

iii. Limits in Addressing the Fundamental Problems Facing Energy Consumers

Some interviewees were concerned that ADR bodies had limited powers to deal with fundamental injustices within the energy market. An example related to pre-payment meters in the UK. The ombuds could receive complaints about this; however, it was unable to consider pricing. The fact that pre-payment meters were more expensive and that this could potentially be the cause of underlying debt presenting in a complaint was not something the ombuds service could do anything about:

> [T]he prepayment meter is generally for the poorest in society, but it's one of the highest tariffs, in terms of cost per unit. So, I mean, whether that's something that's fair, I don't know, I think that's how these things usually are, isn't it? … in terms of pricing, it isn't for us (UK Ombuds 6–10).

In relation to the potential for challenging unfair terms and conditions, some interviewees said that the ombuds service was empowered to handle this, while others pointed out that this fact was not necessarily widely known in the organisation or that they had been told the opposite:

> [S]ometimes even within our business, it's getting that message out, that we can, actually, challenge terms and conditions. Because, I think, sometimes, you think they're like law, don't you, well, you know, you've agreed to that term and condition, so that's that (UK Ombuds 6–10).

Another limitation, mentioned by UK Ombuds 1, was that the service's role ends abruptly with a decision being provided on a complaint. She suggested that more could be done for vulnerable people in advising them how to access other services after a complaint had been concluded. This could involve working with the energy company or third-sector providers to make sure that underlying issues in the complaint, such as debt or other vulnerabilities, could be addressed in a more fundamental way:

> [T]here's a lot of work as an ombudsman that we could do to actually work in partnership with people, so that PCs [participating companies] have the right partnerships working with them, around outstanding debt. Because our role is to make a decision, and once we've done that, it's actually, can we connect? I think there's a real opportunity for the Ombudsman to work closely in that area. So, it's not, we've done our

> bit, we're off. Actually, we, not hand hold, but work closely with the right people to get the companies, the relationships built back up. Which then helps everybody (UK Ombuds 1).

In jurisdictions such as Catalonia and Bulgaria, interviewees reported that the public ombuds played a prominent role in relation to energy issues. This role was not restricted to directly considering energy disputes (the bulk of which were dealt with by more specialised ADR bodies), but also included raising issues of general concern and advocating for the rights of energy consumers in order to bring about policy changes:

> Maybe a month ago or something like that, the ombudsman of Bulgaria came up with … [a] proposal to the government that instead of this subsidy in cash, it would be much better if the energy-poor households received, for example, vouchers for purchasing energy-efficient heating appliances … She wrote something like a memorandum or a letter with proposals to the government (Bulgarian Policy 2).

In these jurisdictions, the public ombuds took on a more political role and systemic role, which involved challenging the status quo and seeking to affect wider causes of injustice in energy provision:

> Effective? I mean, she's not, let's say, part of the government establishment … she is quite active and over the past year she has tried to tackle the problem of energy monopolies in Bulgaria … She has been quite active in … in protesting or raising the issue of electricity prices (Bulgarian Policy 2).

D. The Need for ADR to Develop Partnerships and Systemic Approaches

i. *The Importance of Partnership*

Questions around the proper limits of the ombuds' role led interviewees to identify two main ways in which ADR could develop to enhance how it helped vulnerable and energy-poor consumers. On the one hand, this involved ADR bodies becoming more systemic and vocal actors in changing systems and, on the other, it involved better partnership working and coordination among actors who could each offer different things.

> We are in permanent contact, we have regular meetings with NGOs, with municipalities … with elderly people … and it's a way to share our vision around or related with the problem and it's a way to detect special situations if we need to act … (Catalan Ombuds 1 and 2).
>
> Part of the response I think needs to be a policy one that's about how do we … put them [issues] in the right places; whether that be with the regulator, whether that be Citizens Advice, whether that be us taking a more vocal position on some things. But you've got, you know, what are the things that we might be able to do to change the system? (UK Ombuds 2).

UK interviewees pointed out that there was an established tripartite relationship between the regulator, Citizens Advice, and the ombuds service. This was seen as important in dealing with vulnerability:

> You can see people like the Extra Help Unit, the companies themselves, the energy suppliers, and then people like us, who are also in partnership in that sector, all starting to come together to deal with vulnerability. And that's when it will start to have an impact. (UK Ombuds 1).

Similarly, in Catalonia the partnership approach was also seen as key to delivering a more systemic approach. The Catalan Ombuds, for example, described their advocacy work in relation to issues facing energy consumers as a method of consensus building:

> We are trying to put … [around the same] table companies, NGOs … administration and also we are [at] the same table, and it's a very interesting discussion … the actors that are in the same situation but in different ways and how is the best way to approach it … So what we are putting as a conclusion and as recommendations, it's okay, it's our proposal, but … you are not asking … [for] something that is impossible, you are asking … [for] something that [around a] table … we agree that it is a good way to approach it (Catalan Ombuds 1 and 2).

Generally, a focus on partnership was important because the issue was often that solutions were being offered by various organisations and institutions, but these were not working well together:

> So, is the problem that you're not offering the right solution as an ombudsman, or I'm not offering the right solution as a company, or that we're not working properly together? (Catalan Policy 3).

Despite participants recognising the importance of partnership, there were mixed views about how much this was achieved in practice:

> I think it is the time to work together, the companies and the National Commissioner, and the ombudsman, and the public administration, because sometimes … the solution that one party is saying, has nothing to do with the thinking in another party. So, that's why there is not an understanding among us (Catalan Policy 3).

ii. Third-Sector Partnerships

Partnership with the third sector and local government services was also seen as being particularly important. Catalan Ombuds 1 and 2 commented on the key role that these services played in helping energy-poor and vulnerable consumers access justice:

> There are a lot of NGOs that have helped a lot of people, give advice on how to complain against a bill, how to act against when they're having a problem, things like that, and they have done a lot of work … A lot of municipalities are doing a lot of work on that, not only the main administration, the government, but also the city halls is where the problems are really solved (Catalan Ombuds 1 and 2).

Catalan Policy 1 also commented on the key role of NGOs and groups working with vulnerable people. These were crucial because they provided a link between this group of consumers and the energy companies:

> They really know about vulnerable consumers. But, because we, as electrical companies, we don't know nothing about them. We only have lists of thousands or millions … of contracts and we know … we don't know who is behind. They really know about vulnerable consumers … They speak both languages … They know about vulnerable consumers and they know about … energy companies (Catalan Policy 1).

Partnership was seen as important not only in ensuring that people are able to access justice, but also to ensure that people's problems are dealt with holistically rather than piecemeal. A consumer advocacy organisation in the UK expressed a frustration that, although it could often resolve the immediate issues with an energy supplier, that would not resolve underlying issues of fuel poverty, debt, employment problems, barriers to claiming benefits, housing matters and so on, that were often the root cause of people's difficulties:

> An awful lot of our consumers are in fuel poverty, but a lot of the issues we deal with are compliance related, if that makes sense. So, again, we're wanting to do more in the space of, you know, could we provide some more financial advice to consumers when they come here? … I think the dream would be to … go into your local [Citizens Advice] bureau, [and] they can have all the details there. We've solved your energy complaint, and now they can look at income maximisation. That kind of thing … I think there's ways in which we can make the service a little bit more inclusive (UK Complaint Handling Organisation 1).

The need for more integrated service provision was also highlighted by other third-sector actors. For instance, UK Third Sector 1 noted that having to refer people to other services could be inefficient and lead to a lack of continuity for individuals. They were looking therefore at the possibility of more joined-up approaches:

> We're trying to look at whether we can be that one-stop shop and not have to pass [things on] … We're actually looking, starting to address those things about whether we can offer that wider service and also, not just broker those links but actually handle [cases] throughout that process so we do get to see what happens on the other side (UK Third Sector 1).

The data in the current study echoes findings of Deller and Waddams Price that there can be particular challenges for third-sector organisations not only when contributing to partnership and policy processes as a result of limited resources, but also when trying to help consumers see through potential complaints to ADR bodies.[4]

> Because we don't have a network, [other] organisations that we work in this field, we are too small and we spend our time acting but not networking. We mean to do it but … at

[4] D Deller and C Waddams Price (eds), *Fairness in Retail Energy Markets? Evidence form the UK* (CCP, 2018), available at: competitionpolicy.ac.uk/documents/8158338/18232983/CCP+%26+UKERC+-+Fairness+in+Retail+Energy+Markets+Report.pdf/6499c409-10c9-8f5a-73a3-0290b5ab022f.

> the end we focus on our projects and we work on them, then we don't have the time or the space to share (Catalan Third Sector 1 and 2).
>
> We probably don't know enough about the role of ombudsman services … There's a chance it [a case] might get handed over to the ombudsman to kind of take a view. At that point, we kind of lose a bit of visibility of what happens (UK Third Sector 3).

iii. Partnerships with Energy Suppliers

Good relationships with energy companies were considered to be crucial by Catalan Ombuds 1 and 2. The ombuds was seen as having prestige which energy companies responded to, as well as a constructive approach to asking for changes:

> I think we are proud to work with them and companies also I think … we sometimes detect some situation that they haven't detected, no, and if I can say our prestige, how do you say, our professionality, our experience … it's a guarantee for the companies when they receive a complaint or they receive some claim from us because they know that that situation has been examined … They trust in our work and they like the way we approach it (Catalan Ombuds 1 and 2).

Good relationships with partners also allowed the Catalan ombuds to carry out policy advocacy work where legislative or policy change was required:

> The ombudsman … can analyse the situation and tell to public authorities … its points of view, its conclusions … and give information to the parliament (Catalan Ombuds 1 and 2).

The UK energy ombuds discussed the potential of intervening 'upstream' with energy companies as being potentially much more effective than thinking about expanding access to the ombuds service or developing its support functions to provide more assistance to vulnerable people:

> Isn't the key to this about … taking it upstream into the companies? So, if you start thinking about the more natural place to go … Your best place to start is the companies, rather than, perhaps, trying to set up a bit of civil society [in the ombuds service] that people don't come to. Because, you know they're at the company, they must be, that's how they got to the Ombudsman in the first place. So, a lot more of what we're trying to do is to go, how can we build partnerships within the companies? And how can we use our data, and our different perspective, to shift some of that mind set and behaviour at a company? … You're then going with the grain of the customer journey … Why not just go back earlier in the journey and fix it here, would be what we're trying to do (UK Ombuds 2).
>
> Our role is to do ourselves out of a job … in the end, that's kind of what it is. It's to try and get the companies to improve their processes, their systems, how they deal with things. So, that in future, that kind of complaint won't come up again (UK Ombuds 6–10).

In France, in addition to the national energy ombuds, some companies also operate an organisational ombuds scheme. French Policy 5 commented that organisational schemes had potential advantages in terms of bringing about change in company practices. Organisational ombuds can identify the best way to respond to specific issues, and their decisions are sometimes more progressive than those of a national ombuds. The closer relationship with the supplier, meant that an organisational ombuds could act as a spur for the supplier, helping to pinpoint malfunctions. An organisational ombuds has greater expertise and knowledge of people, businesses and processes and knows when and how certain aspects work or not. Thanks to this capability, they can provide a more relevant, quicker and more efficient service, according to French Policy 5.

In the UK, the interview data show that the energy ombuds has started carrying out outreach with energy suppliers, as well as hosting joint training events with the industry and third sector:

> We, specifically, have ombudsmen who aren't just about sitting in the office, and, you know, doing the strokey chin bit. It's about having ombudsmen who are out engaging with companies … who'll be going out and talking to companies about, well, we've spotted this trend. Or, you're needing help with X … So, if we see something, we're going, hang on this doesn't look right, we'll go out and say, this doesn't look right, can we come and work with you? (UK Ombuds 2).

> Over this year, there's four sessions where we [are] sort of putting together companies from the north west, in terms of, we've had a kind of workshops that have had guest speakers and that, so we try to share knowledge across different businesses and charities, things like that, so, we've been involved with that, which has been helpful to learn from others really (UK Ombuds 3 and 4).

One of the potential barriers to greater partnership working was seen as the increasing diversification of the energy industry in some jurisdictions. This meant that system-wide approaches and partnerships were much more difficult to achieve than they were when dealing with a smaller number of big providers:

> In the old days … you just go along to the Big Six and you move six companies … [But] now, if you want to do it, you're trying to move 80 [companies], and counting … how do you raise the standard of how you deal with vulnerability across all of those companies, many of whom were set up to compete on price, and many of whom, if we're honest, a regulator doesn't even really know who they are? … You've got a real mixed bag in there. Some great performers, and some who are in it for a quick buck (UK Ombuds 2).

III. Discussion

In this part of the chapter, we discuss the empirical findings presented above and seek to draw some conclusions on ADR and access to justice.

A. The Access to Justice Challenge

The findings of our study support the evidence in the existing literature on the demographic characteristics of people who use ADR and ombuds schemes.[5]

[5] Creutzfeldt (n 3); B Hubeau, 'The Profile of Complainants: How to Overcome the "Matthew Effect"?' in M Hertogh and R Kirkham (eds), *Research Handbook on the Ombudsman* (Edward Elgar, 2018);

ADR's claims to supporting access to justice cannot be maintained while it continues to serve such a narrow demographic of consumers. As Hubeau has pointed out, not only are certain groups and individuals excluded, but the effect of more powerful individuals and groups being able to secure access to an ombuds is that their existing advantages are boosted, while others are left further behind.[6] ADR could potentially be monopolised by middle-class users,[7] and the effect on the industry could be that their interests are prioritised to avoid the cost and reputational damage of complaints that go to ADR. As we noted earlier, the energy sector is characterised by different types of consumers, with a small minority actively engaged in the market and a larger disengaged majority.[8] The danger is that ADR tends to serve only those who are already active in the market. Our data show that at the same time as most consumers remain passive in pursuing ADR, a small minority are increasingly active and challenging. In that sense, the expansion of ADR can be seen as following the logic of European consumer and energy market policies generally, where the expectation and market logic is that consumers will be active in searching for the best deals and pursuing their rights. As we have already argued, that expectation appears seriously flawed, and the findings above in relation to access to justice barriers give further weight to that view.

Thus, our data inform us that there remain problems with consumers' awareness and low usage of ADR. While ADR undoubtedly helps some consumers who reach it, in reality not many consumers do manage to access it. While we did not collect statistical demographic data in this project, the qualitative findings suggest that ADR use is currently not as extensive as it could be. The fact that only 5.2 per cent of energy consumers who experience a problem refer a complaint to ADR indicates that ADR has not, to date, been the transformative access to justice vehicle that its proponents have claimed.[9] As we will argue below, there is, of course, a debate to be had about how many people should be accessing ADR directly: a system that is overused would be inefficient and indicate serious problems with the way the industry was handling disputes. But that is not the current situation. Many consumers have not had their complaints settled satisfactorily

J Dahlvik, A Pohn-Weidinger and M Kollegger, 'High Official at Street-level: A Multi-method Study on the Consultation Days of the Austrian Ombudspersons' in M Groves and A Stuhmcke (eds), *Ombudsmen in the Modern State* (Hart Publishing, forthcoming); Department for Business, Energy & and Industrial Strategy (BEIS), *Resolving Consumer Disputes: Alternative Dispute Resolution and the Court System* (BEIS, 2018), available at: assets.publishing.service.gov.uk/government/uploads/system/uploads/attachment_data/file/698442/Final_report_-_Resolving_consumer_disputes.pdf.

[6] Hubeau (n 5).

[7] A Hastings and P Matthews, *Sharp Elbows: Do the Middle-Classes Have Advantages in Public Service Provision and if so How?* (Project Report, University of Glasgow 2011), available at: eprints.gla.ac.uk/57021/.

[8] M Ioannidou, 'Effective Paths for Consumer Empowerment and Protection in Retail Energy Markets' (2018) 41 *Journal of Consumer Policy* 135.

[9] European Commission, *Consumer Conditions Scoreboard: Consumers at Home in the Single Market* (European Commission 2019), available at: ec.europa.eu/info/sites/info/files/consumers-conditions-scoreboard-2019_pdf_en.pdf.

by energy suppliers,[10] and customer satisfaction is low compared with other sectors,[11] yet many grievances do not reach ADR. Coupled with the fact that those who use ADR are not currently representative, the conclusion has to be that major efforts are required to extend the reach of ADR if access to justice is to be realised.

B. The Barriers that Stand in the Way of Accessing ADR

Our findings confirm the existence of social, cognitive and procedural barriers to access to justice for energy consumers. Not only is the demographic usage of ADR narrow, but our findings show that vulnerable individuals face particular barriers in referring complaints to ADR. The nature of some people's lives, living on low incomes and suffering from multiple forms of disadvantage, can be 'hectic' and 'crazy', meaning that complaining to ADR would simply not be an option. For others, the social stigma associated with complaining and seeking help for problems presents an insurmountable barrier. It is clear that, for such individuals, even the simplest and most accessible of ADR procedures is unlikely to be triggered. This echoes Errington's findings in relation to the emotional nature of energy poverty, with people not necessarily passive and disengaged, but instead being active in other ways: reducing their energy use and seeking practical short-term help with debt problems.[12] There are suggestions here that some consumers may engage more in self-help and be more willing to pursue informal strategies, such as contacting third-sector bodies or complaining directly to energy suppliers.

Certainly, direct negotiation with energy suppliers seems to be the overall preference of energy consumers.[13] More generally, the European Commission's *Consumer Scoreboard* shows that trust in retailers is higher than trust in consumer organisations and state bodies.[14] This may reflect the greater accessibility of energy suppliers (where individuals have an existing relationship) and third-sector bodies (which are based in the community). But it may also reflect a generalised lack of trust in 'the system'. Some of our findings provide indications of this, with cynicism expressed that ADR could overcome the interests of powerful companies in order to provide justice. Rather than helping energy consumers, the peripheral nature of ADR could therefore be seen as part of a system that effectively supports the continued 'illiteracy' of consumers in relation to their rights. Points made by interviewees about language are particularly interesting in showing the physical and relational distance between ADR and vulnerable energy consumers. ADR was referred to as being 'closed' and remote from the problems people experience,

[10] ibid.

[11] BEUC, *Consumer Rights in Energy Market*, BEUC Position Paper (BEUC, October 2013).

[12] E Errington, 'Just Regulation? Access to Policy Formulation for Affordable Energy in GB' (2019) CCP Working Paper 19-2 2019.

[13] European Commission, *Consumer Conditions Scoreboard* (n 9).

[14] ibid.

while ADR and energy suppliers spoke a different language from that of ordinary people – 'we speak French but we don't understand' as one interviewee put it. The language gap was reflected in the very name of ADR institutions, with one interviewee commenting on the difficulty in using the word 'ombudsman' for public understanding of the institution. The combination of legal language and technical terminology was reflective of the distance between vulnerable individuals and the professionals working in the energy and ADR industries (we explore these points in greater depth in chapter six).

Other barriers related less to individual orientations to complaining or people's position in society and more to features of the ADR process. Regulations could impose barriers, such that a complaint could only be made to the UK energy ombuds eight weeks after submitting a complaint, or the low level of redress made available to consumers through ADR in Italy. But, more generally, despite the claims made for the superior accessibility of ADR as an access to justice mechanism, the barriers to access appear to remain considerable. Indeed, our findings suggest that there is an inherent formality arising from the evidence-based process operated by ADR bodies, which requires consumers to submit evidence to support their case. Many of those leading the kind of chaotic lives referred to above are unlikely to be able to do this effectively. At an ESRC Just Energy workshop held with European third-sector energy bodies in 2019, one participant told us that even asking a consumer to fill out a form or sign a consent slip for someone to act on their behalf could be too much. Although ADR is frequently lauded for its non-legal approach, the reality of some modern ADR schemes is that they constitute relatively large-scale bureaucracies (the UK Energy Ombuds has around 400 staff, albeit they cover telecoms and other smaller sectors as well as energy).[15] Thus, while processes may not require legal expertise and legal skills, they may require familiarity with bureaucratic practices and a certain ease in dealing with formal and official communication. UK Ombuds 5 said their current process was not tailored for the needs of vulnerable people and took instead a 'sausage factory' approach. This adds some weight to the concerns of ADR critics that ADR for consumers represents a form of second-class justice,[16] as well as those who are concerned that the institutionalisation of ADR robs it of much of its value as a means of delivering flexible, creative and more human-centred outcomes.[17]

The growth of technology was seen as potentially improving the customer experience, but this was balanced against suggestions that this could lead to further exclusion. Our findings show that, especially for the most vulnerable, online contact can be difficult and that even providing availability by telephone might

[15] See: www.ombudsman-services.org/careers-at-ombudsman-services.

[16] L Nader, *The Life of the Law: Anthropological Projects* (University of California Press, 2005).

[17] M Palmer, 'Formalisation of Alternative Dispute Resolution Processes: Some Socio-legal Thoughts' in J Zekoll, M Bälz and I Amelung (eds), *Formalisation and Flexibilisation in Dispute Resolution* (Brill Nijhoff, 2014).

not be enough to fulfil people's need to 'talk to a human'. Again, the physical and psychological distance between ADR and vulnerable people is significant, with ADR operating through a centralised call-centre model rather than in people's localities. One potential problem is that before consumers reach ADR they will already have spent some time fighting to get through the equally distant and bureaucratic call centres of energy companies. Consumers often have poor experiences there, so that they are already fatigued by the time they could potentially make a referral to ADR. Poor practice among energy companies, either in relation to not providing information about rights and ADR, or by handling complaints poorly in the first place, represents a major barrier to access. As Ramsay[18] and Van Loo[19] have suggested, internal complaint mechanisms within firms are a major site of access to justice. However, the current situation is that they often fail to deliver justice directly, and that the existence of ADR as a safety valve to deal with unremedied cases remains inadequate.

C. Adapting Services to Deal with Vulnerable Users

As shown in chapter four, the vulnerabilities presented by some consumers from an organisational perspective are significant. Making sure that ADR staff have the skills and expertise to deal with people who are not familiar with bureaucratic practices, who are from deprived communities, who lead chaotic lifestyles, who may have health problems, as well as emotional and behavioural issues, represents a serious challenge. Interviewees from the UK energy ombuds told us about their plans to develop a vulnerability strategy – with options including specialist teams, greater use of technology to spot and then support vulnerable people, timescale changes, and greater use of early and negotiated approaches to avoid formality. These developments will be interesting to follow in future. Such approaches are likely to be key to demonstrating that ADR mechanisms are 'for' vulnerable people and in closing the relational distance between ADR mechanisms and vulnerable individuals and groups. At the same time, particularly in relation to the greater use of 'early resolution', there is a danger that settlements lead to unfair outcomes and fail to deal with underlying issues.[20]

A particularly important development, however, is that, in addition to responding to the vulnerabilities being presented by current users, ADR bodies need to pay much more attention to the needs and characteristics of non-users.

[18] I Ramsay, 'Consumer Redress and Access to Justice' in CEF Rickett and TGW Telfer (eds), *International Perspectives on Consumers' Access to Justice* (CUP, 2003).

[19] Comment by Rory Van Loo cited in E Deason, M Green and D Shestowsky et al, 'ADR and Access to Justice: Current Perspectives' (2018) 33 *Ohio State Journal of Dispute Resolution* 303.

[20] M Doyle, V Bondy and C Hirst, 'The Use of Informal Resolution Approaches by Ombudsmen in the UK and Ireland: A Mapping Study' (Ombudsman Research, 2014), available at: ombudsmanresearch.files.wordpress.com/2014/10/the-use-of-informal-resolution-approaches-by-ombudsmen-in-the-uk-and-ireland-a-mapping-study-1.pdf.

Institutional design must be inclusive,[21] and ADR needs to be ready to cater for a more diverse set of needs and users if it is to fulfil a broader access to justice role. Of course, such developments would come at a cost, and this represents a major tension in the low-cost nature of the consumer ADR model as it relates to access to justice. The truth is that access to justice – if by that we mean significantly extending the reach of justice to the excluded and making sure that non-emerged disputes see the light of day – is not a cost-saving enterprise. In fact, the opposite is true: real access to justice is a costly endeavour. This insight is crucial, and yet it reveals one explanation for the strong interlinking of ADR and access to justice in policy narratives. The kind of magical thinking whereby costs to the state (and non-state actors) can be reduced while at the same time extending the reach of justice has had an obvious appeal to policymakers the world over. That is not to say that ADR cannot achieve access to justice goals, and indeed we will argue in chapter seven that well-designed ADR can do just that. However, doing so is likely to involve investment rather than cost-saving, at least in the short-term. While ADR should certainly be cheap from the perspective of a consumer, we need to revise the narrative of cheapness to government and industry if we are serious about tackling access to justice.

D. Questions about the Proper Role of ADR

One of the issues that arose from our findings related to the proper role and functions of ADR. While the UK energy ombuds, for example, planned various adaptations to its service to help deal with more diverse users, there were also limits to how far it could go in doing so. While more support and personalisation could be provided, as an impartial adjudicator, there were limits to how far the organisation could provide advice and support to one of the parties. And while there was recognition that ADR could perhaps go further in seeking to resolve people's problems holistically, ADR bodies could not become social workers or replace the role of third-sector advice. Part of the problem here seemed to be that consumers often expect ADR to deliver a different kind of service. Rather than an impartial body that will adjudicate their case, they perhaps expect a consumer champion, someone who will straightforwardly believe them and fight their corner. They also seem to expect a high level of support from ADR that may not be possible to reconcile with its ultimately adjudicative function. Previous literature has commented on the need for expectations management in relation to dampening down and correcting public expectations of ADR.[22] Another way of looking at this, however, is that ADR could be doing more to meet public expectations, rather than trying to dampen them.

[21] RL Sandefur, 'Fulcrum Point of Equal Access to Justice: Legal and Nonlegal Institutions of Remedy' (2009) 42 *Loyola of Los Angeles Law Review* 949.

[22] S Gilad, 'Accountability or Expectations Management? The Role of the Ombudsman in Financial Regulation' (2008) 30 *Law & Policy* 227; Creutzfeldt (n 3).

Indeed, impartiality is an interesting issue in the context of the 'inherently flawed' energy market. The large power imbalances that exist between suppliers and consumers may call for an approach which is more proactive in supporting the needs and interests of the weaker party. Strict impartiality may well be a fundamental requirement of justice and the rule of law where parties have equal strengths and resources. But where social relations are fundamentally and structurally unequal, impartiality may simply have the effect of preserving the status quo and maintaining existing power relations, particularly in contexts such as the present one where legal advice is not expected to be available. This speaks to some of the broader debates about where ADR sits in relation to the achievement of social justice. Context is key here. And, in an energy sector featuring significant levels of consumer detriment, there may well be a justification for ADR not to deny some of the common expectations of consumers (that ADR bodies will be 'allies' and 'advocates')[23] but to seek to realise them. Certainly, this fits with the logic of the holistic vision of access to justice that we are seeking to outline in this book. This would lead to a quite different perspective, whereby consumer expectations were not bureaucratic problems to be 'managed' but legitimate claims for assistance in the redressing of the fundamental problems arising from the operation of energy markets. This question about how ADR is to operate in an unfair world and in unequal markets was reflected in data from interviewees stressing the limitations of ADR in redressing injustices: for instance, not being able to challenge energy suppliers' pricing, uncertainty over whether terms and conditions could or could not be challenged, and the fact that the poorest consumers often faced the highest pre-payment tariffs and were therefore unlikely to reach ADR.

A further question over whether and how ADR's functions should be expanded relates to cost. Among ADR providers there was a need to maintain an eye on efficiency and dealing with complaints in a cost-effective fashion. Providing more support and advice and more differentiated services would clearly come at a cost, as we have noted above. It also seems clear that ADR bodies are constrained by aspects of the operation of energy markets and the needs of suppliers. In the UK, for instance, the fact that energy providers pay for the energy ombuds is a boon to government, but also places inherent limits on the extent to which ADR can pursue access to justice goals. The energy ombuds has to be mindful of the cost constraint on the retail energy sector, and there will be strong pressure from companies for those costs to be minimised. Similarly, ADR bodies have to deal with the charge that – if they do seek to expand their services beyond their current limited and status quo-preserving niche – they are ambulance chasing or empire building. As has been pointed out by Gilad,[24] ADR bodies have to carefully negotiate the legitimacy of their 'domain' between regulators, courts and industry, and

[23] See Creutzfeldt (n 3).

[24] Gilad (n 22).

this requires a very fine balancing act. While we might be critical of role limitations that result from industry pressure and the desire of governments to shift the costs of dispute resolution away from the public purse, our findings show there are also more pragmatic reasons for ADR having only a limited and peripheral role in the resolution of energy disputes. The points made by some interviewees about it being inappropriate for mass disputing to be provided directly by ADR providers seem compelling.

There is, therefore, a question about how much access to ADR represents enough access to justice. Currently, the figure is 5 per cent, and this seems rather low, especially given that current access is unrepresentative. There is scope for increasing direct access to ADR, but that can only be part of the solution, and there must ultimately be a limit on how many people we should expect to use ADR. The example of how public ombuds have intervened in relation to energy disputes in Catalonia (chapter ten) and Bulgaria (chapter nine) is interesting and shows that one way of overcoming the difficulty in increasing usage of ADR is to take more systemic approaches. The public ombuds in Catalonia and Bulgaria adopt the kind of advocacy approach that, as we noted above, is likely to be appropriate in the context of widespread structural inequality, as well as seeking to influence government and industry actors to resolve problems at source. As we will discuss in chapter seven, these kinds of approaches represent key design options for ADR – seeking, on the one hand, to increase direct access to ADR to a more acceptable and representative level, while, in parallel, adopting more systemic and preventative approaches.

E. Partnership and Systemic Working

An aspect of developing a more systemic and holistic approach for ADR involves the need to develop partnerships. However designed, ADR should not be all things to all people. As noted above, there is a sense that there should be some clear limits set on the role of ADR. Partnership is one way in which the complexity and multifaceted nature of the issues facing energy consumers could be dealt with, while recognising the inherent limitations of any single organisation. Our findings highlight the importance of partnerships between ADR and regulators, consumer advice and third-sector bodies, and energy suppliers. In relation to the third sector, partnership is important in two ways. First, it is a means through which vulnerable groups can be reached and assisted to secure direct access to ADR. Given the difficulties inherent in some vulnerable individuals and groups reaching ADR, intermediaries are hugely important. They can potentially assist vulnerable people by signposting them to ADR and provide them with the kind of support that would be needed to overcome some of the formalities and difficulties inherent in complaining. A limitation on relying on the third sector in this way, however, is that these organisations are often stretched and sometimes do not themselves have sufficient familiarity with ADR.

Another potentially powerful approach to partnership involves going beyond referrals and towards the provision of more integrated services. Providing a service that could not only deal with a presenting energy problem, but at the same time manage other underlying issues such as debt, unemployment, family problems, or housing issues could be a powerful way of dealing with people's 'everyday justice' problems. This would recognise that people's problems do not arise in neat categories that match the remits of particular ADR bodies and other sources of third-party help and advice. Instead, these problems are clustered and dealing with only one part of them is unlikely to provide a long-term solution for individuals. A bottom-up approach that begins by looking at people's problems and the nature of their everyday justice needs would require more integrated and joined-up services. This has been suggested in the civil justice context,[25] with possible examples including the co-location of ADR and community law centres, or the integration of health and consumer advice services. There were signs that this approach was recognised as having potential in our findings, although at present there is little evidence that such integrated approaches exist on the ground.

One area where partnership is being used is policy development. Here, partnership approaches can allow various actors to contribute their voices in ways that could inform regulators and industry. Examples of successful partnerships include the UK's tripartite meetings between the energy ombuds, the regulator and Citizens Advice. In Catalonia, the ombuds took on a very proactive policy advocacy role but stressed that this relied on building coalitions with stakeholders and reaching consensus about the need for change. Partnership was therefore seen as essential to the ombuds having a more influential and powerful systemic role, as it gave legitimacy to its recommendations and calls for change. Wider systemic and policy-advocating roles were more common among public ombuds (Bulgaria, Catalonia) or energy ombuds with a statutory basis (France), although the UK energy ombuds was also considering developing a more 'vocal' role and delivering system change through partnership.

Perhaps the most important partnership, given the importance of internal complaint handling in the context of consumer disputing, was the relationship with energy companies. This could include providing the results of aggregate data, as well as regular communication on issues arising from casework. In the UK, examples were given of consultancy-type arrangements, with the energy ombuds working with suppliers to improve their processes and arranging joint training events for staff of the ADR body and energy suppliers. Such approaches were seen as ways in which ADR could influence what happens 'upstream' among the many complaints that never reach ADR. More generally, the importance of building good relationships with energy suppliers, based on trust and expertise, was seen as valuable. In Catalonia, these good relationships were considered to be part of

[25] L Ojelabi, 'Community Legal Centres' Views on ADR as a Means of Accessing Justice' (2011) 22 *Australasian Journal of Dispute Resolution* 103.

the reason for the ombuds' influential position; the institution was respected in part because it developed expertise in relation to energy problems and because it built partnerships with other expert stakeholders to push issues forward. As Van Loo has noted 'the corporation is a courthouse, to some extent',[26] and this insight – along with the limited number of people who are, can, and perhaps should be, directly accessing ADR – suggests that part of the response to the access to justice challenge involves ADR taking a much greater role in the way in which energy suppliers handle complaints themselves.

IV. Conclusion

This chapter has provided a set of empirical insights that illustrate both the problems and potential in ADR delivering access to justice. Most crucially, the chapter has identified that the access to justice challenge remains largely unanswered by ADR as it currently operates for vulnerable and energy-poor consumers. It remains little used, and those who use it are from a narrow and privileged demographic. Our findings have also reaffirmed the multiple and extensive barriers that stand in the way of accessing justice. Some of these relate to the design of institutions and processes, but many also arise from social conditions that are much harder to address. Our findings have, however, identified a number of areas where there is significant potential for ADR to be enhanced. This includes providing service adaptations to respond to consumer vulnerability, offering additional support and advice, taking on more vocal and systemic roles, and engaging in greater partnership working. While the development of additional functions was viewed with some caution in our findings, they nevertheless point towards some important ways in which ADR might develop from being seen as a 'frenemy' of access to justice towards becoming a major means of realising it.

The next chapter discusses additional routes to access justice for vulnerable and energy-poor consumers. Our data revealed the crucial role that local actors play in fighting energy poverty and supporting access to justice. These local actors should not only be seen as intermediaries with formal institutions but as sites of access to justice in themselves.

[26] Comment by Rory Van Loo (n 19).

6

Everyday Experiences and the Role of Local Actors

I. Introduction

As we argued in chapters one and three, energy poverty and consumer vulnerability are multifaceted social problems, existing alongside a range of other challenges that affect people's daily lives, all of which create substantial barriers to accessing justice. Vulnerable and energy-poor consumers have complex needs, and EU-level and national legislation has only begun to address the problem (see chapter three). Other, complementary solutions need to be found, often beyond the law and formal state action. Our fieldwork shows how distant and inaccessible laws, regulations and state-provided mechanisms for consumer redress can seem to those facing injustice in relation to their energy problems. As one interviewee put it, state-sponsored actors set up to help people are 'closed up' in their offices, and the most vulnerable consumers are not 'knocking on the door' of either ADR providers, energy companies, or local government for help (Catalan Policy 3). Ordinary people are alienated by the world of formal laws and institutions – 'we speak French but we don't understand' (French Policy 3) as one interviewee put it – and are faced with a system that renders them 'illiterate' (Catalan Third Sector 1 and 2). This chapter is, therefore, concerned less with the legal frameworks and formal institutions that seek to secure access to justice and, instead, considers the routine experiences of vulnerable and energy-poor people seeking justice. As we have argued throughout the book so far, lived experiences of vulnerable individuals and groups, and those who assist locally, are an essential aspect of understanding the complexity of the issues at hand. Only once we understand what it means to live with vulnerability and energy poverty can we start to address the situation with an appropriate range of measures.

This chapter begins by introducing two frameworks through which the experiences of vulnerable consumers and their relationships with the energy market and the systems which govern it can be understood: legal alienation and relational distance. Legal alienation is an aspect of legal consciousness research, which is interested in the extent to which people know about and identify with the law and legal institutions. Those who identify with the law can be conceptualised as 'legalists' and 'loyalists', while those who do not are 'cynics' and 'outsiders'.[1] The relationships of energy consumers to the market and the state-provided mechanisms that oversee it are fundamentally conditioned by law, in terms of the consumer contracts that set the terms of their relationships with suppliers and the public law framework through which the energy market is overseen and regulated by public authorities. We argue, however, that vulnerable consumers do not identify with the law, nor do they believe that many of the systems in place to deliver justice in the energy sector are 'for them'. Instead, they are passive, apathetic and cynical about the operation of the market and using the law to bring about change. One of the reasons for this, we suggest, is the high relational distance[2] between vulnerable consumers and formal institutions – energy suppliers, ADR providers and public authorities. Consumers are spatially, culturally and psychologically remote from these formal institutions, and there is a lack of mutual understanding. On the one hand, vulnerable people do not understand the complex legal and bureaucratic systems that operate in the energy market, while formal actors know very little about the daily reality of people's experiences and the problems they face. Legal alienation and relational distance, we argue, provide us with a language and framework with which to understand consumer experiences and identify particular barriers that confront consumers facing significant, systemic injustice, but who are largely passive in response.

The chapter then turns to our empirical data and shows the lack of identification between consumers and key actors in the energy market. Consumers and formal institutions can be characterised as speaking different languages and operating in different worlds, far removed from each other. Vulnerable consumers are alienated by technical and legal language, legal and bureaucratic practices, and the use of communication channels (online and call centres) that they find difficult to access. The world of form-filling and documentary evidence that formal institutions are comfortable with is alien to many vulnerable people who are afraid of bureaucracy and recoil from any kind of formality. Our data show therefore a stark contrast and high relational distance between formal institutions and the daily reality of vulnerable consumers' lives.

We then consider billing as an illustrative example of the relationship between consumers and the market. Billing was the main problem reported in our dataset. Ombuds' annual reports confirm it as the main source of complaints in the energy sector.[3] When people are not able to keep up payments, bills have a direct

[1] M Hertogh, Nobody's Law: Legal Consciousness and Legal Alienation in Everyday Life (Palgrave Macmillan, 2018).

[2] D Black, *The Behaviour of Law* (Academic Press, 1976).

[3] Ombudsman services, 'Complaints at a Glance' (2019), available at: assets.ctfassets.net/46t2drav2f3e/1BKiBlkBxdVCWtI4vrjYFe/02b62def58c8e0224801fd8f7680c3d3/Overall_Sector_Data_Publishing_-_Q3_2019.pdf>; Le mediateur national d'energie, *Rapport d'activite 2019*, available at: www.energie-mediateur.fr/wp-content/uploads/2020/RA-MNE-2019.pdf; Sindic Catalonia, *Annual Report 2019*, available at: www.sindic.cat/site/unitFiles/6898/Annual%20Report%20 2019_eng_ok.pdf; Autoria di Regolazione per Energia Reti e Ambiente, *Annual Report 2019*, available at: www.arera.it/it/relaz_ann/20/20.htm.

impact on energy poverty.[4] There are regulations in place in the European energy market that set out details of billing and what consumers can do to access justice and advice (see chapter three). These require that the bills that customers receive must explain, in simple terms, information about payment and where to seek help and redress. Bills are a tangible first point of contact between the consumer and the energy company. These documents, despite being such an important vehicle for information and signposting, are typically very difficult to read and to understand and leave consumers confused and disenchanted. A study by the European Commission showed that 41 per cent of customers find their electricity bills difficult to understand.[5] Consumers in financial difficulty are significantly less inclined than others to consider these bills to be clear and understandable. We therefore consider billing to be a site of alienation, where the relational distance between legalistic and technical institutions and vulnerable people is particularly high. We conceptualise these as alienating experiences, where consumers are confronted with bureaucratic, technical and legal language and practices that render them 'illiterate'. Overall, our data show a sense of apathy among the most vulnerable consumers, who believe there is no point in complaining, that nothing will change, and that the system is against them. As Catalan Policy 5 noted, the persistence of unjust practices in the energy sector can lead to the cynical conclusion that 'justice does really not protect the vulnerable'.

Thus, vulnerable and energy-poor consumers can feel remote from formal sources of support and develop an outlook which sees the 'system' as a whole – government, ADR providers, energy companies – as fundamentally unaligned to their own interests and as not being 'for them'. Our data, in keeping with previous research on access to justice, shows the important role that local actors can play here. By local actors we mean NGOs, charities, community groups, local hubs, volunteers and community organisers. They can act not only as referral and information providers but can also provide the bridge between the world that consumers live in and the formal, legal–bureaucratic world inhabited by government agencies, regulators, ADR providers and energy companies. In the words of one interviewee, local actors are crucial because 'They speak both languages … They know about vulnerable consumers and they know about … energy companies' (Catalan Policy 1). Therefore, local actors can address some of the cognitive barriers that prevent consumers from taking action – providing an avenue through which alienation and passivity can be overcome. Moreover, while the literature on access to justice already stresses the importance of such actors as intermediaries with the justice system, we emphasise the role that they play in the direct

[4] S Pyne, A Dobbins and C Baffert et al, 'Energy Poverty and Vulnerable Consumers in the Energy Sector across the EU: Analysis of Policies and Measures' (INSIGHT_E 2015) ec.europa.eu/energy/sites/ener/files/documents/INSIGHT_E_Energy%20Poverty_Appendices.pdf.

[5] European Commission, *Second Consumer Market Study on the Functioning of the Retail Electricity Markets for Consumers in the EU* (European Commission, 2017), available at: ec.europa.eu/newsroom/just/item-detail.cfm?item_id=53331.

delivery of justice on the ground. Thus, we argue that local actors should not only be seen as intermediaries with formal institutions but as sites of access to justice. They provide an essential preventative and problem-solving role that is crucial to the realisation of a more bottom-up, more holistic and more therapeutic vision of access to justice. It follows that local actors are a key part of the holistic approach to access to justice that we outlined in chapter two and which we will return to in chapter seven.

The remainder of this chapter is divided into three parts. Section II outlines the theoretical concepts of legal alienation and relational distance. Section III presents data on consumer experiences, and section IV considers the role of local actors.

II. Legal Alienation, Relational Distance and Access to Justice

As explored elsewhere,[6] legal consciousness is a framework to explain what motivates people to act in a certain way with regard to law and legal institutions. As Ramsay has argued, legal consciousness approaches are important in relation to access to justice debates because they highlight ideological barriers to access to justice in addition to more pragmatic concerns, such as cost or institutional design. What people think and believe about the law and the mechanisms provided by the state to secure justice may be just as important as cost and procedural barriers.[7] Legal consciousness research, therefore, involves examining the 'images of laws and legal institutions that people carry around in their heads and occasionally act upon'.[8] Ewick and Silbey suggest such images can be seen in terms of three cultural schemas within which people respond to law: a sense of the majesty of law; law as a game to be played; and law as a capricious and oppressive force.[9] At the same time, legal consciousness provides a framework for understanding people's own beliefs about justice and calls for a more pluralistic approach than merely considering responses to narrowly defined state law.[10]

In this chapter we apply legal consciousness broadly and are concerned not only with responses to law, but also with the way consumers understand and interact (or do not interact) with the whole range of formal actors in the energy market.

[6] C Gill and N Creutzfeldt, The 'Ombuds Watchers': Dissatisfaction, Collective Dissent, and Legal Protest amongst Users of Public Service Ombuds' (2018) 27 *Social & Legal Studies* 367.

[7] I Ramsay, 'Consumer Redress and Access to Justice' in CEF Rickett and TGW Telfer (eds), *International Perspectives on Consumers' Access to Justice* (CUP, 2003).

[8] DM Engel, 'How Does Law Matter in the Constitution of Legal Consciousness?' in BG Garth and A Sarat (eds), *How Does Law Matter?* (Northwestern University Press, 1998).

[9] P Ewick and S Silbey, *The Common Place of Law: Stories from Everyday Life* (Chicago University Press, 1998).

[10] M Hertogh, 'A European Conception of Legal Consciousness: Rediscovering Eugen Ehrlich' (2004) 31 *Journal of Law and Society* 475.

Indeed, consumers' relationships in the energy market are inherently structured and conditioned by law: supranational and national legislation provide the framework for the operation of liberalised energy markets; legal contracts, themselves heavily regulated, govern the basis on which energy is supplied to individuals; public authorities set the rules which regulate the energy sector's practices and are responsible for overseeing suppliers; and courts and ADR providers constitute state-procured machinery for the settlement of disputes. Thus, we apply legal consciousness here in a broad sense, which encompasses how consumers interact with formal sources of authority in the energy market, all of which are ultimately sanctioned or conditioned by law.

Our interview data suggest that people feel isolated and alienated by their situations and by their experiences with energy companies and government bodies and, ultimately, in accessing justice. Genn, in her study on the legal experiences of ordinary citizens in England and Wales, concludes that '[r]espondents' views of the legal system often conveyed a sense of alienation from the institutions and processes of the law'.[11] Hertogh, when describing public officials' attitudes to the law, offers a model of legal citizenship, focusing on legal alienation, which considers the degree to which individuals 'identify' with the law and the degree to which they have knowledge of the law. Those who identify with the law are referred to as 'loyalists' and 'legalists', while those who do not are 'cynics' or 'outsiders'.[12] This conceptualisation resonates strongly with our data, which show a lack of identification among vulnerable consumers with the whole system for helping them deal with their problems. Rather than laws and regulations, legal institutions, regulators and ADR being perceived as mechanisms to achieve justice, they are seen either fatalistically, as impotent in changing the status quo, or as aspects of a system that has been designed to be oppressive and act against their interests.

Legal consciousness and legal alienation have previously been applied to the study of ombuds, albeit in the public sector. Hertogh, for example, found that public ombuds do not restore public trust in government, in part because loyalists and legalists were most likely to engage ombuds processes and complain. These groups believed that the ombuds and the protections of administration law were there to help them and that complaining would ensure that the system would remedy the injustice they had experienced. They believed that the law was for them and with them and, therefore, were willing to seek help and redress. Hertogh found that outsiders and cynics, on the other hand, were much less likely to engage the ombuds process – they did not identify with and feel close enough to the law and its values.[13] Hertogh concluded that 'complainants with fairly high levels of

[11] H Genn, Paths to Justice: What People Do and Think about Going to Law (Hart Publishing, 1999) 216.

[12] M Hertogh, 'What's in a Handshake? Legal Equality and Legal Consciousness in the Netherlands' (2009) 18 *Social & Legal Studies* 221; Hertogh, *Nobody's Law* (n 1).

[13] M Hertogh, 'Why the Ombudsman Does not Promote Public Trust in Government: Lesson from the Low Countries' (2013) 35 *Journal of Social Welfare & Family Law* 345.

trust in the justice system (and in politics) are able to take better advantage of the ombuds than those with low levels of trust'.[14] Outsiders and cynics, therefore, may find it hard to relate to the work of formal institutions and be less likely to engage with them. Gill and Creutzfeldt suggested, in the context of citizens' experiences of ombuds schemes in the UK, that a sense of alienation from dispute resolution systems formed part of a broader disillusionment with institutions of the state, which were seen as pitted against the interests of individuals.[15]

A further notion that is helpful in conceptualising the gap between consumers' experiences and the systems available to help them is that of relational distance. Relational distance has been used to explain the relationship between law, government and social control.[16] In *The Behaviour of Law*, Black predicts that the quantity of law in a given instance of conflict (the extent to which a matter will become subject to legal processes), can be explained by the location of the parties in social space: 'the social structure of a case predicts and explains how it will be handled'.[17] Relational distance according to Black refers to 'the degree to which people participate in one another's lives', while he uses law in a broad sense to refer to 'governmental social control … governmental authority applied to a particular case'.[18] He argues that his theory applies not only to law, but any form of third-party intervention in a conflict:

> Just as law varies directly varies with relational distance, for example, so does every form of intervention: *Third-party intervention varies directly with relational distance* [footnote omitted]. The likelihood and degree of authoritative intervention thus increases along a continuum of relational distance between the adversaries, from therapy to mediation, arbitration, and adjudication [footnote omitted]. Closer adversaries are more likely to seek mediation than arbitration or adjudication, for instance, and third parties are more likely to mediate than arbitrate or adjudicate closer conflicts.

Relational distance has also been used in a range of other contexts in order to understand how the relative position of individuals and institutions shape social phenomena.[19] The literature on relational distance suggests that it has several dimensions: structural distance, status distance and psychological distance.[20] Structural distance refers to physical distance, frequency of interaction and the channels of communication between individuals; status distance refers to demographic differences (age, class, etc) and social differences (relative power, social standing, cultural norms); and psychological distance refers to the quality of the relationship and how it is perceived.

[14] ibid 255.

[15] Gill and Creutzfeldt (n 6).

[16] Black, *The Behaviour of Law* (n 2).

[17] D Black, 'The Epistemology of Pure Sociology' (1995) 20 *Law & Social Inquiry* 829, 830.

[18] Black, *The Behaviour of Law* (n 2) 40–41.

[19] eg: L Erskine, 'Defining Relational Distance for Today's Leaders' (2012) 7 *International Journal of Leadership Studies* 96; O Ibert, 'Relational Distance: Sociocultural and Time: Spatial Tensions in Innovation Practices' (2010) 42 *Environment and Planning A* 187.

[20] Erskine (n 19).

Black's main theoretical prediction is that the closer the relational distance between people, the less likely it is that the law will condition their relationship.[21] The consumer context we have described in this book fits imperfectly with Black's theoretical predictions: it appears that despite high relational distance, consumers are more willing to pursue informal negotiation strategies with energy suppliers or seek help from advice agencies, than they are to engage the law. While it is the case that their relationships with suppliers are heavily conditioned by law, therefore, in relation to justice-seeking behaviour, consumers' preference seems to be geared towards informal relations and away from any kind of formal third-party intervention. In many cases, consumers take no action at all and, therefore, either do not perceive themselves to be in a potential conflict situation or are fatalistic about any potential resolution. While Black's overall theory, therefore, may have limited purchase in the context of energy consumer disputes, the main value of his work for our present purposes is his elaboration of the concept of relational distance as an important variable in understanding the presence and function of law (and other third-party intervention) in society. Indeed, we use the concept of relational distance here as a means of illustrating the barriers to accessing justice that arise as a result of the distance between consumers, energy suppliers, public authorities and ADR providers. While consumers may be more likely to engage legal or quasi-legal processes than people in a dispute within personal relationships (as per Black's theory), on the other hand it appears that those in a position of lower relational distance (legalists and loyalists in Hertogh's terms) are more likely to engage ADR and formal third-party intervention. Consumers who are remote from formal, legal–bureaucratic systems (cynics and outsiders) are least likely to take any kind of action or, if they take it, are more likely to use informal approaches. Certainly, the greater propensity of certain social groups to make complaints suggests that they are comfortable with the system and believe it serves their interests. As noted by UK Ombuds 2, those who complain to ADR are 'people like me': in other words, they are close together in social status and position. Vulnerable individuals and groups, on the other hand, being further away from the legal and bureaucratic world, are less likely to believe that complaining is worth it. Therefore, we suggest that relational distance – although it appears to function differently from Black's prediction in our context – is a useful concept for understanding consumers' detachment and alienation from the laws, policies and institutions that are – in theory – available to help them deal with their energy and justice problems. Relational distance is also helpful to our discussion of intermediaries and local actors, since they can potentially play a part in reducing relational distance and facilitating access to formal institutions. We now turn to consider our empirical data and analyse the way in which alienation and relational distance arise in the everyday experiences of consumers.

[21] Black, The Behaviour of Law (n 2).

III. Vulnerable and Energy-Poor Consumers, the Energy Market and Formal Institutions: Stories of Alienation and Disconnection

This section presents two themes in our data, namely: alienation and relational distance between consumers, the energy market and formal institutions; and an in-depth look at billing as a particular site of alienation in consumer experiences.

A. Alienation and Relational Distance in Our Data

i. Apathy, Cynicism and Disconnection

An interviewee from Bulgaria noted a situation where consumers were uninformed, lacked engagement and were discouraged by a system of energy supply and state oversight which they did not trust. The result of this was a sense of alienation, not only from institutions but from each other. Help and justice were potentially available, but not to the most vulnerable:

> Most people don't know their rights and have little enthusiasm to change things, they are discouraged, have low trust in the governments and institutions. This has led to more and more individualism, people trying to find solutions for themselves, not working as a community. People just don't know where to turn to: they can write letters to NGOs, ombudsman, or ministries, however usually the people who know their rights are the least vulnerable (Bulgarian Policy 2).

Bulgarian Policy 2 noted that the problem was not simply one of education. This point is important because many access to justice and energy market interventions assume that, with the right information, consumers will be able to participate better. In Bulgaria, however, the issue was described as one of widespread apathy, resulting from a lack of faith in state institutions and relational distance that is extensive; the state is remote and uncaring:

> The problem in Bulgaria is also not just knowing the rights, but quite widespread apathy and this giving up, thinking that nothing can be changed, that the state institutions cannot really be trusted, that they don't care about people (Bulgarian Policy 2).

The particular situation in Bulgaria (see chapter nine) is acute, but similar themes were raised in other jurisdictions. Catalan Policy 5, for example, commented on the lack of justice for vulnerable people that resulted from inherent unfairness in the energy market. Energy suppliers were powerful actors, and the law was a tool for them to enhance and abuse their positions of power rather than a tool for vulnerable consumers to secure their rights. While those rights existed in theory, energy companies had the means to use law, whereas most consumers did not:

> Oh, justice does really not protect the vulnerable. So, the real power of utilities are really high, and they have hundreds of lawyers to make things as they want … And about

> ombudsmen and these organisations … they're doing their best … but I'm not sure if it's very useful in practical terms (Catalan Policy 5).

State-provided justice mechanisms, as we saw in chapter five, were peripheral in addressing this fundamental imbalance. Catalan Third Sector 1 and 2 pointed to the systemic nature of these problems. Consumer problems can often be presented as aberrations, individual issues where things have gone wrong. The reality, however, is that the imbalance that was noted within the energy market reflects broader social conditions where injustice leads to alienation and disconnection. Consumers do not know their rights, nor do they have the ability to use them and, as a result, they are disempowered. Rather than helping, the justice system is part the establishment that excludes and renders consumers effectively 'illiterate' in justice terms:

> [W]hat our movement is fighting for is just empowerment of the population, because in the end it's just a thing of knowing which are your rights and then using them in order to have a dignifying life … in terms of access to justice and dispute resolution we are illiterate consumers in general. And the systems make us illiterate and we have to fight (Catalan Third Sector 1 and 2).

Alienating language and practices – alongside the idea that consumers and formal institutions exist in different worlds, speaking different languages – was an important theme in our data. UK Consumers 11–17 noted that bureaucratic systems, driven by call centre technology, meant that consumers end up frustrated and disempowered when trying to contact energy suppliers for help. The use of automated triage systems was a particularly dislocating experience, as they represented inflexible systems that did not respond to people's needs and the problems they faced:

> I want to interact with someone, and get something sorted out properly. Whereas, you're talking on a computer, the computer can't explain to you what's going on, it's just like, it's just basically like, what's your address, what are you phoning for (UK Consumers 11–17).

The vulnerable consumers we spoke to believed that energy suppliers literally spoke a different language from them. One issue related to local accents, which caused problems of communication as a result of some call centres being based abroad and because automated systems were unable to understand what consumers were saying:

> I think you'd find more challenges with an automated service, it sounds silly, but where your accent is stronger … Because it depends on, say, like the company's in London, and the person has done the recorded message, and then you try and do it from the northeast, and you say something, it's like, she'll say something completely different to what you've said, and then you go, no. And then she says … (UK Consumers 11–17).
>
> They'll [call centre staff] say something, and I'm like, no, and then I'll repeat it, and then they're like, oh, and I'm like, no. And then in the end, I say, look, I'm not sounding rude, but is there anyone there that speaks English, I say, because you're not understanding a single word I'm saying (UK Consumers 11–17).

We will return to the issue of language below as it was an important symbolic representation of the distance that existed between vulnerable consumers and formal institutions.

ii. High Relational Distance: The Different Worlds of Consumers and Formal Institutions

A community organiser in the UK (UK Third Sector 8) commented that at the root of many consumers' inability to secure help was a 'lack of humans'. The absence of a relationship with energy suppliers and other sources of help, and the bureaucratic approaches they adopted, meant that people were left isolated. Their circumstances were not understood, and they had no meaningful way of engaging with formal institutions:

> [I]t tends to be the lack of humans, [for] want of a better word ... We're having to refer into services that are stretched, because the majority of them cases is because of the lack of human interaction (UK Third Sector 8).

The lack of a human dimension and the non-existence of any kind of relationship between vulnerable consumers and sources of help outside their direct localities and communities was commented on by other interviewees. According to an NGO in Barcelona, the issues were often not technical, but were about finding ways to relate to people:

> It's not only a question of 'paying your bill', it's finding the way to talk, understand, engage with the people and then use social measures when needed ... the human dimension is missing (Catalan Third Sector 1 and 2).

The distant nature of the relationship between consumers and formal institutions was described as an issue of scale and a feature of modern bureaucratic societies. Lack of understanding and alienation arise as a result of the impersonality of bureaucratic institutions, their large size and remoteness from communities, with individuals just one of 'thousands of contracts'. Catalan Policy 1's comment showed that a high relational distance was perceived on both sides, with energy suppliers knowing nothing about consumers' situations and their experiences on the ground:

> [W]e, as electrical companies, we don't know nothing about them. We only have lists of thousands or millions ... millions of contracts ... we don't know who is behind [them] (Catalan Policy 1).

An interviewee from an energy company in Italy commented in similar terms that a lack of mutual understanding between energy suppliers and consumers was problematic and resulted from the fact that privacy rules prevented companies from knowing information that might then be used to assist people:

> [Energy company] can't get inside the homes of its clients, can't know how much the people earn, how much they spend for heating ... If a consumer doesn't make his way to [energy company], there's no way to know it (Italian Policy 4).

A further feature that created distance between consumers and formal institutions related to mechanisms for help that required proactive and knowledgeable action on the part of consumers. In France, the example of accessing energy-related state benefits – the Cheque Energie – was discussed by interviewees. While it is a potential source of help to make energy efficiency savings and, therefore, reduce energy costs, the design of the scheme effectively excluded many vulnerable people. For example, the scheme was promoted via direct mailings containing seven pages of information. As noted before, the most vulnerable consumers struggle to engage with any element of formality. Moreover, in many cases vulnerable consumers do not even read the information that is sent to them, simply not trusting that help is available to them or that any formal communication could contain good news:

> [A]n energy-poor household must understand what to do with the Chèque énergie … some people thought it was advertising (7 pages long) and some people don't open the mail because 'the mail only carries bad news' … The system is too difficult for a number of people (French Third Sector 1).

The assumption of policymakers that consumers are self-reliant and will be able to navigate complex legal and bureaucratic systems of support to help them resolve or alleviate their problems is often misguided. For consumers, the perceived costs of acting and having to engage with bureaucratic form-filling is off-putting. Even where help is potentially available, consumers remain apathetic and do not trust that the potential benefits of acting outweigh the costs of living with their situation and doing nothing. An interviewee from an energy company in Italy told us:

> There is no automatic mechanism for obtaining the bonus, the consumer has to be proactive and ask for it. The bonus is not tailored to the needs of the situation of the families … the limited beneficiaries of the bonuses may come from a fundamental disinformation about the way to ask for it, the costs of the process … The consumer perceives a certain cost of dealing with the bureaucracy, the involvement of the city, of filling forms. This is also linked to the uncertainty of getting the bonus (Italian Policy 4).

iii. An Insight into the Lives of Vulnerable and Energy-Poor Consumers

The world of rules, forms and of the expectation that people read their mail, was far removed from the daily reality of consumers in acute poverty and in particularly vulnerable circumstances. One of the consumers we interviewed in France described severe problems linked to his housing conditions, where even calling for help to deal with a fire was problematic due to the fact that he did not own a telephone:

> It was slippery, we've already fallen in front of the entrance … When there was a leak in the bathroom, it would leak everywhere. We were embarrassed. The washing machine was flooding us. We've had fires a few times, 30 years ago and more recently. We tried to put the cast iron stove up for sale, 1200 euros, but it won't go away. The fireplace caught fire one Christmas Eve. We wanted to call the fire department, but we didn't

> have a phone, the neighbour called. The walls were black from the smoke from the fires (French Consumer 1).

Also in France, a third-sector interviewee gave another example of the way in which alienation and high relational distance arose for consumers. For many, such alienation is a fact of life, even before thinking about resolving their problems or engaging with bureaucratic systems. Their living conditions are poor, and their social characteristics make them isolated from others. Old age was a particular example, where elderly people could become socially isolated and, as a result, not be able to gain the help from friends and family that is often an essential step in obtaining more formal sources of help and advice:

> People of a certain age isolate themselves. When you see the facades of some houses, you don't know what's going on inside. Even in rural areas or villages where there is certain solidarity, 'sometimes nobody cares any more' (French Third Sector 12).

A further example of the daily reality of vulnerable consumers' experiences and the gulf that could exist between them and professionals working to help to them was provided by UK Third Sector 3. She referred to the differences in perspective between herself, her organisational mandate and the multiple problems that people faced, which put them in 'really bad places'. Consumers would often have different priorities and a different sense of their needs when compared with what help could be provided for them: 'gas and electric might not be their priority although it's yours'. The result was that interventions could only scratch the surface and go so far in reaching individuals and their problems:

> I mean, it is difficult, because obviously some of the people that we go to see are in really bad places. A lot of them are unwell – a lot of them particularly have mental health issues – so we have to be very super aware of that. You can sort of go in with your focus, which is sorting out the gas and electric, but you've got to be very mindful that they've got other things going on in their lives. Gas and electric might not be their priority although it's yours, so sort of being sensitive to that. And then obviously, being aware that okay, you're never going to be able to solve usually a problem in one visit. Often it is going to need someone going to help, meters read, bills updated, payment plans in place. You know, if you're doing a tariff switch, are you going to need to help them read the meters in a couple of weeks? (UK Third Sector 3).

A community organiser in the UK (UK Third Sector 8) meanwhile reported the severe impact that austerity policies had on people in her community. She lived in an area that had high, multigenerational unemployment, a lack of local industries, high levels of crime and stretched and inadequate local services. She described things already being stretched prior to the implementation of various budget cuts. For many people, the resulting poverty was something they could not ultimately cope with, leading to a rise in suicide cases among local people:

> We see a range of, like, complex needs, there's a lot of it, a lot of it is harder, because of the poverty element, because a lot of people are accessing food banks, now, more than they've ever done before … I'd been supporting a young lass for 18 months … on the

> Friday, she'd came to the food bank to get a parcel from us, and we'd given her the food. I'd popped round to see if she needed anything else doing after that, she was quite well, she was doing well. The difficulty was that she couldn't see how well she was doing herself. Like, you could see the progress she was making, but it's difficult when you're in a situation where it's hard, and you can't see it yourself. So, I'd finished the food bank on Friday teatime and gone home, and then got a message on Saturday morning, that she'd killed herself (UK Third Sector 8).

The same interviewee gave another example of people in her community who were left adrift as a result of a lack of effective social services. She spoke about a young man with learning difficulties, living on his own, who was unable to cope with many routine aspects of life, but also would not contact services unless they put in the effort from their side:

> He can't ring anybody, like, if there's an issue … Because he can't contact people, and he doesn't know what he needs to sort out. We'd found out that some stuff had gone on, that shouldn't have gone on, and got him to speak to some people about it. But nobody's monitoring the situation with him … unless someone's breathing down his neck and saying, look, we need to do something for him, because he's struggling (UK Third Sector 8).

B. Billing: A Site of Alienation and High Relational Distance

Energy bills are not easy to understand, with 41 per cent of European consumers finding them hard to comprehend.[22] Bills, after the formation of contracts, are one of the crucial communications between consumers and energy suppliers and are the major point of reference through which consumers come to understand the energy market and any problems that they experience within it. Despite their content being regulated, they are the subject most complained about to energy suppliers and ombuds.[23] As a result, understanding how consumers perceive their energy bills and the information they contain is crucial to understanding how they react to energy problems and their propensity to seek justice where they arise. Bills are also important because we know that the energy sector is particularly subject to market-based vulnerability (see chapters one and three): that is, the complexity and technical nature of the market itself present challenges that mean that many more consumers are likely to be disadvantaged.

In an event organised by ASSIST[24] held in Rome on 23 January 2020 ('Energy rights – asking for a social bonus to fight energy poverty'), local vulnerable

[22] European Commission, *Consumer Study on 'Pre-contractual information and billing in the Energy market – Improved Clarity and Comparability'* (European Commission, 2018), available at: ec.europa.eu/info/sites/info/files/final_report_2_july_2018.pdf.

[23] See: www.which.co.uk/news/2020/02/energy-complaints-wouldve-hit-almost-6-9-million-in-the-last-year-did-your-gripe-go-unheard/.

[24] ASISIT is a project on energy poverty financed by EU funds (2017–20), and coordinated in Italy by AISFOR, available at: www.assist2gether.eu.

groups were invited to inform ASSIST about their energy problems. One of the issues highlighted at the event was that vulnerable consumers were often afraid of bureaucracy and computer illiterate. Online systems as well as understanding bills were huge hurdles. One of the participants said it was 'challenging to find the information about the [social] bonus on the invoice, so people don't know if they get it or not'. A further obstacle was that all invoice layouts are different, which made it tricky to compare suppliers. One of our interviewees also pointed out that energy bills in Italy were particularly complicated as they feature a range of other costs unrelated to energy: 'Energy bills have many costs not related to energy consumption (eg television tax, smart meters, and disarmament tax after WW2)' (Italian Policy 2).

Generally, vulnerable consumers lacked understanding of the complexities of the energy market and of energy as a product. As a result, they were unable to navigate the market, pay their bills, understand them, or know where to seek help. An energy company that we interviewed in Spain[25] stated:

> People don't understand the difference between the various tariffs offered in the regulated vs free market. This becomes problematic when people are not able to pay their bills (Catalan Policy 1).

Bills pose different challenges to different groups of vulnerable people. The following shows common examples of everyday challenges. As noted in chapter one, being over the age of 65 was one of the aspects of vulnerability most often identified in the energy sector.[26] Common problems the elderly face include understanding the transition to online billing, changing tariffs and a paperless world. Most energy companies have taken these measures to save money, to serve a liberalised and fast-changing market and to be seen to be more efficient.[27] However, this may not work for their vulnerable customers:

> I'm 70 years old, I'm a retired pensioner and I live in a studio flat which is very small. It's like I've got a bedsit with a separate kitchen and bathroom, and I don't have a TV, I don't have hardly anything that uses electricity. And I was completely … well, just overwhelmed by this bill. So … one of the problems I had was that they insisted that my account had to be managed online (UK Consumer 9).

Despite the bill including information about how to complain, UK Consumer EHU 9 was 'overwhelmed' by the bill and unable to relate it to her actual experience of consumption. This was then compounded by the energy supplier's online practices, which further excluded her from taking effective action to resolve the problem.

[25] See ch 10 on Catalonia in part II: there is a different type of complexity in countries that have a mixed model of public–private provision.

[26] European Commission, Second Consumer Market Study (n 5).

[27] S Ali, M Maroof and S Hanif, 'Smart Energy Meters for Energy Conservation and Minimizing Errors' (2010) Joint International Conference on Power Electronics, Drives and Energy Systems and 2010 Power India, New Delhi, 1.

Practical constraints may also leave consumers feeling unable to access the systems and help that is supposedly available to them. In the case of UK Consumer EHU 1, problems accessing her meter meant that she was not able to read it and was left uncertain in relation to her energy consumption and bills. Poor practice by the energy supplier left her feeling anxious, stressed, frightened and, ultimately desperate:

> I'm 80 years of age and I have an artificial knee; my meters are in a cupboard on the floor and I can't get in to look at it … for a year I got absolutely no indication and no statements or anything from them of what I owed or what I was using … And in desperation … I was getting a little bit frightened as well, because what I didn't want was one day a very large bill coming through my doorway with me not knowing why I had got a very large bill; so somebody suggested I got in touch with the CAB [Citizens Advice Bureau], and I did, and I told them the story, and I said, you know, at my age I don't need this amount of stress, this is just not fair, and I need the answers (UK Consumer 1).

One of our elderly interviewees in Catalonia reported that she was unable to understand what she owed and why she paid so much. She told us the bills were in a format she could not understand. She saw this as part of a system that was fundamentally unfair. She pointed out that companies made millions in profits from people who were very poor and failed to provide the information and customer service required to help people:

> Some companies use the vulnerability of people to get them to sign contracts. Companies don't provide information, and they are really poorly organised (Catalan Consumer 2).

As noted above, language was a key issue in relation to bills. Consumers 'don't know what is a kilowatt hour, they don't know how to understand their energy bills' (Catalan Third Sector 1 and 2). This reflected a wider problem with language used both by energy suppliers and other formal institutions. There was a lack of 'plain language' used by companies (Catalan Third Sector 1 and 2) and the whole system was seen as talking a different dialect from that of ordinary people: 'we speak French but we don't understand anything' (French Third Sector 3). UK Consumers 11–17 pointed out that understanding forms and formal communications was challenging, because organisations were

> using words that people can't understand, and [we are] basically having to get a dictionary out to understand what they're saying in a sentence, when they could have just explained it more simply (UK Consumers 11–17).

This was reflected in the complaint system too, where language could be alienating and frustrating even for professionals working in the field:

> I had to complain once and it was difficult for me … It's not logical … it's not easy … It shouldn't be so juridical or so legal in terms of language (Catalan Third Sector 1 and 2).

In the UK, a sign of the barriers which language could create between formal institutions and vulnerable consumers related to the word 'ombudsman', which some people could not say, let alone understand:

> What does the word ombudsman actually mean? A lot of people can't even say the word … It's an old, ancient way of working, but actually the ombudsman is there to help you (UK Ombuds 5).

C. Summary

The data above and presented in the book so far highlight the significant relational distance that exists between vulnerable energy consumers and various sources of help. Energy companies' practices, state benefits and ADR mechanisms all fail to reach the most vulnerable. Apathy, lack of trust and cynicism are features of a market that is unequal and of formal institutions perceived as remote and not aligned to people's interests. The law is a tool for the powerful and does not prevent poor practices by energy suppliers. Indeed, people are alienated in their everyday interactions with energy suppliers, through practices and communication which does not meet their needs. Vulnerable consumers inhabit a different world, where their problems are unrecognised and not catered for. Overall, there is a lack of mutual understanding between formal institutions and consumers. Bureaucratic practices – be that the 'sausage factory' approach of ADR, or the use of automated call centre triage by energy suppliers – are unable to interact meaningfully with vulnerable consumers. Instead, the latter are isolated and without a 'human' connection. Even where sources of help are available, consumers are afraid of bureaucracy and put off by even the most routine and basic bureaucratic demands (the giving of consent, form-filling, the submission of evidence in the form of paperwork). Online systems, or systems that require high levels of engagement, are beyond the reach of people facing multiple acute problems.

We have described these experiences in terms of legal alienation and high relational distance. Consumers are remote from formal institutions spatially, in terms of their relative status and power, and psychologically, in terms of the ways in which they perceive their problems. This high relational distance means that the interactions between consumers and formal institutions are heavily conditioned by law, in the absence of the possibility of a closer and more human dimension, but at the same time consumers are passive in using their rights and using the law to change their situations. They are subjects of law in the sense that their relationships in the market and the practices they are subject to are regulated. However, the law is not seen as in instrument which they can use as a means of bringing about change. Vulnerable consumers are often uninformed of their rights in the first place but are also sceptical of the apparent help available to them through formal institutions and do not believe the system is there for them. Many vulnerable consumers, therefore, can be characterised as cynics or outsiders. Laws and regulations that are meant to help them are ineffective, and consumers do not believe that engaging mechanisms such as ADR will be worth it. The ultimate outcome for many vulnerable consumers is passivity, apathy and alienation.

IV. Local Actors: More than Intermediaries

In beginning to address the problems highlighted above, we turn to one set of actors who have the potential to bridge the gap between vulnerable consumers and the means to secure access to justice: local actors such as NGOs, charities, volunteers, local hubs and community groups. These local actors, usually accessed at a point of crisis, are confronted with an array of issues that have caused, or contributed to, energy-related problems. Local actors are often part of a local community network that steps into action once mobilised. This mobilisation can occur through social workers, GP surgeries, word of mouth, charities and advice bodies. The value of local actors is that they form part of and are embedded in communities. As a result, sources of help and support arise in the mundane everyday encounters where people come together for informal exchanges.

> Well, I was in the hairdressers and my hairdresser is always up to date on all these things; she said, you've got to ring the CAB [Citizens Advice Bureau], they will help you; and that's how I got hold of them (UK Consumer 1).

The most vulnerable are in fact often found by local initiatives, rather than actively seeking solutions to their problems. For instance, neighbours, church workers, schoolteachers or friends are key sources of help. Local actors can assist in accessing help, support and advice through various channels and can assist individuals in developing agency and combating passivity and apathy. This has the potential to help people regain trust in the system and overcome the alienation and isolation that characterises their relationships with formal institutions.

We argue, therefore, that these actors can play a potentially significant role in addressing access to justice challenges. In part, this is because they can act as intermediaries, referring cases to appropriate authorities to deal with specific problems. Indeed, local actors are important in this respect because they understand the divergent worlds we have described above: they understand both the isolating and acute nature of vulnerability for people living alone, in poor housing, with poor health, and they also understand the world of the call centre, the online form, the lawyer and the bureaucrat. As such, local actors, close to the ground and the experiences of vulnerable people, are able to act as interpreters, working in two languages:

> They really know about vulnerable consumers … They speak both languages … They know about vulnerable consumers and they know about … energy companies (Catalan Policy 1).

Local actors are in a unique position, therefore, to bridge the relational distance between consumers, energy companies, ADR and the state. Local actors can help address lack of trust and alienation by translating complex concepts into a local and friendly language. Our interviews revealed that vulnerable people were more likely to search for, and trust, direct contact (through a social worker, charity, local church) rather than formal institutions, which are remote and are often seen as being the problem rather than the solution.

A limitation of local actors as intermediaries, is that they are often under-resourced and not well informed about how to make referrals to ADR or other sources of help. Indeed, seeing local actors purely as vehicles to make referrals into formal systems is restrictive. Instead, we suggest that local actors should be seen as a component of access to justice systems. Fitting with the approach described in chapter two, a more bottom-up, holistic and preventative attitude to access to justice would place more emphasis on either making sure problems do not arise or curing them at source. Many of the local actors we spoke to in the course of field-work expressed the view that formal institutions were too slow, too legalistic, too bureaucratic and too distant to help deal with the problems of vulnerable people. This view presents a challenge to the idea that local groups could fulfil a larger role as intermediaries, but at the same time shows the potential value of such groups in a system reoriented towards grass-roots justice. In a truly bottom-up system, the aim of access to justice would no longer be in thinking of ways to make sure that problems emerge as disputes and are appropriately steered towards formal institutions of justice. Instead, direct action at a local level could be the principal means through which justice is achieved in everyday life. In the rest of this chapter we present three examples from our case study jurisdictions which highlight the work of local actors and show their potential in delivering access to justice. As with the potential of ADR (explored in chapters four and five), such local action is not a *panacea*, but is a key element of the approach to enhancing access to justice we argue for in this book, with a focus on preventing and treating systemic injustice, on the practices and complaint handling of energy companies as a key site of access to justice, and on developing grass-roots, integrated and problem-solving approaches to people's difficulties.

A. Community Action in the North-East of England

In the North East of England, we spoke to a community organiser (UK Third Sector 8) and a group of vulnerable women, who met on a weekly basis in the local community centre. UK Third Sector 8 played a key role in helping people access different local services, as well as personally providing people with help. She, along with a network of local services, provided a safety net for vulnerable people who struggled to access services directly:

> So when you come into areas like [place], and you probably see it in parts of [place] as well, where people just don't know, or it's a fear of, like, places, to be forced into a Jobcentre, if you've not been into one, and expecting them to go in there and know how to navigate that environment. It's so different.

UK Third Sector 8 provided the type of help that might otherwise be given 'more easily, by neighbours, friends, or like, this type of setting'. She dealt every day with vulnerable people and 'groups of people [who] are already isolated, and [who] find the social element of sorting things out like that difficult'. UK Third Sector 8 was a lynchpin in the local community, finding people and referring them into various sources of help:

> [P]eople who come to me with, like, different issues, and I'm referring them into the right services, because I go to the network, and things, to make sure if anything's new, I know of it, and I work with the services to make sure I know what they need, and where to go. But the problem is, is they're so stretched, that they're not getting back in touch with these people.

UK Third Sector 8 stressed the importance of partnerships having been developed at a local level. This allowed for better links into local services and formal sources of help. It also worked the other way, in that social workers would now call UK Third Sector 8 in order to provide emergency help to some people:

> Today, I've got agencies ringing me, like, social workers, saying, I have a family that needs a bed. And a family that needs a bed, or a family that needs a washer, or a family that needs a fridge-freezer, or bedding, we haven't got the resources, can you help? … And then I'll take a list of what they need, and get them the items that they need, by putting a callout through the community.

One of the roles that UK Third Sector 8 fulfilled through her group was to inform formal organisations, such as local authorities, about the reality of people's lives and what was really going on at a local level. This was the reason why they agreed to participate in our research:

> We will meet anybody that will come in and listen to the stories, and the proper stories, rather than what people think they are. So, what happened was, the Council started listening, and we started creating partnerships with the agencies.

UK Third Sector 8, along with members of the community, was supporting people in acute need who would otherwise fall through the cracks. This involved everything from assistance when people ran out of money in their pre-payment meters, to helping people move house:

> I think we've moved, in the last, I'd say in the last 18 months, we've done 14 house moves, and they're kind of bigger families, and single people. So, we, me and [name] relocated a young man with learning disabilities, and complex support needs. Because the services are just not there for him, and he's living by himself, trying to manage everyday stuff, when he should really have a decent care package in place, but they just don't have the resources to do it.
>
> I'll give you an example of how bad it gets. Last winter, it was cold, and we had families sat in the dark, in the cold, because if you can't afford to put your gas on, your boiler goes off, too …. So that affects, obviously, your heating, your radiators, and things like that. So, we had a family, and it was seven, half seven at night, and they were sat in the dark, with no electric, and no gas. And then, we'd sorted them out, managed to get them

> some kind of temporary, like, lighting. You can get, you know the wind-up ones, where you wind them up and they do it themselves. And then we sorted out getting them food, and things like that.

UK Third Sector 8 acted as a key point of information and referral within the local community, working with a range of other local actors, and providing a personal link between the community and service providers:

> We'll go to, like, networking seminars, and different things, to find out what's there, and what's going on, if there's anything new that can support us to support people there … So, we're always kind of looking for what's available, and what's going on. And then obviously, through food bank, we do a lot of signposting, and a lot of kind of work on that end of it as well. So, they know they can start here. Someone in need, I'd say, like, somebody, kind of, back and forth things with, because some families are completely stand alone, they've got no aunties, uncles, grandmas, granddads, or anything. So, I'm Auntie [name] to all the kids around.

One of the distinguishing features of the help provided by UK Third Sector 8 was that there was no limit to her remit or, more precisely, she did not have a remit. This meant people could approach her with anything and would not be turned away and told they had come to the wrong place. Rather than being removed from the community, in an office or a call centre, she lived and worked among the people who needed help:

> There's no limit to it. There's only kind of one rule. If you can get to me, I'll help you. We don't refuse any help, anywhere … people know who I am, now, I live here, they see me about, I'm available every day.

B. Energy Advice and Intervention in Catalonia

We held an interview with a female participant who is 25 years old and lives with her husband, her mother, her two sisters and four children (between 3 and 11 years old) in Barcelona. She first approached a local energy advice service (the Service) when her energy company threatened to and then did cut off the electricity supply for three days. But with her mother depending on dialysis and four children at home, they could not cope with the pressure. They even received very aggressive calls and letters from the company's lawyers.

The first thing the agent of the Service did was to block any disconnection and then set up a payment plan to pay off the debts. This came as a huge relief for the family. They are still at risk regarding the increase in their rent (from €750 to €840 a month). But now, social services are helping them more than before. The Service gave information on how radiators work and how to save energy at home because theirs is very cold in the winter. The Service also helped them get a better contract. Having cheaper invoices make a huge difference: 'We can buy food for the kids and us.'

They discovered the Service through information in their mailbox and an advertisement on the street. However, information on getting access to rights and redress is missing. Schools have a part to play. For example, they can be more aware: teachers are always asking for money for books, lunches and excursions, for instance. The family's new social worker also assisted with tips on how to ask for support schemes for transportation. However, even though the mother is very sick, the family feel that the hospital does not care about her overall wellbeing. Doctors and nurses knew that the mother could not get her treatment if she had no access to electricity, but they only proposed to get her a manual dialysis machine.

C. Charity Work in the North of France

We now present data from an interview held with a 48-year-old male participant in the countryside of northern France (French Consumer 1).[28] We visited his home together with the founder of an innovative non-profit association (the Association) that helps energy-poor homeowners navigate the complex process of accessing services and service providers to carry out deep energy renovations.[29] Since his parents' deaths, French Consumer 1 has been living alone in the house that his family bought when he was 10 years old. Almost four decades later, not much has changed. The electricity wiring is dangerously old and, with few outlets, he relies on a network of power bars to connect appliances and equipment like a TV and clock radio.

While there is a wood-burning stove set into the original fireplace, he has been advised against using it because it produces dangerously high levels of carbon monoxide (CO). In fact, it is likely that only the combination of poor insulation and air leaks around doors and windows has saved him (and earlier the whole family) from CO poisoning. At present, French Consumer 1 relies solely on an electric heater, but to keep costs down, he turns it on only at night – and only in the room in which he sleeps. During the day, the indoor temperature hovers around 9°C. As the house does not have a hot water system, French Consumer 1 uses an electric induction stovetop plaque for both cooking and all hot water needs.

We learned from the volunteer assisting the participant that he has been struggling to get help to renovate his house to make it liveable. A passable exterior hides the reality of what it is like to live in. Leading up to 2016, the Mayor of the Commune visited several times and advised him of the need to carry out works. The man did not disagree but saw no way of going ahead with the project, given the gulf between the scope of work needed and his personal circumstances.

[28] ESRC Justenergy project website: esrcjustenergy.wordpress.com/blog/.

[29] The Association first helps people gain access to financial aid schemes offered by the French agency for housing (Agence nationale de l'habitat) and other public agencies, as well as private actors (mostly foundations) that provide other types of support, including personal assistance and financial aid. In turn, the Association acts as the coordinator of renovation projects, collaborating with a network of local suppliers ranging from builders and insulators to those with expertise on efficient heating systems, windows, lighting and appliances and equipment. The Association aims – to the greatest extent possible – to use environmentally friendly and bio-sourced materials. Beyond these technical aspects, collaborators are engaged from the financial community, volunteers, donors and local businesses who offer discounted or donated goods and services.

Once the Association evaluates a house and deems it likely to be eligible for various social assistance schemes, volunteers take on the critical role of guiding people like French Consumer 1 through the processes and paperwork that would otherwise be overwhelming – and almost certainly a barrier to their accessing help that is designed for their situations.

V. Conclusion

In this chapter, we conceptualised the relationship between vulnerable consumers, the energy market and the public authorities who oversee it as one of high relational distance and alienation. Vulnerable consumers are far removed from legal–bureaucratic processes and institutions. Vulnerable consumers inhabit a different world from these formal institutions and processes, and they speak a different language. Routine experiences in the energy market are alienating. Simply receiving a bill – a key interaction and one that is regulated by law – can be a cause of disempowerment, confusion and frustration. Billing shows in a microcosm the gulf that exists between vulnerable consumers and the market and its regulators. Rather than seeing the law and the existence of rights (such as the ability to complain to ADR) as a means of changing their situation, vulnerable consumers remain passive and isolated. They do not believe that the system is for them, they do not understand legal language and terminology, and they are afraid of bureaucracy. Any degree of formality and bureaucratic practice appears to be anathema to many vulnerable people. All of this implies a high degree of distrust in the state and the market and a lack of identification with law as a vehicle for protection and meaningful change. Law is more likely to be seen as peripheral to people's acute daily problems or as an instrument for the use of powerful companies rather than the vulnerable.

The reality of vulnerable and energy-poor consumers' experiences is central to deepening our understanding of access to justice barriers and challenges. Overcoming alienation and high relational distance represents a complex problem, with no single solution. Part of the answer, however, is likely to be around the involvement of local actors. We have outlined the important role they can play as intermediaries, bridging the gap between individuals and formal sources of help, as well as showing the direct action they can take on behalf of consumers to get problems resolved 'on the ground'. Thus, local actors should be seen not only as intermediaries, or referral agencies, but as bottom-up access to justice actors who can play a key role in delivering a more preventative, local and therapeutic system of access to justice. If we see access to justice as the resolution of problems at the earliest stage, rather than as the mechanism through which disputes reach formal justice institutions, then the crucial role of local actors becomes much clearer. To this end, we suggest that they could form part of a more holistic vision for access to justice.

7

Towards a More Holistic System of Access to Justice

I. Introduction

Part I of this book has brought together questions about access to justice, alternative dispute resolution (ADR) and vulnerable and energy-poor consumers. Our central concern has been to explore barriers to access to justice, how access to justice should be understood, and the role of ADR as an instrument for achieving access to justice. Our overall conclusion is that, despite ADR now being the dominant form of dispute resolution available to energy consumers, it fails to reach the most vulnerable and those most in need of justice. Rather, ADR is an 'elite' remedy that serves a narrow demographic and which is largely reactive to the needs of individuals with significant intellectual, financial and personal resources.[1] While ADR can make a difference for those who use it, this helps only the rare consumers who make it all the way to an ADR body. There are a number of barriers that stand in the way of using ADR, and many of the theoretical benefits of ADR have yet to break those barriers down. As a result, ADR does little to reach vulnerable and energy-poor consumers.

The first section of this chapter draws together the arguments developed in part I of the book with regard to problems and solutions in delivering access to justice for vulnerable and energy-poor consumers. The second section presents design options for a reformed system of access to justice, with a particular focus on the part that ADR can play in delivering a more holistic access to justice. The third and final part reflects on the limitations of this study and directions for future research.

II. Recapping the Argument of the Book

In the course of the preceding chapters, we have developed a comprehensive set of arguments about access to justice for vulnerable and energy-poor consumers.

[1] B Hubeau, 'The Profile of Complainants: How to Overcome the "Matthew Effect"?' in M Hertogh and R Kirkham (eds), *Research Handbook on the Ombudsman* (Edward Elgar, 2018).

Chapter one introduced the access to justice challenge, exploring the gap between the ideal and reality of access to justice. Meaningful access to justice is illusory for billions of people around the world. In the European energy sector, consumer detriment is high, and consumers are largely passive in their market engagement and in the pursuit of their rights. Vulnerable and energy-poor consumers face particularly acute barriers to accessing justice. Chapter one argued that many of the access to justice barriers facing people in general apply equally to the context of vulnerable and energy-poor consumers. These consumers face significant challenges at the naming, blaming and claiming phases of Felstiner et al's conceptualisation of the dispute emergence process. Structural social conditions (race, class, demographic characteristics, etc), cultural and social norms, individual cognitive processing and practical features of institutional design (such as the availability of advice or the complexity of procedures) add up to significant challenges across most civil justice contexts.

We argue, however, that access to justice for vulnerable and energy-poor consumers presents additional challenges. The nature of the liberalised energy market, for example, and its reliance on the existence of active consumers, creates problems for individuals and groups who are unable to engage fully with energy services or seek solutions when things go wrong. The low value, in relative terms, of many consumer problems represents a significant challenge and results in passivity and rational apathy. Not only are the direct costs of seeking resolution likely to be considered by consumers, but also the costs in terms of stress and time involved in pursuing disputes. Indeed, how consumers perceive conflict and complaining represents a barrier to access to justice. Legal consciousness research has shown that people have different understandings of the law, and that the images of the law they carry around in their heads shape their responses to their everyday problems. Many consumers are also socially, culturally and personally predisposed to avoid conflict-seeking and complaining behaviour. Drawing on our data, we argue that the lived reality of consumers' experiences powerfully illustrates the barriers that stand in the way of access to justice. At the same time, these experiences represent the key starting point for thinking about access to justice, how it should be defined and how it might be achieved.

In chapter two, we set out our proposal for a holistic vision of access to justice. The chapter claims that, despite early accounts of access to justice taking a broad view of the concept, there has been a reversion – driven partly by ideological preference and partly by pragmatism – towards narrow definitions of access to justice. Such narrow approaches to access to justice equate justice with the concept of 'legal justice', involving access to legal assistance in the form of legal advice and access to resolution in the form of legal institutions. We argue for a broader view, with non-legal advice provision, alternative forms of dispute resolution, internal complaint-handling arrangements within firms, and a broader range of social and community actors being recognised as important to the delivery of access to justice in practice. We also argue that an emphasis on narrow procedural justice is inadequate. Simply giving people theoretical access to procedural remedies is not sufficient to 'tick the box' of access to justice. Instead, consideration needs to be given to questions around the achievement of substantive justice. Having argued that narrow conceptions of legal justice are unhelpful, we argue that the achievement of social justice should be a goal of any system for accessing justice. Indeed, we argue that the relationship between access to justice and social justice is inextricable, existing both as a necessary precondition of access to justice and as the ultimate prize of an effective and accessible system of justice.

Overall, chapter two argues for a holistic vision of access to justice that involves recognition of: the (often non-legal) reality of people's everyday justice problems and the need, as a result, to take a broad view of the actors and institutions that might deliver access to justice; the importance of collective interests in relation to people's justice problems and the need to see access to justice as facilitating the achievement of social justice, remedying the substantive conditions that leave people vulnerable and energy poor; and, finally, the need for policy and institutional design processes to recognise, involve and engage those who are excluded from justice.

Chapter three considered the law and policy framework of the European Union (EU), with a particular emphasis on the extent to which it recognises and seeks to protect vulnerable and energy-poor consumers and the development of ADR as part of the possible solution to the access to justice challenge. We argue that EU law currently provides only limited protection of the needs and interests of vulnerable and energy-poor consumers. While there is a growing policy interest in providing additional protections, the energy market and its regulation remain dominated by understandings of consumers as active market participants. A lack of standardised definitions of consumer vulnerability and a failure to adopt the kind of modern, holistic definitions that often feature in academic discourses limit the extent to which vulnerability is useful as a tool to focus attention and direct resources. While there has been more recognition of vulnerability for energy consumers than consumers more generally, it is unclear that this has resulted in interventions that have significantly improved their situation. The position with regard to energy poverty is worse still, with very few countries adopting a definition of energy poverty to date. Thus, while there is increasing rhetorical recognition of the needs of vulnerable and energy-poor consumers, major stumbling blocks currently exist in terms of how the concepts should be defined and operationalised. And a particular missing link in EU policy debates so far has been in making connections between vulnerability and energy poverty agendas and access to justice agendas.

The development of ADR for energy consumer disputes, taking place in the context of a significant growth of ADR in civil justice systems generally, and consumer disputes specifically, has been presented in part as a measure addressing access to justice. The aim of providing mechanisms for the private enforcement of rights that avoid the formality, cost and complexity of courts has been one of the drivers behind the development of ADR. At the same time, however, cost-reduction has been an important motivation, with the obvious potential for conflict with the aim of bringing about greater access to justice. A key issue here is whether ADR is primarily a vehicle for transferring existing cases away from courts, or whether it is a mechanism that seeks to expand access to justice to new populations. Other drivers, including self-regulatory impulses by industry and the interest of regulators in dispute resolution as an aspect of market regulation, can be seen to have been prominent in the context of consumer disputing. The relationship between ADR and access to justice is therefore complicated. Also complicated are the arrangements for the delivery of ADR that exist in practice across the EU. ADR mechanisms include a bewildering mix of ombuds, regulators, conciliators, arbitrators, adjudicators and complaint boards, and include a mix of statutory and non-statutory designs.

Chapter four considered the problems and potential associated with ADR as an access to justice measure, noting that it has been described as a 'frenemy' of access to justice. Given the scale of the challenges outlined in chapter one, we argue that a sanguine approach to the potential for ADR to provide access to justice needs to be adopted. The claims made for ADR (similarly to the counter-claims made for courts) are often hyperbolic and ideologically driven. The reality is that ADR, even before considering how it operates empirically, is not currently designed to overcome the barriers to dispute emergence that occur at each of the naming, blaming and claiming stages. The starting point for considering the contribution of ADR to access to justice has to be one of realism, which resists the overly enthusiastic accounts presented in some policy and scholarly narratives. Chapter four considered two sets of arguments in the literature on access to justice and ADR. One set of arguments questions the effectiveness of ADR and its ability, inter alia, to reduce costs, simplify processes for parties and lead to the kind of more flexible and creative conclusions that are assumed to form part of ADR. The other set of arguments revolves around ADR and settlement, and the extent to which ADR provides access to substantive justice. Overall, we argue that ADR can contribute to access to justice, including in its substantive dimension and can perhaps do so more effectively than courts, as a result of its ability to look beyond legal justice. This is not an empirical argument – it remains unclear to what extent any mechanism of dispute resolution (including courts) provides substantive justice in practice. However, we argue that a well-designed system of ADR should be able to deliver substantive justice goals.

Chapter five returned to our empirical data and examined the extent to which ADR currently provides access to justice for vulnerable and energy-poor consumers. Our findings confirm the results of previous studies and existing data that suggest that ADR has a limited reach in relation to delivering access to justice beyond a white, middle-class, male, and wealthy demographic of users. We found that consumers faced a range of barriers to accessing justice in the energy sector, including lack of awareness of rights and ADR; the poor practices of energy suppliers, regulatory and technological barriers, and psychological barriers. In terms of the role that ADR is expected to play, we found that consumers often wanted something different from ADR than what it actually provided: they wanted someone to believe them and fight their case for them rather than an impartial adjudicator. ADR providers themselves were uncertain about the limits of their role, particularly in terms of providing the kind of extra support that vulnerable and energy-poor consumers might need and in being able to address fundamental, substantive issues in relation to consumers' problems. Important themes in terms of the effectiveness of ADR included a need to work in partnership and in a more systemic way, with closer relationships particularly required with the third sector and energy suppliers.

Finally, chapter six returned to the barriers facing vulnerable and energy-poor consumers and introduced two important frameworks to help conceptualise the access to justice problem: legal alienation and relational distance. Legal alienation provides an important framework for understanding situations where people have limited understanding of their rights and limited identification with the laws and state-provided systems to assist in realising them. Relational distance meanwhile was posited as a way of describing the large gap that exists between the lived experiences of vulnerable and energy-poor consumers and the world inhabited by lawyers, bureaucrats, regulators and ADR bodies. Together, a lack of mutual understanding and identification between consumers, energy suppliers and the institutions that regulate the market are argued to represent an important barrier to accessing justice. Our data show how apathy, cynicism and alienation arise in consumer experiences. A lack of trust in public institutions, a general passivity in response to unfair systems, a perception that the law supports the interests of the powerful, all contribute to alienation. Rather than assisting consumers, formal protections are seen as part of a system rendering people 'illiterate' through complexity and a lack of meaningful access. Communications between consumers and formal institutions are a particular site of alienation, with consumers and market actors effectively speaking different languages. The sense that vulnerable and energy-poor consumers inhabit a different world from that occupied by the actors who are part of the legal framework to assist them is reflected strongly in the data. The relationship between consumers, energy suppliers and justice/regulatory bodies is a distant one, which often fails to provide a human touch and recognise people's individual circumstances. There is little understanding of, and insight into, the often acute and desperate situations that people find themselves in. Billing provides a particularly useful illustration of the problems facing energy consumers and their relationship to the energy market and the laws that regulate it.

Chapter six argues that one of the ways in which alienation and relational distance might be overcome is through the intervention of local actors such as NGOs, charities, volunteers, local hubs and community groups. These actors are able to provide a bridge between formal institutions and vulnerable and energy-poor consumers. They face both ways and are able to speak the language of each party and interpret for them. As such they can potentially play a key role in mitigating feelings of legal alienation and reducing the relational distance between consumers and market actors. At the same time, however, the limited resources of many of these actors and the stretched nature of third-sector, charity and community services mean that the extent to which they can assist in delivering access to justice is currently limited. Our data reveal the potential for this role to be developed in future, but also show that local groups should be seen as more than intermediaries when it comes to access to justice. Indeed, our holistic vision of access to justice is based less on the idea of maximising the number of problems that are transmitted through to ADR systems for resolution, and as much on the idea of avoiding problems arising in the first place and dealing with them as close as possible to the point at which they arise. Here, our data show the important problem-solving work carried out by local actors, who are able to deal with people's problems holistically and provide the kind of immediate support and help they need.

III. Dispute System Design and the Delivery of Holistic Access to Justice

ADR may or may not enhance access to justice, and much depends on the particular form of ADR that is deployed and the motivations behind that deployment.[2] If access to justice is a principal driver and sufficient attention is paid to principles of good Dispute System Design (DSD), then our view is that ADR has significant potential to improve access to justice. DSD is a field of enquiry that involves two aspects: it examines the processes through which dispute systems are designed and evaluated; and it examines the substantive principles and design options available to those designing systems for resolving disputes.[3] DSD has mainly been developed by North American scholars, writing in the context of organisational dispute resolution. However, there has been recent interest in applying these ideas in the context of European consumer disputing.[4] Indeed, much of the literature on consumer ADR is inherently concerned with design issues, considering both the operation of current systems and making recommendations for improvements.[5] Gill et al's[6] DSD model for consumer disputes stresses the importance of access to justice in the goal-setting phase of designing dispute resolution schemes, with decisions made about the goals of the scheme (and trade-offs between goals) influencing a range of design choices around organisational systems and processes. As part of the model's first-order system design choices, accessibility is one of five key

[2] A Nylund, 'Access to Justice: Is ADR a Help or Hindrance?' in L Ervo and A Nylund (eds), *The Future of Civil Litigation: Access to Courts and Court-annexed Mediation in the Nordic Countries* (Springer, 2014) 327.

[3] C Gill, J Williams, C Brennan and C Hirst, 'Designing Consumer Redress: A Dispute System Design (DSD) Model for Consumer-to-Business Disputes' (2016) 36 *Legal Studies* 438.

[4] ibid; P Cortes, The Law of Consumer Redress in an Evolving Digital Market: *Upgrading from Alternative to Online Dispute Resolution* (CUP, 2017).

[5] C Hodges, I Benöhr and N Creutzfeldt-Banda, *Consumer ADR in Europe* (Hart Publishing, 2012); P Cortes (ed), *The New Regulatory Framework for Consumer Dispute Resolution* (OUP, 2016).

[6] Gill, Williams, Brennan and Hurst (n 3).

areas that are highlighted for attention by designers. Gill et al argue that the key design choice in relation to accessibility is the degree to which an ADR scheme is proactive in reaching out to groups that would not ordinarily use ADR and how far those who do complain are supported with help and advice to make their complaints.[7]

A. A Developing Consensus Around the Ombuds Model

While literature on consumer ADR remains divided between its proponents and its detractors, among those who accept the potential value of ADR in the consumer context, a strong consensus has developed around the leading form of ADR. Indeed, the ombuds institution, and its potential to deliver added-value features, is strongly endorsed by academic commentators.[8] As we have seen in chapter four, the ability both to provide advisory functions to consumers and feedback to industry and regulators are seen as key value-adding features, which go beyond more basic models of ADR that focus only on dispute resolution. Hodges has probably been the leading proponent of the ombuds model:

> [A] strong case can be made that the consumer ombuds model is the more advanced form [of consumer ADR], as it offers a number of advantages, notably the ability to offer advise and assistance to consumers, to aggregate individual claims (collective redress), to aggregate data on case types and incidence, and to provide feedback that drives behaviour change.[9]

From an access to justice perspective, we support the emerging consensus around the added value of the ombuds model and its superiority in most consumer-disputing contexts. Particularly in the energy sector, given its status as a service of general concern and the important consumer interests involved (as well as the public stake in the energy supply), the ombud's more developed features are required. The advisory function has the potential to help vulnerable consumers who lack knowledge of their entitlements about how to go about securing them, while the feedback function potentially helps to inform regulators and ensures that industries raise their standards, leading to fewer injustices arising in the first place.

If the ombuds is accepted as the leading model for ADR from the perspective of access to justice, it is problematic that the model is very much in a minority

[7] ibid.

[8] Cortes, *The Law of Consumer Redress* (n 4); C Hodges, 'Consumer Redress: Implementing the Vision' in P Cortes (ed), *The New Regulatory Framework for Consumer Dispute Resolution* (OUP, 2016); N Creutzfeldt, *ADR in the Energy Sector in Europe* (National Energy Ombudsmen Network, 2015), available at: www.neon-ombudsman.org/2015/03/12/independent-ombudsmen-and-adr-providers-building-bridges-in-the-energy-market/; C Gill and C Hirst, *Defining Consumer Ombudsman* (Ombudsman Services, 2016).

[9] C Hodges, 'The Private Sector Ombudsman' in M Hertogh and R Kirkham (eds), *Research Handbook on the Ombudsman* (Edward Elgar, 2018).

and that complaint handling by regulators is the dominant approach to ADR in the energy sector.[10] As Hodges et al[11] have pointed out, issues around perceived independence may arise where regulators carry out this function. Creutzfeldt has argued that, while complaint handling by regulatory authorities may be seen as sufficiently independent in some jurisdictions, there are examples where this has not worked well.[12] One of these is in Germany, where, prior to the creation of a bespoke energy ADR body, complaints were dealt with by the regulator. A lack of focus on complaint handling and a narrow approach to eligibility of complaints led to high levels of dissatisfaction. Another issue with regulators performing complaint-handling roles is that this reduces the potential for checks and balances within the system. An advantage of independent ADR – particularly if provided on a statutory basis by a public body – is that it can potentially identify problems that stem from regulatory failures or regulatory inaction. In most settings, ADR is in a subservient position to regulators and seen as a tool or policy instrument of market regulation. This is problematic given the potential for regulatory capture of regulators by industry. Indeed, while many commentators argue that ADR should be embedded within regulatory systems to ensure efficient feedback and cooperation, we argue that a greater degree of independence for the ADR body would allow for a more powerful approach.

While we support the development of a fully independent ombuds, the notion that the ombuds' added-value functions provide value in practice and enhance access to justice has yet to be proved empirically. As Creutzfeldt has pointed out, a major theme in the literature on consumer ADR is that theoretical claims are yet to be supported by a clear evidence base.[13] In relation to the potential for standard-raising activity, Gill has suggested – albeit in relation to the public sector – that a cautious approach should be taken to claims that ombuds can play a significant role in helping those they oversee to learn from complaints and improve services.[14] In the specific context of energy disputes in the UK, some concerns have been raised about the limited and narrow focus adopted by the energy ombuds, which was found to be focusing only on its core case-handling role.[15] Cortes meanwhile has noted that 'ADR entities' role in sharing intelligence is far below its full potential in many economic sectors'.[16] There is also a great deal of variety both in how

[10] Kirkham has noted that ombuds feature principally in Belgium, the UK Ireland, France, Germany and Malta: RM Kirkham, 'Regulating ADR: Lessons from the UK' in P Cortes (ed), *The New Regulatory Framework for Consumer Dispute Resolution* (OUP, 2016). In the energy sector meanwhile, Creutzfeldt, *ADR in the Energy Sector in Europe* (n 8), found a similar situation.

[11] Hodges, Benöhr and Creutzfeldt-Banda (n 5).

[12] Creutzfeldt, *ADR in the Energy Sector in Europe* (n 8).

[13] N Creutzfeldt, 'Ombudsman Schemes' in P Cortes (ed), *The Transformation of Consumer Dispute Resolution in the European Union: A Renewed Approach to Consumer Protection* (OUP, 2016).

[14] C Gill, 'What Can Government Learn from the Ombudsman?' in M Hertogh and R Kirkham (eds), *Research Handbook on the Ombudsman Research* (Edward Elgar, 2018).

[15] Lucerna Partners, *Review of Ombudsman Services: Energy* (Ofgem, 2015), available at: www.ofgem.gov.uk/sites/default/files/docs/2015/09/review_of_ombudsman_services_energy_2.pdf.

[16] Cortes, *The Law of Consumer Redress* (n 4) 269.

individual ombuds operate and in the range of ADR mechanisms available in the consumer context, so that not all ADR provides value-adding features, nor is there equal consistency and quality across the board.[17] The data presented in chapters five and six suggest that access to justice remains limited, even in those jurisdictions that feature the ombuds model: the model is preferred, therefore, but is not a panacea. We need to go further.

Thus, we argue that there is a need not only to converge towards the ombuds model as the form of dispute resolution best suited to the resolution of energy disputes, but to reimagine the ombud's role and powers in order to deliver access to justice. The data presented in chapters five and six show key ways in which current approaches could be enhanced: the provision of greater support; the personalisation of services to cater for diverse users and potential users; the development of a more systemic and vocal role in relation to raising standards and redressing injustice; the greater use of partnerships and potential for the provision of more integrated and holistic services; and the focus on complaint handling by energy suppliers as a major site of access to justice for energy consumers. The access to justice challenge, therefore, requires more in our view than the adoption of the ombuds model. That model, despite its potential, has largely failed to date to move beyond being 'a middle-class remedy for middle class people'. What we need, therefore, is to consider design options for an ombuds that has access to justice at the heart of its mission and, moreover, that seeks to deliver the more powerful and holistic vision that we set out in chapter two. Not only must the ombuds provide a procedural remedy and a basic standard of legal justice, but the ombuds must raise its ambitions and seek to deliver collective justice and contribute to redressing the systemic injustices that characterise the energy sector. Fulfilling that more powerful substantive vision of access to justice requires the design of a more powerful ombuds model.

B. Towards a More Inclusive, Preventative and Therapeutic Access to Justice

A particularly valuable feature of the ombuds model, and of the design proposals we make below, is that it has the potential to provide a combination of top-down and bottom-up solutions to access to justice.[18] Top-down approaches focus on the design of institutions provided for the remedy of grievances and reducing

[17] C Gill, N Creutzfeldt and J Williams et al, *Confusion, Gaps, and Overlaps: A Consumer Perspective on Alternative Dispute Resolution between Consumers and Businesses* (QMUL, University of Westminster, Citizens Advice, 2017), available at: www.citizensadvice.org.uk/Global/CitizensAdvice/Consumer%20publications/Confusiongapsandoverlaps-Original1.docx.pdf.

[18] C Albiston and R Sandefur, 'Expanding the Empirical Study of Access to Justice' [2013] *Wisconsin Law Review* 101, 119.

procedural barriers to access these; bottom-up approaches are more concerned with reducing the barriers that people experience on the ground and that have less to do with the design of institutions and more to do with social inequality, and cognitive and cultural barriers. Potentially, a reimagined ombuds model could tackle both sets of barriers – enhancing processes to provide as much direct access to the institution as possible, while taking broader systemic action (both to educate consumers and improve standards) so that problems either do not arise in the first place or are more likely to be resolved quickly if they do. Sanderfur's[19] suggestion that access to justice requires inclusive institutional design, therefore, fits well with our holistic vision of access to justice and the proposals we make below with regard to an expanded ombuds model. In looking at the ombuds model, we need to move beyond recognition of its potential 'added-value' features and towards a more powerful notion of 'inclusive design'. Indeed, the creation of a more 'inclusive access to justice' has recently been recommended by Riefa and Saintier as essential to ensure access to justice for vulnerable consumers.[20]

In setting out our approach below, we are influenced by literature on therapeutic jurisprudence[21] and preventative law.[22] Creating a more therapeutic access to justice system might involve dealing with people's problems holistically; responding to people's expectations as legitimate demands for justice in an unfair marketplace; and recognising vulnerability, difference and diversity. Current systems take insufficiently seriously the idea of 'recognition justice',[23] a key part of the energy justice framework, and fail to cater appropriately for those who are denied justice, both procedural and substantive, within energy markets. A more therapeutic system here is one that seeks to address this and shift its focus to address the needs of the most vulnerable and excluded individuals and groups. At present, and despite a growing recognition of the needs of vulnerable and energy-poor consumers, the policy focus is on those most able to make use of the market and realise their rights. Preventative law approaches meanwhile chime with proposals for ADR to shift towards systemic and collective approaches to delivering justice. Hodges[24] has recently argued for the whole civil and administrative justice systems to be redesigned to incorporate preventative principles and ensure that dispute resolution systems not only resolve disputes, but also contribute to helping people resolve

[19] RL Sandefur, 'Fulcrum Point of Equal Access to Justice: Legal and Nonlegal Institutions of Remedy' (2009) 42 *Loyola of Los Angeles Law Review* 949.

[20] C Riefa and S Saintier (eds), *Vulnerable Consumers and the Law: Consumer Protection and Access to Justice* (Routledge, 2020).

[21] D Wexler and B Winick, *Essays in Therapeutic Jurisprudence* (Carolina Academic Press, 1991).

[22] AK Schneider, 'The Intersection of Therapeutic Jurisprudence, Preventive Law, and Alternative Dispute Resolution' (1999) 5 *Psychology, Public Policy, and Law* 1084.

[23] K Jenkins, D McCauley and R Heffron et al, 'Energy Justice: A Conceptual Review' (2016) 11 *Energy Research & Social Science* 174.

[24] C Hodges, *Delivering Dispute Resolution: A Holistic Review of Models in England and Wales* (Hart Publishing, 2019).

their own problems and minimise the sources of conflict that lead to disputes in the first place:

> It is not enough for a State to ensure that the disputes that arise are justly and fairly resolved. It is important to use the information gathered to reduce the incidence of similar problems and the risk of future problems. Users have related to a number of agencies that they want the system to change and improve.[25]

A similar approach has recently been suggested by Cohen and Alberstein[26] who offer a preventative law model for dispute system design, albeit one that is focused on disputes that take place in the shadow of courts. Their approach draws inspiration from the field of public health and suggests that a focus on dispute resolution institutions as sites of access to justice is unhelpful, and that, instead, a whole systems approach is needed that seeks to either avoid conflicts arising or to deal with them effectively at source:

> Our access to justice conflict resolution perspective transcends the focus on the individual dispute and the focus on the past, in favor of a social perspective on the nature of disputes and a focus on primary prevention. It is a comprehensive approach, which presents law as focusing on primary prevention through relationship building, and on altering the social conditions that produce legal conflicts while digging deep into their source. Such a public health approach to law can be elaborated through the use of DSD methodologies.[27]

Our proposals, therefore, call for more therapeutic, preventative and inclusive approaches to access to justice.

C. Consumer Participation in the Design of Access to Justice Policies and Institutions

In keeping with the 'all-affected principle' and the energy justice framework's focus on the participation of affected individuals in policymaking processes (see chapter two), an important aspect of reforming current approaches is to involve vulnerable and energy-poor consumers in policymaking. There are very significant challenges in doing this, particularly given the general passivity we have noted as a feature of consumer behaviour in the energy market and the limited propensity for consumers to pursue their rights. Offering greater opportunities for participation,

[25] C Hodges, 'Delivering Dispute Resolution: Recent Review on the Resolution of Disputes in England and Wales' (Foundation for Law, Justice and Society Policy Brief, 2019) 11.

[26] H Cohen and M Alberstein, 'Multilevel Access to Justice in a World of Vanishing Trials: A Conflict Resolution Perspective' (2019) 47 *Fordham Urban Law Journal* 1.

[27] ibid 40.

however, could lead to the design of more consumer-focused policies, processes and institutions, which in turn could help ensure that these mechanisms are triggered by consumers when they have a problem.

IV. From Added Value to Inclusive Design: Overview of Design Options

Table 7.1 presents an overview of options for designing ADR. In presenting the options, we have conceptualised access to justice as a problem which involves supply and demand.[28] We argue that there are three broad sets of approaches. The first involves making changes that would improve the supply of ADR – making the service more attractive to potential and current users by enhancing the 'offer' of the ADR service. The second involves measures that seek to increase the demand for ADR services directly – aiming to increase the numbers of individuals accessing the ADR service in the first place through outreach, education and partnership working. The third, counterintuitively, involves measures that seek to reduce demand for ADR – aiming instead to deal with problems at a collective level or working in partnership with others to ensure problems do not escalate to the ADR body.

These options are not mutually exclusive, albeit limited resources and the need to prioritise mean that some options may be preferred over others. It is also important to note that some of the options are uncontroversial and already form part of the approaches of some ADR bodies. In presenting these broad design options we have sought to suggest how access to justice can be mainstreamed as a priority for ADR in the energy sector and how it might be transformed as part of a more holistic approach to access to justice. As noted above, other values and goals also need to be balanced with that goal. Brennan et al note that the extent to which access to justice can be prioritised as a goal of an ADR system is hemmed in by contextual factors and the existence of other potentially conflicting goals.[29] It is also important to note that not all options will be as applicable, depending on jurisdictions. However, the overall approach we propose should be of value in thinking about ADR design across a range of contexts. While our predominant focus is on ADR, the suggestions we make also refer to the roles of other actors, such as the local actors we discussed in chapter six, and other important stakeholders in the regulatory landscape (see chapter three).

[28] Albiston and Sandefur (n 18).

[29] C Brennan, T Sourdin and J Williams et al, 'Consumer Vulnerability and Complaint Handling: Challenges, Opportunities and Dispute System Design' (2017) 41 *International Journal of Consumer Studies* 638.

Table 7.1 Overview of design options

Reform option	Possible reform measures	Reform rationale/ assumption	Limitations
Improve the supply of ADR	Identify consumers' needs and provide service adaptations Increase the provision of advice and support by the ADR body	The simpler and more responsive the ADR mechanism, the more people will use it and the better it will be able to respond to diverse needs. Main emphasis on reducing 'claiming' related access to justice barriers. Top down assumption that the design of procedural remedies is key to access to justice	Does not address the 'naming' and 'blaming' barriers to access to justice. Requires people to know about and access ADR in the first place. A focus only on this aspect may benefit existing, over-represented groups at the expense of the excluded
Increase demand for ADR	Increase consumer outreach and education programmes provided by ADR bodies Work with stakeholders to increase complaint referrals	The more people are aware of their rights, the more they will complain. Increasing the number of people using ADR will automatically enhance access to justice. Given the distance between ADR and vulnerable individuals, working with intermediaries is likely to be key	Only partly deals with 'naming' and 'blaming' barriers: no outreach programme can overcome the social inequalities or individual level cognitive barriers that limit complaining behaviour. Does not deal with the limited powers and role of the ADR body to bring about just outcomes. Reliance on intermediaries requires a well-funded/ better informed third sector

(continued)

Table 7.1 ***(Continued)***

Reform option	**Possible reform measures**	**Reform rationale/ assumption**	**Limitations**
Decrease demand for ADR	Work with other service providers to provide 'holistic' response Develop an advocacy role Work with businesses 'down-stream' Shift emphasis from individual to collective redress	Increasing access to ADR, beyond a certain point, is inefficient and reduces access to justice. Naming, blaming and claiming barriers are, effectively, insurmountable. Access to justice is realised by addressing problems at source and reducing demand for dispute resolution. Access to justice in the context of high levels of detriment and an unequal marketplace involves placing more emphasis on substantive justice	Involves ADR mechanisms taking on the roles of other consumer protection stakeholders, eg, consumer agencies, regulators, competition authorities. Politicises ADR mechanisms. Overly paternalistic approach to consumers and militates against consumer participation and engagement (and, potentially, against market efficiency)

A. Option 1: Improve the 'Supply' of ADR

This option involves developing the procedures used by ADR bodies to provide greater flexibility and greater sensitivity to diverse and vulnerable consumers' needs. This would require knowing more about the circumstances of consumers, both those who are currently using ADR and those who are currently not using it. It would also require the adoption of clear definitions of consumer vulnerability and energy poverty, which can be operationalised and used to target effort and resources. In terms of making such consumers central to ADR processes, inspiration could be drawn from human-centred design approaches, which take people's needs and experiences as the starting point for institutional design.[30] More flexible,

[30] C Gill, 'Re-imagining Public Sector Complaint Systems' (2018), available at: ukaji.org/2018/10/03/re-imagining-public-sector-complaint-systems/.

more inclusive and less legalistic and bureaucratic processes have the potential to be more attractive to a broader range of users who might currently feel that seeking third-party help is not for them. Brennan et al, in considering how complaint processes could be designed to meet the needs of vulnerable consumers, argue that important features include ADR bodies having as broad a jurisdiction as possible, the use of inquisitorial techniques that remove the burden on consumers, and the involvement of vulnerable people in ADR scheme design.[31] Creutzfeldt notes that the ombuds model offers consumers 'a level of representation during the dispute resolution process' and that 'consumers like to participate in processes where the third party neutral shows greater "empathy" and helps the consumer to bring the claim forward through an inquisitorial process'.[32] Such approaches could be mainstreamed and extended.

Not only could the process of dispute resolution be enhanced, but the resources devoted to providing advice and support could be increased. While chapter five suggested that there are limits to how far ADR bodies can provide support to one of the parties, in the context of the structural power imbalance characteristics of the energy sector, pure impartiality may need to give way to a model that prioritises the interests of the structurally disadvantaged party. The role of the ADR body should be to look at things from the perspective of the consumer and, where there is any discretion, the benefit of the doubt should be in their favour. In relation to advice, this should not simply entail a signposting service. Advice could also include tips for making effective use of complaints procedures, and substantive advice in relation to the issues in any given case. These proposals take seriously the idea that, rather than 'managing' consumer expectations,[33] ADR bodies could do more to meet them. Strict impartiality in the context of fundamentally unequal social and energy market relations is, in effect, a means of preserving the status quo.

While an expanded advisory function, a more supportive and consumer-oriented role and a more personalised approach to vulnerability are likely to benefit people who reach energy ADR bodies, these measures do little to target the 'naming' and 'blaming' barriers to dispute emergence. Providing an inclusive service, which is seen as effective and meeting the needs of all consumers, is likely to have some impact on encouraging people to use the service, but most people will remain ignorant of ADR regardless of how well it is seen to operate. While inclusive processes are important, therefore, other options need to be considered. Indeed, a focus only on the design of dispute resolution processes has been criticised as

[31] Brennan, Sourdin and Williams et al (n 29).

[32] Creutzfeldt, 'Ombudsman Schemes' (n 13).

[33] S Gilad, 'Accountability or Expectations Management? The Role of the Ombudsman in Financial Regulation' (2008) 30 *Law & Policy* 227; N Creutzfeldt, *Ombudsmen and ADR: A Comparative Study of Informal Justice in Europe* (Palgrave Macmillan 2018).

being reductive and failing to address the multiple barriers that lie in the way of people accessing justice.[34]

B. Option 2: Increase the 'Demand' for ADR

This option involves seeking to stimulate demand for ADR among vulnerable and energy-poor consumers. This might involve direct outreach and education interventions (such as advertising, roadshows, the production of leaflets etc) as well as seeking to work more closely with intermediaries. Despite the low public profile of ADR, attempts at raising awareness have been relatively limited. Many ADR schemes have been reluctant to take proactive measures to increase complaint numbers in order to avoid accusations of ambulance chasing and empire building. Promotion could also lead to surges in demand that would present significant operational challenges for ADR bodies. The effect has been that ADR bodies tend not to be well known, and this position has been largely accepted rather than considered a priority for change. Indeed, the relatively low usage of ADR and the narrow demographic of users does not seem to have been at the forefront of ADR bodies' concerns. As we have seen, usage of ADR in the energy sector is low.

Given the difficulty of reaching vulnerable consumers and of raising awareness, working with intermediaries is an important additional approach. Brennan et al emphasise the key role of intermediaries in consumer disputing and recommend that ADR should develop closer links to third-sector organisations.[35] Intermediaries are in a critical position, speaking the language of vulnerable consumers, on the one hand, and the ADR body, on the other. An issue here, however, is that intermediaries often have a number of acute priorities and may be more focused on emergency responses than on pursuing complaints that inevitably produce results over a longer timescale. They may also simply not have the resources to inform themselves and consumers about the options relating to ADR and how to use it. And where there are questions about the effectiveness of the ADR service and whether their processes are designed to cater for more diverse groups, intermediaries may not perceive ADR as a meaningful route to solutions for people.[36] As Ojelabi points out, 'referral fatigue' is a barrier to accessing justice and, as a result, a reliance on third-party referrals to ADR may not be ideal.[37] Vulnerable people, especially where their lives make keeping paperwork and appointments difficult, need to be offered solutions as close as possible to the point at which they seek help. Working more closely with intermediaries is likely to be

[34] M Palmer, 'Formalisation of Alternative Dispute Resolution Processes: Some Socio-legal Thoughts' in J Zekoll, M Bälz and I Amelung (eds), *Formalisation and Flexibilisation in Dispute Resolution* (Brill Nijhoff, 2014).

[35] Brennan, Sourdin and Williams et al (n 29).

[36] L Ojelabi, 'Community Legal Centres' Views on ADR as a Means of Accessing Justice' (2011) 22 *Australasian Journal of Dispute Resolution* 103.

[37] ibid.

key, therefore, but also requires overcoming barriers that are in themselves likely to be highly significant.

C. Option 3: Decrease the 'Demand' for ADR

This option involves reducing the demand for ADR by seeking to ensure that, as far as possible, problems do not arise in the first place. This would involve a number of aspects. The first again involves working with intermediaries and the third sector. Some of these actors will have cross-cutting agendas (such as general consumer advice, debt, housing) while others may have energy-specific remits (for example, energy charities and NGOs). Rather than seeing these organisations as referral agencies that can signpost to ADR, attention could be given to creating stronger and more integrated links. Since people's problems do not occur within neat forms that match up with the remits and responsibilities of particular organisations, a key part of providing meaningful justice for vulnerable and energy-poor consumers is for organisations to collaborate to deal with issues in a more holistic way. As one interviewee pointed out, this raises the question of whether problems in accessing justice in the energy sector are down to issues with specific actors or a failure to cooperate and take joint action. The latter might involve the co-location of services (for example, having ADR staff working within local advice services, providing ADR outreach in local communities etc) or formal agreements that would allow multiple actors to consider consumers' energy issues at the same time. Such approaches could ultimately reduce demand for ADR by seeking to resolve the root causes of issues – dealing with debt or housing issues that create the potential for long-running problems and that might underlie specific energy complaints. This could be a key part of adopting preventative and public health approaches to people's problems.[38] Hodges charts developments in some jurisdictions towards 'problem-solving' approaches, where the emphasis is not simply on providing legal solutions, but dealing with a person's circumstances holistically. He gives the example of Family Drug and Alcohol Courts 'where judges, social workers, and psychologists support parents to quit addictions so as to prevent removal of their children'.[39] In order to deal with people's 'everyday justice' problems, therefore, energy ADR bodies (or at least the means to access them) need to be based within local communities, where acute problems are most likely to be experienced.

Other proposals in relation to option 3 draw on inspiration from the way in which public ombuds operate. There is widespread agreement in the literature that access to justice in the consumer context cannot be realised through individual dispute resolution alone.[40] Instead – and in keeping with our holistic vision

[38] Cohen and Alberstein (n 26).

[39] Hodges, *Delivering Dispute Resolution* (n 25) 4.

[40] I Ramsay, 'Consumer Redress and Access to Justice' in CEF Rickett and TGW Telfer (eds), *International Perspectives on Consumers' Access to Justice* (CUP, 2003); C Graham, 'Consumer ADR and

of access to justice – an emphasis is needed on the delivery of collective redress, as well as individual dispute resolution. Discussions here have focused either on class/collective actions (the model which dominates in the United States) or public enforcement action by regulators and competition authorities (the model which dominates in Europe).[41] Little attention has been given to the role of ombuds in delivering collective justice, beyond simply aggregating individual case data.

There are three aspects of public ombuds' role that we consider should be explored in the consumer context: a policy advocacy role; a systemic investigation role; and a Complaints Standards Authority (CSA) role. The first approach involves ADR becoming more 'vocal' in policy debates. Going in tandem with a higher public profile and a more obviously pro-consumer orientation, ADR bodies in the energy sector should have a role in advocating the rights and interests of consumers to industry, regulators and government. This would be similar to the role of some public ombuds in advocating human rights or children's rights.[42] It would also reflect the role that public ombuds with an energy-sector jurisdiction have adopted in relation to energy rights (see chapter nine on Bulgaria and chapter ten on Catalonia). That role recognises that such rights routinely remain unrealised in society and that they require promoting by institutions directly interested in bringing them to life. That would require a significant ideological shift in how consumer ADR in the energy sector is conceptualised, but one that would be potentially powerful both in bringing issues to the attention of those with the power to act on injustice and publicly signalling to consumers that ADR is 'for them'. It would also fit with the approach that we have recommended above in relation to the process of dispute resolution – one whose take on impartiality recognises the fundamental problems and inequalities that exist in the energy market and broader society, rather than one that ignores these in the pursuit of formal impartiality.

The second approach involves adopting a model used by ombuds in Scotland, Wales, and Northern Ireland – the so-called Complaints Standards Authority. This involves the ombuds setting complaint standards, monitoring their implementation, and promoting best practice in complaint handling within government.[43] Developing this role has huge potential to enhance access to justice in consumer contexts where 'the corporation is the courthouse'.[44] Most people who complain do so to their energy supplier rather than an ADR body. It may also be that,

Collective Redress' in P Cortes (ed), *The New Regulatory Framework for Consumer Dispute Resolution* (OUP, 2016): I Benöhr, *EU Consumer Law and Human Rights* (OUP, 2013), C Hodges and S Voet, *Delivering Collective Redress: New Technologies* (Hart Publishing, 2018).

[41] Hodges and Voet (n 40).

[42] L Reif, *The Ombudsman, Good Governance and the International Human Rights System* (Martinus Nijhoff, 2004).

[43] C Gill, 'The Evolving Role of the Ombudsman: A Conceptual and Constitutional Analysis of the "Scottish Solution" to Administrative Justice' (2014) 4 *Public Law* 662; C Gill, T Mullen and N Vivian, 'The Managerial Ombudsman' (2020) 83 *Modern Law Review* 797.

[44] Comment by Rory Van Loo cited in E Deason, M Green and D Shestowsky et al, 'ADR and Access to Justice: Current Perspectives' (2018) 33 *Ohio State Journal of Dispute Resolution* 303.

perhaps surprisingly, consumers trust businesses more than third parties such as consumer agencies or public authorities. For example, the European Commission's *Scoreboard* for 2019 reported that consumers' trust in traders surpasses trust in consumer protection authorities and in consumer organisations.[45] Working behind the scenes with energy companies rather than seeking to attract consumers directly may, therefore, be more effective. The potential for internal redress to deliver justice has been a controversial feature of administrative justice debates,[46] and some of those concerns apply here. Internal mechanisms can impede justice as much as they can help people access it. Again, the solution involves good design and oversight – providing the ADR body with such design and oversight functions, therefore, is a powerful way of ensuring that the potential of internal mechanisms to deliver 'everyday justice' is realised. Gill et al have suggested, however, that a CSA function needs to be appropriately calibrated.[47] The original model developed for Scottish public services has been criticised for being overly focused on efficiency and the managerial disposal of complaints, rather than more profound value-based approaches. Given our inclusive vision, it would be important that access to justice values are embedded in the design of CSA powers so that they can deliver access to justice goals in the energy sector. A particular concern here is likely to be on strategies for dealing with, and encouraging, complaints from vulnerable and energy-poor consumers.

Finally, the ombud could be given the kind of own-initiative investigation powers that most public ombuds have. This would allow for system-wide issues to be investigated without a complaint from a consumer having been received. Again, examples in Catalonia and Bulgaria show the potential value of such approaches in the energy context.[48] Gill,[49] arguing for the granting of own-initiative powers to public ombuds in the UK, identifies three reasons for doing so: passive complaining behaviour and the significant unremedied detriment that results from this; the particularly low likelihood of complaints being made by vulnerable individuals

[45] European Commission, *Consumer Conditions Scoreboard Consumers at Home in the Single Market* (European Commission 2019), available at: ec.europa.eu/info/sites/info/files/consumers-conditions-scoreboard-2019_pdf_en.pdf.

[46] S Halliday and D Cowan, *The Appeal of Internal Review: Law, Administrative Justice and the (Non-) Emergence of Disputes* (Hart Publishing 2003); R Thomas and J Tomlinson, 'A Different Tale of Judicial Power: Administrative Review as a Problematic Response to the Judicialisation of Tribunals' *Public Law* (forthcoming).

[47] Gill, Mullen and Vivian (n 43).

[48] While the role of public ombuds in the energy sector is influential in some jurisdictions, there are limitations to relying on the public ombuds to pursue advocacy and systemic functions. Indeed, given the breadth of remit of these organisations, it is unlikely that they are able to give sustained focus to energy issues. There is also a need to integrate these advocacy and systemic roles as part of a holistic approach to providing citizens with ADR and seeking to intervene strategically through internal complaints mechanisms. Thus, the model we favour would be an energy-sector specific ADR body (ideally an ombuds set up on a statutory basis) with a full range of powers to deliver access to justice for vulnerable and energy-poor consumers.

[49] C Gill, 'Own Initiative Powers' in R Kirkham and C Gill (eds), *A Manifesto for Ombudsman Reform* (Palgrave, 2020).

and groups; and the potential to capitalise on under-developed added-value features of the ombuds institution. The particular value of giving the ombuds such powers, in a public sector context that features a range of other mechanisms such as audit, inspection and (some) sectoral regulation, is that the ombuds has a unique focus on fairness in administrative processes and also has an important role to play in examining and troubleshooting internal redress mechanisms. These arguments apply equally to the energy sector, given its status as a service of general interest, the strong public interest in energy, and the substantial element of public regulation of the energy market. Own-initiative investigations could be launched based on a range of triggers, including media reports, political debate, intelligence from complaints, information from regulators, and working closely with civil society and third sector-actors. The aims of systemic investigation in the energy sector are likely to be twofold – to provide collective redress where there appears to be an issue causing widespread detriment to vulnerable and energy-poor consumers and to identify systemic problems in the energy market and recommend changes to prevent future injustices. The collective element of such investigations would therefore involve both *ex post* and *ex ante* features. Graham has suggested that there is little appetite for ADR providers to take on these kinds of collective redress powers, and he describes the systemic approach used by the Parliamentary and Health Services Ombudsman in the first decade of the twenty-first century as an 'aberration'.[50] That said, Graham recognises that questions around the extent to which ADR should be fulfilling more collective and systemic functions is an important and 'difficult' question in terms of the future development of ADR: 'The most difficult issue is whether CADR schemes will develop a greater focus on systemic issues, either through communication to a regulator or a general enforcement agency or through developing the means of deciding on collective cases'.[51]

D. Functional Overlaps, Partnership and Domain Legitimacy

The idea that the ombuds could deliver a multifunctional role is not new and, indeed, Hodges has praised the ombuds model for being able to contribute to other parts of the consumer protection landscape.[52] Gill and Hirst[53] and Creutzfeldt[54] have suggested that, even without the proposals for an expanded role we make above, ADR has a legitimate role to play in relation to other 'pillars' of consumer protection such as advice, advocacy, information and education, and enforcement. As a result of potential overlap with other actors, however, there is a need

[50] Graham (n 40).
[51] ibid, 445.
[52] Hodges, 'The Private Sector Ombudsman' (n 9).
[53] C Gill and C Hirst, *Defining Consumer Ombudsmen* (Ombudsman Services, 2016).
[54] Creutzfeldt, 'Ombudsman Schemes' (n 13).

for ombuds to carve out what Gilad has referred to as a legitimate 'domain'.[55] This is a space for legitimate action in the context of a landscape involving other institutional actors. The question for ADR is how far it could and should go in expanding its functions where existing institutions already have a role to play. In the energy sector, a range of actors have a consumer protection role, including regulators, competition authorities, general consumer enforcement bodies, consumer advice organisations and various third-sector organisations.

General arguments in favour of an expanded role for ADR in the energy sector – particularly in relation to the development of more regulatory functions – include the provision of systemic redundancy, the provision of checks and balances, and enhancing the potential for partnership. In relation to redundancy, the argument is that overlaps between institutional actors are not necessarily problematic. While there is a danger of regulatory overload from the perspective of those who are subject to oversight bodies, a greater danger results from gaps that result from overly narrow remits and a lack of 'joined-up' action between stakeholders. As one of our interviewees suggested, issues in relation to access to justice in the energy sector may be due to a lack of concerted action as much as limitations in the competences of particular organisations. Ensuring an element of overlap between regulators, competition authorities and ADR, therefore, could be a way of ensuring that issues are more likely to be picked up and acted upon. It also allows for checks and balances to be deployed within oversight systems themselves. There should be accountability not only for the energy suppliers, but for the actors who intervene within that market. It should be possible for the ADR body, therefore, to conclude that problems in energy markets are caused by regulatory failures and to recommend changes in that regard. Currently, in many jurisdictions, ADR is commissioned and overseen by energy regulators (a feature of the development of ADR as an aspect of market regulation rather than an aspect of the justice system). While we agree that close cooperation with energy regulators is essential, independence from regulators is equally important. ADR bodies need to have their own distinct source of legitimacy and operate free from regulatory interference.

Finally, a degree of overlap could enhance cooperation between actors in the energy sector rather than lead to conflict or inefficiency. Where institutional remits are narrowly drawn, it becomes easier for issues to fall between the cracks, and a lack of joined-up action on cross-cutting issues is a major issue for modern, increasingly integrated service delivery. Gaps are, therefore, more likely to be an issue than overlaps. Indeed, overlaps may force cooperation by requiring joint action and negotiation in a greater number of areas. Tightly drawn remits allow for lip service to be paid to joined-up working while an institution concentrates on its core business. Greater overlap requires coordinated action and the development of stronger partnerships. Indeed, in keeping with the general points we

[55] S Gilad, 'Exchange without Capture: The UK Financial Ombudsman Service's Struggle for Accepted Domain' (2008) 86 *Public Administration* 907.

have made above in relation to partnerships, a key element of our proposals is that an expanded role for ADR needs to involve closer working with other consumer protection bodies and other energy market actors. This might involve, for example, consulting with regulatory authorities before launching systemic investigations and potentially instigating joint enquiries depending on the issues. Thus, in our view, there are some general arguments to be made for an expanded role that overlaps with the roles of other consumer protection actors operating in the energy sector.

A further argument is that such an expanded role allows for a unique and additional contribution in each area – thus overlap should not involve replication of functions, but the provision of distinctive additional protections and benefits for vulnerable and energy-poor consumers. What should be the unique contribution of ADR? In our view, this comes down to a concern with justice, a matter which other energy-sector actors are likely to be interested in, but which is the unique locus of ADR (particularly in a context where the ambition is to replace courts and the public interest functions they have traditionally been seen as delivering).[56] In relation to advice provision, ADR can add value through its expertise in complaint handling and complaint systems, providing specialist information to energy consumers on access to the informal justice system. There is also significant potential here for the development of integrated and co-located models, as well as other forms of collaboration such as the provision of training and support to other advice providers on complaint issues. A stronger connection between formal institutions, such as ADR, and local actors working on energy issues is likely to be important in bridging the high relational distance that currently exists between energy consumers and market actors.

The greatest potential for overlap involves proposals to allow ADR to effectively regulate internal complaint procedures of energy suppliers and carry out systemic investigations. In relation to a CSA role, the key argument for this sitting with ADR rather than a regulator relates to the expertise of ADR in complaint matters, as well as its institutional focus on dispute resolution and justice. ADR bodies live and breathe complaints and routinely assess the quality of complaint handling as part of their casework. That expertise is key in helping to design effective processes in the first place and in being able to identify where there may be flaws in their operations. Moreover, the institutional focus of ADR on complaints means that access to justice within energy companies will be prioritised. Energy regulators keeping oversight of multiple issues in a complex market may not be in a position to prioritise internal complaint handling by energy suppliers. If the corporation is indeed the courthouse for most consumer disputes and the place where they access (or do not access) justice, then there is a good argument for ADR bodies taking on the role of overseeing this aspect of energy suppliers' operations. Drawing on the broad approach taken to administrative justice

[56] Cortes, *The Law of Consumer Redress* (n 4).

(which includes first-instance decision-making by public authorities and internal redress arrangements), complaint handling by energy suppliers should be seen as a justice issue that requires the attention of the ombuds.

Another answer is that a systemic investigation role would fit well with the proposed CSA role. Providing ADR with a more dynamic 'upstream' role overseeing internal complaint handling by energy suppliers will provide ADR bodies with much better intelligence about where problems exist for vulnerable and energy-poor consumers and where injustices are arising. As well as being able to deal with individual energy suppliers, the potential to look across the whole energy market is likely to be beneficial where potential systemic issues are indicated. There could also be a distinction between systemic investigations and collective redress. Systemic investigations may involve the provision of collective redress but might also be more focused on the development of best practice or the investigation of emerging issues with the potential for creating consumer detriment in the energy sector. Systemic powers should also be tied clearly to access to justice goals and deployed in those circumstances where vulnerable and energy-poor individuals and groups are not complaining, but there is good reason to consider that they may be subject to detriment. This will allow ADR bodies to make a distinctive contribution to access to justice in the energy market and not overstep their legitimate domain. Another way of seeing the collective redress issue is to question whether it is best situated with enforcement and regulatory agencies in the first place. It might be argued that redress is more clearly in the territory of ADR, and that, as ADR systems develop in sophistication and become a more settled part of justice and regulatory systems, there should be a natural migration of collective redress functions towards ADR.

V. Limitations and Directions for Future Research

Given the growth of ADR within justice systems and its particular prominence in consumer disputing, it seems critical to us to focus on the extent to which the growth of this institution had advanced access to justice. Much weight has been placed on the shoulders of ADR as an instrument of justice reform. Knowing more about how ADR is fulfilling its promise (or not) is, therefore, a crucial issue. At the same time, the focus we have adopted in this book has excluded detailed discussion of a range of other mechanisms and actors. In seeking clarity of focus and prioritising ADR as an urgent issue, we have inevitably not been able to consider other aspects of the access to justice landscape in as much detail. And while partnership and whole system approaches have been highlighted as particularly important, we were only able to touch on how more cooperative and integrated approaches could be developed among stakeholders in future. There were also some methodological limitations in relation to our data. Securing access to research participants was easier in some jurisdictions than in others, and this made detailed comparisons between different jurisdictions difficult. Indeed, in this book, our emphasis has been on highlighting the main themes arising from our research, and we have left the discussion of jurisdictional differences largely to the jurisdictional experts who have contributed to part II of this book. We plan to follow up on these insights, with jurisdiction-specific publications in due course.

In terms of future research, a number of areas suggest themselves. More theoretical research is required to explore the connection between ADR and the delivery of substantive justice. We have made the argument in this book that ADR can deliver this through an emphasis on social justice, but these insights need to be followed up and developed further. There is also an empirical dimension here, and the theoretical potential of ADR to deliver substantive justice needs to proceed in tandem with socio-legal work on the ground.[57] A major effort of future research should be to investigate the practices of energy suppliers in relation to handling complaints. Internal mechanisms are hugely important in determining the degree to which people access and achieve justice. But, at present, little is known about how these systems operate and – to the extent that they have been studied – the research has been driven from marketing standpoints concerned with customer retention. A public justice outlook is needed to complement these perspectives. The role of local actors should also be subject to more research in future. The literature on intermediaries could be developed with more emphasis on both the referral and direct problem-solving functions. Finally, an important area for future research, is to investigate the links between aspects of the system, rather than considering institutions and processes in isolation. Creutzfeldt et al have suggested the potential value of nodal governance as a framework for investigation of the role of local actors in relation to energy poverty.[58] A network analysis approach would be valuable in studying how current players in the access to justice landscape interact with each other and the effect that these interactions and networks have on the delivery of access to justice.

VI. Conclusion

This chapter has summarised the arguments developed in preceding chapters in order to provide the basis for outlining a set of design options for a more holistic system of access to justice. An important conclusion has been that much of the

[57] Charlie Irvine's work on lay people's perceptions of justice in the context of mediation of small claims disputes points the way to a very fruitful avenue of future research: C Irvine, 'What Do "Lay" People Know about Justice? An Empirical Enquiry' (2020) 16 *International Journal of Law in Context* 146.

[58] N Creutzfeldt, C Gill, R McPherson and M Cornelis, 'The Social and Local Dimensions of Governance of Energy Poverty: Adaptive Responses to State Remoteness' (2020) 43 *Journal of Consumer Policy* 635.

potential of ADR in delivering access to justice for vulnerable energy consumers remains unrealised and depends on the way in which ADR is designed. The literature on DSD and consumer ADR provide a number of insights here, one of which revolves around the superiority of the multifunctional ombuds model. We agree with the developing consensus that the ombuds represents the most powerful model of ADR for delivering access to justice in relation to consumer disputes. We have argued that there are significant benefits in the ombuds' ability to fulfil not only core dispute resolution goals, but also to contribute to market regulation and add value to each of the pillars of the consumer protection landscape. That said, three issues arise. The first is that the potential value of the ombuds model has not yet been shown empirically, and its benefits remain largely theoretical. The second is that there remain significant variations in practice among ombuds, so that, although a broad model can be identified, there is likely to be significant variation in terms of how much 'added value' particular ombuds aim to deliver. The third, and most important, is that there is little evidence that the access to justice challenge is being grasped and prioritised by ombuds: like other aspects of the ADR landscape, they remain little used and the demographic of users remains stubbornly narrow and unrepresentative.

Beginning with this latter insight, this chapter has sought to reimagine ADR with the aim of maximising the chances of access to justice being delivered for vulnerable and energy-poor consumers. The adoption of the ombuds model is a good starting point, but we have argued that ADR could go further in three respects: first, by improving the 'supply' of ADR (ie, by reforming its dispute resolution processes); second, by increasing 'demand' for ADR; and third, by decreasing demand for ADR. The first option involves reforming ADR processes to deliver more advice and support to complainants, as well as departing from strict impartiality and extending equitable concepts to redressing structural imbalances, as well as avoiding the unduly harsh outcomes of law. Rather than seeking to 'manage' consumers' expectations of a more powerful and status quo-changing institution, ADR bodies could see such demands as legitimate claims for justice in the context of an inherently flawed and unequal marketplace. The second option involves seeking to develop outreach programmes to engage more people in directly using ADR and working with intermediaries to ensure referrals are made. The third option involves a range of measures that could reduce direct demand for ADR by taking preventative approaches that seek to resolve complaints as close as possible to the point at which they arise in everyday life. Part of the solution here might be to involve a problem-solving approach, with more integrated service provision and ADR co-located with advice provision and a range of other actors. Other solutions involve a similar holistic approach but at a systemic level. Here, inspiration may be drawn from the way in which public ombuds operate, with suggestions being advanced about a role for ADR in providing policy advocacy, the regulation of internal complaints procedures, and systemic investigations. In relation to each of these proposals, we have emphasised the need for partnership as a key feature of the system, proposing an extended role for ADR, but recognising that effective coordinated action across the consumer protection landscape is essential to delivering access to justice goals.

In bringing part I of this book to a close, we re-emphasise that the findings and arguments we have presented in this volume do not represent the whole story of access to justice for vulnerable and energy-poor consumers. We have presented an overview of our key findings, and these will be followed up in future work which will delve deeper into specific aspects of our data and the jurisdictions we have considered. We were fortunate to engage with a range of experts in the course of this project, and part II now considers their perspectives on access to justice for vulnerable and energy-poor consumers. The chapters that follow highlight some of the challenges and opportunities that stand in the way of the holistic vision we have proposed here.

PART II

Access to Justice, ADR and Energy Poverty in Five Countries

8

Introduction to Part II

Part II of the book provides a complementing view on the theoretical and empirical discoveries of our *Just Energy* project. It is made up of a repository of five country chapters. For all those readers who are interested in an in-depth country-specific dive, part II is where to find it. We invited national experts to write about access to justice, alternative dispute resolution (ADR) and energy poverty to highlight the different approaches and perspectives towards these topics in each country. Therefore, the following chapters portray a range of national approaches to energy policy, the complexity of vulnerability, the different roles of ADR and ombuds schemes. The chapters, while covering broadly the same themes, have different foci, reflecting the variation in national interpretations and implementations of legislation on energy poverty and ADR.

I. Outline of Chapters

Chapter nine: 'Energy Injustice in Bulgaria', by Teodora Peneva, critically reviews the mechanism for access to justice in the energy sector in Bulgaria. The chapter discusses the national Ombudsman which carries the function of protecting vulnerable consumers across all service sectors (including energy), the municipalities' Ombudsman, and Ombudsmen in energy companies. Bulgaria is the country with the highest level of energy poverty in the EU. Numerous problems reinforce poverty issues that lead to social distress regarding energy consumption. This chapter concludes that citizens in Bulgaria meet high levels of energy injustice which they have to fight with inefficient consumer protection mechanisms, whose efficiency depends on the individuals in charge rather than on legal and administrative processes.

Chapter ten: 'Energy Poverty and Access to Justice in Catalonia', by Anaïs Varo and Enric Bartlett Castellà, discusses the advanced legislation on energy poverty. The chapter analyses the Spanish electrical system and considers the main mechanisms to combat injustice that energy poverty represents. Further, the impact of the Spanish state strategy against energy poverty on Catalonia is discussed. The European definition of energy communities, as viable non-profit alternatives to traditional actors in the provision of energy services, captures and tries to enhance a cooperative experience of more than a century. Social innovation and community-based initiatives usually puts energy vulnerability and environmental justice at the centre of their concerns. The energy transition, which citizen communities promote, can and should be a catalyst to eradicate energy poverty. Additionally, Energy Communities propose a new scenario for traditional ADR, which will have to innovate and adapt to new possible types of conflicts.

Chapter eleven by Marine Cornelis is about access to justice and energy poverty in France. This chapter describes fuel poverty and its drivers in France, discusses the policies at national and local level to help vulnerable consumers and concludes by arguing for a more prominent role for ADR in the energy sector. For access to justice (including ADR) to help vulnerable and energy-poor consumers, a simplification of existing systems and clear signposting is necessary. However, in a state as centralised as France, where each administration, company and service is keen to defend their own sector, the framework does not yet seem to be ready to provide aid centred on the needs of the individual, in particular those who need it most.

Chapter twelve: 'Access to Justice for Vulnerable and Energy Poor Consumers in Italy: Policy Measures and the Role of ADR', by Sarah Supino and Benedetta Voltaggio, argues for a new angle to understand energy, namely considering it as indispensable good. The chapter discusses Italy's vast ADR system for energy, valued by consumers. This system represents a combination of consumer associations and companies working together to inform and support consumers. However, it is not entirely clear how vulnerable consumers can access ADR. Despite ADR providers being capable of providing services for the energy poor, there is room for improvement. These shortcomings are due to the fact that Italy has no action plan to protect vulnerable consumers (nor coordinated ADR policies).

Chapter thirteen: 'Access to Justice in Energy: UK' by Cosmo Graham focuses on energy policy and the tensions it encapsulates in the UK. This tension lies between access and availability for all, and the idea that energy supply should be coming from a competitive market without much government intervention. The chapter concludes by suggesting that the technocratic, centralised system has not addressed access to energy justice. Therefore, a better alternative would be a decentralised, populist system with greater scope for those affected to have a voice in decision-making as well as a move away from market mechanisms. Underpinning this argument is a further argument about changes to the energy system in pursuit of a major policy goal of decarbonisation.

9

Energy Injustice in Bulgaria

TEODORA PENEVA

I. Introduction

Bulgaria is the country with the highest level of energy poverty in the European Union (EU). Over 58 per cent of households in Bulgaria spent more than 10 per cent of their net income on energy in 2017.[1] This figure is persistent and is impacted by changes in the economic cycle, fluctuating up and down by some 2–3 per cent year on year. There were 41 per cent of households in 2017 with a net total income, after energy costs, below the poverty line with energy cost above 10 per cent. In this situation, people are exposed to many risk factors of energy poverty – low income, high energy costs, low energy efficiency of buildings[2] and energy injustice.

The mechanisms for access to energy justice in Bulgaria have a strong foundation, but also numerous problems, which together with persistent poverty issues lead to social distress regarding energy consumption. Bulgaria has had a National Ombudsman since 2005, ombudsmen in municipalities in about 14 cities in the country (out of 256),[3] some of which have been in existence since 2000, and an energy ombudsman for the electricity supplier CEZ for western Bulgaria, since 2013. In addition, the Commission for Consumer Protection (CCP) has been engaged in mediation activities since the enactment of the Consumer Protection Act in September 2005.[4] Alternative dispute resolution (ADR) commissions in different sectors were attached to the CCP in 2013, after

[1] T Peneva, 'Influence of different types of heating on energy poverty', presentation at the conference 'Energy Efficient Heating as a Measure for Clean Air' (2020), available at: www.zazemiata.org/materiali-konferencia-bitovo-otoplenie/.

[2] T Peneva, *Energy Poverty: The Bulgarian Case* (Washington, DC, International Association for Energy Economics, 2014).

[3] S Kazasian, 'Out of 265 municipalities in Bulgaria, only 14 have local public mediators' (*BNT News*, 23 April 2018), available at: bntnews.bg/bg/a/ot-265-obshchini-v-blgariya-samo-v-14-ima-mestni-obshchestveni-posrednitsi.

[4] Consumer Protection Act (SG) (2005), available at: mi.government.bg/en/library/consumer-protection-act-1-c25-m258-2.html.

the ADR Directive (2013/11/EU)[5] and the ODR Regulation (EU) No 524/2013[6] were enacted. All these legal mediators between the government, businesses and consumers/citizens have different rights and solve different types of problems.

None of them is officially authorised to terminate or impact decisions of the main energy regulator – the Energy and Water Regulatory Commission (EWRC).[7] The EWRC examines and resolves issues related to the regulation of business plans and prices of energy, water and sewerage services and also manages complaints in these two sectors.

The EWRC's work on regulating energy prices is critical, as households in Bulgaria have few measures to control energy expenditure. Energy efficiency is not a good choice for cutting costs, as it requires enormous investment and Bulgarian citizens have limited or no financial help for this; the only workable solutions currently are either to cut consumption, or to switch to solid fuel for heating in the winter, which has a lower average monthly cost.

In February 2020, the Ministry of Regional Development and Public Work published a *Summary Review and Analysis of the National Housing Stock in the Republic of Bulgaria*,[8] which reviewed energy consumption using data from energy audits of residential buildings for 2015–19 maintained by the Agency for Sustainable Energy Development. According to the report, the amount of buildings with the worst energy performance (classes E, F and G) is high – over 90 per cent – and the average temperatures of air-conditioned spaces are low (10–15 degrees celsius) in residential buildings due to under-consumption of energy. In terms of consumption habits, households in Bulgaria are characterised by exceptional savings, lack of comfort and reasonable energy consumption. Energy deprivation is typical, which is clearly seen when comparing the energy consumption in the household sector per square meter and per person.

Data from the National Statistical Institute in Bulgaria analysed by Peneva shows that the percentage of low-income households using solid fuels increases each year, while higher-income groups are more likely to switch to electricity.[9] In Bulgaria, nearly 60 per cent of the population use electricity for heating, and over a quarter use solid fuel. The use of central heating falls below 2 per cent for low-income groups which represent nearly 40 per cent of the population, while it accounts for 20 per cent of households with the highest yield, a share that

[5] Directive 2013/11/EU of the European Parliament and of the Council of 21 May 2013 on alternative dispute resolution for consumer disputes and amending Regulation (EC) No 2006/2004 and Directive 2009/22/EC (Directive on consumer ADR), available at: eur-lex.europa.eu/legal-content/EN/TXT/?uri=celex%3A32013L0011.

[6] Regulation (EU) No 524/2013 of the European Parliament and of the Council of 21 May 2013 on online dispute resolution for consumer disputes and amending Regulation (EC) No 2006/2004 and Directive 2009/22/EC (Regulation on consumer ODR), available at: eur-lex.europa.eu/legal-content/EN/TXT/?uri=celex%3A32013R0524.

[7] Energy and Water Regulatory Commission: www.dker.bg/en/home.html.

[8] Ministry of Regional Development and Public Works, *Summary Review and analysis of the national housing stock in the Republic of Bulgaria* (2020), available at: www.mrrb.bg/bg/pregled-i-analiz-na-nacionalniya-jilisten-sgraden-fond-v-republika-bulgariya/.

[9] Peneva, 'Influence of different types of heating on energy poverty' (n 1).

increased to nearly 30 per cent in 2017, along with rising inequalities. In 2015, when the winter season recorded the lowest temperatures at the beginning of the year, the low-income groups using solid fuel increased sharply by an average of about 6–7 per cent, from 31 per cent in 2014 to 37–38 per cent in 2015, and back to 36 per cent in 2016. All this shows the strong link between incomes and the structure of consumption, and the more active use of switching heating type to cut energy cost, compared with any other instrument.

Figure 9.1A Share of energy used by household by resource type 2014–17 – gas

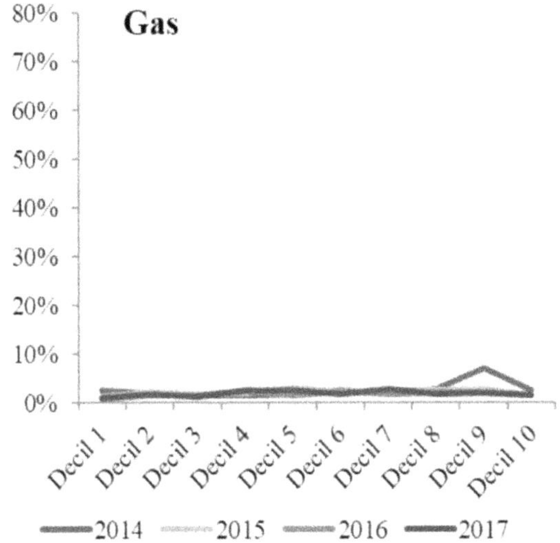

Figure 9.1B Share of energy used by household by resource type 2014–17 – central heating

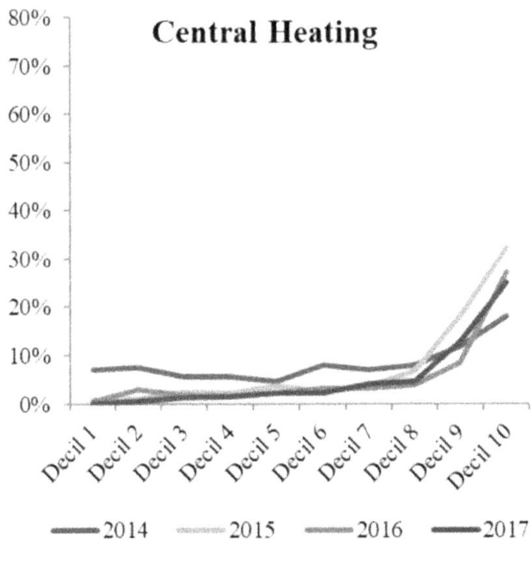

Figure 9.1C Share of energy used by household by resource type 2014–17 – solid fuel

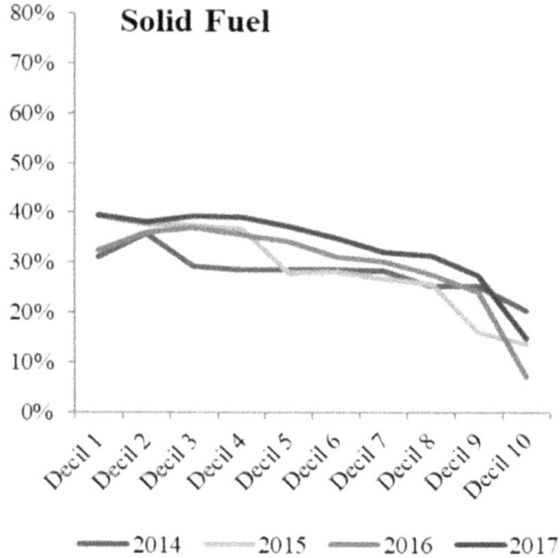

Figure 9.1D Share of energy used by household by resource type 2014–17 – electricity

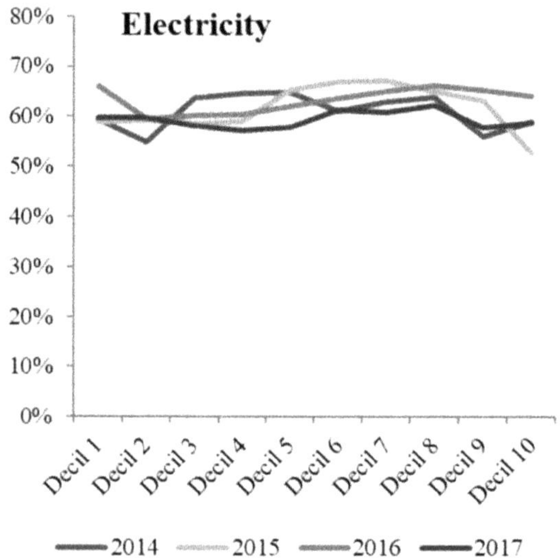

Given all these considerations, the lack of effective mechanisms to address the injustice in price formation and consumption additionally puts pressure on vulnerable consumers. According to Article 14(1) (suppl SG 18/05) of the Energy Act 2003[10] 'interested persons' – state bodies, organisations, energy enterprises,

[10] Energy Sector Act 2003, last amend and suppl SG 83/9 October 2018, available at: www.me.government.bg/en/library/energy-act-256-c25-m258-1.html.

WSS operators (operators of water supply and sewerage services), clients, privileged consumers and consumer organisations – can only assist the EWRC in performing its functions.

The Ombudsman, for example, is not explicitly cited as an 'interested person' in the Energy Act; rather the law refers to consumer organisations which are officially authorised to participate in public discussions of upcoming implementation of EWRC decisions. At the same time, consumer organisations in Bulgaria are regulated by the Consumer Protection Act. This protects consumer rights against violation by suppliers, with a specific focus on 10 sectors[11] – the energy sector is not included. Complaints recorded and addressed in the CCP's annual report in relation to energy include the proper energy efficiency labels on electric appliances, as well as the completion of energy efficiency measures in buildings. The CCP receives complaints against energy suppliers; however, the organisation states that this is not its main competence. Yet, it has issued several public statements on the most popular conflict areas for energy consumers, being unclear and unfair calculations of heating bills for users of central heating. It has further participated in inspections organised by the Ombudsman to cease consumers' rights violation.

This chapter discusses the most common problems encountered in the energy supply system that, intentionally or not, drive people into energy poverty. It goes on to discuss the main barriers that ombudsmen and other providers of consumer protection face.

II. Energy Poverty in Bulgaria

Consistent work and efforts to protect consumer rights have contributed to a fairer relationship between energy suppliers and consumers during the past 15 years. However, the fourth pillar of energy poverty in Bulgaria – energy injustice – cannot be eradicated alongside the other three, namely low income, high energy bills and poor energy efficiency.[12] The latter three pillars of energy poverty in Bulgaria are highly persistent and sustained. Although the country's economic development was extremely stable in the years after 2008, there are signs of increasing energy poverty levels, due mainly to higher income inequalities, lower building efficiency, with few measures to improve these factors over the years, higher consumer debts with increased supply and competition in the finance sector.

People in Bulgaria have the lowest income among all EU countries, high relative energy prices (measured as a share of the energy expenditure in the total

[11] Alcohol products, tobacco products, electric appliances, automobile tyres, aerosol vials, crystal glass products, textile products, shoes, household appliances, new passenger vehicles, touristic services, e-trade, insurance services, real estate agencies, posts, telecommunication services.

[12] H Thomson, 'The EU Fuel Poverty Toolkit: An introductory guide to identifying and measuring fuel poverty' (University of York, 2013) 4.

household income, averaging 13–15 per cent of the total income for the last 20 years) and low quality of buildings with a low budget for energy efficiency measures.[13] High energy bills have been a big burden, especially in the lower income groups. Rising income inequalities (see Table 9.1) have also enhanced conflict between users and energy suppliers in the last few years. Problems with debt collection and issues for institutions dealing with consumers' rights protection have also increased.

Table 9.1 Average share of energy expenditure in households' total net income

Decile Group	2014	2015	2016	2017
Decile 1	24.1%	17.9%	24.1%	20.8%
Decile 2	18.4%	15.8%	18.3%	17.0%
Decile 3	15.8%	14.7%	17.1%	14.8%
Decile 4	14.7%	15.0%	15.6%	14.6%
Decile 5	14.3%	14.3%	14.8%	13.1%
Decile 6	14.1%	14.0%	14.8%	11.2%
Decile 7	12.9%	13.1%	14.8%	11.0%
Decile 8	12.3%	12.2%	12.2%	9.7%
Decile 9	11.6%	10.5%	12.3%	9.5%
Decile 10	9.4%	9.0%	11.0%	7.7%
Total	**13.6%**	**13.3%**	**15.1%**	**14.0%**

The fourth pillar – energy injustice – is additional to high energy bills, low income and poor building quality. Many people have had to pay higher charges for their heating and risk being sued for postponing bill payment. There were no standard rules for charging interest on unpaid debt, so in some cases additional penalties were multiplied tenfold, a hundredfold or even more than the amount of the unpaid bill. There will probably never be an objective estimate of the injustice pillar due to lack of public data. However, it does exist, and problems also still persist with central heating suppliers of the old installation system, for example.

A general idea of the size of this pillar was obtained from data on the number of court cases in Sofia, published in different media over a period of 4–5 years. In 2011 over 60 per cent of the cases in the largest court in Sofia related to the central heating company. Each month, 150–200 central heating cases were heard in the court, according to Racheva.[14] In 2012, the heating company spent

[13] Peneva, *Energy Poverty: The Bulgarian Case* (n 2).

[14] K Racheva, '60% of the cases heard in court in Bulgaria are related to Toplofikacia' (*bTV News*, 3 November 2011), available at: btvnovinite.bg/1644389578-60_na_sto_ot_delata_v_naygolemiya_sad_v_Bulgaria_svarzani_s_Toplofikatsiya.html.

over BGN130 million on court cases with over 30,000 consumers, according to Kurlev and Mavrova.[15] Kadiiska notes that of the 600–700 court debt-collecting cases per day in 2018, some 100–200 involved the heating company.[16] In Sofia in 2015, the heating company's legal fees amounted to BGN6.11 million, increasing to BGN10.22 million in 2016 and BGN11.84 million in 2017, according to the company's financial statements stated by the Ombudsman in a discussion session in the National Assembly.[17]

All this is an additional burden on the already high levels of energy poverty. There is no official definition of energy poverty in Bulgaria; however, applying the most popular definitions based on anonymous data from the Household Budgets Survey, one can gauge the high persisting and increasing levels of poverty in the years up to 2017 (see Figure 9.2).

Regardless of the definition used, energy poverty in Bulgaria is high. The only existing definition is absolutely inadequate for the country's specifics – Low Income High Cost (LIHC)[18] has limited implications because people with income below the official poverty line could rarely afford high-cost energy as they have to keep costs to a minimum. These households are seen rather as an exception, which in favourable economic conditions averages 10 per cent of households and in worse conditions could reach more. The situation in the lower three decile groups by income is critical. In the last decade, most low-income groups have switched to wood heating in order to control costs and reduce the proportion of energy spending in their total income, according to a Peneva's analysis.[19]

Figure 9.2: (1) 10 per cent rule: a household is energy poor if its energy expenditure exceeds 10 per cent of net income; (2) Poverty after energy consumption measures households with net income after energy cost under the official poverty line; (3) LIHCs-households with a net total income after energy cost below the poverty line and a share of energy cost above 10 per cent); (4) LIHC-households with a net income below the poverty line and energy expenditure above the median for the country. The poverty line for the three definitions is calculated as 60 per cent of the median equalised income of the sample for the respective year.

[15] M Mavrova and P Kurlev, 'Toplofikacia-Sofia raises the price of hot water to compensate fewer consumers of heating, states a lawyer' (*Darik News*, 20 March 2012), available at: dariknews.bg/novini/biznes/toplofikaciq-sofiq-vdiga-cenata-na-toplata-voda-za-da-kompensira-otliva-ot-parno-tvyrdi-advokat-873019.

[16] M Kadiiska, 'Debt collectors flood Themida with 700 cases a day' (*Monitor*, 18 September 2018), available at: www.monitor.bg/bg/a/view/sybirachi-na-dylgove-zalivat-temida-s-po-700-dela-na-den-144535.

[17] National Assembly of the Republic of Bulgaria, Commission for Monitoring the Activities of the Energy and Water Regulatory Commission, *Protocol of Discussion with the participation of Ms Maya Manolova, Ombudsman of the Republic of Bulgaria on the topic: 'Protection of consumer rights in their relations with district heating companies'* (2016), available at: parliament.bg/bg/parliamentarycommittees/members/2349/steno/ID/4285.

[18] J Hills, *Getting the Measure of Fuel Poverty* (Centre for the Analysis of Social Exclusion, 2012).

[19] Peneva, 'Influence of different types of heating on energy poverty' (n 1).

Figure 9.2 Energy poverty in Bulgaria

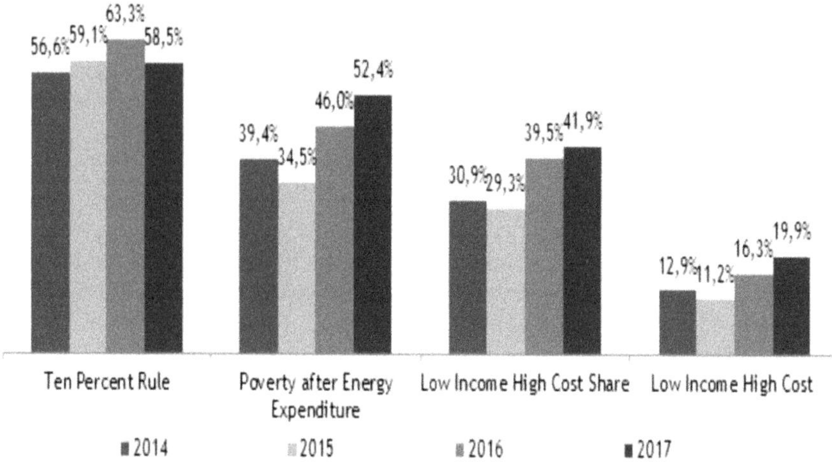

III. Consumer Protection Mechanism

As already mentioned in the Introduction, Bulgarian consumers have several choices if they cannot directly solve their problems with energy suppliers. First, they would, in the best case, refer to the EWRC, which, however, has limited power. The second option, which has emerged as the most efficient in recent years, is going to the Ombudsman of the Republic of Bulgaria. Alternatives to the National Ombudsman are local ombudsmen in municipalities located in the provinces. However, they only operate in 14 out of 256 cities in Bulgaria. If a local ombudsman cannot solve the issue, they can ask the National Ombudsman for support. The next level and option are consumer protection organisations, which in Bulgaria are not specific to the energy sector. These organisations cover all economic sectors, with a focus on 10, and, whenever a consumer asks for help, he or she is transferred to the Ombudsman's office.

Each of these legal institutions is regulated by different laws – the Ombudsman Act for the National Ombudsman, the Consumer Protection Act for consumer organisations, the Energy Act for the EWRC and the Local Government and Local Administration Act[20] for the Local Ombudsman. ADR commissions are attached to the CCP and are not popular in the country, as since their inception, they have failed to provide solutions for consumers. When the National Ombudsman cannot solve a problem directly with the supplier or with the EWRC, it will very often contact other state bodies, such as the Ministry of Energy, the National Assembly and even the Ministry Council, to address problems.

[20] Local Government and Local Administration Act 1991, last amend and suppl SG 9/26 January 2017, available at: www.mrrb.bg/en/local-government-and-local-administration-act/.

Figure 9.3 Consumer Protection Mechanism in Bulgaria

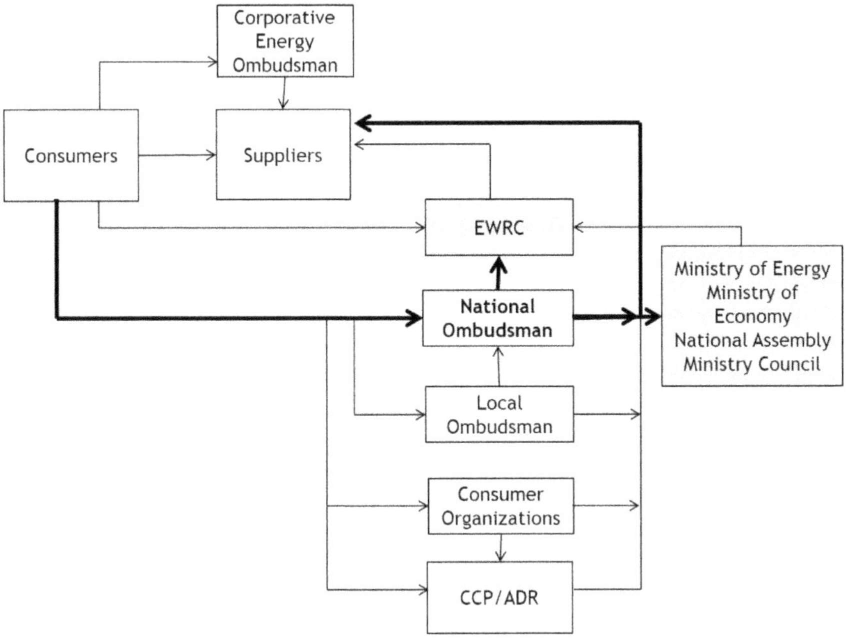

Source: Author's own representation.

It is not easy to estimate the extent of each route to access energy justice. There is only a limited amount of data for all institutions between 2012 and 2015. However, the situation is dynamic, with different factors impacting on the effectiveness of each method – changes in the regulatory framework, restricting or enhancing the rights and power of a specific institution, consumers' attitudes and trust in the institution, time of establishment, etc. It is difficult to draw conclusions without understanding all factors impacting on the flows of in/justice. This chapter can only provide an overview of the different factors and attempts to put the pieces of the puzzle together, sector by sector.

A. Heating Supply

There was an average of 590,700 residential heating consumers in Bulgaria in the years between 2012 and 2015, according to the EWRC's annual reports (2012, 2013, 2014, 2015).[21] This number is constantly decreasing, due to the inability of consumers to control their bills, due to poverty, problems in the regulatory

[21] Annual Reports of the CEWR for 2008–18, available at: www.dker.bg/bg/za-kevr/godishni-otcheti.html.

framework, and problems with individual measurement and rising injustice. In 2012, there were 12,277 complaints about heating suppliers in 15 cities, 371 complaints against heating suppliers at the EWRC and 280 to the National Ombudsman, according to the Ombudsman's annual report (2012).[22]

The same year, the CCP received a total of 17,736 complaints for all economic sectors (compared with 5,331 to the Ombudsman), of which 44 per cent were about public services, according to the CCP's annual report (2013). There was no specific breakdown of each service and issues relating to heating supply and consumer relations are mentioned as problems beyond the competence of the CCP, and thus were transferred to other institutions.

In 2012 there were 873 applications for conciliation proceedings. No data on the electricity commission complaints were provided, although the only available data for 2017 show a total of four complaints about electricity (not even heating) suppliers. In 540 conciliation cases, the proceedings were terminated due to the energy provider's failure to attend; 26 of the proceedings were terminated due to the applicant's failure to attend; 68 were terminated because no agreement was reached; and only 56 cases reached an agreement, according to the CCP's annual report (2012).[23]

According to the EWRC's annual report (2008), the average number of complaints against heating suppliers was 18 per 1,000 consumers. This number increased to 20 in 2012, according to the EWRC annual report (2013), and declined to 17 in 2015. Unfortunately, information about the number of complaints on the supplier side in the years after 2015 was not collected by the EWRC.

B. Electricity Supply

In 2013 and 2014 respectively, there were 4,837,224 and 4,329,527 household users of electricity in Bulgaria, according to data from the EWRC annual reports (2013, 2014). Electricity suppliers received 62,313 complaints in 2013 and 29,527 in 2014. The National Ombudsman received 540 complaints in that year, according to its annual report (2013), the only year with more complaints for electricity than for heating (526).

According to the EWRC report, in 2008 the average number of complaints against electricity suppliers was six per 1,000 consumers. Calculation of data from the 2013 and 2014 reports shows increases in the average number of complaints against electricity suppliers to 13 per 1,000 consumers in 2013 and seven per 1,000 in 2014. The 2013 year was an exceptional year for drawing the attention of the media and the government to energy poverty in the country. It was a year with low temperatures, higher heating needs and longer billing periods by suppliers, sometimes lasting 1.5 months. All this resulted in huge energy bills. People were protesting on the streets and burning their energy bills in front of the media.

[22] Annual Reports of the National Ombudsman for 2005–19, available at: www.ombudsman.bg/reports/415?page=6#middleWrapper.

[23] CCP, Annual Reports for 2012–14, available at: kzp.bg/aktove-old/old.kzp.bg/indexed81.html.

There were 17,834 incoming complaints for all economic sectors in the CCP in 2013, of which 6,020 were directed to other competent authorities, as stated in the annual report (2013). One could perhaps suggest that a certain proportion of these redirected complaints were coming from either heating or electricity consumers, but there is no concrete information on this.

According to the same report, there were 515 applications for ADR for all economic sectors at the CCP in 2013, with only 28 reaching an agreement. Of the total amount, 323 were terminated because 261 suppliers did not attend, 16 consumers did not attend and in 46 cases both parties failed to reach an agreement, according to the CCP annual report (2013). This situation is not broken down by sectors or issues. The mechanism is officially reported as ineffective in the CCP annual report (2014). Citizens' trust in this mechanism decreased further in the following years. The CCP annual report of 2019 states that there were just 113 applications for ADR in all sectors in 2019, of which 73 did not have enough documentation to start the official procedure. Of the remaining cases, there were 60 companies, providers of goods or services, that did not respond at all. Just eight cases reached an agreement. This clearly shows the ineffectiveness of ADR in the country.

IV. Key Areas of Energy Injustice

No matter which routes are used, all complaints concern similar problems. Some of the persisting key areas of injustice are shown but not limited to the list in Figure 9.4.

A. Heating Supply

Problems in the supply of heating can be summarised as old installations, high heating losses, unfair and unclear heating measurement, infringement of the rights to pay for actual consumption, consumer distrust in the measurement and in heating accountants, low debt collection and high interest, and court expenses for consumers. The majority of complaints relate to disagreements with what has been done by the heating accounting companies in multifamily buildings. Often, consumers complain about unfair distribution of heat used in common building installations. Each of these problems needs a specific explanation, because these are not always problems of the heating suppliers, but are a result of the system's inability to adapt to new European rules for individual measurement coupled with high levels of poverty in the country that has arisen since the 1990s.

At least 10 per cent of complaints lodged with the EWRC every year disagree with the legal framework, including the provision of Article 150, paragraph 1 of the Energy Act, according to which the sale of heat for household purposes is made under public terms and conditions without signing individual contracts, according to the EWRC annual report (2016). Other important categories of

Figure 9.4 Key energy injustice areas in Bulgaria

Central heating supply	Electricity supply	Water supply
- lack of individual contracts between the heating suppliers and consumers - infringed right to actual measurement and reporting; - violation of the right to pay for actually used service - wrong calculations of the heat energy per unit share in substations - numerous conflicts in regulating common consumption in multifamily buildings - poor quality of service provided - sued consumers for delaying payment with improper calculations of interests charges on debts - the decision of the EWRC for setting electricity and natural gas caps, is an individual administrative act and cannot be appealed to by citizens in court	- poor quality of the delivered electricity frequent shortages resulting in broken electric appliances - unilateral correction of terms by companies of consumer accounts - inspections and replacement of commercial measuring instruments in the absence of the client - improper calculations of taxes for disconnecting electricity supply and charging interests on the debt - unreasonable price increases	- water shortages in many cities in Bulgaria, particularly in 2019 – severe problems - poor quality of the provided plumbing service - unfair distribution of consumption of 'common consumption' water by lots of users in multifamily buildings - economically unjustified increase in the cost of water and sewerage services - huge losses in the network, nearing 60% of the end-price

Source: Own summary from Ombudsman's annual reports 2005–19.

consumer objections are disagreements with the court's decisions on amounts due but unpaid for heat, and the application of the limitation period of obligations, etc, for which the CCP is not responsible.

B. Electricity Supply

The largest number of complaints in this area relate to accounting and invoicing of electricity. Problems reported to the EWRC include allegations of inaccurate reporting or lack of an actual report, inaccurate operation of metering switches, errors when billing the reported quantities and charging for network services. The second issue is the quality of the low-voltage electricity delivered to connection points, frequent power outages and failures at electrical appliances. The checks carried out by the EWRC in this regard show a high percentage of justification resulting from insufficient speed and lack of commitment on the part of companies, according to EWRC annual reports (2012–16). Additional problems also reported to the Ombudsman include unilateral correction by companies of consumer accounts and inspections and replacement of commercial measuring instruments in the absence of the client. Some of these still persist, but in general they are fewer.

C. Water Supply

Most state-owned energy and water supply services in Bulgaria are characterised by inefficient and in some cases low-quality supply, bad management (with huge debts accumulated during the long years of underperformance), low consumption and high consumer debts, resulting in an inability for investment in infrastructure renovation and improvement. The water sector is not an exception.

In the water segment, the role of the EWRC is important because the nature of the problem is more often quality of supply. However, access to justice is not straightforward. According to the procedural rules for handling complaints under Ordinance No 3 of EWRC (2018) on licensing of energy activities, the Commission deals with complaints after they have been sent first to the water suppliers and the complainant has received a reply but is not satisfied with it.

In conclusion, consumers have similar problems, but often they have been transferred from one institution to another. Terms and conditions of energy suppliers under a regulated household market are common for all and complex in nature, and are the responsibility of different ministries, agencies and institutions. The EWRC reports that in some years just 17 per cent of all complaints are within its competence, and each year some 10 per cent of consumers' complaints are transferred to the Ministry of Energy, according to Article 31, paragraph 2 of the Code of Administrative Procedure, and others to different institutions. Moreover, institutions rarely take the initiative to amend the legal framework in order to solve persistent injustice problems. For this reason, the roles of consumer organisations and the Ombudsman are important.

V. The Energy Injustice Labyrinth in Bulgaria

A. EWRC

The State Energy Regulatory Commission[24] was established in 1999 based on Article 11(2) of the repealed Energy and Energy Efficiency Act.[25] The Law on

[24] See: www.dker.bg/en/home.html.

[25] Energy and Energy Efficiency Act, 1999 prom SG, issue 64/ of June 16, 1999, available at: seea.government.bg/documents/ZEE_EN.pdf.

Regulation of Water Supply and Sewerage Services amended the Energy Act and the Commission was transformed into a State Commission for Energy and Water Regulation (SEWRC). In 2015 the election procedure for Commission members changed,[26] and it was no longer a state body within the Council of Ministers but was elected by the National Assembly. Its name changed to the Commission for Energy and Water Regulation (EWRC) in 2015.

A General Department for Complaint Handling and Dispute Resolution was established at the SEWRC in 2011 to ensure that appropriate action is taken to maximise effective responses to the growing issues of consumer needs.

This resulted in changes in the functions of the EWRC in 2012 in the Energy Act,[27] according to which the Commission: (1) issues, amends, supplements, suspends and revokes licences in the cases provided for in this law; (2) adopts and publishes basic guidelines for its activity; (3) adopts the bylaws envisaged in this law; (4) approves the general terms of the contracts provided for in this law; and (5) *approves rules for working with consumers of energy services.*

Yet, when dealing with complaints, the EWRC often had to transfer complaints to other institutions – the National Assembly, the Presidency, the Ministry Council, different ministries, commissions, agencies, regional administration, municipal administrations, and so on. The percentage of complaints sent to the EWRC for transfers was different each year, for example 14 per cent of the total in 2016, sometimes more. In the majority of cases, however, complaints have not passed through suppliers first, which is the regulatory requirement of the Commission. This is because citizens tend to avoid direct contact with suppliers. The Commission accounted for the large number of complaints for transfer by the fact that consumers are not familiar with the charging structures in the energy suppliers' 'Common terms' for service supply, which replaced individual contracts in the country, and therefore escalate their complaint to the highest possible level for solving these issues, according to the EWRC annual report[28] (2015, 83).

The EWRC is empowered mainly to regulate prices and to check the quality of energy supplies, while financial disputes between the supplier and consumers are not in its power. The latter have been transferred to other institutions, but consumers have also gradually learned to request the Ombudsman's help. Analysis of EWRC complaints shows that just 17 per cent in 2016 and 31 per cent in 2017 were within the Commission's competence.

Complaints in the water segment in particular are often transferred to the Ministry of Environment, Ministry of Regional Development and Public Works, Ministry of Economy and Energy, the presidential administration, the Council of Ministers, municipalities, etc, most often by the CCP.

[26] A Georgiev, 'Institutional Independency of the National Energy Regulator in Bulgaria' (PhD thesis, Faculty of Economics and Business Administration, Sofia University, 2015).

[27] Energy Act 2003, last amend and suppl SG. 83/9 October 2018, available at: www.me.government.bg/en/library/energy-act-256-c25-m258-1.html.

[28] Annual Reports of the CEWR for 2008–18, available at: www.dker.bg/bg/za-kevr/godishni-otcheti.html.

Figure 9.5 Number of complaints at the EWRC

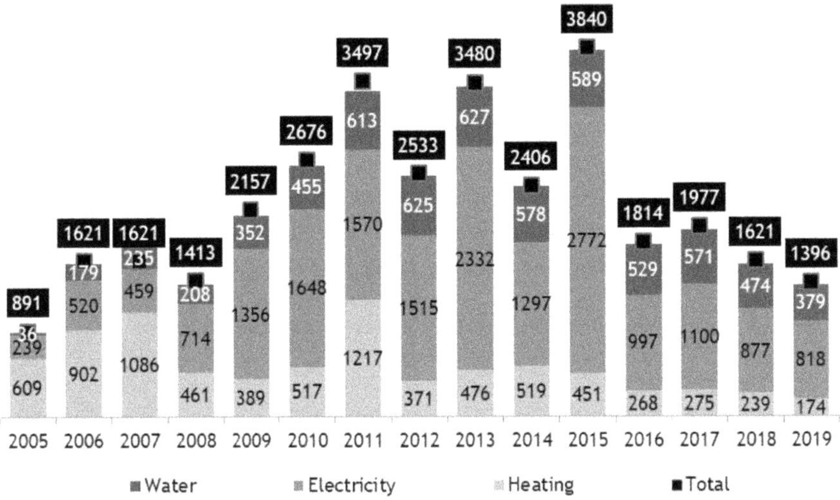

Source: EWRC Annual Reports (2005–19).

After sending a complaint to the EWRC and if no effective solution is found, consumers then send complaints to the National Ombudsman – an institution that has gained their respect and trust over the years.

B. National Ombudsman

The National Ombudsman has been the institution that receives the largest number of complaints about electricity, heating and water suppliers in the country since its establishment.[29] This is also the institution that most actively addresses proposals for amendments in the regulatory framework concerning energy consumer rights. It is the only consumer protection organisation that has had some impact on improving energy justice in the sector. Small steps were achieved over 15 years (2005–2019), including clearer bills, explicit citing of how consumption was calculated in the bills, fewer unfair bills, fewer fines and a more transparent way of charging interest on debts, a more orderly market and better supplier attitude. During the mandate of Ombudsman May Manolova (2015–19), central heating users in Sofia (over 400,000 households or nearly 70 per cent of all central heating consumers in the country) were given the right not to be sued for bills lower than the official minimal salary (BGN560 in 2019), which marked a huge step towards energy justice in the city.[30]

[29] Annual Report of the National Ombudsman for 2005, available at: www.ombudsman.bg/reports/415?page=6#middleWrapper.

[30] Annual Report of the CEWR for 2015, available at: www.dker.bg/bg/za-kevr/godishni-otcheti.html.

The Ombudsman as an institution protecting consumer rights has gained consistent recognition in Bulgaria, as the data on the total number of complaints in the period between 2005 and 2019 shows, according to annual reports.[31] The areas covered have grown to include all fields where citizens suffer rights violations. In general, public services complaints have made up nearly one-third of all complaints since the institution was opened. In the few years up to 2019, this share has slightly declined to 23 per cent, but in fact the real number of complaints increased. The decline was due to more complaints against insurance and finance services emerging, and the new battlefield for the Ombudsman for bringing in a personal bankruptcy law to protect people from excessive manipulations.

Figure 9.6 Number of complaints at National Ombudsman of Bulgaria

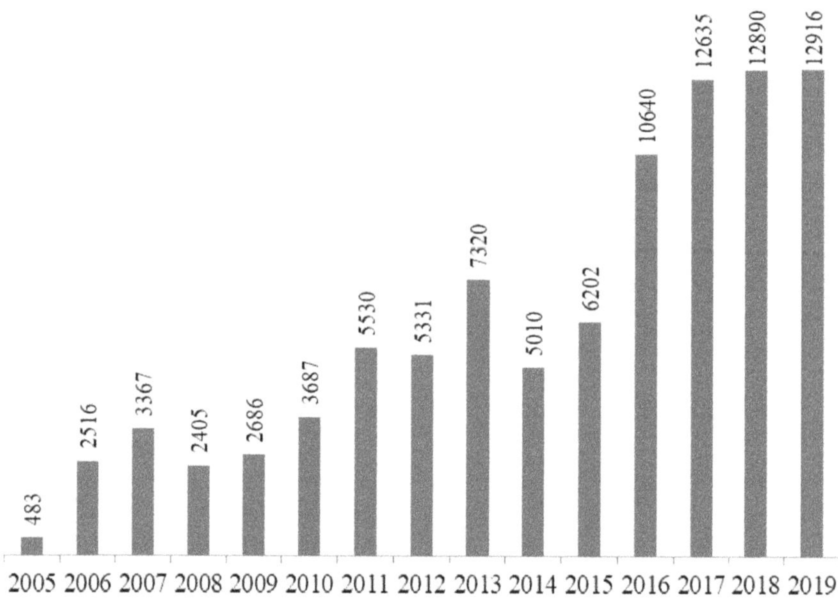

Source: Annual Reports of National Ombudsman of Republic of Bulgaria.

The period between 2005 and 2015 was marked by numerous attempts by the Ombudsman to summarise and address all the problems in the energy sector with all the relevant institutions at all levels, according to its annual reports from the period. Some changes were made during the period, mainly in improving the information in energy bills and explaining the methodology of heating accountants. Some overcharging practices also stopped, but many consumers still continued to carry the burden of high energy bills, resulting in numerous court cases, the

[31] Annual Reports of the National Ombudsman for 2005–19, available at: www.ombudsman.bg/reports/415?page=6#middleWrapper.

suspension of the bank accounts of vulnerable consumers, and huge debts that did not correspond to real consumption.

The battle over these problems continued more actively after 2015. Figure 9.7 shows a twofold increase in the number of complaints to the Ombudsman as result of the nomination of Maya Manolova to the post. She managed to bring several important court cases to completion during her mandate and provide more justice to consumers. In 2016, the Ombudsman sued Toplofikatsia – the heating supplier in Sofia with nearly 70 per cent of all heating customers in Bulgaria in over 400,000 households, according to an article on *News.bg*[32] – thus protecting consumers from expensive court cases for unpaid bills up to the minimal salary threshold.

Figure 9.7 Number of complaints at heating, electricity and water suppliers

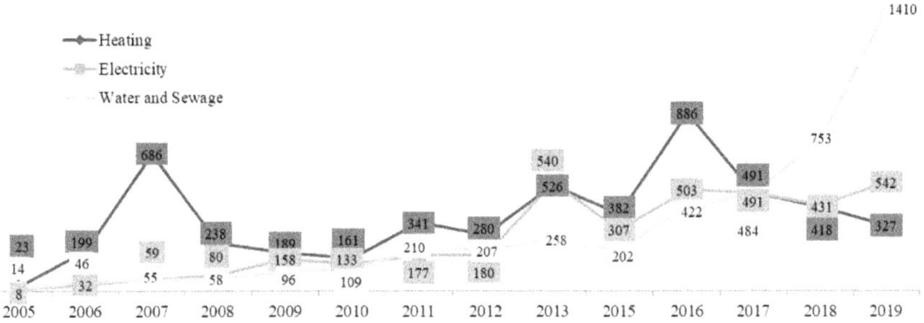

Source: Annual Report of National Ombudsman of Republic of Bulgaria.

C. Local/Municipalities Ombudsmen

Prior to the Ombudsman Act, in the period between 1999 and 2000, a dozen pilot projects were launched with the appointment of public mediators in Sevlievo, Plovdiv, Varna, Shumen, Razgrad, Smolyan, Stara Zagora, Kazanlak, the Mladost metropolitan area and Sofia. Local ombudsmen, however, were not included in the Ombudsman Law. They were termed 'Public Mediators' and the positions had a non-obligatory character. The municipal mediator should be elected and dismissed by a qualified majority of the municipal council, by the votes of two-thirds of the total number of municipal councillors. This makes the procedure long and painful.

Several different annual reports of local ombudsmen (Sofia 2019, Plovdiv 2017, Kyustendil 2019, Shumen 2019, Batak 2011) show that not all of them get involved in problems with public services providers. The Sofia Ombudsman explicitly does not accept complaints relating to public services suppliers. The public mediator in Plovdiv, the second largest city in Bulgaria, as of 2019, does accept complaints

[32] 'The ombudsman sued Toplofikacia Sofia for the legal consulting fees' (*news.bg*, 2019), available at: news.bg/crime/ombudsmanat-osadi-toplofikatsiya-sofiya-za-yuristkonsultskite-honorari.html.

about energy suppliers, and even provides some suggestions and measures for improvement. Others are more involved in problems with the public administration, which in general was the purpose for the establishment of the position – to carry out anti-corruption and controlling functions with regard to the local administration.

In 2015 the National Ombudsman started a national campaign for election of local public mediators. The purpose of the campaign was to promote the institution of the local public mediators and to convince every local authority of its need to protect the civic interest at the local level. At that time, there were only 14 local ombudsmen in 265 municipalities in the country.

In 2018, together with the National Association of Local Public Mediators, the Ombudsman submitted to the National Assembly draft amendments to the Local Government and Local Administration Act, which regulates the choice and powers of public mediators in the municipalities.

This draft law, however, has not moved forward. If passed, it would possibly enable the National Ombudsman to create a more efficient system to protect consumers and allocate more problems to the local institutions.

D. Energy Ombudsman at the Electricity Supplier CEZ

The position of the Energy Ombudsman at CEZ was created in March 2013, in respect of Directive 2009/72/EU[33] of the European Parliament, regarding the rules for internal electricity markets, aimed at improving the quality of client servicing and ensuring the efficient work of CEZ in Bulgaria. The Ombudsman's role and organisation of its work are specified in the Rules for the Status and Activities of the Energy Ombudsman of CEZ in Bulgaria.[34] According to the Rules, the Energy Ombudsman should revise cases in which clients had sought help from the supplier but were not satisfied. The Energy Ombudsman should be neutral regarding these cases.

In 2018, there were 752 items of incoming correspondence, of which 19 per cent were complaints, according to the report. The remaining were mostly enquiries about information and investigations. It is clear then that the Ombudsman plays an important role in providing clients with information. Most enquiries were about meters and bill calculations, as well as about quality problems in the distribution network. Of the complaints, 83 per cent were about electricity distribution and 17 per cent about electricity supply.

[33] Directive 2009/72/EC of the European Parliament and of the Council of 13 July 2009 concerning common rules for the internal market in electricity and repealing Directive 2003/54/EC, available at: eur-lex.europa.eu/legal-content/EN/ALL/?uri=celex%3A32009L0072.

[34] CEZ, *Rules for the Status and Activities of the Energy Ombudsman of CEZ in Bulgaria* (2013), available at: www.cez.bg/edee/content/file-other/bulgaria/ombudsman/cez-bulgaria_ombudsman_pravila_20130328_bg_sp_kv.pdf.

Figure 9.8 Incoming correspondence at the Energy Ombudsman of CEZ

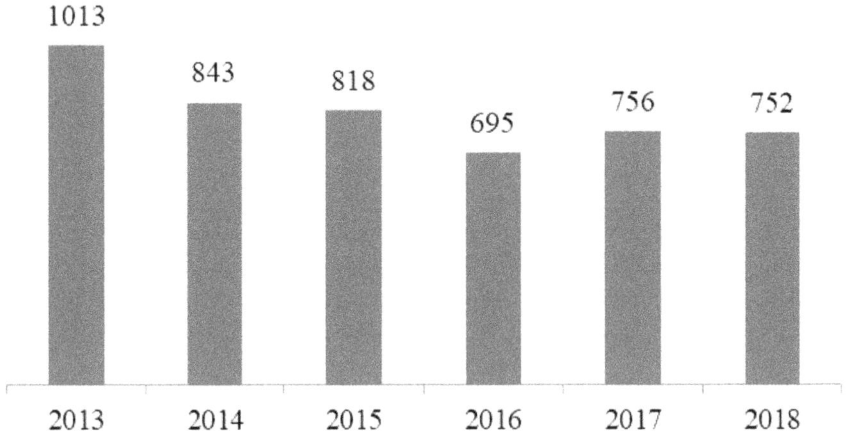

Source: Annual Report of the Energy Ombudsman at CEZ for 2018.

E. Consumer Organisations

According to the List of Qualified Organisations issued by the Ministry of Economy,[35] qualified consumer organisations which have a legal interest in bringing an action for suspension or prohibition of acts or commercial practices that are in the violation of the collective interests of consumers are as follows:

1. Commission for Consumer Protection.
2. National Association 'Active Consumers'.
3. Regional Union of Consumers – 98 – Vidin city.
4. National League – Service Users.
5. Association 'Help for the Consumer'.
6. Federation of Consumers in Bulgaria.
7. Association for Legal Help for Consumers.
8. National Association for Consumer Protection.
9. Association 'Legal Clinic for Consumers'.

However, unlike the CCP, the other organisations do not have active publications and initiatives in protecting consumers in the energy sector.

According to Article 165 of the Consumer Protection Act, the CCP consists of three members, including the chair, who are appointed for a term of five years by a decision of the Council of Ministers and appointed by the Prime Minister.

[35] Ministry of Economy of Bulgaria, List of Qualified Organizations in the Republic of Bulgaria, which have Any Legal Interest to Accept Claims for Discontinuation or for the Prohibition of actions or Trade Practices Which are in Violation of the Collective Interests of Consumers (2020) approved by order No RD-16-1053/10.12.2009, available at: www.mi.government.bg/bg/library/spisak-na-kvalificiranite-organizacii-v-republika-balgariya-koito-imat-praven-interes-da-predyavyavat-729-c293-m0-7.html.

The method of election of the Commission chair and members is subject to discussion in the same way that it is for the EWRC. Over the years, the institutional independency has been questioned, in the same way that it is with other state commissions for control over a certain sector. Sources of financing, members' election methods, etc, are factors for a critical review in all countries with regulated sectors of the economy.

The CCP's activities in the field of consumer protection in the energy sector are minimal and inefficient. A summary of the Commission's work in the energy sector shows more activity around the organisation of public events (for example, working groups and public discussions) and fewer specific activities around draft law proposals, suing of suppliers and legal amendment proposals, which seem to be more effective. No data and analysis of consumer complaints was provided in the annual reports of the CCP, which suggests less work on individual cases.

F. ADR

ADR was introduced to Bulgaria in 2012, to include 12 general conciliation commissions in different cities and 14 sectorial conciliation commissions.[36] All these commissions are within the structure of the CCP. Among the sectorial commissions, one is engaged in the electrical energy sector and there are no commissions on heat and water. Problems in these fields need to be addressed to the general Commission.

Data from the CCP's 2017 annual report show that the Commission received a total of 23,303 written complaints and 216 applications for ADR, of which four were sent to the electrical energy ADR commission.[37] All were resolved.

In 2014, the CCP received a total of 17,903 complaints, of which 10 per cent related to public services: 507 conciliation proceedings were instituted in 2014, of which 205, or 36 per cent were terminated according to Article 21, item 2 of the Criminal Code of the Republic of Bulgaria[38] (1968, amended 2017) in which the supplier did not appear or did not send a representative. In fact, a large number of suppliers receive their notifications, the duly signed return is returned to the CPC but, due to the voluntary nature of the conciliation proceedings, suppliers do not appear and do not send a duly authorised representative. In these cases, the chair of the Conciliation Commission has no choice but to suspend the proceedings. The number of cases in which agreement was reached was 70 or about 14 per cent of the total.

The situation in previous years was very similar. Disputes in 2012 were mainly about mobile operators and telecommunication service providers, according

[36] CCP website, 2020: kzp.bg/.

[37] CCP, Annual Reports for 2012–14, available at: kzp.bg/aktove-old/old.kzp.bg/indexed81.html.

[38] Criminal Code of the Republic of Bulgaria 1968, amended 2017, available at: www.legislationline.org/download/id/8395/file/Bulgaria_Criminal_Code_1968_am2017_ENG.pdf.

to the annual report.[39] In 2013, there were 515 applications of which an agreement was only reached in 28. In 261 cases the supplier did not attend; in 16 the consumer did not attend; and in 46 both attended but did not reach an agreement. This is for all economic sectors. No specifics are provided on any of the sectors or types of dispute.

This mechanism is not well received or popular in the country. Indeed, the CCP itself states that the mechanism is not effective for the country's needs.

The National Ombudsman has expressed the view that these ADR mechanisms are inefficient, criticising the voluntary nature of reconciliation proceedings and the low number of agreements reached.

The Ombudsman summarises the following areas for critical review of the ADR conciliation mechanism:

1. Voluntary participation of suppliers in the procedures.
2. ADR does not necessarily include a member with legal education.
3. The debt limitation period shall be suspended when a conciliation procedure is instituted before a general or sectorial conciliation commission.
4. Confusion about which consumer protection method to use if necessary – Voluntary Dispute Settlement Procedure with EWRC, Payment Disputes Commission, sectorial ombudsmen, etc.
5. Most of the consumers' problems cannot be solved by ADR because the terms of services are legally regulated in the suppliers' 'Common terms' for all users and are subject to persistent bad practices or the result of poor legislative decisions.
6. A large part of the citizens' problems with the supplying companies is in the phase of forced debt collection. The process often begins without the debtor being notified at all and is accompanied by the charging of expenses, including huge legal fees and private enforcement agents' fees.

VI. Constraints for Energy Justice in Bulgaria

A. Heating Supply

There were central heating supply companies in 15 cities in Bulgaria as of 2019. Central heating grids were designed and developed in the 1980s in Bulgaria, when the government subsidised a big part of energy prices and the usage in the multi-family panel buildings reached 100 per cent of households.[40] After removal of state subsidies and an increase in prices, many users cancelled the service, which resulted in higher distribution costs for those remaining in the buildings. Families who cancelled the service were still obliged to pay for common building costs,

[39] CCP, Annual Report for 2012, available at: kzp.bg/aktove-old/old.kzp.bg/indexed81.html.
[40] Peneva, *Energy Poverty: The Bulgarian Case* (n 2).

and their refusal to do so resulted in numerous court cases and huge debts at the heating supplier. At the same time, the bills of users became unpredictable and uncontrollable.

All the problems of the heating supply sector are described in the National Program for Stabilization and Development of the District Heating Sector in the Republic of Bulgaria.[41] The primary effect, of old installations leading to lower quality and high price, coupled with the secondary effect, of fewer users and lower consumption, hampered the general development of the most price cost-effective and environmentally friendly type of heating. The sector faces huge challenges to survive in conditions of high levels of energy poverty and a strong consumer wish to control consumption and bills.

Moreover, lower usage has resulted in higher heating losses in a network designed to work with optimal maximum usage in all buildings in the area covered. Lower debt collection and lower bills pushed heating supply companies towards bankruptcy or near-bankruptcy. To compensate, heating supply companies started suing consumers and charging unfair taxes for legal services. Bankruptcy now faced everyone in the chain.

Centralised heating systems in the majority of residential units do not allow commercial measurement in each individual apartment, but only in the building's heating station (vertical installation type). In order to promote the savings in the district heating apartments, devices for regulating consumption and devices for distributing the reported amounts of heat at the heating station among its users were introduced. This system, which has been operating successfully in a number of European countries, according to the National Program,[42] has proven to be unsuitable for Bulgaria, not for technical but for neighbourly reasons – free use of heat in part of the apartments at the expense of the others. The well-deserved distrust of the neighbours was redirected to the heating accountants and hence to district heating suppliers. This was an additional reason for refusal of the service. The old method of distribution based on heated volume, which does not encourage savings but prevents the billing of the accounts of the correct customers, is not allowed by European directives and rules.

The report points out additional reasons for the financial burden on the companies. In specific periods, such as from 2006 to 2009, natural gas prices increased every three months or more frequently, while the regulatory framework does not allow changes in the heating price for households more than once a year. All this led to additional financial losses on top of the heating losses caused by poor infrastructure and lower consumption in buildings. To compensate for these losses, in 2020 the EWRC designed a mechanism for allocating finance

[41] Ministry of Economy, Energy and Tourism, *National Program for Stabilization and Development of the District Heating Sector in the Republic of Bulgaria* (2011), available at: mi.government.bg/files/useruploads/files/proekt_programme_dht.pdf.

[42] Ministry of Economy of Bulgaria, *National Program for Stabilization and Development of the District Heating Sector in the Republic of Bulgaria until 2020* (2011), available at: mi.government.bg/files/useruploads/files/proekt_programme_dht.pdf.

for a 40 per cent gas price decrease for Bulgaria provided in March 2020 by the Russian government, starting six months before the announcement and favouring heating suppliers. On 1 April 2020, the Commission announced a 42.78 per cent price decrease for natural gas and just 21.8 per cent price decrease for central heating, according to Katanska Gocheva.[43] A month later, on 1 May 2020, a new price announcement indicated an average heating price decrease of less than 5 per cent, according to *bTV News*.[44] This triggered a new accusation from the energy consumer protector – the Ombudsman. It is the second time that this situation has occurred in Bulgaria. In 2016, the gas price decreased by 23 per cent while the heating price for household consumers only decreased by an average of 5 per cent.[45]

All this indicates significant system distortions: distortions in the supplier–consumer relationships, in the supplier's expenditure–income balance, and in consumers' consumption–expenditure balance. These are systemic problems, in which each part of the supply chain is deprived of a certain type of natural right. Removing one injustice is often offset by the introduction of a new one. Energy injustice is still present in the country and takes various forms and occurs in different ways each year.

B. Electricity Supply

In general, injustice in the supplier–consumer relationship in the electricity sector is less prominent than in other sectors. This is observable from the lower numbers of complaints compared with other sectors – namely, heating and water. These problems in the early years after privatisation were related to lack of clear information on bills, poor quality of the delivered electricity, unilateral correction by companies of consumer accounts, and inspections and replacement of commercial measuring instruments in the absence of the client and others. Some of them still persist, but in general are much fewer. It is important to note that the household segment in Bulgaria's electricity sector is still regulated. Liberalisation has not begun, hampered mainly by energy poverty. While the Commission still protects consumers from increasing prices, the Ombudsman believes that prices are too high. However, heating suppliers claim that prices are too low and are a reason for the replacement of central heating with electric heating.

This replacement is not a welcome development, as the electrical grids are not designed for the electrical loads required for heating homes that have given up

[43] The price of natural gas decreased by 42.78%, of heating, by 21.84% (*Capital*, 1 April 2020), available at: www.capital.bg/biznes/energetika/2010/04/01/4049109_cenata_na_prirodniia_gaz_poevtiniava_s_4278_na_parnoto/.

[44] 'CEWR set lower price of heating and hot water' (*bTV News*, 1 May 2020), available at: btvnovinite.bg/bulgaria/kevr-opredeli-po-niski-ceni-na-parnoto-i-toplata-voda.html.

[45] D Petkova, 'From April 1, the price of natural gas falls by 23%' *Investor's News* (31 March 2020), available at: www.investor.bg/ikonomika-i-politika/332/a/ot-1-april-cenata-na-prirodniia-gaz-pada-s-23-214196/.

central heating. Moreover, the use of solid fuels, where that is possible, will result in air pollution creating health risks. In addition, carbon dioxide emissions will increase by at least two million tonnes a year due to the higher carbon intensity of alternatives – electricity or coal – according to the sector's National Program.[46]

C. Water Supply

Recent changes in the water supply sector concerning water price increases since 2018 have elevated water poverty in the country. This was coupled with severe water shortages in several large cities, bringing people onto the streets at the end of December 2019. Causes for water shortages include long-term lack of investment in renovation of the water supply infrastructure and the drying out of neighbouring water supply dams.

Most state-owned energy and water supply services in Bulgaria are characterised by inefficient, and in some cases, low quality supply, bad management (with huge debts accumulated during long years of underperformance), low consumption and high consumer debts, resulting in an inability for investment in infrastructure renovation and improvement. The water sector is not an exception.

There is a reference price for households, which is a percentage (4 per cent) of the average household's income in the relevant region. However, the maximum water price in Bulgaria is not fairly applied and exceeds the 4 per cent recommended by the European Court of Auditors.[47] There are also concerns about the Prime Minister's decision in January 2020 to set a uniform water price for the entire country due to low incomes in villages, remote and less developed regions, and lower water supply cost.

Yet, having this cap, or reference price, is seen as relatively fair by the Ombudsman and has been used as an argument in cases in specific cities with high and economically not reasonable price increases. A similar case was seen in Dobrich, for which in January 2018 the Ombudsman sent an opinion to the EWRC asking for indication of the average monthly household income used. According to the Ombudsman, the data should be taken from the monitoring of household budgets because the numbers used in this case showed higher values in order to justify the unfair increase in the cost of the service.[48]

After a severe water shortage in 2019, the Prime Minister announced the setting up of a nationwide state-owned water supply holding applying a single standard price for all Bulgarian consumers. This was attacked by many consumer

[46] Ministry of Economy of Bulgaria, *National Program for Stabilization and Development of the District Heating Sector in the Republic of Bulgaria until 2020* (2011), available at: mi.government.bg/files/useruploads/files/proekt_programme_dht.pdf.

[47] European Court of Auditors, *Publications on Implementing the Drinking Water Directive* (2017), available at: op.europa.eu/webpub/eca/special-reports/drinking-water-12-2017/bg/.

[48] Annual Report of the National Ombudsman for 2018, available at: www.ombudsman.bg/reports/415?page=6#middleWrapper.

rights organisations, mainly the Ombudsman, believing that in places where the gravity water is supplied at very low cost, consumers will have to pay extra to compensate other regions. These regions in general are remote, with much lower income levels than the country's average.

D. Legal Limitations to the National Ombudsman's Rights

There are fundamental legal provisions that lead to energy injustice in Bulgaria, resulting in numerous complaints and the inability to solve individual disputes even in courts. A summary of these problems now follows.

As stated at the beginning of this chapter, the Ombudsman is the key institution to provide protection for energy consumers in Bulgaria, but it is not officially entrusted to impact on the decisions of the EWRC, which designs and amends the regulatory framework governing the relationship between suppliers and consumers of energy. The Ombudsman's legal power is limited. Even mobilising all possible sources to lobby for legal changes has turned out not to be enough to protect consumer rights during all three of his terms until 2019.

The CCP mechanism does not cover the energy sector. Instead, ADR has been introduced to it, reducing the possibility of enhancing consumer rights in the field. In addition, the Local Ombudsman network is not well developed. It has the potential to be a very strong support for the National Ombudsman and therefore consumers, but is encumbered by that fact that, first, local ombudsmen are regulated by totally separate legal provisions distinct from the Ombudsman Act and, second, their network development is hindered by legal limitations for tough election requirements. The Ombudsman Act does not include clauses on the activities of local ombudsmen or the interaction between local and national ombudsmen.

Corporative ombudsmen could help to ease some of the energy injustice but are mainly effective in areas of providing information, investigations and checks in specific cases. Such ombudsmen cannot solve legal disputes or issues concerning court cases. In addition, many suppliers do not have ombudsmen.

E. Questionable Status of the EWRC

According to the provisions of Article 36a, paragraph 2 of the Energy Act,[49] the decision of the EWRC, which establishes electricity and natural gas caps is an individual administrative act and cannot be appealed by citizens in court.

However, the Ombudsman's request states that the provision of Article 36a, paragraph 2 of the Energy Act in the part 'which is an individual administrative act' contravenes Article 4, paragraph. 1, Article 56 and Article 120, paragraph 2

[49] Energy Act 2003, last amend and suppl SG 83/9 October 2018, available at: www.me.government.bg/en/library/energy-act-256-c25-m258-1.html.

of the Constitution, which is why it should be declared unconstitutional. At the request, constitutional case No 8/2018 was implemented.

According to Article 13 of the Energy Act, the EWRC, as a state body, can take reasoned decisions, which are individual or common administrative acts. But the Ombudsman's request argues in detail that the individual administrative acts under Article 36a, paragraph 2 of the Energy Act, which establish price caps, directly and indirectly affect the rights and legitimate interests of an indefinite number of citizens. This reasoning was also sent to the Chair of the National Assembly.

F. Physical Persons Bankruptcy Act

One of the key issues identified by the National Ombudsman in dealing with numerous court cases for the huge debts of consumers was the lack of a physical persons' bankruptcy Act in Bulgaria. Such a law would be expected to regulate the debt-collecting companies which cooperate with many energy suppliers, in addition to banks and other credit and leasing providers. In a population of less than seven million people, there are nearly two million citizens with overdue loans and bills, having no tools to protect and regulate their relationship with these companies.[50]

In 2018, the current Ombudsman organised a forum on 'Regulation of bankruptcy of natural persons in the Republic of Bulgaria – opportunities and perspectives', at which she presented a concept for a draft law on bankruptcy for individuals. The drafting of the law was one of the priorities for the Ombudsman in 2018, as Bulgaria is the only EU country that does not have legislation on personal bankruptcy, and this is also a socially significant problem for Bulgarian citizens.

Over 81 per cent of Bulgarian citizens want the adoption of special legislation to regulate the bankruptcy of individuals, according to the Ombudsman. This issue had still not been solved in April 2020.

G. CCP, EWRC Members Election

The Energy Act in Bulgaria stipulates that the chair and the other members of the Committee are elected and dismissed by the National Assembly. Despite the legal restrictions on the involvement of politicians in the decisions of the regulator, they have an informal instrument of influence through their proposals for appointing commissioners and chairs, setting annual budgets, the frequency of contacts with commissioners, and more. Business, in turn, can exert influence through contacts with the regulator, as a former or future employer of commissioners, and through

[50] A Kostadinov, 'The Consumer Protection Association supports the Ombudsman's idea of a Personal Bankruptcy Act' (*Darik News*, 1 August 2019), available at: dariknews.bg/novini/bylgariia/asociaciiata-za-zashtita-na-potrebitelite-podkrepia-ideiata-na-ombudsmana-za-zakon-za-lichen-falit-2179732.

other means. If the EWRC worked smoothly, the Ombudsman's work would not be so important.

As mentioned in section II.E, the same problem applies to the CCP Chair and members. Members' election methods, sources of finances and other factors for institutional independency are critical to a review of consumer protection mechanisms in all countries with regulated sectors of the economy.

H. ADR Constraints

ADR appears not to be an effective mechanism to access justice for the problematic energy sector in Bulgaria. All specifics of energy injustice in the country are hindering the application of this mechanism. An analysis by the conciliation commissions conducted in 2014[51] shows that conciliation proceedings are not considered to be an effective procedure due to the voluntary reconciliation/mediation solutions to solve the current problems. The proceedings at the Conciliation Commission take considerable time and resources but, despite this, consumers remain extremely dissatisfied with the institution's actions and the retailers' lack of interest in them. The mechanism does not include an option for administrative penal liability on traders for failure to attend conciliation meetings and for failure to send a representative. Another major drawback is that the Conciliation Commission cannot resolve the core of the dispute, but can only attempt to reach an agreement if the trader is willing to make compromises, which in most cases they are not.

In the field of consumer disputes with heating suppliers, the National Ombudsman states that ADR cannot help either with regard to the aggressive methods used by the collectors, nor with regard to the enormous fees, expenses and legal fees, nor to protect the debtor from arbitrary arbitration.

In the field of public services, ADR may fail in solving problems of this type:

1. Calculations of heating bills of central heating suppliers – including methodology, ways of calculating common expenditure of buildings – are entirely done by suppliers and heating accountants. The consumer has no role and cannot participate in this process due to legal regulations.
2. Calculations of electricity correction for a past period are legal, even though it is often a subject for dispute.
3. The order for charging water consumption for general consumption is clearly unfair and has been the subject of numerous complaints, but it is legally written in Ordinance No 4 of 2004.[52]

Therefore, none of these major disputes can be solved through ADR mechanisms.

[51] CCP, Annual Report for 2014, available at: kzp.bg/aktove-old/old.kzp.bg/indexed81.html.

[52] Pursuant to Article 45 of Ordinance No 4/2004, disputes between operators and consumers are settled by court procedure, and in § 6 of the Transitional and Final Provisions of the Ordinance it is explicitly stated that the Minister of Regional Affairs gives instructions for the implementation of the Ordinance development and public works. Therefore, a dispute between the complainant and the

VII. Conclusions

Bulgaria is an ideal example of energy injustice in conditions of a regulated energy market, combined with high poverty, a complex and imperfect regulatory framework, and numerous uncoordinated consumer protection mechanisms. Consumers do not have direct and efficient access to justice, no matter the willingness of the representatives of each channel to help. Improvements in justice for energy consumers has been a long and tough process, with small steps towards success reached only through the enormous efforts of individuals in positions of responsibility.

The government, on the other hand, has underestimated the poverty issue for a long time. Bulgaria has probably had around 22 per cent of its citizens living below the official poverty line for more than 20 years, according to the Eurostat and NSI databases (2020).[53] Fluctuations around this percentage were related to the economic cycle – increases in overall population incomes in periods of higher economic growth and income decreases in recession periods – and not to the efficiency of government policies. A heating allowance is provided to less than 7 per cent of the population,[54] and this satisfies only a very small part of the heating needs. At the same time, the lowest income groups, accounting for some 30 per cent of households in the country, spend an average of 20 per cent of their net income on energy and in most cases use solid fuel. Moreover, the country's social protection system is failing to help the lowest income groups with their basic needs.

Bulgarian people receive the lowest average income of any EU country. They cannot invest in improving the efficiency of their buildings. They cannot access justice in the cases where suppliers demand extra payments over actual consumption. Their only recourse is to cut consumption, so as to control their bills. In the case of central heating, even cutting individual consumption does not help, so the only solution is to cut building consumption and switch to another heating type. Withdrawal from central heating leads to a new type of energy poverty, where people have to spend much more for other more expensive kinds of heating, such as electricity and gas, with higher costs per unit, or choose solid fuel which is not environmentally friendly and brings other types of problems. This completes the cycle that starts with poverty and ends with deeper poverty.

The role of energy justice in this process is critical. Unfortunately, consumer organisations have limited powers and can only partially solve cases such as individual disputes over unfair billing, excessive interest on debts, the collection of low levels of debt, high legal taxes for court cases, and poor quality services with frequent outages, particularly for water from 2019 to 2020. Mechanisms for

plumbing operator over the implementation of the regulation remains outside the control powers of the CEWR. See: www.lex.bg/laws/ldoc/2135499390.

[53] National Statistical Institute of Bulgaria database: www.nsi.bg/en.

[54] Peneva, *Energy Poverty: The Bulgarian Case* (n 2).

accessing justice cannot provide solutions to the most common problems, such as imposing a cap on electricity prices with reference to incomes, preventing court cases for debts lower than the official minimum salary for all heating suppliers across the country, or introducing individual contracts for all public services.

The regulatory framework does not allow establishment of a network of local ombudsmen – regarded as a solution to many of these issues and which would be a source of support to the National Ombudsman – or relocation of ADR mechanisms to the National Ombudsman. ADR mechanisms in their current status are highly inefficient, not just for the energy sector, but for all issues. In order to be efficient, they need to be binding, and there needs to be a special sectorial commission for heat, for water and for public services. Moreover, it is essential that they should be transparent; unfortunately, the reverse is true and, to date, they are actually the least transparent routes to justice.

The rights and powers of each channel need to be reviewed and optimised, not just ADR, but also the EWRC, the National Ombudsman and the local ombudsmen. In addition, all relevant legal Acts need to be reviewed along with the common terms for supply of energy. Methodologies for energy measurement need to be re-evaluated, and the system needs a better coordination mechanism. In particular, the transfers of complaints from one institution to another needs to end. In short, people have the right to easy access to justice.

10

Energy Poverty and Access to Justice in Catalonia

ANAÏS VARO AND ENRIC R BARTLETT CASTELLÀ

I. Introduction

Energy supply and access to energy services are essential to human life. Energy poverty is understood as the inability to attain the socially and materially necessitated domestic energy services that ensure the wellbeing of a household, allowing its members to participate meaningfully in society.[1] In 2017 the percentage of people living in energy poverty in Spain fluctuated between 7.4 per cent and 17.3 per cent, depending on the indicator used to evaluate the phenomenon.[2] To deal with this situation, several measures and policies have been deployed at different administrative, institutional and governance levels.

The Ombudsman's intervention and the use of alternative means of conflict resolution, such as consumer arbitration, to combat energy poverty in Catalonia, are part of an institutional framework. Catalonia, institutionally, is an autonomous community of Spain, which is a decentralised state, but not a federal one. Catalonia has legislative power and jurisdiction in the sectors recognised by the Catalan Statute of Autonomy (which is a higher-level rule than the law under the constitutional umbrella). In light of the above, legislation from the central State Parliament and that of the Autonomous Community sometimes conflict. With a complex and multidimensional phenomenon, such as energy poverty, Catalonia holds competences in social services and consumer protection, while the central

[1] S Buzar, 'The "hidden" geographies of energy poverty in post-socialism: between institutions and households' (2007) 38 *Geoforum* 224.

[2] The latest available data on energy poverty in Spain was published in the Spanish National Strategy to combat Energy Poverty, launched in 2019. The document compiles the data for four primary indicators proposed by the European Energy Poverty Observatory: the inability to keep home adequately warm; the arrears on utility bills; the low energy expenditure (M/2); and the high share of energy expenditure in income. For more information on energy poverty measures and indicators see: www.energypoverty.eu/.

legislator is responsible for the ground rules of the energy system (though not excluding regional intervention in some aspects, such as quality of supply). The Constitutional Court has the final word on the articulation of those powers. In its judgments, the Court has considered that the state-level competence should prevail for the energy system.

Catalonia has one of the more advanced bodies of legislation on energy poverty, not only taking into consideration all energy supplies but also the water supply. State-level measures on energy poverty include both electricity and gas services. In this chapter, we will focus on the electricity supply for two reasons. First, it is the most important factor both in terms of people and energy supplied; and, second, because energy transition measures to prevent global warming will be achieved through the electrification of the economy.

It is in this context that we begin our analysis by presenting an overview of the Spanish electrical system. Next, we consider the main mechanisms needed to combat the injustice that energy poverty represents. We do this by first reviewing how this crisis has made its way into the centre of Catalonia's political agenda. We then move on to deal with the Catalan legislation, before examining the Spanish state strategy against energy poverty and its impact on Catalonia.

Next, we address in detail the intervention carried out by the Síndic de Greuges, the Catalan Ombudsman. We consider both individual complaints and ex officio actions, paying particular attention to recommendations for regulatory changes. Despite the considerable work that is being done, the Ombudsman's remit does not cover the entire range of consumers living in energy poverty. For this reason, we also dedicate a section to the intervention carried out directly by the local Catalan administrations. Following on from this, we scrutinise the complaint mechanisms of the suppliers themselves and the review process that takes place through consumer arbitration.

After considering the regulatory framework and its implementation, we first discuss the paradigm shift that sees the energy-rights approach targeting specific characteristics of those affected. Second, we look at aspects so far not covered by public policies – the gaps that need filling. Then, having considered both the past and the present, we turn our gaze to the future. We suggest how it would be possible to realise a model of energy justice, its political and legislative implications and, in particular, the role that energy communities defined in European directives can play. Finally, we offer some conclusions.

II. The Spanish Electrical System

Since the middle of the nineteenth century, the supply of energy in Spain has been constituted as a publicly owned service. It was initially locally run by public authorities which provided energy directly or by contracting the provision to a third party. Within the conceptual framework of the theory of public service developed by Duguit and the school of Bordeaux,[3] citizens hold a right to it.

The liberalisation process of the electricity market has been promoted by the European institutions from the 1990s onwards. This policy was based on the assertion that competitive markets would allow for a better provision of service, both in quality and price. The result was that most former public services were changed into regulated services in which the public authorities guarantee the service but do not provide it. These services have been given different denominations. They are termed 'services of general economic interest' in the European Union (EU). With some variation, in general they correspond to the principles of public service: affordability, quality, continuity, equal access and mutability or adaptation to ensure the best performance.

In services provided through networks that respond to the logic of a natural monopoly, in which a single entity is, in economic terms, more efficient than multiple ones, liberalisation attempts to create competitive markets by allowing new operators access to the networks of the former monopolists. In the Spanish electricity and gas sectors, this has resulted in requiring the separation of transport and distribution activities from production and supply activities. However, vertically integrated undertakings are legal, provided that each business is carried out by a company with an independent legal personality. This is the case, for example, for big groups such as Endesa, Iberdrola or Naturgy.[4]

The ultimate justification for liberalisation is that competitive markets allow for a better allocation of resources and, therefore, higher quality and lower prices. Experiences in different countries make it possible to ascertain whether these intended positive results have actually been achieved. As a result, we see an increasing amount of support for a return of the electricity and gas sectors to the public sphere,[5] although these voices are certainly not unanimous. One of the reasons for this failure to achieve the objectives of liberalisation is that the original premise, namely that there would be sufficient competition in the energy markets, was mistaken. The lack of competition is very apparent in the data. The national retail energy markets for households are still highly concentrated, with a value below 2,000 in the Herfindahl and Hirschman index in only seven Member States

[3] eg, L Duguit, 'The concept of public service' (1923) 32 *Yale Law Journal* 425, available at: www.digitalcommons.law.yale.edu/cgi/viewcontent.cgi?article=2948&context=ylj.

[4] eg, the Endesa group is part of Enel – the second largest power company in the world – and at the same time has more than 50 energy companies. These companies' operations range from energy production (renewable and non-renewable) to distribution and supplying.

[5] For an in-depth study, see V Weghmann, 'Going public: a decarbonised, affordable and democratic energy system for Europe. The failure of energy liberalisation' (European Public Services Union, 2019), available at: www.epsu.org/article/going-public-decarbonised-affordable-and-democratic-energy-system-europe-new-epsu-report.

in electricity and four Member States in gas. There is a general understanding that indices of between 1,000 and 1,500 points reflect a moderate market concentration, while with indices above 2,500 points, the market is too concentrated.[6]

The EU average number of active nationwide suppliers per country in 2018 was around 40 in the gas sector and 60 in the electricity sector. The number of electricity suppliers for households that are active nationwide in Spain is 215, the highest in the EU. Even so, like in many Member States, national electricity and gas retail markets are still dominated by a few suppliers.[7] As the Spanish regulator has reported in relation to the retail market, where household consumers are located, in 2018 the three largest electricity trading groups in Spain held a combined share of 86 per cent of consumption.[8] The effect of market share concentration on domestic consumers is negative, as evidenced by the fact that, in standard terms, margins are higher for suppliers linked to large energy groups.[9]

A key indicator of competition is the degree of alignment between the evolution of electricity costs in wholesale markets and the energy component of consumer-billed prices in the retail market.[10] When the energy price implied in the billed amounts is higher than the estimated cost of supply, as has been the case every year in Spain since at least 2011, competition has room for improvement.[11] There is a standard supply contract for small consumers[12] at a regulated rate – known as the voluntary price for the small consumer (PVPC)[13] – which is linked to the wholesale market prices. This contract can only be provided by the eight existing reference suppliers.[14]

The fourth European regulatory package emphasises placing the consumer at the heart of the system, with the opportunity for active choice and participation

[6] Council of European Energy Regulators (CEER), *Handbook for National Energy Regulators. How to assess retail market functioning* (Brussels, 2017) 10, available at: www.ceer.eu/documents/104400/-/-/840b4ce7-9e4a-5ecc-403a-fad85d6ba268.

[7] CEER, *Monitoring report on the performance of European retail markets in 2018* (Brussels, 2017) 7, available at: www.ceer.eu/documents/104400/-/-/5c492f87-c88f-6c78-5852-43f1f13c89e4.

[8] The retail portion is a segment with too much concentration, as it yields a value of 2,791 points, in the Herfindahl and Hirschman Index. See: CNMC Comisión Nacional de los Mercados y la Competencia (National Commission on Markets and Competition), 'Informe de Supervisión del Mercado Minorista de Electricidad' (2019) IS/DE/027/19, 15, available at: www.cnmc.es/sites/default/files/2820666_0.pdf.

[9] CEER, *Monitoring report* (n 7) 22.

[10] ibid 20.

[11] The gross marketing margin, calculated as the difference between the two prices between 2018 and 2017, increased in the domestic segment (23–32 €/MWh, up from 18–27 €/MWh the previous year). Where competition is most intense, SMEs fell slightly (1–10 €/MWh, up from 2–10€/MWh), and where it is larger, the industrial segment remained very small (-6–2€/MWh).

[12] It means, those connected in low voltage with a contracted power less than or equal to 10 kW.

[13] About 11 million of the 28 million household consumers have this tariff. CEER, *Monitoring report* (n 7) 59.

[14] These suppliers comply with the criteria established in Royal Decree 216/2014 (Article 3). The main criteria to fulfil the requirements is having been on the market for three years, having a social capital higher than €500,000 and more than 25,000 customers during the last year. Some suppliers fulfil the criteria and do not apply to be recognised as such because margins in this tariff are very narrow.

in the market.[15] Price and contractual conditions comparison tools are useful for this purpose, but retail consumers hardly ever use them.[16] Some consumers choose to contract the alternative to the PVPC offered by the relevant suppliers. However, this choice sometimes has a higher fixed price all year round than that proposed by the suppliers on the free market in the same group.[17] The example mentioned above demonstrates the difficulty for consumers to make informed decisions. Vulnerable consumers, in any case, should opt for the PVPC so as to enjoy the protective measures provided for in state legislation (discussed in III.C below).

The lack of competition drives up supply prices and contributes to energy poverty. The National Strategy against Energy Poverty (2019–2024), approved by the Spanish central government, defines it (as we will develop in III.C) as 'a situation where a household cannot satisfy their basic needs in terms of energy as a consequence of a non-sufficient income level and, in some cases, can be aggravated further by living in a non-energy-efficient house'. Between 3.5 million and some eight million people, according to the indicator used, are living in energy poverty.[18]

III. Vulnerable Consumers and Access to Energy Justice in Catalonia

In this section we explore the main mechanisms for accessing justice for people living in energy poverty. We examine the main energy poverty measures in Catalonia, their scope and impact, as well as the crucial role of the actors involved in their design, implementation and evaluation.

A. The Emergence of Energy Poverty in the Political and Policy Agenda in Catalonia

It was not until 2012 that the term 'energy poverty' entered the Spanish public lexicon and later made its way into specific regulations and policies. Indeed, the first energy poverty regulations at European level were introduced in 2009 – through the Third Energy Package[19] – and it was in that same year that the first

[15] European Commission, *Clean Energy for All* (2016), available at: www.ec.europa.eu/energy/topics/energy-strategy/clean-energy-all-europeans_en.

[16] The switching rates are 9.3% domestic/27% industrial segments, ibid 43.

[17] CEER, *Monitoring report* (n 7) 37–38.

[18] Ministerio para la Transición Ecológica, 'Estrategia nacional contra la pobreza energética' (2018) 7, available at: www.miteco.gob.es/es//planes-estrategias/estrategia-pobreza-energetica/.

[19] Particularly, through Directive 2009/72/EC of the European Parliament and of the Council of 13 July 2009 concerning common rules for the internal market in electricity and repealing Directive 2003/54/EC [2009] OJ L 211/55.

Social Bond for Electricity was approved in Spain. Despite that, the concept of energy poverty was not yet known and recognised as a social problem.[20] As Sanz-Hernández states in her research, the first appearance of the energy poverty phenomenon in the Spanish press was in 2012, but its politisation did not occur until the engagement of social actors such as social movements in 2014.[21] In Catalonia, the launch of the social movement 'Alliance Against Energy Poverty' (APE) marks a turning point in the proposal and deployment of specific energy poverty policies, as discussed later in this chapter.

Catalan energy poverty measures are highly complex because they interact (and sometimes collide) with national jurisdictions on strategic matters (such as the energy sector or social equality among Spanish citizens)[22] since energy poverty constitutes a multicausal social problem. In this context, a unified strategy can be difficult to pursue in a politically and administratively decentralised country in which each governance level has specific jurisdiction on crucial matters to address the problem.

In 2013, the Catalan Ombudsman published a pioneering report on the situation of Energy Poverty in Catalonia. Two main hurdles to successfully addressing the problem were highlighted.[23] First, despite the valuable knowledge gathered from practical experience of local actors, there was no specific data on energy poverty. Consequently, this knowledge gap also meant a dearth of policies addressing this problem. Thus, second, the report highlighted this lack of public policy as a problem to be urgently addressed. Therefore, in this initial document, the Ombudsman recommends several operative and normative changes.

The first measures in Catalonia were approved in 2013, with the modification to the Consuming Code Act.[24] It incorporated a scheme to protect vulnerable consumers: postponement or payment in instalments in cases of debt, and a ban on basic supplies disconnection in case of non-payment. These measures were pioneering mechanisms to protect vulnerable consumers through extrajudicial means.[25] However, these initiatives were soon suspended, and later cancelled, by

[20] The introduction of the first social bond in Spain responded less to a specific concern for energy poverty than to a political strategy to contain the rocketing citizens' anger at the rise in electricity prices.

[21] A Sanz-Hernández, 'Social Engagement and Socio-Genesis of Energy Poverty as a Problem in Spain' (2019) 124 *Energy Policy* 286.

[22] On the one hand, energy poverty is a complex social problem caused by multiple factors that cannot be solved with only one simple solution. It requires a holistic and interdisciplinary approach that in a decentralised governance structure means a collaborative effort among all the government levels and non-government actors involved. On the other hand, we should bear in mind that, despite the relative normality of these collisions between jurisdictions, the case of energy poverty involves one of the greater lobby sectors in the Spanish context: energy companies.

[23] Síndic de Greuges, 'Informe Sobre La Pobresa Energètica a Catalunya' (2013), available at: www.sindic.cat/site/unitFiles/3530/Informe pobresa energetica definitiu.pdf.

[24] Decret Llei 6/2013, de 23 de desembre, pel qual es modifica la Llei 22/2010, de 20 de juliol, del Codi de consum de Catalunya.

[25] J Ponce Solé and JI Soto Valle, 'La Pobreza Energética: Del Marco Constitucional a La Gestión Administrativa Para La Protección de Derechos. En Especial, El Caso Catalán' in J Ponce Solé and

the Spanish Constitutional Court on the grounds of jurisdiction overlapping with state prerogatives on the energy sector.[26] As mentioned above, big suppliers have a prevalent position in energy sector regulation (particularly at national policy level) meaning they have a strong lobbying position against any regional initiative that could threaten their position.[27]

B. The Catalan Housing Emergency and Energy Poverty Measures Act (Law 24/2015)

In 2014, several social organisations[28] launched a Popular Legislative Initiative (ILP) that collected more than 140,000 signatures with the goal of proposing a new law project on housing and energy poverty to the Catalan Parliament. After months of mobilisation and negotiations, the ILP's proposal achieved unanimity in Parliament, becoming Catalan Act 24/2015 on urgent measures to address the housing and energy poverty emergency.

Immediately after, the Spanish government (made up of members of the Popular Party at that time)[29] filed a constitutional appeal against the popular law, meaning that it was effectively suspended. An exception was the section on energy poverty measures that, due to strong popular support, was excluded from the constitutional appeal.[30]

In terms of its material and territorial scope, the Catalan Act 24/2015 is limited to the Catalan territory. The main novelty of the rule was the introduction of the *precautionary principle* as a basic tool to protect the energy-poor population. The precautionary principle consists in the prohibition to energy suppliers of disconnecting a household for unpaid dues before requesting a social services report assessing the economic and social situation of the specific consumer.[31] Only when the consumer is not considered vulnerable can the supply be interrupted.

JI Soto Valle (eds), *Pobreza energética: regulación jurídica y protección de los derechos de las personas* (Federació de Municipis de Catalunya, 2018).

[26] STC 60/2016, de 17 de marzo de 2016. In this Constitutional Court decision, the specific measures on energy poverty of the Catalan Act were declared unconstitutional arguing that the Spanish State has the prerogative of establishing the ground rules of the energy sector, which was violated by the Catalan regulation.

[27] Ponce Solé and Soto Valle (n 25) 25.

[28] Organisations forming part of the core group were the Platform for People Affected by Mortgages (PAH), the APE and the Centre for Human Rights Observatory DESC.

[29] It is important to bear in mind the complexity of power distribution in a decentralised country like Spain where the political scenario is divided by two different cleavages: the ideologic (right–left) but also the centre–peripheric. This political complexity also affects the policy dimension and helps us to understand the dynamics that made possible the unanimous approval of the Catalan law and the quick reaction from the central government.

[30] The suspension affects the obligation for banks and big real estate entities to propose solutions to the affected families instead of evicting them and the possibility for the public administration to fine the entities that own empty dwellings.

[31] Additionally, it establishes that, in case of non-response from the social services office, the supply cannot be interrupted (Art 6 Llei 24/2015).

Besides these measures, other energy poverty policies have been deployed in the Catalan territory, mostly at the local level. Due to the lack of space in this chapter, we only mention the following as examples of good practice: Energy Advice Points in the city of Barcelona, and the Energy Poverty Programme 'Let's save Energy!' from the Diputació de Girona (a legal public authority that coordinates and provides services to 221 municipalities in the province of Girona). Both have an interdisciplinary and interdepartmental approach to the problem and include direct interventions in energy-poor households, such as energy audits, energy advice and energy efficiency improvements.

C. The National Strategy on Energy Poverty in Spain and its Impact in Catalonia

In April 2019, after a six-month drafting process that included public participation, Spain launched a new National Strategy against Energy Poverty. The new National Strategy consolidates the existing energy poverty policies at the national level and incorporates some novelties, such as an official definition of energy poverty, energy poverty reduction objectives[32] and a new measure: the Gas Social Bond. Overall, from the 19 measures included in the National Strategy, 11 of them refer to improving knowledge about the energy poverty situation and comprehensive awareness measures. From the eight other measures, half of them are financial aids for energy-poor consumers and the rest refer to energy efficiency measures. From this distribution we can see that, despite the compelling announcements in the strategic document, the actual operative measures are disappointing as regards the fulfilment of their own objectives. As previously mentioned, the energy poverty definition adopted in Spain (see section II) highlights the economic burden as the main cause of energy poverty, therefore it is considered only as an alternative expression to general poverty.

Following on from the National Strategy and the state-level energy poverty measures, we now discuss the interactions and compatibility between the Catalan precautionary principle and the current national Electricity Social Bond.[33] The Electricity Social Bond establishes a discount on the bill of either 25 or 40 per cent

[32] The strategy establishes two parallel energy poverty reduction goals (one mandatory, the second desirable) to be potentially accomplished in a 5-year period. They would be a reduction of 25% (50% if possible) of the indicators proposed by the Energy Poverty Observatory.

[33] The current Electricity Social Bond is the third generation of social bonds in Spain. The first tariff reduction was approved in 2009, as a reaction to the rocketing of energy prices after the energy liberalisation process. The measure allowed freezing the electricity rates at the time of its approval. The second Electricity Social Bond implemented a fixed discount of 25% of the bill for all consumers with a low contracted power (<3kW) in their main residences, plus some specific criteria like pensioners, large family status or being part of a household with all its members unemployed. Finally, in 2017, the current Social Bond was approved, expanding the discount rates and incorporating new targeting requirements.

on the regulated rates for vulnerable households.[34] It also includes a ban on disconnection in severe cases, requiring other administrations (regional or local) to fund the remaining 50 per cent of the total of the pending bill, or, since 2018, in vulnerable households with one or more members who are either under 16 years old or have a disability above 33 per cent or a high level of dependency. Enlarging the pool of customers eligible for the Electricity Social Bond, postponing its renewal, and banning residential electricity and gas supply disconnections of first homes are some of the measures adopted to tackle the Covid-19 outbreak, which has changed this framework temporarily. However, it is fair to say that based on their social responsibility commitments, even before these changes took place, suppliers adopted measures to provide relief to customers. The main difference between the Spanish and Catalan frameworks are the eligibility criteria to be a beneficiary. In the case of the Electricity Social Bond, the income upper threshold established is significantly lower than the Catalan one.[35] Without going into greater detail, we can see an actual disparity in the protection scope of both policies regarding their target beneficiaries.

Additional elements for the debate are the funding system of the social bond, on the one hand, and the Catalan disconnection ban's financial consequences, on the other. The Spanish Social Bond is funded by a Solidarity Fund financed by all suppliers (although only the eight main suppliers, considered last-resource suppliers, can offer it).[36] This funding system was negotiated after the suspension of the previous one by a Supreme Court decision[37] promoted by the main supplying companies. In the Catalan case, the funding to ensure the disconnection ban is only vaguely regulated in the law which established that a collaboration agreement would be signed between public administrations and supplying companies to cover the expenses of the measure, but not detailing the economic responsibility distribution. At the time of writing, an economic agreement has not yet been reached.

The new National Strategy establishes the objective of creating a new (fourth generation) social bond with the following elements: universal application to all basic utilities; automatic enforcement according to the households' income level and other specific criteria; and the introduction of coordination mechanisms among regional administrations. In this chapter we will not consider this new measure in our analysis since it is not yet properly designed and implemented.

[34] At 31 December 2018, a total of one million consumers, at the cost of €95 million, were beneficiaries of the social bond. CEER, *Monitoring report* (n 7) 60.

[35] The reason is that the cost of living in Catalonia is more expensive than the Spanish average. Someone has proposed using the income indicators from the autonomous community where the supply point is. ER Bartlett Castellà, 'Pobreza Energética. Una regulación controvertida' in J Ponce Solé and JI Soto Valle, *Pobreza energética: regulación jurídica y protección de los derechos de las personas* (Federació de Municipis de Catalunya, 2018) 55.

[36] The social bond only can be offered by the electricity companies considered 'suppliers of reference'.

[37] STS 4526/2016, and STS 4527/2016, both 24 October 2016. The result of the court sentences has been that the state reimbursed the payments from the enterprises until December 2016. A study of the successive funding systems in Bartlett Castellà, 'Pobreza Energética' (n 35).

D. The Intervention of the Catalan Ombudsman

i. The Institutional Framework for the Ombudsman's Action

The Catalan Ombudsman is part of the institutional framework of the parliamentary Ombudsman, independent of the powers of the state, although linked to the legislative assembly. The Ombudsman is also known as a magistrate of persuasion. He publishes his decisions, but they are not binding. To be successful, the Ombudsman has to convince.[38] Besides the Parliamentary Ombudsman, in Catalonia, there is a network of Local Ombudsmen who play an active role in advising citizens on their rights and assisting in redressing the malfunctioning of the local administration that affects them.[39] They use tools equivalent to those of the Parliamentary Ombudsman while reporting to the city council. When the complaint received involves an administration or service outside their mandate, they send it to the Parliamentary Ombudsman with whom they have a bilateral and cooperative relationship.

In the context of the welfare state, there are increased contacts between citizens and the state itself. More relationships overwhelm the possibilities of traditional means of control of public activity: namely Parliament, the judiciary and other internal control mechanisms (for example, internal review by specialised government services). It has been a driver of the global expansion of the Ombudsman role (first established in the constitution of Sweden in 1809). The Ombudsman's expanding operational powers include public services and, more recently, those of general economic interest.

In Spain, while water remains a public service, electricity is a service of general economic interest. The Catalan Ombudsman is competent to intervene in both sectors.[40] In doing so, he must consider the legal order (commented on at III.B and III.C) which, when assessing the causes of energy poverty, he seems reasonable would distinguish between: (a) those attributable to the market, namely the high price of energy considering the purchasing power of average wages; and (b) personal ones, if the price is affordable, but the individual still lacks the income to pay it. In the first case, liberalisation has not produced the intended result, and it makes sense to impose public service obligations on energy companies, such as financing the social bonus or contributing to energy efficiency funds, until the price becomes affordable through greater competition. In the second case, the solution may be social aid financed from the tax system, to which not only

[38] See an in-depth study in ER Bartlett Castellà, *El Síndic de Greuges. Síndico de Agravios de Catalunya* (Tirant lo Blanch, 2005).

[39] The 'Fòrum de Síndics i Síndiques Defensors i Defensores Locals de Catalunya' raises awareness of their activities www.sindicatureslocals.cat/es/inicio/.

[40] Art 78 of the Statute of Autonomy of Catalonia empowers it to supervise 'public administrations … private companies that manage public services or engage in activities of general or universal interest or equivalent activities in a concerted or indirect manner'.

companies but also a variety of other bodies contribute. The financing fight against energy poverty is a controversial issue. The extra benefits achieved by the concentration of market shares can be redistributed and redirected to combat energy poverty, with public service obligations, but also by attracting taxation. The protection against energy poverty in Spain's framework, and its specificities in Catalonia, makes no distinction between the cause and the increase in tax pressure on companies in the first case, nor with the contribution of public budgets in the second.[41]

The Catalan Ombudsman, upon receiving complaints from citizens, informs them of the legal provisions relating to their case. To carry out its work it asks for information and verifies the response by companies and public administrations. Where appropriate, the Ombudsman proposes other measures, based on legality and fairness. He may also suggest changes in the procedures for action and recommend changes to regulations and laws. The Ombudsman has the competence to initiate *ex officio* proceedings, and he can contact the organisations it deems appropriate for better resolving the matter.

ii. Individual Complaints

Below are two examples of actions referred to in the 2019 Annual Report.[42] In one, the Ombudsman addresses the supplier, in connection with a power disconnection that took place. Three invoices were issued after the cut. The supplier, following the Ombudsman's intervention, transferred the amount of the three invoices owed into the consumer's bank account. On another occasion, despite the consumer's payment, after disconnection for non-compliance with an agreed instalment, the distributor improperly delayed the reconnection. The Catalan administration, at the request of the Ombudsman, held that the distributor must compensate the consumer and verify that the consumer had accepted the compensation.

iii. Recommendations for Regulatory Changes

The Ombudsman's actions to solve specific problems allow him to uncover the causes of energy poverty and propose measures to address it. Further, it can also identify dysfunctions in the application of protective measures for vulnerable people. The Ombudsman has thus recommended the regulatory deployment of Law 24/2015 which, under the precautionary principle, would strengthen the energy-poor protection: in particular, the adoption of the protocol required to

[41] Even in an exceptional situation, such as COVID-19, where vulnerability stems from the cessation of economic activity ordered by the government to tackle the pandemic, the burden on protection measures falls with supplying companies. Art 28 of Royal Decree-Law 11/2020 of 1 April 2020, BOE No 91, 1 April 2020.

[42] Síndic de Greuges, 'Informe al Parlament 2019' (Barcelona, 2020) 194, available at: www.sindic.cat/site/unitFiles/6898/Informe-al-Parlament-2019_cat.pdf.

communicate with social services and for their intervention before granting aid to avoid power cuts in cases of non-payment due to lack of economic resources; and, likewise, a set of modifications of the state regulations establishing the social bond,[43] such as assessing whether all the required documentation is necessary and if the administration has applied the principle of not requesting documentation already in its possession.[44]

Until 2014, the Ombudsman had devoted three extraordinary reports to services of general interest.[45] In 2019, the Ombudsman took it a step further. He not only addressed the right to supply and support measures to those who have difficulty paying for energy, but also the underlying price of electricity supply, which raised the sector's figures to €45,000 M.[46]

The electricity bill covers the energy produced for the supply, the fixed costs of its transmission over the networks, back-up and demand management services, and marketing. But he also contributes to energy policy decisions, such as support for a renewable generation or financing of the system deficit for other years, and taxes, such as VAT and electricity tax. The study contains several recommendations concerning regulated costs and taxation, with the potential to reduce the amount of the current invoice by up to 50 per cent (summarised below).

The cost of transporting energy in high voltage (long-distance travel) and the cost of its distribution at low voltage (up to the point of supply) are two issues directly related to the power supply. They fund the transport and distribution system operators. Both activities are natural monopolies and therefore have no competition. Their determination corresponds to the regulator, not to the market. The generating companies are exempt from these costs, called tolls, although, through their decisions to locate the production plants, they induce investment in new networks and control the conditions of their use. Moreover, by giving higher weight to contracted power over the energy effectively consumed, the relative price of the KW/h is made more expensive, above all for the small consumer. The energy produced is fed into the networks and some gets lost along the way.

[43] A compilation commented on in D Ruiz, 'El Derecho a los Suministros básicos y su garantía real' in J Ponce Solé and JI Soto Valle, *Pobreza energética: regulación jurídica y protección de los derechos de las personas* (Federació de Municipis de Catalunya, 2018) 111–12.

[44] Numerous denials of the social bond are because it is not possible to check income levels for persons who are not required to file a tax return. The State Tax Agency should provide a negative certificate based on its records as verification.

[45] Síndic de Greuges, 'Informe Pobresa Energètica' (n 23); Síndic de Greuges, 'La prestación privada de servicios de interés general y las buenas prácticas corporativas' (2014); Síndic de Greuges, 'El derecho a los suministros básicos (electricidad, agua y gas)' (2014).

[46] €19,000 million corresponding to the energy generated and sold; €7,000 million of networks (tolls), of which €1,700 million for transport and €5,300 million for distribution; 10,000 non-supply-related charges of which €2,800 million relative to deficits in previous years and €7,100 million for regulated remuneration to renewables; €9,000 million of taxes, corresponding to €1510 million to the generation tax, €6,300 million to VAT and €1,300 million to the electricity tax. Síndic de Greuges, 'Informe sobre el derecho al suministro de electricidad: obstáculos y soluciones en el precio, el acceso al servicio y la garantía de su calidad' (2019) 7, available at: www.sindic.cat/site/unitFiles/6104/Informe%20dret%20al%20subministrament%20electric_cast_def.pdf.

These so-called losses build up to a significant amount.[47] Despite not having caused them, consumers (namely ordinary families) cover these losses – especially the low-voltage one.

The Ombudsman proposes to eliminate charges to finance incentives for renewables and cogeneration. He is recommending that the different end-users of energy should finance them proportionately. Because emissions reduction benefits everyone and is a countrywide target, it is reasonable for fossil fuel consumers to also contribute to this endeavour. A tax or price on CO_2 emissions could address this. The tariff deficit, a mismatch between the costs recognised by network use and commitments to support the energy transition, grew to an aggregate amount of €30,000 million, as a result of political decisions. Until 2028 the long-term funding amounts to €2,800 million per year, which the Ombudsman understands must come out of the public budget.

The compensation of extra-peninsular systems guarantees the same cost to the consumer, whether they live on the peninsula or in the Balearic and Canary archipelagos, with higher costs. It amounts to €300 million, collected through tolls and general budgets. The Ombudsman report contends that this compensation could fully fund the budget, supplemented by social policy items. As regards taxation, the tax burdens on energy consumption are high with an electricity tax of 5.11269632 per cent and VAT of 21 per cent. The Ombudsman proposes abolishing the first one and to setting a reduced rate for the second. Although the amount is low, he also proposes to remove the charge for hiring a meter from the invoice. The Ombudsman considers it is not financially justified (lack of cost–benefit analysis) and because the consumer already pays for the meter through the tolls that fund the distribution activity.

Even with a price structure such as that questioned by the Ombudsman, optimising contracts and introducing energy efficiency measures can mean significant savings. Although the Ombudsman may, incidentally, provide some advice, that is not his institutional function. However, some mainly local administrations are carrying out this task. In the fight against energy poverty, strengthening the relationship between the Ombudsman and the local administrations involved would be an institutional win-win that benefits citizens.

E. Other Actors Intervening in Energy Poverty Situations

i. The Intervention of Catalan Local Administrations

Through energy efficiency programmes some municipalities, in coordination with municipal social services, advise consumers on how to reduce their bills.[48]

[47] In 2018, it was 8.93% of total grid-injected power, which is about 25,000 GWh/year. CEER, '2nd CEER Report on Power Loses' (version with Corrigendum published 23 March 2020) C19-EQS-101-03,2020, 146, available at: www.ceer.eu/documents/104400/-/-/fd4178b4-ed00-6d06-5f4b-8b87d630b060.

[48] An example is Rubí Brilla, an initiative of the City of Rubi, located 23 kilometres from Barcelona, with 75,000 inhabitants. See: www.rubi.cat/es/ayuntamiento/proyectos-estrategicos/rubibrilla.

Distribution system operators, who manage the low and medium voltage transmission network which carries electricity to end-consumers, have rolled out 'smart' meters that provide a comprehensive range of new data. However, the full potential benefits derived from this implementation, financed by customers, are on standby as it lacks proper regulation of third-party access to this data with consumer consent. When this bottleneck is resolved, new business models providing energy audits will appear to the benefit of consumers. Likewise, there is the possibility of incorporating self-consumption, with the associated exemption of charges and tolls for the self-consumed energy and advantageous funding proposals in exchange for adding demand from many consumers and participating in flexibility services that the system operator requires. Part IV.C refers to the opportunities provided by energy communities in this regard.

The municipal services are in direct contact with vulnerable people. They deal with the cases that may not reach the Ombudsman (summarised at IV.B–IV.E below). They often show that specific conditions of vulnerability are manifested not only in a limitation of economic resources but in ignorance of one's rights, hence, the importance of frequent exchange of information among all public actors engaged in the protection of rights. Many small and medium-sized local administrations need timely legal advice on issues related to energy poverty which their citizens report. The Ombudsman's cooperation – by providing good practices guides, standard questions and answers, and even tailor-made responses to specific enquiries – could make a difference. On the other hand, local entities can help the Ombudsman fulfil its mandate with mapping, in real-time, energy poverty-related issues arising throughout the country and testing the success and limits of solutions tried.

ii. The Alliance against Energy Poverty: The Right to Energy Approach

The APE[49] is a key social actor in understanding the deployment of energy poverty policies in Catalonia, at both regional and local levels (particularly in cities with APE's local nodes, such as Barcelona).

The APE was launched in 2014 by neighbourhood associations, workers' assemblies and water and housing rights platforms. Their activity can be structured into two main dimensions: collective assemblies of energy-poor people for mutual support and their advocacy of for regulations and policy changes to ensure the right to basic supplies (energy but also water). It also was a key member of the group that promoted the current Catalan Act 24/2015.

We particularly highlight the innovative approach of APE addressing energy poverty situations through the creation of mutual support networks and

[49] For more information see: www.pobresaenergetica.es/index.php/ca/.

empowering energy-poor populations. As James Angel states, the APE approach is antagonistic to the traditional 'casework', promoting a solidarity relationship among members of the Alliance (most of them energy-poor people) rather than charity.[50] At the same time, APE's approach to energy poverty is rooted in the recognition of a right to energy as a basic need. Research on the right to energy and its policy and regulatory implications in the European Framework[51] is still sparse and needs further development.

F. Alternative Resolution of Consumer Disputes and Social Bonus

i. Complaints to Suppliers

The relevant supplier is one that recognises or does not recognise the social bond, based on a binding report by the ministry responsible for energy. A statement is issued by an algorithm, based on the data provided by the consumer that the supplier then enters into a central state administration computer platform. The consumer may appeal before consumer services.

The energy regulator does not resolve claims, but it does monitor that energy companies have effective mechanisms to manage them. The regulator has found that there has been an increase in complaints about the contracting of the social bond (from 10,000 in 2017 to 40,000 in 2018).[52] Modification of the requirements and the obligation to make a new application seem to be the cause of this increase. The regulator is also investigating a lack of diligence in the processing of social bond applications by some suppliers.[53]

It is important to put the above figures into context with the total complaints filed in Spain as a whole: 1,648,443, 9 per cent more than in 2017, of which 1,181,347 were in the electricity sector and 467,068 in the natural gas sector. This amount represents an average of four claims for every 100 electricity customers and six complaints for about every 100 natural gas customers, in annual terms. Those decided in favour of the consumer, in Spain as a whole, were 39 per cent and 31 per cent, respectively.[54] In Catalonia, the data are 220,720 in electricity

[50] J Angel, 'Irregular connections: everyday energy politics in Catalonia' (2019) 43 *International Journal of Urban and Regional Research* 337.

[51] M Hesselman, A Varo and S Laakso, 'The right to energy in the European Union' (2019), available at: www.engager-energy.net/wp-content/uploads/2019/06/ENGAGER-Policy-Brief-No.-2-June-2019-The-Right-to-Energy-in-the-EU.pdf.

[52] Comisión Nacional de los Mercados y la Competencia (CNMC), 'Informe sobre las reclamaciones planteadas por los consumidores a las comercializadoras y distribuidoras de energía eléctrica y gas natural durante el año 2018' Expediente IS/DE/001/19 (2019), available at: www.cnmc.es/sites/default/files/2817336_3.pdf.

[53] CNMC, 'Informe sobre reclamaciones' (2019) 26.

[54] ibid 42. Figures are approximately 20% and 40%, respectively, in those cases where the provider has cut the service due to non-payment. Figs 9 and 10, 19, 20.

and 107,562 in gas, respectively.[55] Data on the percentages of favourable resolution by autonomous filing communities have not been provided.

The most common reasons for claims, nearly half of all received in both sectors, are disagreements in measurement, billing and collection. This is in line with those reported at the European level through the Agency for the Cooperation of Energy Regulators.

ii. Consumer Arbitration in the Face of Disagreement with the Resolution of the Claim

A consumer who disagrees with the decision adopted by the company may go to arbitration. In 2017, the total number of arbitrations requested for both sectors together was 1,579, of which 47 per cent were resolved in favour of the consumer.[56] We do not have data for 2018/2019 when litigation about the social bonus increased. Reviewing the awards of the Arbitration Board for Consumer Affairs of Catalonia, 2017 included, we have not found any award about the social bond.[57]

We have also consulted the 2019 activity of the Catalan Consumer Agency. Of the total awards issued, 422 relate to claims for electricity, gas and water supplies. In the absence of access to the content of each award, we cannot determine whether there are any cases concerning the social bond. From interviews carried out with staff of the local administrations dealing with this subject, there appears to be hardly any use of arbitration. In other words, one of the options that EU law offers to vulnerable consumers – to resolve disputes without going to court – is practically unused.[58]

The EU Directive devotes attention to the professionality of Arbitral Institutions. It tries to ensure they have the expertise, independence and impartiality required. However, it assumes that citizens have the personal skills to defend their rights in such disputes, provided that the procedure is easy and free of charge. The last of these is a very optimistic assumption which does not match with reality. There are a lot of energy-poor citizens who need coaching to drive a formal procedure, even if it is quite simple. So, spreading the use of consumer arbitration requires assisting them with that backing.

It is necessary to provide information that gives citizens awareness of their rights but also to help them to write and choose the documents (contracts, bills, etc) needed for seeking redress. This is not the case for citizens with high school

[55] CNMC, 'Informe sobre reclamaciones' (n 53) 9–11.

[56] ibid 20. Data, segregated by autonomous communities or topics are not provided.

[57] Agència catalana de Consum, 'Recull Laudes Junta Arbitral de Consum de Catalunya 2012–2017' (2018), available at: aplicacio.consum.gencat.cat/documentacio/17082.pdf.

[58] Directive 2013/11/EU of the European Parliament and of the Council of 21 May 2013 on alternative dispute resolution for consumer disputes and amending Regulation (EC) No 2006/2004 and Directive 2009/22/EC (Directive on Consumer ADR) ELI: data.europa.eu/eli/dir/2013/11/oj implemented into the Spanish legal system by Law 7/2017, of 2 November. BOE No 268 of 4 November 2017: www.boe.es/eli/es/l/2017/11/02/7.

or university degrees, but many citizens involved in the problems which we are considering lack these qualifications. Assistance from the public administration, social or consumer services, or from bar associations who agree to supply the service for the last of these, or from pro bono private practitioners or NGOs, is crucial to increase the use of consumer arbitration in the energy poverty field. In all probability, frequent use of these rights would render enough awards favourable to customers that would incentivise an improvement in suppliers' practices where there is room for that.

IV. Energy Poverty: What are the Gaps in the Current Measures?

A. Households' Debt Accumulation and Sustainable Future Solutions

So far, we have identified three principal gaps that need to be addressed. The first refers to the current central demand of the APE: the cancellation of households' debt accumulated since the supplying disconnection ban.[59] As outlined above, the Catalan regulation foresees a collaboration agreement as among the measures that would solve the funding of a dispute, but so far, this agreement has not been reached. In the light of this situation, households are not disconnected from the energy grid but, at the same time, they accumulate debt that can be claimed by the suppliers in the future. In August 2019 the main distribution company, Endesa, sent a letter to all Catalan local authorities requiring them to pay 50 per cent of the debt accumulated by vulnerable consumers in each municipality, threatening them with disconnections in case of non-compliance. Municipalities, social organisations and the regional government (Generalitat de Catalunya) have reached an agreement for a proposal in response to the company's demand. The new proposal presses the distribution company to assume the current total debt and compromises by offering that local authorities would pay 40 per cent of future debt. At the time of writing (May 2020), there is no agreement as yet.

B. Energy-Poor Population Out of Policies' Scope

The second gap is the significant proportion of the vulnerable population that remains out of the scope of the aforementioned policies. As Bazillian, Nakhooda

[59] Although the Catalan law bans energy and water supply disconnections for vulnerable consumers, the cost of consumption during the non-paid period accumulates, creating debt for households. It is currently not clear who should be liable for this debt, the household being the ultimately responsible party.

and Van Der Graaf outline: 'Energy poverty poses at least three requirements of the actors, institutions and processes of energy governance: access, affordability, and quality.[60] In this spirit, we can see that energy poverty policies in Catalonia are focused on the second element: affordability. Although we recognise that affordability is a crucial factor, we can still discern some aspects of energy poverty that are not directly related to it. For example, we can identify people that are irregularly connected to basic supplies, as well as situations of lack of access to energy for reasons of urban and/or infrastructure degradation.

Irregular connections refer to illegal connections (or reconnections after a disconnection procedure) to the electricity grid for very different reasons. Illegal connections to the power supply are fraudulent acts and classified in the Spanish Criminal Code.[61] Although illegal, these connections are more common than one would expect,[62] particularly in recent years as a consequence of the deep socio-economic crisis of 2008. From the insights of the Working Group on Irregular Housing Occupations[63] in Catalonia, we can distinguish different origins for irregular households' connections to basic supplies (namely, electricity and water): (a) non-payment of bills and disconnection (without a real option of cancelling the debt and being legally reconnected);[64] (b) the impossibility of drawing up a supply contract because of being in an irregular housing condition (squatting, non-legal or informal renting agreement, etc); and (c) the impossibility of concluding a supply contract due to the building conditions (in cases in which they don't fulfil the legal requirements for installation of basic supplies). Besides these three situations, there are also irregular connections to basic supplies linked to (d) criminal activities.[65] There needs to be a deeper understanding of these situations since in many cases they do not respond to criminal objectives but social circumstances.

The second type of population excluded from mainstream targeting are communities in areas with electricity access difficulties due to old and obsolete infrastructure. These cases go beyond the classical energy poverty protection policies, normally referring to the inability of households to access energy for economic reasons or building performance limitations. On the basis of Bouzarovski, Petrova and Tirado-Herrero's energy poverty definition, we should consider any

[60] M Bazilian, S Nakhooda and T Van De Graaf, 'Energy governance and poverty' (2014) 1 *Energy Research & Social Science* 217.

[61] Art 255 Código Penal.

[62] Angel (n 50) 343.

[63] This Working Group was created in 2017. Anais Varo, co-author of this chapter, is part of the Working Group as an expert in energy poverty policies.

[64] Although strong guarantees are provided by the Catalan regulation, there are still cases where the precautionary principle is not applied and, therefore, members of the vulnerable population are disconnected. In July 2019, Barcelona imposed a financial penalty for the first time on an electricity supplier for non-compliance with Catalan Act 24/2015. The financial penalty was executed after a court decision allowing the city council to do it (15 July 2019).

[65] As an example of this last category, there are documented police interventions of irregular connections in indoor cannabis plantations.

'situation in which a household lacks a socially and materially necessitated level of energy services in the home'.[66] According to this interpretation, all communities that suffer systemic energy disconnections because of the bad condition of their electricity grid infrastructure (which is not frequent in Catalonia) should be included in the energy-poor population. These situations are usually aggravated by extreme weather events (for instance, the recent storm Gloria caused hundreds of energy disconnections that in certain areas lasted for days)[67] or other factors, such as urban degradation and exclusion.

C. Practices of Recovery Companies Contracted by Marketers

Providers sometimes contract the services of recovery companies to recover unpaid bills. Some of their practices include coming to the house unannounced at any hour of the day and calling neighbours and telling them about the debts of the person concerned. These are mechanisms of pressure that violate the person's right to honour and privacy. They make threats that the person will go to prison for the debt, despite the fact that, in Spain, non-payment is not a crime except in the case of fraud when it may involve crossing the limits of the Penal Code. Moreover, if the claimed debt is under appeal or in litigation, the transfer of the debtor's data to a third party is not appropriate.[68]

D. The Transfer of Debt by Providers

Assigning a collection right to a third party is permitted in the Spanish legal system. It does not require the debtor's consent. However, if a delay has been agreed upon, the credit is transmitted with this postponement. Likewise, the debtor may terminate this arrangement by paying the transferee the price paid (usually less than the nominal), the costs incurred and the interest on the amount since the transferee paid. A vulnerable consumer is unlikely to be aware of these legal provisions. Municipal services can advise, but they do not always have this knowledge.[69] The Ombudsman's work promoting best practice guides that such direct social services

[66] S Bouzarovski, S Petrova and S Tirado Herrero, 'From fuel poverty to energy vulnerability: the importance of services, needs and practices' (2014) SPRU Working Paper Series SWPS 2014-25, 276.

[67] EFE, 'Generalitat starts proceedings against Endesa and Red Eléctrica due to the electricity disconnections during the storm' *El País* (Barcelona, 3 February 2020), available at: elpais.com/ccaa/2020/02/03/catalunya/1580724741_815822.html.

[68] C Bresciano, 'La protección de los derechos de los consumidores de electricidad en derecho español y la lucha contra la pobreza energética' (Master's thesis, Ramon Llull University, 2018) 22–26. The legal advice she provided to Rubi Brilla is the paper's cornerstone.

[69] ibid 27–29.

can use, as it has done in other fields such as protecting minors from abuse or neglect, would be a way to reduce the effects of vulnerability.

E. Aid that does not Reach its Recipients

There are problems in the management of the Thermal Social Bond, a commendable initiative of the Spanish government to combat heating gaps during the winter. This highlights the multiple dimensions of vulnerability. There have been 116,644 families who have lost the bonus because they have neither paid their domestic electricity bills nor responded to the letter sent, nor have they acted upon a subsequent request published in the *Official Gazette* to provide a bank account.[70] For those consumers who have difficulty paying their bills it is better to go to the supplier's offices and settle their issues with them rather than to be exposed to a demand for repayment due to a lack of funds. Access to a bank account is not something many vulnerable people have, despite the facilities given by banks to open accounts without a minimum balance and the simplification of management processes through the internet. The attempt of municipal social services to use a simple computer programme to reconcile data published in the *Official Gazette* with those of people in contact with them, to help citizens open a bank account, was met with the objection that it could violate the General Data Protection Regulation.

F. Registration as a Requirement to Contract Supplies

Consumers need to provide an address of the point of supply at the time of contracting the service. The municipalities, which are competent to carry out and maintain the '*padrón municipal*', the official population record, must ensure the integrity of the data provided and that the legitimate rights or interests of third parties are not harmed. To do this, they often ask for the title, property, or rental documents which legitimise the occupation of the house. However, local authorities are not in a position to judge issues of ownership, urban leases, or, in general, matters of a legal–private nature. Asking for evidence of title is for the sole purpose of providing an element of proof that the individual lives in the address indicated. It is not unusual for vulnerable families to be unable to prove the title. It does not mean that their house occupancy is a criminal offence, but that situations of social fragility have different derivatives. Circumstances like these have pushed local authorities, such as the Municipality of Rubi, to design new protocols to verify residence in a particular home and authorise registration, without which the contract is not possible.

[70] Identified through the identity document of the supply-point holder. BOE Notification Supplement of 18 November 2019.

G. Vulnerable Consumers and Procedural Energy Justice

In regard to the notion of energy justice and connecting it to a wider conceptualisation of 'access to justice', we discuss the procedural dimension as a key factor. Procedural energy justice is defined as 'a call for equitable procedures that engage all stakeholders in a non-discriminatory way'.[71] Hence, guaranteeing access to justice for vulnerable consumers in the energy sector should also include a procedural dimension.

The Ombudsman tracks many characteristics of energy poverty, but even with the citizen-friendly easy access, there are cases that go unnoticed under its watch. So, despite the successful performance that the Ombudsman has delivered in this field, there is still room for improvement. In attempting to fulfil its function of keeping Parliament informed, the Ombudsman encounters difficulties in communicating all the flaws in the framework that is meant to protect vulnerable and needy customers.

An excellent way to bridge this gap would be to reinforce data-sharing on this subject with the local administration by making it happen automatically. In this way, the Ombudsman could immediately directly advise local administrations that sometimes lack the relevant information or push regulators and regional agencies activities to do so. Thus, the local administration and Ombudsman, whilst retaining their roles of supervised and supervisor, would extend their relation in more cooperative ways.

We have already described how the energy-poor population is beyond the scope of policies and detailed the disturbing practices of recovery companies, the transfer of debt by providers, the aid that does not reach its recipients and the difficulties arising from not registering in the official population record. Municipal services need to detect these circumstances, and many more, and this is why the relationship between the Ombudsman and local administrations is so essential. It is necessary for proper diagnosis and developing imaginative solutions. There are innovative local authority initiatives to map energy poverty, comparing data from providers about unpaid bills that led to the suspension of power with the official record on population and the urban cadastre. These techniques allow the calculation of rates of poverty by zones and, as a better diagnosis, more focused solutions.[72] To scale up and spread these initiatives can bring about a change in fighting energy poverty. The Ombudsman could play the role of crucial enabler, backing these projects and sharing ideas to define a methodological approach with municipalities, perhaps through dialogue with the municipal associative organisations.

Considering the legal framework in Spain, consumer arbitration should be the standard procedure to solve disagreements about granting the social bond when

[71] D McCauley et al, 'Advancing energy justice: the triumvirate of tenets and systems thinking' (2013) 32 *International Energy Law Review* 107.

[72] See: www.congrespobresaenergetica.cat/copia-de-sala-assist.

the consumers' demands have been rejected. It would require the provision of advice to consumers who lack the personal skills to drive the arbitration procedure for themselves. Nevertheless, it would be appropriate to amend the bylaw regulating the social bond to state clearly to suppliers that the arbitration award is valid without more steps. It would mean that there would be no need to return to the ministry responsible for energy which had originally given a negative binding report based on the data entered by the supplier into a central state administration computer platform.

An effort needs to be made to include vulnerable citizens and consumers in the designing, population-targeting and implementation of energy transition policies. In this respect, we have identified an opportunity for energy justice in development of the future energy communities' legal framework in the EU (see section V.C).

V. Moving Towards a Just Energy Model: Policy Implications

A. Good Practices in Community-Based Organisations: From Vulnerable Consumers to Empowered Citizens

From the experiences mentioned above, we highlight how community-based initiatives have become crucial for access to justice for vulnerable consumers. The case of the Alliance Against Energy Poverty becomes a paradigmatic example of how a stigmatised situation, such as not being able to afford a basic energy supply, can be transformed into an opportunity for citizens' empowerment. The mutual support networks created by the APE not only work as a social and political network to tackle energy poverty, but also as a means to improve the energy culture in Catalonia.

Other grassroots experiences, as pilot projects, have been developed in the Catalan territory that are examples of good practices. 'Neighbours Communities against Energy Poverty' are self-financing communities with the aim of tackling energy poverty.[73] The aim of these communities is to promote empowerment and self-sufficiency, helping people to avoid dependence on traditional banks and public social assistance, while encouraging energy-saving habits and energy efficiency improvements at home.

B. The Future Catalan Energy Transition Act: An Opportunity

During 2021 the new Catalan Energy Transition Act will be approved. In the winter of 2020, a public consultation process was opened with the goal of gathering

[73] See: www.ecoserveis.net/en/donation/cospe/.

comments, improvements and opinions on the draft bill from social and environmental organisations, as well as from the public. Although it is still at a draft stage, we can draw a few conclusions from the preliminary text.

The draft law includes specific articles on energy poverty (Article 21 and Article 53) and just transition (Article 22). The current draft text includes a guarantee for the vulnerable population to access energy services, but it does not suggest any specific tool or mechanism for this purpose. In addition, there is a specific article on just transition, but its content is limited to the potential job losses that the energy transition could trigger. The transformation of the current energy arrangements is a golden opportunity to move towards a more just and fair energy model, as well as to ensure access to justice for all citizens.

VI. Conclusions

In 2012, the growing number of families struggling to meet their energy needs impacted the political agenda as a public matter. The responses of the Catalan Parliament since 2013, such as the banning of energy disconnections for vulnerable consumers, conflicted with the central government's course of action. The rulings of the Constitutional Court, which prioritises the state-level core competence on the energy sector over regional jurisdiction on 'social services' and 'consumption', weakened Catalan measures without introducing significant central state protection measures until 2017. The new Spanish National Strategy on Energy Poverty tackles some of the unsolved issues, although – as pointed out in this chapter – there are still several gaps that need to be urgently addressed.

The Catalan Ombudsman has dealt extensively with both the definition of the right to energy supply and the measures to protect it. In this regard, we highlight his proposals to reduce the price of supply and to improve the effectiveness of vulnerable consumers' support. Recommendations to improve the state-level measures would be the lightening of the administrative procedures and not demanding documentation that the administration already has. Another improvement would be the normative development of the measures already included in the Catalan law, such as the precautionary principle and the financing mechanisms needed to ensure it.

Besides the economic burden of access to energy services, there are other factors that directly affect vulnerable consumers. The lack of information on energy consumers' rights or the lack of skills and tools to navigate the required paperwork to access available support might be as harmful as the inability to pay bills. The administration's support to compensate these gaps would be more effective if it was deployed at a regional level rather than state level. It requires the proximity and experience of regional and local administrations on social services and consumers' issues that the central government cannot offer. The negligible use of consumer arbitration to challenge denials of a social bonus shows that legal measures alone are not sufficient to protect vulnerable consumers' rights. The legal measures need to be monitored and complemented, both by public administrations and social and community-based organisations. In this same vein, organisations such as the APE have created support networks to empower energy-poor households. Shifting from the role of energy-poor people and aid recipients to promoters of their own rights is a tectonic change.

The European definition of Energy Communities (ECs), as viable, non-profit alternatives to traditional actors in the provision of energy services, captures and tries to enhance a cooperative experience dating back more than a century. Even if they do not replace utilities as larger energy service providers, they can combat vulnerability more effectively than these. Social innovation and community-based initiatives usually put energy vulnerability and environmental justice at the centre of their concerns. The energy transition, which citizen communities aim to promote, can and should be a catalyst to eradicate energy poverty. Additionally, ECs will propose a new scenario for traditional alternative dispute resolution (ADR) means, which will have to innovate and adapt to this new potential type of conflicts. As we have highlighted, although ECs incorporate democratic procedural tools in their very basic structure, ADR systems will be more necessary than ever.

11

Access to Justice and Energy Poverty in France

MARINE CORNELIS

I. Introduction

This chapter describes fuel poverty and its drivers in France, discusses the policies at national and local level to help vulnerable consumers and concludes by arguing for a more prominent role of alternative dispute resolution (ADR) in the energy sector.

In 2018, 11.6 per cent of the French population (approximately 6.7 million individuals) spent more than 8 per cent of their income on paying their energy bills and, as a consequence, were considered as living in 'energy poverty' (*précarité énergétique*), as defined under French Law (law 2010-788)[1] and by the indicators of the National Energy Poverty Observatory.[2]

However, the introduction of a definition of energy poverty in 2010 has not helped to simplify the process of identifying the households affected, nor the mitigation journey. The entities and indicators aimed at evaluating the magnitude of this phenomenon and its consequences within society have multiplied in the past few years, as epitomised by the launch of the Observatoire National de la Précarité Energétique (ONPE) in 2011. In practice, fuel poverty remains highly complex. The drivers, the solutions, the national and the local initiatives are multiple and often intertwined. The main measures are financial support for the payment of bills and multi-layered programmes enabling technical assistance to address the quality of buildings. These are supported by a wide range of actors, including social workers, private organisations, social landlords, energy companies, local structures, but also mediation and ADR schemes.

[1] Loi 2010-788 du 12 juillet 2010 portant engagement national pour l'environnement.

[2] The French Observatory uses two main indicators: the energy effort rate above 8% applied to households in the first three deciles of disposable income per consumption unit; and reporting of cold temperatures during the winter preceding the survey applied to the first three deciles of disposable income per consumption unit. Source: Observatoire national de la précarité énergétique, available at: www.onpe.org/definition_indicateurs/definition_des_indicateurs.

In particular, the public energy ombudsman (Médiateur national de l'énergie) and in-house mediators acting in the energy market have multiplied initiatives to assist vulnerable consumers facing fuel poverty. In this context, can ADR be the missing link between the different actors and policies and facilitate a more effective protection of vulnerable consumers? It does not seem so, since the architecture of support measures remains highly complex. The remit of the intervention of ombuds is limited to contractual relationships and, only more recently, to market practices. Many gaps still need to be filled. So far, consumers urgently needing help to pay their bills or facing many difficulties do not regard ombuds as gateways to the enforcement of their rights or providers of actual relief.

II. Energy Poverty

According to the French National Energy Poverty Observatory, in 2018 11.7 per cent of households (3.4 million) spent more than 8 per cent of their income on paying energy bills for their home making them among the lowest-income households. They are officially 'energy poor'. At the same time, about seven million households were facing 'economic' energy poverty (*précarité énergétique*).[3] These data illustrate the complexity of quantifying the extent of the phenomenon in France.

France adopted an official definition with the law of 12 July 2010: 'A person in a situation of energy poverty is experiencing particular difficulties in his or her dwelling to obtain the energy supply necessary to meet his or her basic needs due to the inadequacy of his or her resources or housing conditions'. The four main factors that can lead to fuel poverty are a low level of resources, low-performance housing (poor insulation and/or inadequate heating equipment when available), energy prices and household practices.[4] Since the end of the 2000s, energy poverty has received more and more attention from the media and policymakers, thanks to the push given by the action of well-organised civic organisations such as the RAPPEL Network created in 2007. An eight-month national debate on Energy Transition took place in 2013. It resulted in a Law on Energy Transition published on 30 August 2015 which provided additional measures, including better targeted programmes (such as the *Habiter mieux* (Living better) renovation programme and Local Contracts of Commitment at departmental level), and the creation of the ONPE.

France's policy priorities for combatting this phenomenon are twofold – curative and preventive: curative to respond to the affordability emergency; and

[3] Observatoire national de la précarité énergétique (2020), *Tableau de bord de la précarité énergétique 2019*.

[4] M Cornelis, *Policy Overview of the Development of Energy Poverty & Vulnerability at EU Level*, ESRC Just Energy (2018); see: esrcjustenergy.files.wordpress.com/2018/12/eu-energy-policy-overview.pdf.

preventive to address the poor quality of the buildings. The first is an aid for the payment of energy bills (not limited to gas or electricity), a dedicated voucher termed the *Chèque énergie* (energy cheque). In 2019 5.7 million households received this voucher, with an average of €200 per household (heating bills cost an average of €1,400 per household per year). The second type of measure seeks to reduce the phenomenon in the long term by limiting overall consumption and increasing the number of high-performance thermal renovation programmes for housing. About 17 programmes co-exist, and some are cumulative. According to the Building Energy Renovation Plan, there are 7–8 million 'leaky homes' in France. Of these, 3.8 million are occupied by low-income households, 1.5 million of which own their own home. In the social housing sector, the objective is to renovate 100,000 leaky homes each year. Thanks to the measures put in place by the state, the National Housing Agency's *Habiter mieux* programme enabled 62,500 privately owned homes to be renovated in 2018.[5] However, members of the RAPPEL network and NGOs consider that the government's retrofitting ambitions are too low,[6] in particular for renters, and the amount of the energy cheque is too small to make a difference for the most vulnerable.[7]

French energy markets have been open to competition since 1 July 2007. However, electricity markets are still highly concentrated. According to the regulator, the Commission de Régulation de l'Energie (CRE), a vast majority of residential and non-residential electricity consumers have remained under regulated tariffs with the incumbent suppliers (Électricité de France (EDF) and ENGIE). As of 30 September 2019, 73 per cent of residential and non-residential consumers remained with regulated tariffs and 27 per cent were on market offers (24 per cent with an alternative supplier). Articles L.337-4 to L.337-9 and R.337-18 *et seq* of the Energy Code govern regulated tariffs. Since 1 January 2016, in mainland France, only consumers subscribing to power less than or equal to 36kVA can benefit from regulated tariffs, ie, only residential consumers and small businesses.[8] Nevertheless, the opposite applies to the gas supply. On 30 September 2019, 65 per cent of residential and non-residential sites were on market offers (35 per cent with an alternative supplier) and 35 per cent under the regulated tariff. Law no 2019-1147 of 8 November 2019 is putting an end to the regulated gas tariffs of the incumbent suppliers in two stages. In the first stage, non-domestic end-consumers using less than 30MWh will no longer be able to benefit from these tariffs as of 1 December 2020. For domestic end-users with an annual reference consumption of less than 30MWh, sole owners of a mainly residential building

[5] Observatoire national de la précarité énergétique (n 3).

[6] CLER (2019) *Loi énergie-climat: Tout reste à faire!* (2019), available at: cler.org/loi-energie-climat-tout-reste-a-faire/.

[7] N Creutzfeldt, C Gill, R McPherson and M Cornelis, 'The Social and Local Dimensions of Governance of Energy Poverty: Adaptive Responses to State Remoteness' (2020) 43 *Journal of Consumer Policy* 635.

[8] CRE, Marché de détail de l'électricité (2019), available at: www.cre.fr/Electricite/marche-de-detail-de-l-electricite.

consuming less than 150MWh per year and associations of co-owners of such a building, the end of the regulated gas tariffs will take place on 1 July 2023.[9]

Energy companies and the National Energy Ombudsman are among the leading actors in the fight against energy poverty. They are both on the front line (through direct contact with customers and sending invoices for the former, and management of the information portal for the latter), but are also the source of crucial data needed to monitor and understand the extent of the phenomenon. However, the complexity of the landscape and red tape makes it difficult for the most vulnerable households to access their support services and therefore 'ensure efficient treatment of complaints and out-of-court dispute settlements'.[10]

III. A Complex ADR Landscape: Divided between the National Public Ombudsman, Company Mediators and Other Public Parties

In this section, three areas of access to justice through mediation will be discussed: these are the public energy ombudsman; private in-house mediators; and organisations addressing the complaints of tenants towards their landlords.

In France, out-of-court dispute resolution can be performed by different bodies: the Médiateur National de l'Energie (National Energy Ombudsman), the statutory public body operating for all suppliers; and incumbent company 'mediators', only accessible to customers of EDF and ENGIE. 'Alternative' suppliers, ie, those who have emerged since 2007, do not have in-house ADR bodies. However, the Ministry of Economy and Finance's Direction générale de la concurrence, de la consommation et de la répression des fraudes (Directorate-General for Competition Policy, Consumer Affairs and Fraud Control: DGCCRF) handles complaints relating to commercial practices. It adds a layer of complexity to the dispute settlement procedure. Moreover, given the importance of housing in the context of the fight against energy poverty in France, access to justice is also reflected in measures addressing the 'decency' of housing and remedies against landlords. In this case, organisations are now specialised in providing legal help for renters.

A. Company Mediators (Internal Company Ombudsman)

France has a long tradition of in-house private ADR. The largest providers are EDF and ENGIE.

The Médiateur du Groupe EDF (EDF Group Mediator) was founded in 1999, seven years before the National Energy Ombudsman (2006). Company mediators

[9] ibid.

[10] Third Energy Package Electricity Directive (Directive 2009/72/EC).

are now subject to the provisions of Title I of Book VI of the French Consumer Code. It stems from the Ordinance of 20 August 2015 relating to the out-of-court settlement of consumer disputes, as well as Decree no 2015-1382 of 30 October 2015 relating to the mediation of consumer disputes and Decree no 2015-1607 of 7 December 2015 relating to the conditions for appointing company mediators.[11]

The Médiateur de la consommation pour le Groupe ENGIE (ENGIE Group Mediator, formerly Gaz de France (GDF)) was approved on 26 February 2016 by the Commission d'Evaluation et de Contrôle de la Médiation de la Consommation (Evaluation and Control Commission for Consumer Mediation: CECM) defined by law. The ENGIE mediator is registered on the list of independent consumer ombudsmen in France and notified to the European Commission.[12] The same applies to the EDF mediator: on 8 April 2016, the service was approved by the CECM and notified to the European Commission.[13]

The EDF Group Mediator handled 1,361 disputes in 2018. In 78 per cent of cases, the mediator fully or partially satisfied the request of the complainant.[14] In 20 years, the EDF Group Mediator has handled 13,000 individual and professional disputes with EDF and its subsidiaries. In 2018, the EDF Group Mediator received 4,444 referrals from consumers (-3 per cent compared with 2017) and recorded a 19 per cent increase in the number of cases eligible for mediation. A vast majority of the disputes relating to contract and invoicing and payment issues (respectively 65.3 per cent and 16.5 per cent of the eligible disputes).[15]

For ENGIE, the total number of requests to the Ombudsman increased in 2018, reaching 6,646 requests (+11 per cent compared with 2017 and +11.5 per cent compared with 2016). Correspondingly, the number of complaints eligible for mediation received decreased, with 327 eligible requests in 2018 (-17 per cent compared with 2017). A total of 387 disputes were handled in 2018, down 8.3 per cent from 2017. Most disputes regarded invoicing (56.1 per cent) and payment issues (18 per cent of the eligible disputes).[16]

The main categories of complaints received by private mediators are quite in line with those of the National Energy Ombudsman. However, when mentioning energy poverty to the EDF Mediator in February 2020, we were told that only a few disputes had actually been lodged by vulnerable and energy-poor households.

[11] Médiateur du Groupe EDF, *Saisir le Médiateur de la Consommation du Groupe EDF* (2020), available at: mediateur.edf.fr/la-mediation-de-la-consommation.

[12] Médiateur du Groupe ENGIE, *Quel médiateur saisir ? Quels médiateurs puis-je solliciter?* (2020), available at: www.mediateur-engie.com/faq/competences/mediateur-saisir-mediateurs-puis-solliciter/.

[13] Médiateur du Groupe EDF (2019), *Le rapport dédié aux consommateurs* (2019), available at: www.energie-mediateur.fr/en/disputes/your-dispute/the-internal-ombudsmen-of-the-edf-and-engie-groups/.

[14] Médiateur du Groupe EDF, *Le médiateur du groupe EDF publie son rapport 2018* (2019), available at: www.edf.fr/sites/default/files/contrib/groupe-edf/espaces-dedies/espace-medias/cp/2019/20190418-cp_edf_le_mediateur_du_groupe_edf_publie_son_rapport_2018.pdf.

[15] See: mediateur.edf.fr/rapport_annuel_consommation/#rapport.

[16] Médiateur du Groupe ENGIE, *Les rapports annuels* (2020), available at: www.mediateur-engie.com/qui-sommes-nous/rapport-annuel.

These big companies have consumer performance departments and 'solidarity advisers' who are able to help at different levels, and therefore the number of cases directly relating to energy poverty is limited.

The two private mediation bodies have signed a convention (memorandum of understanding) with the National Energy Ombudsman to organise their interventions according to their respective competences. Customers of EDF or ENGIE or their subsidiaries can freely contact the company's mediator or the National Energy Ombudsman, but two similar cases cannot be followed up in parallel. On the other hand, if they choose the EDF or ENGIE Mediator, consumers retain the right to later turn to the National Energy Ombudsman if they are not satisfied with the outcome of the procedure. The functioning of the latter is rather similar, but its scope of action is larger, enabling a better, albeit partial, monitoring of the situation.

B. Médiateur National de l'Energie (National Energy Ombudsman)

The Médiateur National de l'Energie (National Energy Ombudsman) was created by the Energy Law of 7 December 2006. The role of the Ombudsman is defined by Articles L. 122-1 to L. 122-5 and R. 122-1 to R. 122-12 of the Energy Code. Besides pure dispute resolution, the Ombudsman informs, advises and assists consumers in the out-of-court settlement of disputes relating to the supply of energy. The Ombudsman also manages the Energie-Info platform, which was accessed by 2.1 million consumers in 2018. Since its foundation, the institution has advocated positions to improve the practices of companies active in the energy sector and consumer protection. In particular, the Ombudsman encourages network suppliers and operators to improve their practices and, if necessary, proposes legislative and regulatory changes.

The National Energy Ombudsman received 16,934 cases in 2018 (against 14,548 in 2017 and 12,260 in 2016), among which 5,530 disputes were admissible in mediation. Household consumers are not the only ones to request assistance from the Ombudsman, as some of them initiate action through third parties: consumers associations, legal protection bodies, social workers or friends and families.[17] In 2018, the proportion of third parties in referrals amounted to 17 per cent. In 2016, insurance companies led this category (6 per cent), taking action for their customers mainly for disputes dealing with the quality of supply. They were followed by the friends-and-relatives category and the co-owners' associations (3 per cent each), public authorities such as the National Ombudsman and law professionals (2 per cent), and finally, social workers (0.75 per cent). Among these third parties,

[17] Médiateur National de l'Energie, *2018 Annual Report* (2019).

about 30 requested the assistance of the Ombudsman more than twice for different consumers.[18]

The National Energy Ombudsman deals with many complaints directly and indirectly relating to energy poverty, such as those related to the application of the energy cheque; problems of unaffordable bills and recurrent unpaid bills; administrative fees and debt collection; disconnection due to unpaid bills; and problems of understanding and literacy and questionable commercial and sales practices affecting vulnerable people. These complaints fall into the broad categories identified in its annual report. The National Energy Ombudsman is therefore a vital observer of the situation of households and the evolution of fuel poverty.

In 2018, among the 5,530 admissible disputes, 44 per cent were about challenging the level of consumption, 9 per cent about price and tariff, 9 per cent about invoicing and 8 per cent about payment and settlement. Only 2 per cent focused on commercial practices. This can be explained by the fact that the National Energy Ombudsman's ability to handle disputes relating to business and market practices is limited, as the organisation's scope under the Energy Code is limited to 'contract execution'. The Ombudsman can inform, advise and guide consumers facing this type of litigation, or even intervene informally with a supplier to cancel a disputed contract, but it cannot issue written recommendations for solutions.

The National Energy Ombudsman is theoretically only in charge of supervising existing contractual relations. All matters relating to commercial practices should therefore be managed by the DGCCRF. The DGCCRF has been quite reluctant to extend of the area of competence of the National Energy Ombudsman to the formation of contracts because the DGCCRF views this as a subject matter that falls within its own legal scope. However, the DGCCRF is currently positioning itself more in the penal field, through repressive investigations.[19] The Ombudsman's activity is different and appears complementary since it champions the quick and amicable resolution of disputes. That is why the Ombudsman has kept on calling for the extension of its area of competence to the formation of contracts.[20] In 2018, the Ombudsman services and the DGCCRF agreed on new rules that 'make it possible to better support consumers while respecting everyone's prerogatives'.[21] Therefore, the two services have agreed that when a signed contract, even if refuted by the consumer, exists (subscription disputes), the case will fall within the Ombudsman's legal field of competence. The Ombudsman also feeds back to the DGCCRF information provided by victims of misleading commercial practices. In 2019, 61 per cent of households received unsolicited contacts from suppliers, compared with 37 per cent in 2017. In 2018, nearly 8 per cent of consumers who contacted the Ombudsman complained about business practices (for example,

[18] Cornelis (n 4).
[19] ibid.
[20] ibid.
[21] Médiateur National de l'Energie, *2018 Annual Report* (n 17).

misleading arguments, aggressive practices, forced sales).[22] The Ombudsman also reports that in March 2019, a court ordered ENGIE to pay €1 million in damages to EDF for solicitations implementing acts of unfair competition. The Ombudsman is monitoring this kind of issue closely, but its scope of intervention remains limited. In response to this phenomenon, in 2020, the newly appointed Ombudsman has taken a clear stance in favour of a complete ban on door-to-door sales of energy contracts. According to the Ombudsman, this phenomenon is set to increase with the arrival of new suppliers and with the end of regulated gas tariffs, scheduled for 2023.[23]

C. Landlord–Tenant Mediation

A third type of access to justice through mediation that can be used in France is based on private law and the relationship between landlord and tenant. In the event of a conflict, often linked to the poor quality of housing, French tenants can turn to associations that will enable them to assert their rights against landlords. There are various mediation associations active in France, the best known of which are the Agences départementales pour l'Information sur le Logement (ADIL) and the Léo Lagrange Federation.[24]

Here, we can see the particular approach adopted by France to deal with the subject of energy poverty. It is not only a question of costs, but also, and even more importantly, of decent or unhealthy housing, two concepts that are enshrined in law. By law, the landlord must provide the tenant with a dwelling that does not affect their safety or health and is equipped with certain elements of comfort. The notions of substandard housing, insalubrity and danger refer to legal provisions and therefore to the administrative enforcement powers exercised by mayors and prefects, within the framework of specific procedures. Mediation associations can intervene in the resolution of rental relations to regularise the contract (amount of rent, duration of the contract) or charges (amount, methods of regularisation) according to the law of 6 July 1989 to improve rental relations; or, in the event of dysfunctions observed in the state of housing, see the decree of 30 January 2002 on the decency of housing.

If the amicable procedure fails, the association may bring the case before the Departmental Conciliation Commission. Representatives of owners and tenants' organisations meet to try to find an amicable settlement. This Commission gives an impartial opinion which is often followed if there is legal action afterwards. In the event of failure, the final step is to refer the matter to the district judge. In the majority of cases, the court will rule in favour of the tenant.

[22] ibid.

[23] 'Energie: Il faut interdire les démarchages à domicile' *Le Monde* (24 February 2020), available at: www.lemonde.fr/economie/article/2020/02/24/energie-il-faut-interdire-les-demarchages-a-domicile_6030572_3234.html.

[24] RAPPEL, Quels dispositifs pour accompagner les ménages en précarité énergétique? (2018).

It is interesting to note that, despite those tools, no outcome data is available: is this the sign of a good policy intention that is hampered by too many barriers rendering access to justice too complicated?

IV. What are the Barriers to Access Justice for Energy Consumers?

When comparing the number of existing energy contracts in France (32.8 million household electricity contracts)[25] with the number of complaints (less than 17,000 per year), it is reasonable to wonder whether the services of the ombudsmen are sufficiently known to the general public. The National Energy Ombudsman is, therefore, carefully monitoring its awareness and reputation in its annual 'barometer'. In 2019, 31 per cent of respondents had heard of the National Energy Ombudsman, 6 per cent more than in 2018. In general, awareness mostly comes from the media (58 per cent of quotes versus 17 per cent for the internet). The Ombudsman also manages the Energie-Info platform, which is known by around a quarter of the households surveyed. The combined awareness of the Ombudsman and its information service Energie-Info is stable, with 43 per cent of respondents knowing one of the two.[26] Although there does not seem to be a specific channel of direct contact with vulnerable households, the National Energy Ombudsman does makes an effort to communicate with them on themes likely to affect them, such as the winter truce, the energy cheque or door-to-door sales.

The implementation of the energy cheque and its expansion to more households since 2018 has sometimes created confusion among operators and families. The Ombudsman notes in its 2019 annual report that some people who were previously beneficiaries of social tariffs would not receive the cheque, and that suppliers were sometimes not sufficiently knowledgeable. Furthermore, the cheque gives the right to other forms of protection, such as the winter truce, and many households are not aware of this. Some consumers do not understand that the difference between the consumption billed and the cheque is not refunded when a person has consumed less than the amount of the cheque. Associations such as the RAPPEL or the Abbé Pierre Foundation still criticise the insufficient level of the payment and complexity of the cheque scheme.[27] Households receive the cheque

[25] Connaissance des Energies, *Le point sur la fourniture d'électricité aux ménages français* (2019), available at: www.connaissancedesenergies.org/fourniture-denergie-le-point-sur-louverture-la-concurrence-en-france-190704.

[26] Médiateur National de l'énergie, *Baromètre Energie-Info du médiateur national de l'énergie* (2019), available at: www.energie-mediateur.fr/wp-content/uploads/2019/11/20191105-synthese-barometre-energie-info.pdf.

[27] Challenges, *Le nouveau chèque énergie laisse les associations sur leur faim* (2019), available at: www.challenges.fr/energie-et-environnement/la-hausse-du-cheque-energie-pas-suffisante-pour-les-ong_650164.

automatically but in a large and intimidating envelope. They are responsible for the management of their cheque, but they may not understand the measures they would need to implement to receive the correct amount and related rights. One of the issues to address regarding the cheque is its scope. For instance, residents who are not subject to a housing tax, such as people who live in rental intermediation housing and therefore do not pay the 'general' housing tax, cannot get any of the benefits of the cheque, even when they are asked to contribute to electricity and heating charges.

The main issue concerning access to justice and ADR for vulnerable and poor households is instead a question of the architecture of support measures. The ONPE website lists no less than 17 different schemes.[28] France simultaneously favours two complementary channels of intervention, both on costs (energy cheques, aid for the payment of debts from insurance and pension funds) and on consumption (aid for energy efficiency of uses, or aid for buildings such as public aid for renovation, private programmes and aid from foundations, etc). The operators of these different measures are not necessarily aware of the work of their peers, and households are, therefore, not in a position to assert all their rights. As noted by Erard et al:

> Public policy to combat fuel poverty is like a policy split into a myriad of actors without precise governance: housing, social and energy actors tackle it without any of them really appearing as leaders on the issue. The fight against fuel poverty is thus symptomatic of a 'silo approach' of public policy.[29]

The territorial difference is also a confounding factor. It is, therefore, the informed intermediary (social worker, volunteer from a third-sector organisation) that will make the difference.[30]

V. What Role does ADR (Ombuds) Play in Accessing Justice for Energy-Poor and Vulnerable Consumers?

A. Access to Advice and Information

One of the fundamental missions of the National Energy Ombudsman is the implementation and management of the Energie-Info platform and the online comparator of the various offers on the market. In this sense, the Ombudsman puts itself at the beginning and the end of the process of legal intervention, allowing not only the resolution of disputes but also their prevention. The slogan of the

[28] ONPE, *Tout savoir sur les dispositifs de prévention de la précarité énergétique en un clin d'œil* (2019), available at: www.onpe.org/tout_savoir_dispositifs_prevention_precarite_energetique.

[29] T Erard, L Chancel and M Saujot, 'La précarité énergétique face au défi des données' (March 2015) IDDRI Study, no 1/15.

[30] Creutzfeldt, Gill, McPherson and Cornelis (n 7).

Ombudsman is, moreover, 'Inform–Advise–Protect'. The Ombudsman believes that the first step for energy consumers to be empowered is to 'obtain the knowledge needed to make informed choices'. In practice, 2.1 million consumers visited the Energie-Info platform in 2018, and it received nearly 188,000 calls through a toll-free number. Among those, 6,200 complex requests (not disputes) were handled by the Ombudsman.[31] The Ombudsman is also very active on social networks (Facebook and Twitter) for which it publishes specific material. In addition, the Ombudsman's services regularly publish short videos to explain the Ombudsman's role, debunk myths about energy markets and inform consumers of their rights.

The Ombudsman has also been collaborating with the ONPE since its creation in 2011. Each year, the Ombudsman publishes a barometer to monitor market developments and consumer experiences. At the ONPE's request, the Ombudsman has added questions relevant to collecting information about energy poverty. The results suggest that 15 per cent of respondents reported having felt cold at home for at least 24 hours during the winter of 2018/2019, the same level as in previous years.[32] Poor insulation in their homes is still the main reason (41 per cent). In the same period, one-third of households restricted heating to avoid having high bills, and 10 per cent of households had difficulty paying some electricity or natural gas bills.[33] The follow-up of unpaid electricity and gas bills is also an important indicator used by the Ombudsman (and the regulator) and transmitted to the ONPE. In 2018, 572,440 interventions were made by suppliers for unpaid invoices: 477,349 for electricity (+4.9 per cent) and 95,091 for gas (+0.8 per cent). These data serve to assess the situation and show that it is becoming increasingly difficult for households to pay their energy bills.[34]

Thanks to these tools, the Ombudsman is therefore a prime observer of market trends and the proper implementation of the regulations. As a result, it must often remind operators of their obligations in terms of proper enforcement of consumer protection (for example, Decree no 2008-780 of 13 August 2008 on the procedure applicable in the event of unpaid electricity, gas, heat and water bills). The Ombudsman does this through recommendations following specific complaints, or through generic recommendations transmitted to the competent authorities, ie, the DGCCRF, the CRE or the Directorate-General for Energy and Climate of the Ministry of the Environment. The Ombudsman is therefore regularly consulted on energy poverty-related topics by Parliament and the government. Indeed, the Ombudsman has been able to support or inspire specific measures to protect vulnerable consumers, such as the winter truce;[35] the limitation of billing catch-up to 14 months;[36] or the replacement of social tariffs by the energy cheque.[37]

[31] Médiateur National de l'Energie, *2018 Annual Report* (n 17).
[32] ibid.
[33] Médiateur National de l'énergie, *2019* (n 26).
[34] Médiateur National de l'Energie, *2018 Annual Report* (n 17).
[35] Article L115-3 du Code de l'action sociale et des familles, version en vigueur au 1 janvier 2018.
[36] Article L224-11 du Code de la Consommation, version en vigueur au 17 août 2016.
[37] Article R124-1 du Code de l'énergie, version en vigueur au 20 mars 2020.

The Ombudsman also participates in various working groups arranged by the CRE. These working groups have set up different market procedures and introduced 'soft law' in the electricity[38] and natural gas[39] sectors.

The Ombudsman also aims to introduce educational communications specifically adapted for consumers, whether via telephone or in written form. Referring vulnerable consumers to the appropriate entities (town hall, social services) and support schemes can also be included in such communications. According to the National Energy Ombudsman and the EDF Mediator, some people were grateful for this personalised approach. A representative of the EDF Mediator said that

> the EDF mediator is a reassuring figure who does not ask for anything in return. Incarnation is important. People often turn to the EDF mediator saying, 'I want to talk to a human'. Today, only humans show empathy and understand the person's circumstances.[40]

B. Energy Companies

Energy companies play an essential role in the fight against energy poverty. The biggest have in-house resources to respond to the phenomenon. For instance, there are more than 500 'solidarity advisers' at EDF who work with social workers and charities. Companies also finance programmes and initiatives to combat energy poverty and housing issues, such as supporting the RAPPEL network and providing funds for housing renovation. All energy producers contribute directly to fund energy-saving certificates (EEC) that pay for energy-saving measures, such as housing renovation. The draft Energy and Climate Plan presented by France to the European Commission in 2019 stated that energy companies should invest more than €2 billion in the fight against energy poverty for the period 2018–2020. The plan for energy-focused renovation of buildings also foresees that the state will allocate €1.2 billion to fight energy poverty.[41]

In practice, there is a strong link between the two 'historical' suppliers and approaches with a strong social and territorial impact. This can be explained by the fact that EDF and ENGIE (as GDF) were until the 2000s purely state-owned companies. To date, EDF is still 80 per cent owned by the French state which also still holds nearly a quarter of ENGIE's shareholding. The leading distribution operators, Enedis (electricity) and GRDF (gas), which are in the front line in meeting the concrete needs of consumers in the territories (for example, in the event of a supply shortage or meter replacement) are also respectively subsidiaries of EDF and ENGIE. This traditional state monopoly has facilitated the early commitment of these suppliers to financing energy poverty alleviation measures,

[38] CRE, Groupe de travail Electricité 2007, available at: www.gte2007.com/referentiel.php.
[39] CRE, Groupe de travail Gaz 2007, available at: www.gtg2007.com/index.php.
[40] In a meeting with the author in February 2020.
[41] Creutzfeldt Gill, McPherson and Cornelis (n 7).

such as the creation of social tariffs.[42] A first 'Solidarity Energy Convention'[43] was signed in 1985 between the state and EDF and GDF to support those with unpaid electricity bills. Ten years later, the Minister for Housing, EDF and GDF signed a Solidarity-Energy Charter (1997–2000) to implement support measures for vulnerable households, such as the maintenance of their energy connection for a period of time necessary for the intervention of social services, the limitation of disconnection for non-payment, as well as other actions and specific services for vulnerable families. To help pay the bills, a Poverty and Vulnerability Fund was set up as early as 1985 and updated in the 1990s. In practice, in each department, the prefect, EDF and GDF, as well as other partners (local authorities, municipal social action centres, social protection bodies, etc), have signed an annual agreement implementing this scheme. An 'energy solidarity fund' was also set up at the departmental level, financed by the departmental directorate of health and social affairs and local representatives of EDF and GDF, with other potential partners.[44]

More recently, the cooperative and 100 per cent renewable-energy supplier Enercoop launched the Energie Solidaire endowment fund, arising from the association Les Amis d'Enercoop (friends of Enercoop). The project has developed innovative collection solutions. In practice, every Enercoop customer can subscribe to the micro-donation, in the form of 0.01 € per kWh consumed. In April 2019, six months after its launch, the programme had nearly 1,750 micro-donors, for a monthly collection of nearly €50,000. Moreover, self-consuming photovoltaics panels producers can donate their unused production surplus instead of reselling it. Once the energy is recovered by Enercoop, the cooperative undertakes to pay back to Energie Solidaire the equivalent value of the energy sold. Those funds are then allocated to local initiatives to help households affected by energy poverty.[45]

Regarding unpaid bills and payment problems, since 2014, energy suppliers must transmit data relative to the measures they are taking to the National Energy Ombudsman and to the national regulatory authority, the CRE.[46] In 2018, the number of procedures for unpaid electricity and gas bills for individuals increased compared with 2017: up by 4.2 per cent. According to the figures they provided to the Ombudsman and the CRE, suppliers made 572,440 interventions for non-payment: 477,349 in electricity (+4.9 per cent) and 95,091 in gas (+0.8 per cent).[47] In 2016, 604,000 actions (cuts, power reductions, contracts terminated by the supplier) were initiated.

[42] S Pye, A Dobbins and C Baffert et al, 'Energy Poverty and Vulnerable Consumers in the Energy Sector across the EU: Analysis of Policies and Measures' (INSIGHT_E, 2015), available at: ec.europa.eu/energy/sites/ener/files/documents/INSIGHT_E_Energy%20Poverty%20-%20Main%20Report_FINAL.pdf.

[43] Later converted into Funds of Solidarity for Housing.

[44] Cornelis (n 4).

[45] See: www.enercoop.fr/content/energie-solidaire-un-lancement-reussi-en-018.

[46] Décret 2014-274 du 27 février 2014 modifiant le décret 2008-780 du 13 août 2008 relatif à la procédure applicable en cas d'impayés des factures d'électricité, de gaz, de chaleur et d'eau.

[47] National Energy Ombudsman, *Annual Report* (2019).

However, not all suppliers are exemplary. In its 2018 activity report,[48] the National Energy Ombudsman noted an increase in complaints relating to the implementation of the energy cheque. Some suppliers were slow to implement it; others did not communicate appropriately on the modalities of implementation. In some cases, the rights associated with the energy cheque were not respected: for example, commissioning and late payment fees are reduced. In addition, suppliers are not allowed to reduce power or cut off supply during the winter truce. In order to claim these rights, low-income households must send their energy cheque to the electricity supplier or provide a certificate if they have used it for other purposes, such as buying domestic fuel. Similarly, the automatic introduction of the energy cheque in 2018 went hand-in-hand with the end of social tariffs. In 2018, the Ombudsman had to deal with complaints where the application of the new scheme did not seem to have been done correctly. Unfortunately, due to delays and process changes, the Ombudsman could no longer check applications retrospectively. Therefore, it was up to ENGIE to grant the social tariff retroactively to close these disputes.

VI. How can Vulnerable Consumers Access Justice?

A. State Level, Private Level, Local Initiatives?

Historically, France is a centralised country, and the energy Ombudsman does not have offices in the territories to enable people to come to it. Most contacts therefore happen through traditional communication tools (mail, internet, telephone) or through intermediaries, such as social workers, as well as members of the RAPPEL network. For instance, in March 2020, during the Coronavirus outbreak and at a time when the French government had announced an extension of the winter truce to 31 May 2020 (as opposed to the usual 31 March), the Ombudsman services contacted the members of the RAPPEL network to check with them that the extensions had been properly implemented.[49]

However, as far as the formal justice system is concerned, French law guarantees accessible and free locations coordinated by the departmental councils for access to the law (CDADs) where people can go to find out about their rights and duties. The French Ministry of Justice acknowledges that many people are unaware of the nature and extent of these rights and the remedies available to enforce them.[50] The 1991 law on Legal Aid ensures equal access to the law for all citizens, especially the most vulnerable.[51] Access to the law was also enshrined in the Act

[48] ibid.
[49] Email received by the author on 18 March 2020, as a recipient of the RAPPEL mailing list.
[50] *cf* French Ministry of Justice, Connaître vos droits: www.justice.fr/connaître-vos-droits.
[51] 203 Loi 91-647 du 10 juillet 1991 relative à l'aide juridique (Law on Legal Aid).

of 18 November 2016 on the modernisation of justice in the twenty-first century as a component of the public justice service.[52] France believes that access to the law is a fundamental element of the 'social pact', thus making it possible to combat poverty and prevent the exclusion of the most vulnerable and/or isolated people. Indeed, access to the law can be the starting point for a series of often overlapping legal, social and/or administrative procedures.[53] The Ministry of Justice leads and supervises activities aimed at enabling access to the law, through the allocation of grants and coordinated actions by the CDAD. It also subsidises associations contributing to the development of access to the law for different groups (young people, people with disabilities or exclusion, foreigners, travellers, etc). In February 2017, to promote access to the law the Minister of Justice signed a national charter with seven associations specialising in the field of exclusion. This charter sets out 'values, common objectives, fundamental principles, implementation methods allowing access to the law and support for most destitute people'.[54]

In addition, every year, the Ministry of Justice organises a national day of access to the law and honours the best initiatives. In 2019, the 'prize for access to the law' was awarded to the CDAD of Dordogne for having produced, with the help of mentally ill people, a series of documents bearing the label 'easy to read and understand' for the attention of people with intellectual disabilities or vulnerable individuals (for example, elderly people whose intellectual faculties are impaired), but also foreigners with a poor command of the French language.[55]

Although the supervision happens at the national level, each department coordinates their own CDAD.[56] The CDAD is placed under the authority of the president of the district court of the Department. It brings together different stakeholders: institutional (prefecture, regional council, departmental council, cities and communities of cities); jurisdictional (president of the district court and public prosecutor at this court); professionals (lawyers, notaries); and associations. Together, they identify needs, define local policy, stimulate action (guides for young people, open days, etc), draft and disseminate an inventory of the actions carried out, and evaluate the quality and effectiveness of the mechanisms put in place to improve access to the law.[57] In this way, the CDADs enable partnerships and networking activities among local actors to support new projects corresponding to specific unmet needs in various fields and contributing to the development of amicable dispute resolution methods.

[52] Village de la Justice, *Citoyens, découvrez les conseils départementaux de l'accès au droit!* (2019), available at: www.village-justice.com/articles/citoyens-participez-journee-nationale-acces-droit,28538.html.

[53] Cornelis (n 4).

[54] Ministère de la Justice, *Charte Nationale de l'Accès au Droit* (2017), available at: www.justice.gouv.fr/art_pix/charte_nationale_acces_droit_20170221pdf.

[55] Village de la Justice, *Citoyens, découvrez les conseils départementaux de l'accès au droit!* (n 52).

[56] Loi 98-1163 du 18 décembre 1998 relative à l'accès au droit et à la résolution amiable des conflits (law on the access to justice).

[57] Cornelis (n 4).

Furthermore, the Houses of Justice and Law are permanent institutions ensuring a local judicial presence. They are placed under the joint authority of the president of the court of first instance and the public prosecutor. For small civil disputes, they promote the amicable settlement of conflicts (via conciliation, mediation) and provide assistance with access to justice.[58]

VII. What can be done to Improve the Situation?

A. EU Level, National Level …

The landscape of the fight against energy poverty in France is complex and multi-faceted. The problems mostly arise from concerns about housing quality and the issue of costs. Energy poverty is usually not the only problem households are facing, and their difficulties may vary from season to season and from year to year. It is also important to note that, when turning to social workers or NGOs for help, some families will ask for something other than direct support to pay their energy bills. Such vulnerable people deprive themselves and make trade-offs (for example, on food or mobility needs) and may not be identified (statistically) as energy poor. Home or school support could make it possible to identify some of the households in energy poverty, but France is still lacking a systemic approach towards this issue.

The fragmentation of problems results in the multiplication of local actors providing partial help to households. Those actors are not always well informed about the missions of other stakeholders and how they could complement each other's work. Despite the political commitment, the very active RAPPEL network and the ONPE, there is no coordination between the different support services. The Ombudsman should, therefore, insist that these stakeholders publicise the Ombudsman services and pass on the baton in the event of a complaint relating to the energy market. Communication and signposting should be targeted not only at (vulnerable) households but also at social workers.

One of the solutions to the problem of raising awareness and reaching out to more people could be to set up local branches, using the network of Energy Information Centres coordinated by the Agence de l'Environnement et de la Maîtrise de l'Energie (Agency for the Environment and Energy Management) or local housing agencies. Physical meetings and information points could help fill the gap between the field experience of users and the potentially intimidating or bureaucratic processes of the Ombudsman.

What is more, consumers often find it challenging to decipher their bills and find apposite information (for example, the contact details of the Ombudsman):

[58] ibid.

a 2017 study by the European Commission showed that 41 per cent of customers have difficulty understanding their electricity bills.[59] Consumers in financial difficulty are significantly less inclined than others to consider these bills to be clear and understandable. The number of billing-related complaints confirms this. At the moment, bills and invoices remain the first contact tool between the supplier and the customer. Simplifying the invoice could be a way to increase access to information and raise awareness about methods of redress.

The 'Clean Energy for All Package' has brought in many new rights for energy consumers, such as the right to use an aggregator without the authorisation of the energy supplier; or the right to join a local energy community. As a result, the Ombudsman will experience new energy relationships and will shortly have to deal not only with complaints from energy companies and end-users, but also with complaints concerning business-to-business and company-to-company, peer-to-peer platforms and new market players. New contractual or regulatory relationships, such as collective self-consumption, will become more accessible and widespread. An increase in the offerings of suppliers of products and services indirectly relating to the supply of electricity or natural gas can be expected. The Electricity Directive 2019/944[60] allows ombudsmen to deal with suppliers of other products and services (Article 26). The French Ombudsman must very quickly become competent in all disputes concerning products and services which are directly or indirectly linked to the functioning of the energy market, whatever the supplier or company offering these products or services. Consumers themselves do not always distinguish between companies, be they energy suppliers or suppliers of other products and services, but having a single point of reference for resolving their disputes is already a first step. The modalities of the Ombudsman's intervention should therefore be adapted. For example, consumers should have the legal option to complain by telephone, in order to further assist (vulnerable) consumers, especially those intimidated by written procedures.

The deployment of smart meters should be seen as an opportunity to ensure that all households are adequately informed about these new technologies and the possibilities they offer. Households should have easy access to information enabling them to monitor their consumption and, as initially planned under French law, recipients of the energy cheque should be provided with a display installed in the dwelling free of charge. Suppliers had argued that the provision of a display in dwellings was expensive, especially as the number of beneficiaries of the energy voucher was increasing, and that internet tracking was sufficient. Nevertheless, remote monitoring was finally dropped in the Energy-Climate Act of 8 November 2019 (Article 13). In parallel, the deployment of smart meters could allow the

[59] European Commission, *Second Consumer Market Study on the Functioning of the Retail Electricity Markets for Consumers in the EU* (European Commission, 2017).

[60] Directive (EU) 2019/944 of the European Parliament and of the Council of 5 June 2019 on common rules for the internal market for electricity and amending Directive 2012/27/EU (Text with EEA relevance) [2019] OJ L158/125.

emergence of 'prepaid' tariffs, but those tariffs should not add to the burden of vulnerable households.

Another way of extending the impact of the National Energy Ombudsman could be to enable it to be accredited for group or class actions (collective redress). This procedure allows individuals who are victims of the same damage, committed by a professional, to bring a collective action before the courts in order to obtain compensation. It was introduced into French law by Act no 2014-344 of 17 March 2014 on consumer affairs. However, to date, the scope of this law is still limited, in particular because the action must be brought before the courts by one of the 15 accredited associations, but also because it is only possible to launch a group action to compensate for material damage exclusively for disputes relating to consumption or competition. To date, the use of collective actions in the energy sector is not an option in the energy distribution and supply sector for consumer associations or the Ombudsman.

VIII. Conclusion

A simplification of the systems providing justice, including those involved in ADR, is necessary to truly be able to help vulnerable and energy-poor consumers access justice and assert their rights. This includes clear signposting and a re-orientation of legal aid. However, in a state as centralised as France, where each administration, company and service are keen to defend its own precinct, there is still no adequate framework to provide aid centred on the needs of the individual, in particular those most in need.

12

Access to Justice for Vulnerable and Energy-Poor Consumers in Italy: Policy Measures and the Role of ADR

SARAH SUPINO AND BENEDETTA VOLTAGGIO*

I. Italian Policies to Tackle Energy Poverty

Energy poverty (EP) is a widespread problem that affects people who are unable to afford adequate energy supplies due to unavailable economic resources. In recent years, Italy has paid great attention to such problems, even mentioning them in the National Energy Strategy 2017 (NES 2017). The NES 2017 also revealed that in 2016 the percentage of Italian families in EP was about 8 per cent (2.1 million families) of the whole population, 14 per cent in the southern regions.

The main drivers of EP in Italy are low income, high energy costs and high consumption due to low energy performing buildings. In Italy the price of energy products is higher than the European average; in the second half of 2015 (i) the average price per 100 kWh of electricity was €21.1 in Europe and €24.3 in Italy; (ii) the average price of 100 kWh of gas was €7.1 in Europe and €9.1 in Italy.[1] This issue is mainly due to the overall tax burden on energy bills (over 30 per cent of the total amount), including either taxes or the so-called 'amounts covering general electricity charges' (which are indeed taxes, according to the Court of Justice of the European Union).[2]

Furthermore, in Italy, about 64 per cent of residential properties were built before the 1980s, when laws on energy saving were not yet in force.[3]

* Benedetta Voltaggio is author of sections I, II.A, II.B and II.C; Sarah Supino is author of sections II.D, II.E, II.F, II.G and III. They are both authors of section IV.

[1] Eurostat New Release, 'Energy Prices in the EU in 2015' (27 May 2016).

[2] Judgment of 18 January 2017, Case C-189/15 *Istituto di Ricovero e Cura a Carattere Scientifico (IRCCS) v Fondazione Santa Lucia v Cassa conguaglio per il settore elettrico and Others*, commented on by S Armella, 'Sono imposte indirette gli oneri generali del sistema elettrico' (2017) 26 *Corriere Tributario* 2059.

[3] Following the energy crisis of the 1970s, the Italian Parliament issued the first law on energy saving (Law no 373/1973), which was subsequently amended and integrated by Law no 10/1991 containing the first real step towards the energy certification of buildings.

When inefficient buildings are inhabited by poor families (as often happens), the heat loss generated by the building entails an increase in energy consumption and – correlatively – in the energy expenses, with a consequent increase in the discomfort caused by EP. This consequence is more and more aggravated when those responsible for paying energy bills (the tenants) are not the same entities as those making the capital investment decisions (the building owner). In these circumstances, neither the landlord nor the tenant may be inclined to make any upgrades to building (this is the issue of so-called split-incentives).

In Italy there is neither a complete action plan to combat EP, nor a public system for measuring and monitoring it. Nevertheless, Italy has introduced some measures to tackle EP.[4]

The most significant measure is currently the social bonus, aimed at reducing the cost of electricity and gas supplies for low-income families.[5] The bonuses are applied[6] upon request of the beneficiary and reduce the overall burden of the bill. The Regulatory Authority for Energy, Networks and the Environment (ARERA or the Authority) has estimated that in 2017 only about a third of the potential beneficiaries actually requested the bonus.[7] This is due to a lack of knowledge and the administrative burden of the application (annual renewal, retrieval of the necessary documents to obtain the proper certificates etc).[8] To solve this problem, starting from 2021[9] the bonus on energy bills will be applied automatically by adopting a rule that allows the necessary exchange of data between the administrations in order to ensure that all those entitled can benefit from the bonuses, abolishing all the bureaucratic steps currently necessary for families.

Another measure to tackle EP is a tax allowance (detraction) for taxpayers who improve the energy efficiency of their buildings (so-called ecobonus).[10] At the beginning, this allowance was aimed at reducing personal income tax, by subtracting a certain amount from the tax to be paid. For this reason, it did not work for poor people, whose taxes are normally lower than the allowed detraction. In these

[4] For an overview of the main measures and their critical issues, please refer to S Supino and B Voltaggio, *La povertà energetica. Strumenti per affrontare un problema sociale* (il Mulino, 2019); S Supino and B Voltaggio, 'Le misure di contrasto alla povertà energetica: lineamenti e criticità' (2019) 3 *Rivista Energia* 22.

[5] The electricity bonus was established with Law no 266/2006 and Art 3, para 9 of Legislative Decree no 185/2008.

[6] Families with an 'ISEE' (ie, a document that indicates the economic status of a family) not exceeding €8,107.50 and €20,000 in the case of families with at least four dependent children can benefit from the bonuses. The ISEE indicator allows taking into account the family's income level, total assets, composition and the presence of people with disabilities.

[7] ARERA, 287/2015/I/COM (2015), available at: www.autorita.energia.it/it/docs/15/287-15.htm.

[8] The ISEE certificate is issued by the INPS following the processing of the data communicated by the citizen regarding the movable and real estate assets of the whole family. The income data are instead automatically provided by the Revenue Agency.

[9] Legislative Decree of 26 October 2019, no 124, Art 57-*bis*.

[10] Introduced in 2007, it is currently governed by Art 14 of the Legislative Decree of 4 June 2013, no 63. The Law of 27 December 2017, no 205 expanded the audience of beneficiaries and facilitated interventions.

cases, the detraction 'doesn't find capacity' in the tax, and thus benefit cannot be applied. To solve this problem, people with low incomes have been allowed to dispose of a credit for the amount of the allowed detraction: such credits can be transferred to banks and to the company carrying out the building renovation. In this way, the assistance is available even for families who may not be able to support the whole cost of the energy-saving interventions on buildings.

Access to energy for Italian families is also protected by other services introduced through the implementation of Directive 2003/54/EC of 26 June 2003 of the European Parliament and Council. An example of this, with reference to the electricity market, is the energy supply envisaged by Article 23 of the Integrated Electricity Arrears Act for customers who carry out activities of public interest[11] and who are recipients of the bonuses:[12] in respect of these subjects, energy can never be suspended, not even for arrears.

Lastly, measures aimed at ensuring access to energy consumption in the national energy system include tax incentives. Energy consumption is subject to excise duty and VAT, but some tax allowances are provided:

a. an exemption from excise duty[13] up to a monthly consumption of 150 kWh[14] for domestic users, with committed power up to 3 kW;
b. a reduction from excise duty on diesel and LPG used for heating in disadvantaged areas;[15]
c. the application of the reduced VAT rate (10 per cent) to supplies of electricity and gas for domestic use, limited to 480 cubic meters per year.[16]

As regards the effectiveness of these measures, the National Plan for Energy and Climate released on 20 January 2020, hypothesised that they could lead to a reduction of about 1 per cent compared with the 2016 incidence of EP in Italy.[17] This estimate was made considering the following factors:

1. The evolution of residential energy consumption which is expected to decrease in 2030 compared to 2016 by 15.5 per cent (-1.4 per cent on an annual basis).[18]

[11] As identified by the resolution of the Inter-ministerial Committee for Economic Planning no 91 of 6 November 1979, and subsequent amendments.

[12] See para 2.2(b) of the Integrated Act, according to which the compensation is recognised for domestic customers, who are in conditions of economic or physical discomfort.

[13] See Art 52, para 3(e) of Legislative Decree no 504/1995 and resolution no 15 of 14 December 1993 of the Inter-ministerial Price Committee.

[14] In case of supplies with committed power up to 1.5 kW and for consumption above 150 kWh/month, the tax-exempt kWh are gradually reduced.

[15] See Law no 448 of 23 December 1998 and subsequent amendment.

[16] For the surplus, as well as for all ancillary charges (contractual and connections) other than consumption, the VAT rate is instead provided in the ordinary measure (22%).

[17] Ministry of Economic Development, 'Integrated National Plan for Energy and Climate' (2019) 98, available at: www.mise.gov.it/index.php/it/198-notizie-stampa/2040668-pniec2030.

[18] With an increase in the electrical component (of 7.2%) against a reduction in gas (by almost a quarter) and a collapse in oil products.

2. The expected trend of the prices of energy products (including taxes) which should increase.[19]
3. The expenditure of households which could grow at an annualised rate of 0.8 per cent.
4. Demographic evolution, in consideration of the constant increase[20] in families less exposed to the risk of EP.

The existing measures are efficient to tackle EP in Italy, but the national and regulatory system still suffers from numerous gaps. For example, an 'official measure' of EP is still missing, so much so that the only existing regulatory definitions – envisaged for the attribution of social bonuses – are based on income and asset indicators, without considering that EP does not depend only on these factors, but also on other elements, such as the energy consumption and costs. The NES 2017 has proposed the adoption of the EP measurement criterion theorised by Faiella and Lavecchia:[21] the hope is that this intention will crystallise as soon as possible in a definitive regulatory recognition.

It is fundamental to know the impact EP has both from a quantitative (number of Italian families that cannot support energy expenditure) and qualitative (characteristics of such families) point of view. Having clear information on the spread of EP is also essential to identify its main causes and, above all, to individuate the proper measures and policies and to verify their effectiveness.

For the same purpose, a National Observatory on EP would be useful. Some private entities already exist, such as the 'Italian EP Observatory',[22] a network of researchers from universities, public and private entities and institutions which carries out research, information and dissemination activities on the issues of EP, at national and international level. However, a public structure – preferably, managed by the Authority – aimed at collecting all available data and monitoring the spread of EP and the effectiveness of the policy measures is still missing.

In sum, to defeat an enemy you must know it, but the regulatory measures adopted in Italy still denote a superficial knowledge of EP. Maybe it is also due to the fact that, in Italy, electricity is not considered as an essential good: the Italian Criminal Court of Cassation recently stated that

> the lack of electricity does not entail any current danger of serious harm to the person, since electricity is not an indispensable good for life …, since it is suitable for procuring ease and opportunity that go beyond the concept of incoercible necessity.[23]

[19] European Commission, 'EU Reference Scenario 2016'. In particular, the final price of electricity would grow by 0.6% per year. Overall, energy expenditure could grow by 1.3% on an annual basis.

[20] According to the forecasts made by the Italian National Institute of Statistics, in 2030 the share of people over 65 would be equal to a quarter of the total and the number of families would increase due to the continuous trend of reducing the average number of components.

[21] I Faiella and L Lavecchia, 'La povertà energetica in Italia' (2014) *Questioni di economia e finanza* 240.

[22] It has been working since 2019. All the relevant information on the Observatory is available at: oipeosservatorio.it/.

[23] Court of Cassation, criminal section, judgment no 39887 of 4 September 2017.

A new reflection should start from the deep meaning of energy, in particular deeming it an indispensable good, as it is.

II. Access to Justice for Vulnerable and Energy-Poor Consumers in Italy: The Role of ADR

A. Preliminary Remarks

It should be noted that discussions in Italy on EP in general are quite recent,[24] while in other countries (such as England or France) the problem has been recognised and examined for a long time.

At the moment, the debate is therefore focused on the effectiveness of the substantial instruments for the protection of energy-poor consumers (bonuses, social tariffs, etc), but there is still no discussion on the judicial protection of such consumers. No one, either in literature or at the political level, has in fact yet questioned the effectiveness of the instruments of judicial protection in relation to energy-poor consumers.

However, in Italy, there are several tools that protect access to justice for poor people in general; at the same time, in the energy sector, there are tools that allow access to justice for vulnerable energy consumers. Despite the fact that the category of EP does not coincide perfectly with that of 'general poverty' or that of 'energy vulnerability',[25] this analysis offers a starting point for verifying whether

[24] The first main Italian study of the EP in Italy is that by Faiella and Lavecchia (n 21). In recent years, public and private initiatives and studies on EP have also multiplied in Italy (among which it is important to mention P Ranci, M Leonardi and L Susani, *Poveri d'energia* (il Mulino, 2016); and the more recent S Supino and B Voltaggio, *La povertà energetica. Strumenti per affrontare un problema sociale* (il Mulino, 2019). In 2017, for the first time the National Energy Strategy mentioned the fight against EP among the national aims, followed by the National Energy and Climate Plans 2018 which also included such a goal among the most important energy aims.

[25] The Electricity and Gas Directives (the 3rd Energy Package) require each Member State to define the concept of vulnerable customers and to ensure there are adequate safeguards to protect vulnerable customers. This definition may refer to the concept of EP where it has been clearly identified. In Italy, the first definition of vulnerable customer in the gas market, introduced by Legislative Decree no 93/2011, referred to civil and non-civil customers with consumption lower than or equal to 50,000 cubic meters per year. The European Commission, however, contested the excessive breadth of this definition, which also included subjects that do not need particular protection. Today, Art 22 of Legislative Decree no 164/2000 provides a more limited notion of 'vulnerable customers' and refers to those who can access the gas bonus, identified in the light of criteria that also take into account income and assets. In Italy, however, there is no definition of energy-poor consumer or EP. The debate on the topic began a few years ago and for the moment the government has only endorsed in the National Energy Strategy a criterion for measuring EP proposed by some researchers from the Bank of Italy, widely based on the low income–high cost criterion (Faiella and Lavecchia (n 21)). In any case, the concepts of 'EP', 'energy vulnerability' and 'general poverty' do not coincide. As in fact also highlighted in the Vulnerable Consumer Working Group Guidance Document on Vulnerable Consumers, November 2013, 'the customers and consumers who are vulnerable may also face energy and/or fuel poverty; although there is likely to be a positive correlation between the two, it may be rather low.

the instruments envisaged in our legal system are suitable for the protection of energy-poor consumers. In such a context, alternative dispute resolution (ADR) tools certainly play a fundamental role, and they have been strongly enhanced following the Third Energy Package.

B. ADR, Right of Defence and Free Legal Assistance

In addition to the substantive tools to combat energy poverty briefly examined, there are some procedural measures in Italy, with particular attention to ADR, that have also been introduced in the energy sector and are aimed at protecting the right to defence of subjects in conditions of vulnerability or poverty.

This constitutional guarantee ensures that people who do not have sufficient income to meet the costs of justice and legal assistance have access to the protection of their rights and interests.

Article 24 of the Italian Constitution provides that 'everyone can take legal action for the protection of their legitimate rights and interests', ensuring defence as an inviolable right in every state and degree of the proceedings. In Italy, therefore, access to jurisdictional protection is constitutionally recognised, and the task of ensuring the means and defence institutes for the poor is left to the ordinary legislator.[26] Article 24, paragraph 3 of the Constitution establishes that 'the means for acting and defending themselves before each jurisdiction are ensured to the poor with specific institutes', and Article 75 of Presidential Decree no 115/2002 on free legal aid limits itself to providing that 'admission to legal aid is valid for every degree and for every phase of the process and for all possible procedures, derived and accidental, however connected'.

Literal examination of these rules would seem to conclude that neither at the constitutional level nor at the first regulatory one is there a provision that includes, expressly and generally,[27] ADR among procedures to which the institution of legal aid can apply.

Having regard to the purpose of ADR, it can be observed that the legislator's objective of favouring the use of ADR tools and of giving the parties the effective

This is also the case with the correlation between poverty and fuel poverty: the poorest people do not always live in the worst housing, especially in Member States where subsidised housing is offered to those who are least well resourced'.

[26] In particular, the free assistance of a lawyer for civil, criminal, tax and administrative processes is guaranteed by Presidential Decree no 115/2002, containing the discipline of free legal aid. The requirements for admission to legal aid are the ownership of a taxable income of no more than €11,493.82 and the unfounded nature of the claim that you intend to assert. If the applicant lives with other family members (also without having contracted marriage), the income is made up of the sum of the income earned by each member of the family.

[27] The application of legal aid is instead provided in some cases in the detailed rules of the individual institutions. For example, Legislative Decree no 116/2005, has expressly established (Art 6) that legal aid is also extended to the mandatory extrajudicial phases of cross-border disputes.

possibility of amicably settling their disputes would be hopelessly frustrated if the party in possession of the requirements for admission to legal aid, who is presumably the weakest party and the one most interested in a quick and friendly solution, cannot have access to such a form of assistance.

The question of the costs of out-of-court procedures is also of crucial importance for the very legitimacy of the instruments, whose full efficiency can only be reached when they are considered as valid alternatives, endowed with dignity equal to the ordinary process and accessible by anyone who wishes to resort to them. The State should, therefore, guarantee ADR's full usability for all citizens, regardless of their financial resources and regardless of the mandatory nature of the procedure.

In this regard, the jurisprudence and the doctrine,[28] on the basis of an interpretation of the current legislation which is both constitutionally oriented and adhering to the Community principles,[29] has also recognised the applicability of legal aid to the defensive activity carried out in extrajudicial proceedings, where the latter are configured by the rules as mandatory. In such cases, in fact, the connection envisaged by the aforementioned Article 75 would in fact be configurable of the extrajudicial phase to the judicial procedure.[30]

With specific reference to the energy sector, the issue has been resolved by providing, as a general rule, a free conciliation service for all customers, regardless of economic conditions. This choice, together with the regulation of the free legal aid provided for the judicial phase, therefore ensures that a vulnerable party in conflict with the operators can access all stages of justice (both extrajudicial and judicial).

In the following, we will show the extrajudicial procedures in force in Italy, with particular attention to the ADR tools introduced in the energy sector, but also in order to verify their effectiveness with respect to subjects in conditions of vulnerability or energy poverty and, above all, in order to assess whether they are suitable for guaranteeing the right to defence of these subjects, as protected by the Italian Constitution.

[28] Cass civ. 19 April 2013, no 9529, Cass civ.23 November 2011, no 24723. In literature, see N Trocker, 'Gratuito Patrocinio' in *Digesto delle Discipline privatistiche. Sezione civile* (UTET Giuridica, 2013) 288, who maintains that 'in Europe after the Second World War there is also awareness that the problem of legal assistance does not end in the need to make the right to judicial protection concrete and effective. This protection must be flanked with equal importance that of protection before and out of court, both in the form of consultancy in the strict sense and in the form of assistance to any out-of-court negotiations, both informal and arbitration, administrative, etc'. For completeness, we acknowledge a contrary orientation of the doctrine according to which the protection offered by Art 24, para 3 of the constitutional charter has a scope limited to the endoprocessive context.

[29] With Council Directive 2003/8/ EC of 27 January 2003 aimed at improving access to justice in cross-border disputes, the European Union has defined some common minimum standards relating to legal aid, all inspired by the general principle according to which legal aid should be granted to all those who do not have sufficient means, if this is necessary to ensure effective access to justice.

[30] In the same sense, the National Forensic Council expressed itself in circular no 25 of 6 December 2013, arguing that the assistance of the lawyer, mandatory for mediation, should be part of legal aid.

C. The Main Types of ADR in Italy are Inadequate to be Applied in Cases of Energy Disputes Involving Energy-Poor Consumers

It should be said that in Italy there are several forms of ADR that are applicable in all the sectors (not only energy) and are also widespread and exploited by disputing parties.[31] The most important ones are:

1. *Mediation*: introduced by Legislative Decree no 28 of 4 March 2010, which implemented EU Directive no 52/2008 – the process carried out in all civil and commercial trials by an impartial third party which is aimed at assisting the disputing parties in resolving their conflict, through the formulation of a proposal for the resolution of the dispute.[32]
2. *Conciliation*: widely used in disputes between businesses and consumers, who can reach a mutually agreed solution thanks to the assistance of a qualified expert (the conciliator).
3. *Assisted negotiation*: an agreement through which the disputing parties undertake to 'cooperate in good faith and loyalty' in order to settle a dispute through the assistance of lawyers regularly registered in a proper public register.[33]
4. *Arbitration:* the parties, through an arbitration agreement (a contract or a clause contained in a contract) provide that, if a dispute should arise in

[31] It has been estimated that the number of mediation procedures in Italy is six times higher than in the rest of Europe (see resolution approved by the European Parliament on 12 September 2017): this can be explained in light of the large delays in Italy's civil justice system. Trials used to conclude on average in five years for each grade of judgment, while the mediation procedure takes no more than three months (that can be extended by parties). This term ensures a fast resolution of the dispute with an executive agreement. According to the EU Justice Scoreboard published on 26 April 2019 by the European Commission, Italy is the Member State with the longest time to resolve civil and commercial cases. The estimated time for resolving these disputes is around 500 days in the first instance, around 900 days in the second instance, while it takes more than 1,200 days for judgments before the Court of Cassation.

[32] In accordance with Art 2, para 1 of Legislative Decree no 28/2010, any dispute in civil or commercial matters can be solved through mediation, except unavailable rights.
There are four types of mediation: (a) optional (or voluntary) mediation; (b) mandatory mediation, when mediation procedure is a mandatory condition for claiming before a court; (c) delegated mediation, when the parties, in the context of a trial, are invited by the judge to attempt the mediation procedure; and (d) agreed (or consensual) mediation, when the parties introduce a mediation or conciliation clause in their contracts, through which they undertake to carry out mediation proceedings before applying to a judge.

[33] It entered into force with Legislative Decree no 132/2014, converted into Law no 162/2014, with the specific aim to 'solve delays and arrears in civil trials'. The party that chooses to begin a negotiation sends an invitation to enter into a negotiation agreement to the other party, through its lawyer. If the invitation is accepted, the negotiation takes place, which can have a positive or negative outcome. In the latter case, the designated lawyers will have to draw up the declaration of non-agreement. In addition to optional negotiation, in some cases the law provides for mandatory assisted negotiation (disputes relating to compensation for damage from the vehicles, payment for any sums not exceeding €50,000 outside the cases in which compulsory mediation is provided). In such cases, the attempt constitutes a condition of admissibility of the subsequent judicial request.

future or has already arisen, it will be resolved by arbitration and not before a court.[34]

However, such procedures are not very suitable when a party is a vulnerable or energy-poor consumer, for several reasons.

First, they are not free of charge. For example, in the case of mediation, in addition to the attorney's assistance costs[35] and the fixed fee of €40 for initiating the procedure, all parties are required to pay an indemnity to the mediation bodies.[36] The same happens in the case of arbitration.

Second, in most of the procedures a decisive and compulsory role is assigned to lawyers. Since the compulsory assistance of one or more lawyers is a key element of some types of ADR (as in the case of mediation and assisted negotiation), such instruments are not appropriate for vulnerable people, who often are not able to pay the lawyers' fees.

Third, this aspect can discourage private individuals from adopting this tool for the resolution of commercial disputes with companies. In fact, big companies (for example, most energy companies) can count on the assistance of expert lawyers on the specific issues relating to the dispute, with less protection for the weakest party (ie, the consumer) during the negotiation.

Further, it is not clear if the disputes involving consumers can be solved through all the ADR types. For example, there have been discussions around whether such disputes are arbitrable. In literature, it is widely believed that the legislator does not prohibit the arbitration agreement of such disputes.[37] However, the introduction of the arbitration clause must respect the principle of protection of the weaker party. In other words, the consumer is required to have given consent to arbitration with effective awareness, otherwise the arbitration clause will be considered vexatious.[38]

[34] In the presence of an arbitration clause, the judicial action is not proceedable. The arbitrators decide according to law, unless the parties allow them to decide according to equity. The decision that is taken by the arbitrator is called an arbitration award and can be 'ritual' or 'non-ritual': the former has the same effects of a judgment pronounced in a court, but it is not automatically enforceable; the latter has the effects of a contract, where the parties give the arbitrators a mere mandate to settle the dispute.

[35] Art 5, para 1-*bis* of the Decree provides that the presence of the lawyer who assists the party is required in the case of mandatory mediations.

[36] The minimum and maximum amount of the indemnities was established by Decree no 180/2010 to the extent, for each party, from €65 up to €9,200, based on the value of the dispute.

[37] G Alpa, 'Le clausole arbitrali nei contratti del consumatore' [2006] *Rivista dell'arbitrato* 619, 623; E Zucconi Galli Fonseca, 'Tutela arbitrale e tecnica del processo: la clausola compromissoria nei contratti di consumo' [2014] *Rivista Trimestrale di Diritto e Procedura Civile* 997.

[38] The vexatious clauses are the clauses that establish, in favour of the person who prepared them, limitations of liability, the faculty to withdraw from the contract or to suspend its execution, or sanction for the other contracting parties forfeiture, limitations on the faculty to oppose exceptions, restrictions on contractual freedom in relations with third parties, tacit extensions or renewals of the contract, arbitration clauses or derogations from the jurisdiction of the judicial authority. If we refer to a contract stipulated between professional and consumer (Art 1469-*bis* and following of the Italian Civil Code) which has as its object the sale of goods or the provision of services, the clauses which, despite the good faith, determine a significant imbalance of the rights and obligations deriving from the contract for the consumer. Vexatious clauses have no effect unless specifically approved in writing.

Among all the aforementioned types of ADR, conciliation is considered the best alternative process for resolving disputes between service companies and consumers, through which the parties can find an adequate solution to their needs and maintain their commercial relationship.

The conciliation can take place before a judge during a trial (a so-called judicial conciliation) or outside a trial (a so-called out-of-court conciliation). It is a very simple procedure which does not require particular formalities. The consumer application generally addresses the company concerned through a consumers' association or through the website of the same company, and the process takes place between the association's conciliator and the company's conciliator. It generally concludes and solves the matter at the first meeting.

This type of ADR is a useful alternative tool to ordinary justice offered to the consumer, where he or she can be freely assisted by a conciliator appointed by the associations and quickly resolve the dispute that has arisen with the company. As in the other procedures, once the conciliation procedure has started, the parties remain free not to reach an agreement; if the outcome of the conciliation is negative, the parties can still go to a court with no limitations.

Finally, this procedure is free of cost for the user, which guarantees access to this form of protection to vulnerable parties who could not bear all the costs of a judicial procedure.

For these characteristics, the Italian legislator has introduced several forms of mandatory conciliation in many sectors involving consumers. The mandatory nature of these proceedings implies that they are conditions for the prosecution of the subsequent (and possible) judicial claim.

As will be seen, also with specific reference to the energy sector, the Italian legislator has introduced a form of mandatory conciliation, which guarantees access to this form of protection to vulnerable parties who could not bear all the costs of judicial or other ADR procedures. In particular, domestic conciliation has been considered the best model to implement Directives 2009/72/EC and 2009/73/EC of the European Parliament and Council of 13 July 2009 (included in the so-called 'Third Energy Package'), which provided that Member States must establish an independent mechanism to ensure efficient handling of out-of-court settlements relating to electricity and natural gas services. In particular, the general conciliation model has been adapted to the energy sector's needs and modified to fulfil the principles provided for in the aforementioned Directive.

In this respect, it must be highlighted that the introduction of such conciliation has been preceded by several initiatives by ARERA which has paid great attention to this issue and has promptly accepted the requests coming from the European Union, either strengthening the existing types of ADR, or introducing new measures, as well as disclosure obligations for energy companies in order to ensure that consumers are properly informed about the available types of ADR. Most of these initiatives are still working alongside the conciliation procedure, which is in any case the main ADR procedure in force.

It can be said that ARERA and the Italian legislator have been working together for a long time (and are, indeed, still working on the issue) to build an ADR system fit for the energy sector and for vulnerable consumers in particular.

D. Own Initiatives of the Authority: Memoranda of Understanding and Joint Negotiation

The issue of out-of-court dispute resolution in the energy sector was first mentioned in ARERA's Establishing Law, dating back to 1995.[39] Article 2 of that law provided that:

- The Authority assesses complaints, requests and reports submitted by consumers, either individual or groups, to verify if energy companies comply with the public prices and the quality levels provided by law.[40]
- The government issues proper regulations to define the criteria, conditions, terms and methods for conciliation or arbitration proceedings before the Authority, in the event of disputes between users and energy companies.

The latter provision has never been implemented,[41] as the regulations at stake have never been enacted by the government. Nevertheless, ARERA has launched its own initiatives to facilitate conciliation between energy consumers and suppliers.

Among such initiatives, in 2001[42] the Authority signed a memorandum of understanding with the National Council of Consumers and Users, whose purpose is to promote consumers' access to ADR. In 2003, the same Authority approved the 'Memorandum of Understanding between the Authority for Electricity and Gas and the Italian Union of Chambers of Commerce, Industry, Crafts and Agriculture on the conciliation of disputes between consumers and energy distributors and suppliers';[43] at the same time, it promoted numerous meetings with the energy companies in which many operators (and their associations) joined to encourage the development of ADR.

In the following years, the Authority has increasingly promoted[44] the development of initiatives aimed at spreading out-of-court conciliation procedures deriving from memoranda of understanding stipulated between companies and their associations (on the one side) and consumer associations (on the other); moreover, it began to financially support such programmes,[45] especially after the

[39] Law no 481, 14 November 1995.
[40] Para 12(m).
[41] Para 24(b).
[42] With resolution no 226/01, renewed in 2009.
[43] Resolution no 146/03.
[44] G Gioia, 'Il nuovo "pacchetto" della Commissione europea sull'ADR' [2012] *Corriere giuridico* 709.
[45] Resolution no 35/07.

liberalisation of energy markets, which has highlighted the importance of ADR to settle any dispute between suppliers and consumers.[46]

The procedures envisaged by the memoranda of understanding, which abide by specific regulations defined within the same memoranda, are called 'joint negotiation', as the case is overseen by a commission composed of conciliators representing all the parties (company and consumer).[47] The procedures can be activated only if the formal complaint to the energy supplier fails.[48] At the end of the procedure, the commission draws up a report containing a premise of agreement, which is submitted to the customer for approval. In case of acceptance of the proposal, the report is the agreement between the parties; in case of non-acceptance of the proposal, the commission draws up a non-agreement report, which leaves the parties free to take the dispute to a court.

Some memoranda of understanding limit the possibility of negotiation to a given number of listed topics and require voluntary adherence of the company to the same memoranda.[49]

Such procedures do not have explicit costs for end customers, as they constitute a service offered by the consumer associations to their members (or potential members). Consumers can benefit from a flat-rate reimbursement drawn from some funds available at ARERA; however, the reimbursement is recognised only in the case of a positive conclusion of the procedure.[50]

E. The Third Energy Package: The ARERA Conciliation Service and the 'Smart Help Service'

i. *The Conciliation Service*

Directives 2009/72/EC and 2009/73/EC of the European Parliament and Council of 13 July 2009 (included in the so-called 'Third Energy Package') provided that Member States must establish an independent mechanism to ensure efficient handling of out-of-court settlements relating to electricity and natural gas services.

[46] Art 11-*bis* of the Legislative Decree no 35/2005, as amended by Law no 244/2007, provided that the amount deriving from the payment of the sanctions imposed by the Authority would be destined for a fund to finance projects for the benefit of electricity and gas consumers.

[47] See S Iannicelli, 'La conciliazione stragiudiziale delle controversie: modelli differenti e dubbi interpretativi', [2008] *Obbligazioni e contratti* 152; M Marianello, 'I procedimenti complementari di risoluzione delle controversie' [2011] *Obbligazioni e contratti* 537.

[48] In the electricity and gas sector, the term 'complaint' refers to two distinct but related types: the request addressed directly to the operator (first instance complaint) and the one filed at the so called 'Sportello del Consumatore', maintained by 'Acquirente Unico S.p.A.', a stock company whose shares are totally held by the Ministry of the Economy and Finance established for the benefit of the proper functioning of the energy markets, pursuant to Legislative Decree no 163/2006 (second instance complaint). See ARERA, GOP 28/08, GOP 71/09 and 72/09 resolutions.

[49] Similar protocols have been negotiated between companies and associations representing non-domestic customers; on the other hand, conciliation procedures are also available at the Chambers of Commerce, Agriculture, Industry and Crafts according to Law no 580/93.

[50] ARERA, resolution VIS 98/11 of 27 October 2011.

Italy has transposed the aforementioned Directives with the Legislative Decree no 93 of 1 June 2011, entrusting the Authority with various tasks, including that of ensuring the development of ADR in the energy sector (Article 44, paragraph 4).

As the existing tools (ie, the memoranda of understanding) were not accessible to all consumers, being available only if the supplier had voluntarily adhered to the same memoranda, the Authority implemented this task by establishing the Energy Customer Conciliation Service.[51]

Unlike previous instruments, the Conciliation Service is configured as a 'universal' conciliation system, with reference both to potential users and to the topics covered by the procedure. It is also provided by ARERA and is registered in the public register of ADR bodies.

With reference to the potential users, the procedure can be activated by electric and gas users and in particular by:

i. all domestic customers;[52]
ii. non-domestic customers with some limitations;[53]
iii. *prosumers*.[54]

On the other hand, all the companies operating in the electricity and gas market, as well as the GSE distributors,[55] are obliged to take part to the procedure. In a first phase, participation was not mandatory for companies operating in the liberalised market because they were bound to participate only if they voluntarily registered themselves in a special list on the Authority's website. However, in the last years, ARERA has progressively extended such a duty for all operators.[56]

Both parties can be represented by a delegate (not necessarily a lawyer) with the faculty to reconcile and settle the dispute. Users' delegates often belong to a consumers' association.[57]

With reference to the topics, the procedure can be activated for all claims, with the exception of tax disputes and claims concerning the topics reserved to 'Smart Help' (described below). As will be seen in section III of this chapter, the issues

[51] Resolution no 260/2012/E/com of 21 June 2012.

[52] With reference to the gas sector, even a condominium is entitled to opt for the Conciliation Service if the domestic consumption does not exceed 200,000 cubic meters per year.

[53] In the electricity sector, it can be activated by non-domestic customers connected in low voltage (LV) with fewer than 50 employees and annual revenues not exceeding €10 million. In the gas sector, it can be activated by non-domestic customers with consumption not exceeding 50,000 cubic meters per year.

[54] The *prosumer* is the operator that simultaneously consumes and produces energy.

[55] The 'Gestore dei Servizi Energetici' (GSE) is an Italian regulatory agency. It has been identified by the state to pursue and achieve environmental sustainability through the two pillars of renewable sources and energy efficiency.

[56] The duty is provided under Art 9, para 9.4, of the Integrated Text on Conciliation, 'TICO' (Annex A to resolution 209/2016/E/com as supplemented and modified by resolution no 383/2016/E/com of 14 July 2016, and by resolution 355/2018/R/com).

[57] The procedure has a maximum duration of 90 calendar days starting from the presentation of the application, which can be extended for no more than 30 days upon initiative of the parties or upon request of the conciliator who recognises the complexity of the dispute. The parties themselves can jointly request from the conciliator the formulation of a proposal, which they are free to accept or not within the term of 7 days.

most often claimed are related to invoicing (especially in the gas sector), contracts and claims for damages (especially in the electricity sector).

The Conciliation Service is called the 'second level' of protection, because to access the service the customer must have previously submitted a complaint to his or her energy supplier, which was either not followed by a response within 40 days or followed by an unsatisfactory response. Only if the response to the complaint is unsatisfactory, partial or even completely absent, may customers access the second level, represented by the Conciliation Service.

The conciliation request is submitted online or (in some limited cases) by post. The first meeting takes place 30 days after the application. All conciliation meetings take place in virtual rooms[58] where the user and the operator (or their delegates) meet a third-party conciliator, provided by the Conciliation Service and equipped with specific experience on the subject of the claim. The conciliator does not decide the dispute but assists the parties in finding an agreement for the settlement, also by formulating a non-binding proposal. Every conciliator is assigned to the procedure in compliance with criteria of impartiality, professionalism and competence.[59]

On average, conciliations are completed in 45 days (in any case, their duration can never exceed 90 days). If the parties find an agreement, they sign a report that has the value of an enforcement order: that is, it can be invoked by the parties before the competent judge if the parties do not respect it. In the event that an agreement is not reached or when the operator does not participate even if obliged, the conciliator draws up a report stating that the attempt was unsuccessful. In these cases, the client may possibly contact the judge (as will be seen below, the attempt at conciliation has become a mandatory step to claim before a court). If the customer does not come to the meeting, the question is archived, and the attempt is not considered carried out.

Lastly, it should be noted that most of the companies suspend the actions to recover the arrears while a conciliation is pending, developing a best practice for the benefit of the customers among their self-regulation activity.[60]

ii. The Consumer Help Desk and the Smart Help Service

The same decree – no 93/11 – required ARERA to create offices to provide consumers with all the relevant information regarding available ADRs. Consequently, the Authority has renewed the existing 'Consumer Help Desk'.[61]

[58] Exceptionally, meetings can take place via conference calls.

[59] The Conciliation Service adheres, through the Authority, to the National Energy Ombudsmen Network (NEON) which is the European network between ADR bodies and mediation services active in the energy sector.

[60] M Marianello, 'Le ODR nel settore dell'energia' [2015] *Persona e Mercato* 77.

[61] Which had been already introduced with deliberation n GOP 28/08. The Consumer Help Desk, established in 2009 by the Authority and managed in collaboration with the 'Acquirente Unico S.p.a.'

Since 2012, such a front office has also provided the so called 'Smart Help Service', which handles some disputes on five specific issues:

1. Electricity and gas bonuses in case of non-acceptance of an application or delayed delivery of the bonus.
2. Return to the previous supplier in the event of a contract incorrectly concluded by non-domestic customers.
3. Arrears payment (CMOR) charged by a supplier in a bill.
4. Double invoicing following a supplier change.
5. Failure to provide automatic compensation due by the supplier.

Disputes concerning these issues cannot be brought before the Conciliation Service. Rather, it is necessary to contact the Smart Help Service because ARERA believes that these claims deserve faster handling through a privileged channel.[62]

The Service can be activated, directly or through a delegate, by all end customers of electricity and gas for the resolution of disputes against sellers and distributors. The transmission and management of a claim take place *online* and require a prior complaint to the seller (as in the Conciliation Service) in all the five listed cases, except for the first one (social bonuses claims). The procedure differs according to the subject of the complaint; here, it is appropriate to dwell on the complaints concerning bonuses, which are the main Italian measure to counteract energy poverty and vulnerability (see section I above).

With reference to social bonuses, ARERA has defined a special procedure[63] which is easier and faster than the Conciliation Service.[64] This procedure was introduced for the benefit of energy-poor consumers and provides for more favourable rules. Specifically, the customer who encounters problems concerning the recognition of the electric and/or gas social bonus can send a direct request to the Smart Help Service, without involving the supplier; the presence of irregular documentation does not constitute a sufficient element to consider the request for resolution inadmissible; it is not necessary to send a previous complaint to the supplier;[65] if the customer is right, the help desk orders the supplier to credit the sum in the next available invoice, giving feedback to the customer or end-user within 10 working days; the suppliers must reply within 20 working days.

(a stock company whose shares are totally held by the Ministry of the Economy and Finance established for the benefit of the proper functioning of the energy markets) provides information and assistance to end customers on regulation in the electricity, gas and water sectors.

[62] If at the end of the Smart Help the customer wants to claim for damages, he or she can still apply before the Conciliation Services only for this specific claim.

[63] Deliberation no 286/2014.

[64] Deliberation no 383-16, Annex A, Appendix 2, Art 2.

[65] In the case of the bonuses procedure, even if a prior complaint to the supplier is normally required, the absence of such a complaint does not hinder the start of the procedure. This exception has been provided for taking into account the complexity of the bonus payment procedure. As will be seen in para 3, data show that most of the users who claim for bonuses do not send a prior complaint.

iii. Overview of Advantages of Main ADR Tools

At this point, it is possible to draw some first conclusions on the main ADR tools available in the energy sector and on their suitability to protect vulnerable and poor consumers.

First, these tools, unlike those provided in general in the Italian system (see section II.C above), are entirely free of charge. In this way, they can also be used by subjects who do not have adequate economic resources to support the costs of justice.

Second, the presence of a lawyer is never mandatory, but users can also be represented by consumer associations. This aspect is very important because consumer associations have a fundamental role in the fight against EP, in terms of monitoring, measuring and contrasting it. Often, they are strongly influential in their locality by flagging up to public bodies the families that need support. They can therefore act as intermediaries on behalf of energy-poor consumers not only in identifying and helping families in EP, but also in assisting them in the subsequent litigation phase and suggesting the best tools available for them.

Finally, despite the absence of lawyers, the highest standards of quality, professionalism and reliability of the conciliation services are always ensured, precisely because they are carried out under the surveillance of ARERA.

F. Directive 2013/11/EU and the Attempt at Conciliation as a Mandatory Condition for any Subsequent Appeal to the Court

The aforesaid framework was integrated with Directive 2013/11/EU of the European Parliament and Council of 21 May 2013, implemented in Italy by Legislative Decree no 130 of 6 August 2015. This Decree made some changes to the Consumer Code,[66] replacing Article 141 with a whole new Title 'II-bis' called 'Out-of-court dispute resolution'. The new rules aim at promoting high-quality consumer ADR schemes in line with EU standards and provide that ADR bodies should comply with several binding requirements. These are, among others, criteria of impartiality, expertise, transparency and accessibility, as well as of fairness, timeliness and effectiveness.

Such minimum harmonisation criteria also became applicable to procedures carried out by the Authority, as well as to all types of ADR under its supervision, including those available in the energy sector.

Moreover, Legislative Decree no 130/15 provided that the Conciliation Service – as well as the alternative procedure before the Consumer Help Desk – governed by ARERA was an indispensable condition for any subsequent appeal to the court and attributed to the Authority the full power to regulate it in line with

[66] See Legislative Decree no 206 of 6 September 2005.

the 2013 EU Directive (as already seen, this power had been originally entrusted to the government but never implemented).

To reorder the relevant regulation, the Authority approved the Integrated Text on Conciliation (TICO),[67] effective from 1 January 2017, in order to adopt a comprehensive governance of extrajudicial dispute resolution.

In the TICO, the Authority found that the Conciliation Service, operating since 2012, was already in line with EU standards; hence, this procedure was elected as one of the indispensable ones for any subsequent juridical action and became the main ground for resolving issues between the parties in the energy market. As an alternative, ARERA established that mandatory conciliation could also be attempted before other bodies envisaged by the same TICO, including joint negotiations of consumer associations registered in the list of the Authority's ADR bodies and some listed Chambers of Commerce[68] that have joined a special agreement between ARERA and Unioncamere.[69]

In line with the new rules, from 2017 domestic and non-domestic electricity and gas customers, including *prosumers*, must turn to conciliation to settle disputes which have not been solved at the complaint level before appealing to a court. The mandatory condition for any subsequent appeal is considered fulfilled even if the first meeting ends without agreement, including cases of non-appearance of the energy operator. Carrying out the obligatory conciliation attempt may not preclude the granting of interim and protective court measures by the judge in favour of the customer.

To improve consumer awareness on the most suitable choice of ADR measures, the companies must inform their customers about the Conciliation Service and any free access conciliation entities whose procedures they participate in. All the relevant information on the matter must be published on their website, in their contracts and in their responses to complaints that have not been resolved.

G. The 'Third Level' of Protection: ARERA as a Decision-Making Body

As seen above, the consumer protection system is structured on two levels:

1. The first level of protection is based on a written complaint, which aims to settle the dispute at the very beginning and is submitted by the customer to the energy company.
2. If the response to the complaint is unsatisfactory, partial or even completely absent, customers may access the second level, represented by the Conciliation

[67] Annex A to resolution 209/2016/E/com as supplemented and modified by resolution no 383/2016/E/com of 14 July 2016, and by resolution 355/2018/R/com.

[68] The list is available at: www.arera.it/it/consumatori/conciliazione_CC.htm.

[69] Unioncamere is the Italian Union of Chambers of Commerce, Industry, Crafts and Agriculture. It is the public body that unites and institutionally represents the Italian Chambers system.

Service and by the other authorised entities in the ADR list, which is a mandatory condition for any subsequent claim to the courts.

In these two levels, the Authority is responsible only for creating offices and methods for resolving disputes and for pursuing the widest knowledge and accessibility to consumers.

However, for more complex cases, the Authority has established a third level of protection,[70] which can be activated voluntarily for disputes not resolved in the first two levels. This level prefigures the Authority to intervene upon a party's request to directly settle certain disputes, playing a decision-making role.

In the initial phase,[71] ARERA excluded this third level for disputes on debt collection and taxes. Moreover, to begin this procedure some conditions must be met: among others, the parties must not have appealed to a court on the same facts and must start the procedure within 30 days of the conclusion of the compulsory conciliation attempt. The decision of the dispute is taken by the Board of the Authority with its resolution (published on the Authority website), which also sets the deadline within which the parties are required to comply, under penalty of any sanctions.

The 'third level' is not a preliminary condition for an appeal to the court but an alternative to this, without prejudice to the right to judicial protection even after it has taken place. The parties remain free to appeal before the judge to claim the greater damages, as well as to appeal against the Authority's decision. The 'three levels' system is schematised in Figure 12.1.

III. Data on ADR Procedures in the Energy Sector

A. The Conciliation Service

As announced in the ARERA press release of 21 February 2020,[72] in 2019 the Conciliation Service allowed energy customers to save over €8.5 million, resolving disputes with the sellers of electricity, gas and water (a sector to which the service was extended in 2018). By way of example, the total amount of €8.5 million in 2019 (the value of which will increase once the pending procedures have been completed) represents what has been returned from suppliers to customers as refunds, indemnities, recalculation of incorrect invoices or expenses and interest. This value increased significantly compared with €5.6 million in 2018 and is divided between non-domestic (57 per cent) and domestic (43 per cent) customers. The number of applications presented by domestic customers is higher (over 70 per cent of the total), but their overall economic value is lower than those submitted by non-domestic customers.

[70] Resolution no 621/2016/E/COM.
[71] Resolution no 639/2017/E/COM.
[72] See: www.arera.it/it/com_stampa/20/200221.htm.

Figure 12.1 The 'three levels' system

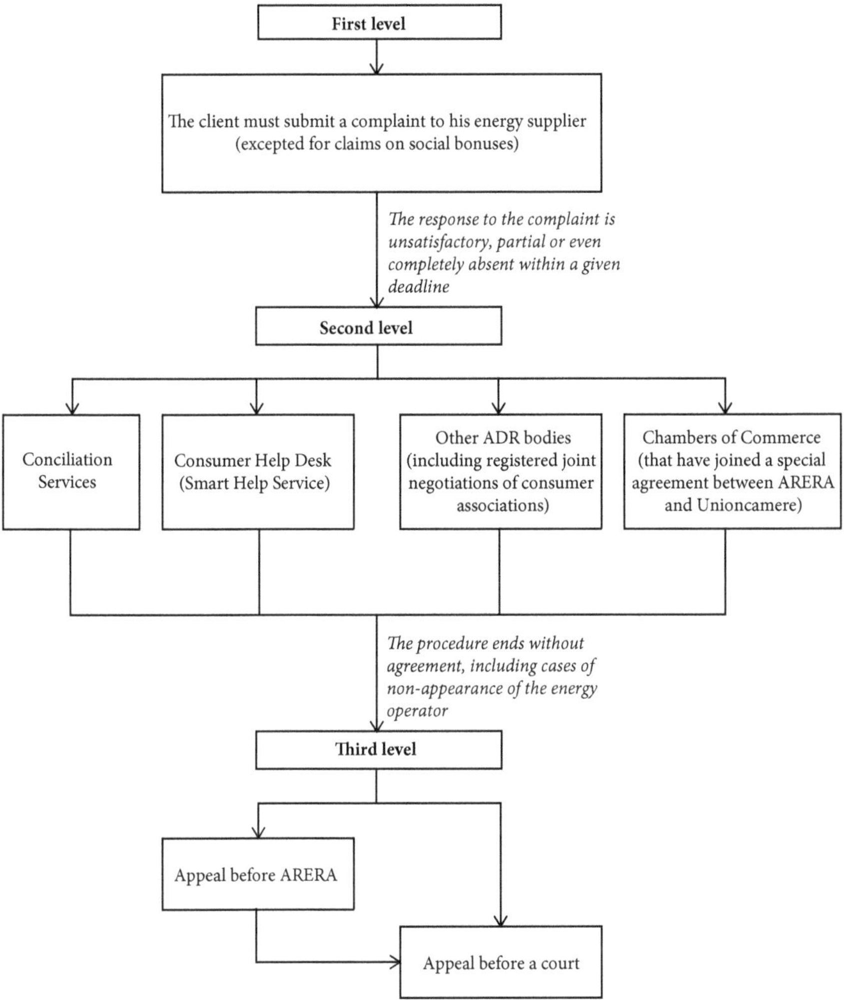

The number of applications has grown in time, from 11,000 (in 2018) to over 16,000 (in 2019), with about 70 per cent of agreements concluded positively; 95 per cent of users who completed the final evaluation questionnaire reported they were very satisfied with the service. The vast majority of applications concern cases relating to the electricity (8,165) and gas (5,167) sectors. See Figure 12.2.[73]

[73] Source: ARERA Conciliation Service, Annual report, last updated 10 January 2020, available at: www.arera.it/allegati/consumatori/raconciliazione19_eng.pdf.

Figure 12.2 Amount of conciliation applications (2019)

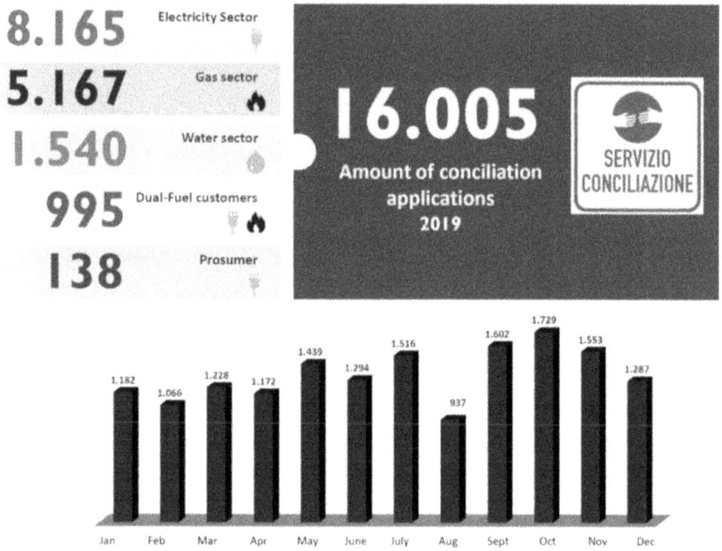

As the data show, the Conciliation Service is enjoying great success, considering that only three years before 2019, ie, in 2016, the total applications had been 3,360 and, in 2015, 2,496.[74]

The issues most often claimed are those relating to invoicing (especially in the gas sector), contracts and claims for damages (especially in the electricity sector), as shown in Figure 12.3.[75]

Furthermore, in about 68 per cent of the applications, customers preferred to be represented by a delegate (for example, a consumer association), as shown in Figure 12.4.[76]

Finally, it should be noted that about 20 per cent of the applications were not admitted to the procedure, mainly because the customer decided not to complete the application or for procedural reasons (missing documentation, expired deadlines, topics falling outside the scope of the conciliation, etc).

The percentage of admitted applications is higher with regard to applications submitted by consumer associations (89 per cent of applications admitted), followed by other delegates (80 per cent) and by end customers who act without a delegate (72 per cent).

[74] ISDACI, 'Tenth report on the spread of alternative justice in Italy' (ISDACI, 2018).

[75] Source: ARERA Conciliation Service, Annual report, last updated 10 January 2020, available3 at: www.arera.it/allegati/consumatori/raconciliazione19_eng.pdf.

[76] ibid.

Figure 12.3 Conciliation topics by sector (2019)

Electricity Sector			Gas Sector		
Topics	**%**	**No.**	**Topics**	**%**	**No.**
Invoicing/billing	48.1	3,925	Invoicing/billing	61.8	3,192
Damages	16.3	1,329	Contracts	9.8	508
Contracts	11.9	971	Late/non-payment and disconnections	8.3	431
Other	8.4	682	Other	7.8	403
Late/non-payment and disconnections	5.8	477	Metering	5.4	279
Connection and technical quality	4.6	377	Connection and technical quality	4.2	215
Metering	3.6	298	Damages	1.6	85
Market	0.9	75	Market	0.8	39
Commercial quality	0.4	31	Commercial quality	0.3	15
Total	**100%**	**8.165**	**Total**	**100%**	**5.167**

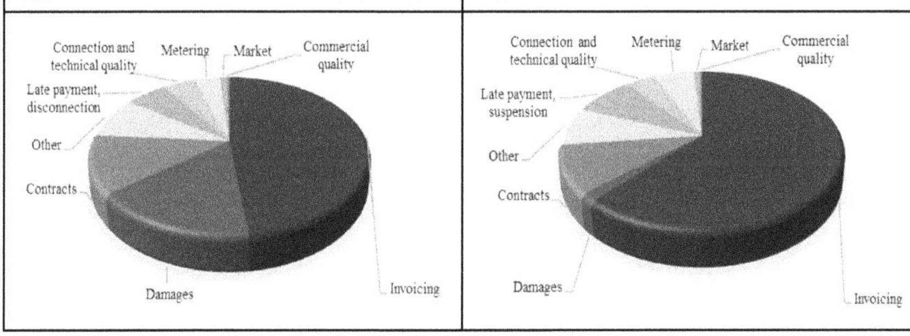

Consumer associations also have the best results with reference to the agreements reached in the Conciliation Service: the procedures submitted by such associations conclude with an agreement in 81 per cent of cases. However, the same percentage is lower for applications submitted by other delegates (55 per cent) and by the direct customers (62 per cent).

Such data are summarised in Table 12.1.

Table 12.1 Admitted applications and conclusions (2018)

Applicant	Submitted applications (no.)	Admitted applications (%)	Reached agreements (%)
Direct user	3,862	72	62
Consumer associations	3,062	89	81
Other delegates	3,777	80	55
SME associations	4	100	100

Figure 12.4 Type of applicant (2019)*

Type	Customer	Consumers Associations	Others	SME Associations	Total
Domestic	3,650	3,659	4,467	–	11,776
Non-domestic	1,497	585	2,140	7	4,229
Total	**5,147**	**4,244**	**6,604**	**7**	**16,005**
% vs tot.	**32%**	**27%**	**41%**	**0.04%**	**100%**

* Information declared by the applicants at the time of the application.

AVERAGE AGE AND
APPLICATIONS ISSUED BY
CUSTOMERS DELEGATE

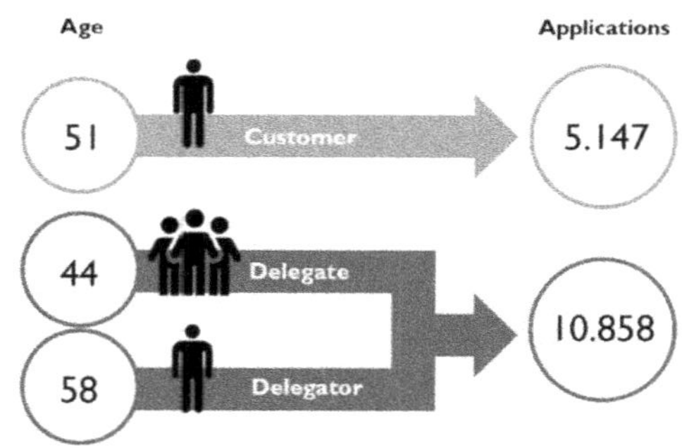

B. The Smart Help Service

With reference to the Smart Help Service,[77] in 2018 customers activated 7,247 procedures spread across the five different issues (see section II.E.ii above), most of which (86.6 per cent) concerned the electricity and gas bonus which is – as already pointed out – the most important Italian measure in favour of vulnerable consumers. The special procedures gave very good results both in terms of ease of use (86 per cent of accesses were made directly by end customers without the use of delegates) and of resolution times (from five to 18 working days).

The social bonus (6,280 cases received in 2018, 2,110 of which referred to the electric bonus, 5,598 to the gas bonus and 572 to both bonuses) is the main topic covered in the Smart Help Service, as shown in Figure 12.5.

Figure 12.5 Smart Help Service claims (2018)

Topics	%	No
Requests on bonuses	**86.6**	**6,280**
Electricity bonus	29	2,110
Gas bonus	49.6	3,598
Electricity and gas bonus	8	572
Requests on other topics	**13.4**	**967**
CMOR	9.5	686
Return to the previous supplier	1.8	128
Double invoicing	2	148
Failure to provide automatic compensation	0.1	5
Total requests	**100%**	7,247

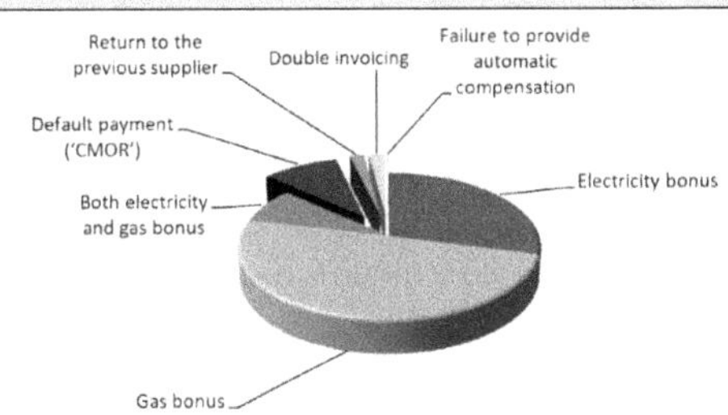

The same data are also confirmed for the first five months of 2020:[78] customers activated 3,488 requests before the Smart Help Service, most of which (84.1 per cent) concerned the social bonus.

[77] All data described in the following are taken from the ARERA Annual Report on the processing of complaints and the resolution of disputes of electric and natural gas customers, 2018, approved with deliberation no 331/2019.

[78] Data available at: www.sportelloperilconsumatore.it/lo-sportello/numeri.

It should be remembered that for 2018 the reference audience (families benefiting from social bonuses) was made up of around 800,000 families with an electricity contract and 520,000 families with a gas contract and that in about 65 per cent of cases the families concerned benefited from both bonuses.[79]

The procedure for the recognition of the social bonus includes several steps which lead to different operators (including public entities, such as the Municipalities), and it is not always easy for the end customer to understand at what point in the procedure the disservice may have occurred. In this regard, the timing of disbursement of the bonus still represents the main cause of complaint by end customers (56 per cent of cases), followed by delays in validating the application by the distributor (32 per cent of cases), while the remaining tranche of cases deals with the end of the bonus disbursement (2 per cent) and the non-admission of the bonus application by the Municipalities, as shown in Figure 12.6.

Figure 12.6 Claims concerning social bonus (2018)

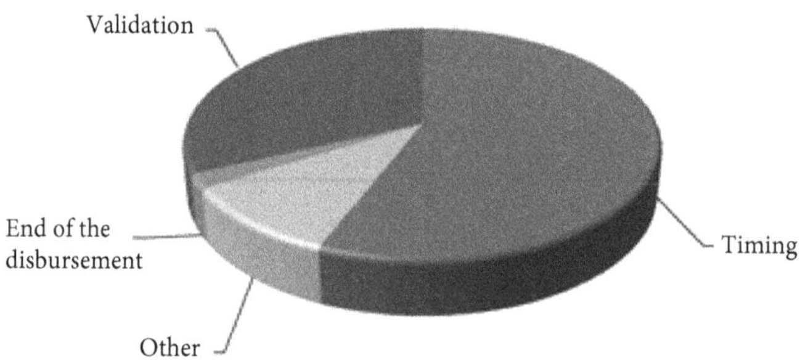

It is important to remember that, in the case of the special bonus procedure, even if a prior complaint to the supplier is normally required, the absence of such a complaint does not hinder the start of the procedure. This exception has been provided to take into account the complexity of the bonus payment procedure already illustrated. In this regard, it can be observed that most of the users who claim for bonuses do not send a prior complaint: specifically, the number of cases registered in the Smart Help Service (6,280) is much higher than the cases declared for the same topic by sellers (1,700) and distributors (around 700).

IV. Conclusions

Italy has a substantial ADR system in the energy sector. This system represents for many a pilot model of ADR in Italy, which could be extended to other sectors.

[79] See ARERA, 'Il bonus sociale elettrico e gas: stato di attuazione per l'anno 2018 relazione al ministro dello sviluppo economico ai sensi dell'articolo 1 comma 4 del decreto del ministro dello sviluppo economico 29 dicembre 2016', Relation no 279/2019/I/com.

Furthermore, users have provided an excellent response, also due to the communication activities carried out by consumer associations and companies; all consumers acknowledged that through ADR they can obtain rapid and free protection, with subsequent cost saving for them, as well as for the energy suppliers.

However, it is important to ascertain, also in the light of the data illustrated in section III, whether these procedures guarantee the protection of vulnerable and energy-poor consumers as well. The data do not dwell on the characteristics of users who submitted the application, and therefore it is not possible to know whether such applicants are vulnerable or energy-poor consumers. However, the data do offer some elements from which it is possible to draw conclusions on the effectiveness of the aforementioned ADR procedures with respect to these categories of users.

First, it is possible to note that the Smart Help Service procedure is used almost exclusively for claims relating to electricity and gas bonuses. Being the bonuses provided exclusively for the category of vulnerable users, we can already conclude that this procedure is very effective and highly appreciated by such users.

Moreover, the ADR procedure concerning claims on bonuses is much less complex precisely to help vulnerable consumers, to prevent them from remaining unprotected for reasons relating to the procedure and not to the issue of the claim. To give just one example, although the law provides for the prior submission of the complaint to the supplier before activating such a procedure, only a third of the applicants claiming bonuses take this step (as shown by the data in section III). In any case, ARERA has provided that, in cases of bonus claims, the prior submission of the complaint is not a condition of admissibility for the subsequent conciliation (as it is for the remaining topics that can be claimed before the Smart Help Service and the Conciliation Service). If the provision of the complaint as a condition of admissibility had not been repealed, the remaining two-thirds of the applications concerning bonuses would have been inadmissible.

However, this protection is provided only for disputes regarding bonuses. For other disputes, the general and more complex procedures apply. This happens precisely because the system protects some given 'objects' (such as bonuses) and not some given 'subjects' (such as vulnerable and energy-poor consumers).

In this regard, data show that many of the requests submitted directly by end customers to the Conciliation Service are not allowed due to formal errors. It is reasonable to think that precisely the most vulnerable subjects are more exposed to this risk, being often also the least informed on the procedures. It can therefore be concluded that the ADR methods envisaged in Italy in the energy sector have characteristics that make them suitable for protecting vulnerable energy-poor consumers, but also that in some respects they can be improved.

The positive aspects (as already highlighted more widely in section II.E.ii) certainly concern the fact that they are completely free of charge, that the presence of a lawyer is not mandatory and that they are supervised by ARERA, which makes experts highly qualified in energy matters available to users.

The negative aspects can be summarised in one sentence. Namely, they take no account of the subjective characteristics of users. Even where simplified procedures are provided (as in the case of the Smart Help Service), these simplifications relate to the topic of the complaint and not to the user who applies. In this respect, vulnerable consumers will find protection only if their complaints concern such 'preserved' objects, and not in all other cases.

This shortcoming is due to the absence of an Italian action plan to protect vulnerable and energy-poor consumers. Despite the pressures coming from Europe,[80] there is not even a definition of EP[81] for all purposes, even though for Italy NES 2017 proposed the adoption of the measurement criterion of EP theorised by researchers at the Bank of Italy.[82] The absence of a regulatory notion of EP clearly makes it impossible to identify energy-poor consumers and, consequently, to provide for specific forms of protection for them.

Once an action plan is adopted, it will also be easier to monitor its effectiveness. In fact, it is expected that ARERA will collect data relating to vulnerable subjects and energy-poor consumers who submit requests, from which it will be possible to better highlight the gaps in the system and the aspects to be improved.

Among these forms of protection, an important role in the ADR procedures should be assumed by consumer associations which, as seen, achieve the best results in the ADR procedures in terms of admitted applications and reached agreements. Such associations have a fundamental role in the fight against EP, since they are major actors in their local territories and able to flag up to public bodies the families that need support. Their role in ADR should be improved, since they could act as intermediaries not only in identifying and helping families in EP, but also in assisting them in the subsequent litigation phase and suggesting the best ADR tools available to them.

It is therefore appropriate that the improvement of ADR mechanisms should be included in the current (and very recent) Italian debate about the fight against EP as a whole, in order to coordinate the solutions reached both with respect to substantial measures and with regard to subsequent procedural measures.

[80] The European Commission's 'Vulnerable Consumers Working Group Guidance Document', drawn up in November 2013 and published in January 2014, highlighted the need to introduce specific protection tools in favour of individuals who are subject to EP, leaving each state the task of identifying a proper definition. Lastly, the European Parliament, in resolution 2015/2323 (INI) of 26 May 2016, called for reinforced coordination between EU Member States to combat EP by sharing best national practices and developing a broad common definition of EP.

[81] As seen, there is only the definition provided for the purposes of access to the bonuses, according to which energy consumers who do not meet a given threshold of income and property are vulnerable. However, this is an insufficient definition, since EP does not depend only on income and property, but also on other factors, such as energy costs and energy consumption. See Faiella and Lavecchia (n 21).

[82] See Faiella and Lavecchia (n 21); and I Faiella, 'Povertà energetica: come si misura, come si combatte, atti del convegno Bonus sociale, fuel poverty e clienti vulnerabili: il contesto italiano' (Rome, 3 November 2015), available at: www.autorita.energia.it/it/eventi/151103bonus.htm.

13

Access to Justice in Energy: United Kingdom

COSMO GRAHAM

I. Introduction

Energy policy in the United Kingdom (UK) encapsulates a tension. On the one hand, access to energy is seen as essential and should be available and affordable to all. On the other hand, policy for about the last 30 years has been based on the idea that energy supply is best provided through competitive markets and that there should be little, if any, direct government intervention in the energy markets. Energy markets are, however, too important to be left unregulated, so this job has been given to a regulator that is independent from the elected governments and makes its decisions within a statutory framework.

This chapter focuses on those policies which are designed to ensure that the supply of energy is available and affordable to everyone. In order to do this, the chapter first sets out the legal framework for the regulation of energy in Great Britain[1] which is then followed by a section discussing the current structure of the energy industry. This is followed by an examination of a major policy area aimed at securing energy justice, namely fuel poverty and one aimed at ensuring fairness; the vulnerability strategy of the regulator. Having covered these issues, it then looks at the arrangements for how complaints by consumers are handled in the energy sector. The theme running through these areas is the variable effectiveness of different policies, which is not surprising given the starting point.

II. The Legal Framework of Energy Regulation in Great Britain

The regulation of the energy market in Great Britain (GB) is the responsibility of the Office of Gas and Electricity Markets (Ofgem), a non-ministerial government

[1] Northern Ireland is, for these purposes, a separate jurisdiction.

department which has operated as an independent national regulatory authority under the EU Directives.[2] The governing legislation, the Electricity Act 1989 and Gas Act 1986, has its origins in the privatisations of the energy industry, although it has been heavily amended over the years. When carrying out its functions, Ofgem is required to protect the interests of existing and future consumers which are defined as including an interest in the reduction of greenhouse gases, security of supply and a variety of obligations included in the Electricity Directive which include high standards of public and universal service and contributing to the protection of vulnerable consumers.[3] In carrying out its functions, Ofgem is required to have regard to the need to ensure that reasonable demands for energy are met, that energy companies can finance their activities, and the needs of sustainable development. In addition, Ofgem is required to consider whether promoting competition is the most appropriate way of carrying out those functions or some alternative is better. Furthermore, Ofgem is required to consider the interests of the disabled or chronically sick, people of pensionable age, those individuals with low incomes and individuals residing in rural areas, although they may also consider the interests of other groups of individuals. Ofgem is also obliged to consider the guidance on social and environmental matters issued by the Secretary of State, which currently dates back to 2011.

These are a complex set of duties which are often in tension. They can be seen as a legislative version of what is referred to as the 'energy trilemma': affordability, security of supply and decarbonisation. Because the legislation is not prescriptive and does not provide priority ordering, this gives Ofgem some discretion to decide upon its actions. This is subject to Ofgem acting in a manner which is consistent with government priorities, the formal expression of which is the social and environmental guidance. There is, however, evidence that government has had informal influence in the past on issues with high political salience, such as affordability, and there is provision in current legislation for the government to issue strategy and policy statements to Ofgem, although this legislation has yet to be brought into force. Energy justice issues, discussed more fully in chapter one, therefore compete with other policy issues.

In terms of functions, the centrepiece of the regulatory system is that anyone who wishes to be involved in the energy market must apply for and be granted a licence to operate. Licences set down legally binding requirements and it is Ofgem's role to ensure that licensees adhere to the terms of their licence, and it has been given enforcement powers, which include the power to fine companies that are in breach of their licence conditions as well as the power to enforce competition law,

[2] Directive 2009/72/EC concerning common rules for the internal market in electricity: Art 35. Energy regulation is not a devolved matter [2009] OJ L211/55 and Art 39 Directive 2009/73/EC of the European Parliament and of the Council of 13 July 2009 concerning common rules for the internal market in natural *gas* [2009] OJ L211/94.

[3] The current plan is not to change these obligations but to remove the EU element: The Electricity and Gas etc (Amendment etc) (EU Exit) Regulations 2019 (draft).

concurrently with the Competition and Markets Authority (CMA). Ofgem also has the power to alter the licences, either individually or for all the licences in a class, subject to following certain procedures.

III. The GB Energy Industry

The GB energy supply market has a number of characteristics which set it apart from most energy markets in EU countries. It is a market which has become increasingly competitive over the last 10 years. When the CMA did its report into the retail energy markets it looked at concentration levels from 2011, using the Herfindal-Hirschmann Index (HHI), a standard method for measuring concentration. At the beginning of this period, the HHI for gas was around 2,450 (highly concentrated) and around 1,800 (concentrated) for electricity.[4] By the middle of 2019, the HHI was down to 1,224 in gas and 987 in electricity.[5] To give some further context, at this point there were 64 active licensed suppliers.[6] At the same time, there appears to be a significant level of switching by domestic consumers between suppliers with an annual switching rate of around 20 per cent.[7]

A second unique characteristic of the UK domestic energy market is the very low rate of disconnection for debt (six in 2018) and the significant use of pre-payment meters (PPMs). There are around 4.3 million people using PPMs, representing 15 per cent of the domestic market.[8] These two phenomena are connected because the standard practice of energy suppliers is not to disconnect consumers for failing to pay their bills but instead to provide them with a PPM. PPMs are controversial because the price of energy is higher when provided via a PPM,[9] PPM users are less likely to switch supplier, and there are concerns that people may self-disconnect or ration their use of energy supply and that this is much less easily identified than disconnections. On the other hand, most users of PPMs are happy with them, although they recognise that they are paying more for their energy than if they were on another tariff. They are also generally less engaged with the energy market than consumers overall.[10]

A third issue to explain is the political importance of debates over the affordability of energy supplies. This came about because of a steady rise in the price of energy, which peaked in around 2014, although there were various high-profile political interventions between 2012 and 2013. As a result, the energy retail market

[4] CMA, *Energy Market Report* (CMA, 2016) para 8.155. The Herfindahl-Hirschman Index is calculated as the sum of the squares of the market shares of the companies in a market.
[5] Ofgem, *State of the Market Report 2019* (Ofgem, 2019) para 3.5.
[6] ibid para 3.6.
[7] ibid para 3.14.
[8] ibid para 3.56.
[9] ibid para 3.60.
[10] ibid para 3.63.

was investigated jointly by Ofgem and the then Office of Fair Trading (later to become the CMA) which found, among other things, that there was weak competition among incumbent suppliers. This led to a market investigation reference to the CMA which found that there were features of the energy retail market that led to an adverse effect on competition and which allowed the energy supply companies to make excess profits. The CMA came up with a package of remedies to address its concerns.[11] One remedy that the majority of members of the CMA group did not pursue was a price cap on standard variable tariffs for a limited period, which was proposed by the dissenting member of the group.[12] They did recommend a temporary price cap on pre-payment tariffs.[13]

Affordability of energy supplies remained controversial after the CMA investigation and became an election issue in 2017, featuring in both the Conservative and Labour Party manifestos. The CMA had implemented its recommendation for a price cap for pre-payment meter customers and Ofgem extended this to customers who received the Warm Homes Discount. Following the election, a bill was introduced into Parliament which became the Domestic Electricity and Gas (Tariff Caps) Act 2018. The Act required Ofgem to introduce a temporary price cap on standard variable and default tariffs for Great Britain until 2020, with the possibility of an extension up to 2023.

After consultation, the price cap on standard variable and default tariffs was introduced at the beginning of 2019. According to section 8 of the Act, the tariff cap will end in 2020 unless the Secretary of State publishes a statement to the effect that the conditions are not yet in place for effective competition in the domestic supply market. If that is the case, then the conditions continue through 2021. This scenario may be repeated until 2023, when these powers will cease. To assist the Secretary of State, Ofgem must carry out a review in 2020 in order to ascertain whether the conditions are in place for effective competition which will consider the progress made in relation to smart meters. The report must contain a recommendation from Ofgem to the Secretary of State as to whether it thinks that the tariff cap conditions should be extended.

Ofgem has developed a framework for assessing whether or not competition is effective in the energy markets which looks at structural changes in the market, the functioning of the competitive process and whether or not there are fair outcomes for consumers.[14] It is likely, given the coronavirus pandemic, that any decision on whether to lift the tariff caps will be delayed until sometime in 2021, particularly in light of the need to focus on protecting the supply of energy to consumers who are spending more time in their homes.

A final point is the much publicised roll out of smart energy meters which was originally planned to be completed by 2020 but has now been delayed until

[11] Summarised in CMA, *Energy Market Investigation – Final Report* (CMA, 2016) paras 20.21–20.31.
[12] ibid 1415. The dissenting member was Professor Martin Cave, who is now Chair of Ofgem.
[13] CMA, *Energy Market Investigation – Final Report* (n 11) paras 11.73–11.102.
[14] Ofgem, 'Framework for assessing whether conditions are in place for effective competition in domestic supply contracts' (Ofgem, 2019).

2024. This programme has been controversial[15] but smart meters are an important element in the further development of competition in the energy retail markets through, among other things, offering the possibility of innovative tariffs.

IV. The Fuel Poverty Strategy

Fuel or energy poverty has been a policy issue in the UK since the early 1990s.[16] By the beginning of the twenty-first century its eradication had become a cross-party consensus and targets to eradicate fuel poverty within 15 years were enshrined in legislation based on a definition of fuel poverty which involved a household spending more than 10 per cent of its household income on energy.[17] It was accepted that there were three issues responsible for fuel poverty: household income, energy prices and the energy efficiency (or lack of it) of the housing stock. The aim of this strategy was to seek an end to fuel poverty and to end it for vulnerable households by 2010. Vulnerable in this context meant older householder, families with children and those with a disability or long-term illness.

The policy was not, however, successful, largely due to rising international energy prices[18] and there have been significant changes to it since 2010.[19] First, there was a major debate over the appropriate definition of fuel poverty which culminated in the Hills Report[20] which recommended moving from the established definition of spending more than 10 per cent of household income on energy costs to obtain a satisfactory level of heating to a low income/high costs (LIHC) measure. On this yardstick, a household is fuel poor if they have required fuel costs above the national median level and, were they to spend that amount, they would be left with a residual income below the official poverty line. Income includes welfare benefits relating to disability which, it has been argued, should be excluded from the calculation of income because its inclusion understates

[15] See British Infrastructure Group, 'Not So Smart' (2018), available at: www.britishinfrastructuregroup.uk/wp-content/uploads/2018/07/BIG-Not-So-Smart-Full-Report-Updated.pdf. The NAO is investigating the programme: www.nao.org.uk/work-in-progress/smart-meters/. There have been several inquiries by parliamentary committees: Energy and Climate Change Committee, *Smart meter roll-out* (HC 2013–14, 161); Energy and Climate Change Committee, *Smart meters: progress or delay?* (HC 2014–15, 665); Public Accounts Committee, *Update on preparations for smart metering* (HC 2014–15, 103); and Science and Technology Committee, *Evidence Check: Smart metering of electricity and gas* (HC 2016–17, 161).

[16] The starting point is B Boardman, *Fuel Poverty: From cold homes to affordable warmth* (Belhaven Press, 1991).

[17] Warm Homes and Energy Conservation Act 2000, s 2, 'The UK Fuel Poverty Strategy' (Department of Energy and Climate Change, 2001).

[18] For an overview up to 2008, see M Kidson and E Norris, *Implementing the Fuel Poverty Strategy* (Institute for Government, 2012), available at: www.instituteforgovernment.org.uk/sites/default/files/publications/Implementing%20the%20Fuel%20Poverty%20Strategy%20-%20final_0.pdf.

[19] See L Middlemiss, 'A Critical Analysis of the New Politics of Fuel Poverty in England' (2017) 37 *Critical Social Policy* 425.

[20] J Hills, *Getting the Measure of Fuel Poverty* (Centre for the Analysis of Social Exclusion, 2012).

the number of disabled people with low income.[21] Second, there is no longer a UK-wide strategy; responsibility for this policy rests on the devolved administrations so there are separate policies for England, Scotland, Wales and Northern Ireland. Although the LIHC definition has been adopted in England, the devolved administrations continue to apply versions of the 10 per cent of household income definition.[22] This means that it is not possible to provide UK-wide statistics. In England, the proportion of households in fuel poverty remained relatively stable at between 10–12 per cent up until 2015, about 2.5 million households on the LIHC definition.[23] By contrast, in Scotland, over a comparable period between 16 to 38 per cent of households have been in fuel poverty, with the current rate being 26.5 per cent or 649,000 households. The difference between the two is not just an artefact of different measurements: Scotland has always had a higher incidence of fuel poverty than England. In Wales, the number of households in fuel poverty declined significantly between 2008 and 2018 – from 332,000 to 158,000 for reasons which are not clear.[24] However it is measured, fuel poverty remains a significant policy issue in the UK.

Most importantly, the target has changed from the eradication of fuel poverty as far as reasonably practicable among households in England, Scotland and Northern Ireland by 2016, and Wales by 2018 to ensuring that as many fuel poor homes in England as is reasonably practicable achieve a minimum energy efficiency rating of Band C by 2030.[25] As can be seen, the emphasis is now upon achieving energy efficiency in the household stock.[26] This, it has been argued, redefines the problem as one which cannot be solved and ignores the contribution of the energy market.[27] Even if that is not accepted, the Committee on Fuel Poverty is, however, very concerned that there has been no real progress.[28] Finally, this strategy was constructed under the Coalition government and it was not incorporated into the Social and Environmental Guidance which still retains the old, and by now failed, targets. What will happen going forward is unknown as the results of the consultation on a new strategy for England have not been announced and the development of policy in Scotland and Wales has stalled.[29]

[21] ibid 92.

[22] For Scotland see: The Fuel Poverty (Targets, Definitions and Strategy) Act 2019.

[23] Department for Business, Energy & Industrial Strategy (BEIS), *Annual Fuel Poverty Statistics 2017* (2015 Data) (BEIS, 2017) 10 and Figure 2.1.

[24] Wales Audit Office, *Fuel Poverty* (Wales Audit Office, 2019) paras 2.12 –2.21.

[25] HM Government, *Cutting the Cost of Keeping Warm* (Cm 9019, 2015) 12.

[26] ibid; see also, Department for Business, Energy & Industrial Strategy (BEIS), Committee on Fuel Poverty, *Annual Report 2017* (BEIS, 2017).

[27] Middlemiss (n 19).

[28] Department for Business, Energy & Industrial Strategy (BEIS), Committee on Fuel Poverty, *Annual Report 2018* (BEIS, 2018).

[29] Department for Business, Energy & Industrial Strategy (BEIS), *Consultation on the fuel poverty strategy for England* (BEIS, 2019). There is a draft fuel poverty strategy 2018 for Scotland available at: www.gov.scot/publications/draft-fuel-poverty-scotland-2018/. The Welsh government is developing a new strategy which was originally planned to be consulted upon in spring 2020. For background see: National Assembly for Wales Climate Change, Environment and Rural Affairs Committee

A. Income Measures

There are several schemes which provide some form of income support or rebates to domestic customers. The most important is the Warm Home Discount which applies to those suppliers with more than 250,000 customers and has been running since 2011.[30] The scheme provides rebates on the electricity bill, currently £140 plus a variety of indirect support for low-income consumers, such as energy saving advice, debt assistance, benefit entitlement checks and referral to other support organisations.

To obtain benefits under this arrangement, consumers must fall within one of two groups. The first is the 'core group' which covers those customers who are in receipt of state pension credit and receive their rebate automatically. The second is referred to as the 'broader group' which is selected by the suppliers based on criteria which must be approved by Ofgem. These criteria target persons who are on certain means tested benefits and, in particular, have children under the age of five living with them or receive certain benefits which have a disability related element.[31] Suppliers may also expand these criteria if they are able to show that they are targeting households in fuel poverty. People within the broader group must apply for the rebate which is provided on a 'first come, first served' basis. There is a third category of 'industry initiatives' where the industry spends money on issues such as energy efficiency advice, debt assistance and benefits checks.

In the most recent year for which information is available, the spending target was £347 million, divided into £194 million for the core group, £154 million for the broader group and £40 million for other industry initiatives.[32] The core group is composed of around 1.1 million customers while the broader group received around 1.1 million rebates.[33] Most of the money is focused on pensioners, due to the eligibility rules.

There has been a long-running system of Winter Fuel Payments for pensioners. This provides a one-off payment of between £100 and £300 to anyone over, roughly, the age of 64. This policy has been controversial for some time, as it is not targeted at the fuel poor or vulnerable consumers.[34] It is, however, distributed to just under 12 million people at a cost of around £2 billion per annum but only 10 per cent of this is received by fuel poor households.[35] There is also a system of cold weather payments for those on certain benefits and if the temperature in

'Fuel Poverty in Wales' (National Assembly for Wales, 2020) available at: www.assembly.wales/laid%20 documents/cr-ld13147/cr-ld13147-e.pdf.

[30] Warm Home Discount Regulations 2011, SI 2011/2013.

[31] ibid, Sch 2.

[32] Ofgem, 'Warm Home Discount Annual Report 2018–19' (Ofgem, 2019) 8.

[33] ibid, Figure 2.1 and para 3.19.

[34] See House of Commons Energy and Climate Change Committee, *Fuel Poverty* (HC 2009–10, 424-I) paras 31–35; Committee on Fuel Poverty, *Annual Report 2017* (n 9) 6.

[35] Department for Work & Pensions, Winter Fuel Payment: data for winter 2016–17, HL Deb 28 April 2016 col 1236. Department for Business, Energy & Industrial Strategy (BEIS), Committee on Fuel Poverty, *Annual Report 2016–17* (BEIS, 2017) 6 and 33.

their area is recorded as, or forecast to be, zero degrees celsius or below for seven consecutive days. This triggers a payment of £25 for every seven-day period. from 2017 to 2018 it was estimated that there were around 3.7 million recipients receiving payments of £118 million.[36]

What can be seen is that there is very limited help for those who are most disadvantaged. In monetary terms, the main scheme is Winter Fuel Payments, which is poorly targeted. Fuel poverty measures are focused more on improving energy efficiency than the welfare of households, and the effectiveness of policies has been mixed.

B. Ofgem's Vulnerability Strategy

With the creation of Ofgem in 2000 came the first explicit Social Action Plan which created a work programme which was aimed at tackling fuel poverty.[37] By 2005, this had become a Social Action Strategy which, although still highlighting the importance of fuel poverty, now seemed to focus more on vulnerable customers.[38] The strategy focused on four areas of work:[39]

- The [companies] need to comply with regulatory obligations.
- Encouraging best practice among energy suppliers.
- Influencing the debate about the best measures to help tackle fuel poverty.
- How to best inform consumers about ways to lower energy bills.

Ofgem had committed itself to a review of the Social Action Strategy in 2010 and seems to have begun this review around 2011. At this point, one of the themes coming out from the Energy Supply Probe and the Retail Market Review[40] was that there were certain types of consumers who were less likely to benefit from a competitive market. Given this information, there seems to have been a widespread feeling that Ofgem should take a different, wider, approach to social issues. Ofgem consulted widely[41] on this issue over the course of 2011 and 2012 and developed a vulnerability strategy going beyond the groups explicitly mentioned in the legislation. Ofgem felt able to do this because although required to have regard to the interests of certain groups of consumers, the legislation added that regard may also be had to *other* types of consumers.

It was within this context that Ofgem became the first regulator in the UK to create a consumer vulnerability strategy which was updated at the end of 2019.[42]

[36] See: www.gov.uk/government/statistics/cold-weather-payment-statistics-2017-to-2018.
[37] Ofgem, 'Social Action Plan' (Ofgem, 2000).
[38] Ofgem Social Action Strategy' (Ofgem, 2005) para 1.8.
[39] ibid 1.
[40] Ofgem, Energy Supply Probe' (Ofgem, 2008); Ofgem, 'Retail Market Review' (Ofgem, 2012).
[41] Ofgem, 'Proposals for a new consumer vulnerability strategy' (Ofgem, 2012).
[42] Ofgem, 'Consumer Vulnerability Strategy' (Ofgem, 2013) and (Ofgem, 2019).

It is important to note that where the government wishes to take social measures which would have significant financial implications for consumers or regulated companies, this is a matter for government, not Ofgem and that this places limits on what can be done under a vulnerability strategy.[43] The strategy describes how the regulator defines and approaches the complex issue of vulnerability. Its objective is to protect and empower consumers in vulnerable situations in the energy market and to ensure equality of access to market benefits. Consumers should not be at a disadvantage because of their situation. Rather than relying on a list of assumed 'vulnerable groups', the strategy is based on a broad understanding of the range of contributory factors and these include the role of the market: Ofgem's approach was based on looking at risk factors that contribute to vulnerability which stem from personal circumstances as well as from the energy market itself: 'Consumer vulnerability also recognises that vulnerability can be complex, multidimensional and transitory. Vulnerability is not just about an individual; the market can cause or exacerbate vulnerability, and different consumers may be vulnerable in different situations'.[44] While recognising that any consumer can face detriment in a market, Ofgem's work under the strategy focuses on those consumers in vulnerable situations who are most in need of protection or support. Vulnerability is defined as when a consumer's personal circumstances and characteristics combine with aspects of the market to create situations where he or she is:

- significantly less able than a typical consumer to protect or represent his or her interests in the energy market;
- and/or significantly more likely than a typical consumer to suffer detriment, or that detriment is likely to be more substantial.[45]

The strategy recognises that the causes of vulnerability are complex and multidimensional, and that vulnerability can be transitory, ongoing or long-term.

Following on from the strategy, after a consultation process, Ofgem amended and reordered the standard supplier licence conditions. The first condition has the objective of ensuring that all domestic customers, including those in vulnerable situations, are treated fairly. An action in relation to a customer is not fair if it would give rise to a likelihood of detriment, unless the detriment is reasonable in all the relevant circumstances.[46] This is followed by several general standards of conduct which deal with suppliers' behaviour, the provisions of information, customer service arrangements and the treatment of customers in vulnerable situations. Regarding this final point, suppliers must seek to identify customers in a vulnerable situation in an effective and appropriate manner and apply the

[43] Social and Environmental Guidance (2011) para 22, available at: www.ofgem.gov.uk/ofgem-publications/74203/file37517-pdf.

[44] 'Consumer Vulnerability Strategy' (2013) 6.

[45] ibid 12.

[46] Electricity Supply Licence Standard Conditions 0.9.

standards of conduct which take into account the vulnerable situation a domestic customer may be in.[47]

A vulnerable situation is defined as meaning:

> the personal circumstances and characteristics of each Domestic Customer create a situation where he or she is:
>
> (a) significantly less able than a typical Domestic Customer to protect or represent his or her interests; and/or
>
> (b) significantly more likely than a typical Domestic Customer to suffer detriment or that detriment is likely to be more substantial.[48]

This definition of vulnerable circumstances focuses on the characteristics of the customer, with no mention of external factors, although they might be considered in terms of their relationship to the customer's characteristics. Little guidance is given as to what is expected in terms of policies and procedures of the suppliers with the focus being on outcomes. Evidence collected by the Commission for customers in vulnerable circumstances from 2018 to 2019 suggested that the picture across the energy industry was mixed and that there was an urgent need for improvement.[49] Ofgem has also expressed concerns that not all companies are taking sufficient steps to identify vulnerability and treat customers fairly and that smaller suppliers show a poor understanding of vulnerability.[50]

V. Complaints against Energy Companies

The basic legal framework is found in the Consumers, Estate Agents and Redress Act 2007 (CEAR) which allows the Secretary of State to make regulations requiring energy providers to be members of an external redress scheme which is approved by Ofgem. Further regulations provide that energy companies must have a company complaints procedure in place which meets certain standards. Under these provisions Ofgem approved Ombudsman Services: Energy (OS:E) in 2008 to be the provider of an external redress scheme in the energy sector and it became a recognised alternative dispute resolution (ADR) entity under the ADR Directive.[51] CEAR also created a special set of arrangements for vulnerable consumers, defined broadly, and complaints about disconnection. Handling of these cases has become the responsibility of the Extra Help Unit, which is part of Citizens Advice and is based in Scotland, although its remit is UK wide.

The relevant regulations set out that providers must have a complaint handling procedure and certain general requirements for such procedures.[52] The regulations

[47] ibid 0.3.d.
[48] ibid 0.9.
[49] Commission for Customers in Vulnerable Circumstance, *Final Report* (Energy UK, 2019).
[50] 'Consumer Vulnerability Strategy' (2019) 40–42.
[51] Directive 2013/11/EU on alternative dispute resolution for consumer disputes [2013] OJ L165/63.
[52] Gas and Electricity (Consumer Complaint Handling Regulations) 2008, SI 2008/1898.

provide that complaint handling must be adequately resourced and that information about complaint handling procedures should be provided to consumers. The procedure must be accessible either orally or in writing, which includes email. The consumer should be informed of the process and timescale and there must be an internal review stage. Consumers should also be given information about independent help, advice and information as well as being signposted to the redress scheme. There are also obligations on the suppliers to record information in relation to complaints.

A. Complaints and Consumers in Vulnerable Circumstances

All of this applies to the generality of complaints. The only specific reference to vulnerability in the regulations is to complaints made under sections 12 and 13 CEAR. These two sections apply to complaints made by or on behalf of a vulnerable person or where the complaint is in relation to the disconnection of an energy supply. The power to investigate such complaints is vested in Citizens Advice and the day-to-day work is handled by a body called the Extra Help Unit (EHU), based in Glasgow and run by Citizens Advice Scotland, although its remit is UK wide.[53] The Act deliberately does not provide a definition of vulnerability[54] but says instead that a consumer is vulnerable if Citizens Advice is satisfied that it would not be reasonable for the person to pursue that complaint on their own behalf.[55] The explanatory notes to the bill said:

> This might apply to persons who are unable to pursue a complaint by reason of a mental or physical disability, a lack of basic skills (such as literacy) or due to their personal circumstances (such as a recent bereavement).[56]

The EHU takes a very broad approach to vulnerability and that, in practice this is not challenged by suppliers.

If Citizens Advice thinks that it is appropriate to do so, it can either give advice to the complainant or make representations on their behalf to the company complained against. The regulations say that if a reference is made by the EHU to a supplier, the supplier must take such additional steps as it considers necessary or appropriate with a view to assisting the vulnerable consumer and resolving the complaint in an appropriate and prompt manner. Unlike OS:E, the EHU will advocate on behalf of the consumer, although they cannot take any decision binding on the company.

[53] This role was originally carried out by Consumer Focus, renamed Consumer Futures (2013) and transferred to Citizens Advice 2014.

[54] See HL Deb 30 January 2007, vol 689, col 151 (Lord Truscott).

[55] Consumers, Estate Agents and Redress Act 2007, s 12(2).

[56] Consumers, Estate Agents and Redress Act 2007, Explanatory Notes to s 12, available at: www.legislation.gov.uk/ukpga/2007/17/notes/contents.

Table 13.1 below details the amount of individual complaints handled by the EHU on a yearly basis showing a steady increase since 2014. Note that it is not possible for an individual consumer to have direct access to the EHU; they must be referred to it, typically from Citizens Advice.

Table 13.1 EHU complaints

Year	Complaints
2018–19	8,755
2017–18	7,771
2016–17	6,943
2015–16	8,397
2014–15	7,405
2013–14	4,759
2012–13	4,561
2011–12	3,618
2010–11	4,465
2009–10	5,468

Source: EHU.

B. Company Complaint Handling

Although there is a framework in place for complaint handling, there have been significant concerns over the years about how effective energy suppliers are in handling consumer complaints. This can be illustrated in several ways. First, the absolute number of complaints to companies is very high, although it does appear to have been falling. To give an example, in 2019 the six largest energy companies recorded around 2.4 million complaints.[57]

Second, Ofgem's regular research into company complaint handling consistently shows a high level of dissatisfaction with the companies' efforts. The most recent research found that complainants were more likely to be dissatisfied than satisfied with the handling of their complaint (57 per cent of domestic consumers were dissatisfied) and satisfaction levels had risen only slightly from 2016 (from 27 per cent to 32 per cent).[58] This seems to have been driven by the failure of staff

[57] Source: Company complaints data via Ofgem website: www.ofgem.gov.uk/consumers/energy-supplier-comparison-data/compare-supplier-performance-complaints. This includes SSE figures for 2018–19 and Npower only reported numbers of complaints not resolved on the same day; a smaller number than total complaints.

[58] Ofgem, 'Consumer Satisfaction with Energy Supplier Complaint Handling 2018' (Ofgem, 2018) 19.

to taking ownership of a complaint and acting proactively to resolve it, as well as contributing to the view that resolution timescales are too long and that staff do not get back to the complainant as promised.[59] These findings are in line with previous research, starting from 2010 which shows that a majority of customers, with the exception of the 2012 survey, are dissatisfied with the handling of their complaint by the energy company. The research done on company complaint handling has also found what it calls a 'resolution gap', that is cases where the company records the complaint as resolved, but the complainant does not regard it as resolved. This has consistently been the case for about 40 per cent of the people surveyed.[60] Despite this dissatisfaction, research commissioned by Ofgem has found that only around 5 per cent of consumers escalate their complaint to OS:E.[61]

Third, between 2010 and mid-2017, there were 10 cases where Ofgem took enforcement action for a breach of licence conditions against energy suppliers in relation to complaint handling issues.[62] Subsequent to this, as a result of the 2018 complaints survey Ofgem entered into compliance engagement with three energy suppliers and asked seven others to submit plans to improve how they deal with complaints – this action covered all bar one of the largest six energy suppliers and a number of the medium-sized ones.[63] There were also two cases of small suppliers not meeting their obligations under the complaint handling regulations (both of which have since ceased trading). Ofgem also has, since September 2018 at least, a compliance case open against Scottish Power in relation to its complaint handling procedures and stated, in March 2020 that it was 'disappointed with the lack of progress' by Scottish Power.[64]

The Scottish Power case illustrates that there are significant differences in complaint handling between individual companies. Scottish Power is an interesting case, as problems with its complaint handling systems arose first around 2014 when it changed its billing system. Since that time its performance has lagged significantly behind the other large six energy suppliers whether on the Citizens Advice complaints handling performance scorecard,[65] Ofgem statistics on resolution of complaints[66] or OS:E's statistics on the number of cases it receives

[59] ibid 8.

[60] ibid 39.

[61] GfK, 'Complaints to Ombudsman Services: Energy' (Ofgem, 2013), available at: www.ofgem.gov.uk/sites/default/files/docs/2013/12/ofgem_gfk_complaints_to_ombudsman_services_energy_report_2013_0.pdf.

[62] See: www.ofgem.gov.uk/investigations/investigations-and-enforcement-data.

[63] Ofgem, 'Retail Supplier Compliance and Enforcement Report 2019' (Ofgem, 2019) 10.

[64] See: www.ofgem.gov.uk/publications-and-updates/ofgem-takes-compliance-action-over-scottish power-s-complaints-handling.

[65] This covers complaints to CA, the EHU and ES:O, available at: www.citizensadvice.org.uk/Global/CitizensAdvice/Energy/Energy%20Consultation%20responses/Domestic%20complaints%20handling%20performance%20(Updated%20January%202020)%20(1).pdf.

[66] See: www.ofgem.gov.uk/consumers/energy-supplier-comparison-data/compare-supplier-performance-complaints.

from Scottish Power.[67] To be fair, it does not seem to receive more complaints per 100,000 customers than some of the other largest energy companies, but it seems to find it more difficult to resolve them. Nevertheless, this is a problem that was identified back in 2014 and limited progress appears to have been made.

As the energy market has become more competitive and a greater number of smaller suppliers have entered, it has become evident that there is a wider range of performance in complaint handling. Sometimes this may be indicative of a failing company, as in the case of Extra Energy, which had almost 10 times the number of complaints per 100,000 customers submitted to OS:E in 2018 as compared with the sector average. According to Ofgem data, large and medium suppliers have a range of complaints per 100,000 customers, from 160 to 2,341. At the other extreme, there are small suppliers with 11,550 (Nabuh Energy); 4,000 (Yorkshire Energy); and 4,660 (Green Star Energy) per 100,000 customers. It is also notable that OS:E have stated around 40 per cent of their complaints are from smaller suppliers.[68]

One response is to say that this is what would be expected in a competitive market, where there are numerous suppliers offering differing price/quality combinations. This seems too sanguine. First, the energy market is one where a homogeneous service is offered, with little scope for variations of quality. In a competitive market, less dispersion of the offerings would perhaps be expected. Second, it is not clear how competitive this market is currently, given the existence of tariff caps and this allows for the variation observed.

Regardless of which interpretation is correct, regulatory policy is to achieve some minimum standard of complaint handling. The evidence discussed above suggest that, if the policy is aimed at improving company complaint handling, it has failed. Perhaps the starkest illustration is Ofgem's research on customer satisfaction with company complaint handling, summarised in Table 13.2 below. This shows a consistent failure, over more than a decade, of energy companies providing what consumers regard as satisfactory complaint handling and the situation may be worse with smaller companies which are taking an increasing share of the market.

Table 13.2 Satisfaction with company complaint handling – domestic consumer

	2010	2012	2014	2016	2018
Very or quite satisfied (%)	27	40	30	28	32
Neither (%)	15	12	13	12	11
Quite or very dissatisfied (%)	56	47	57	60	57

Source: Ofgem Research on company complaint handling.

[67] See: www.ombudsman-services.org/about-us/annual-reports/complaints-data/energy-complaints-data.

[68] See: www.ombudsman-services.org/news/energy-ombudsman-statement-on-ofgems-complaints-survey.

C. The Role of Ombudsman Services: Energy

When energy companies are unable to resolve complaints, customers have the option of taking their complaint to OS:E. OS:E is part of a wider group, Ombudsman Services, which was founded in 2002 and is a not-for-profit company, limited by guarantee which provides independent dispute resolution services to several sectors, such as communications. At the end of 2018 the wider company had 568 employees, so it is a sizeable operation.

OS:E is a service which is free to use for consumers who may, however, only access it after the energy company has had a chance to resolve the complaint within eight weeks. It is a remote service, available by telephone and email. The decisions that it takes are binding on its company members but not on the consumer and it may make financial awards. Since it launched a new website in 2018, limited information is available about its procedures. It seems to operate some version of a three-stage process. There seems to be a first stage where it is decided whether or not the complaint is within the jurisdiction of OS:E. The second stage involves some level of what has been called informal resolution, possibly without investigation. As of 2014, this seemed to involve around 50 per cent of the cases.[69] The third stage involves a more formal decision. The entire process seems to take about a month.[70] It is accredited under the ADR Directive by Ofgem, which is the competent authority for this purpose and has entered into a Memorandum of Understanding (MoU) with Ofgem.[71]

Tables 13.4 and 13.5 below gives some very basic information on complaint handling by OS:E.[72] It is important to understand that not all contacts are necessarily complaints but that this figure will also include enquiries and that a significant proportion (around 50 per cent) of such enquiries may relate to matters outside the jurisdiction of OS:E or are discontinued. The main reasons for this are either that the consumer has not contacted the energy company before contacting OS:E; that the consumer has failed to provide sufficient information or is outside the time limits.

There is also a significant drop-out rate as regards complaints to the energy companies when looking at complaints which go to OS:E. Ofgem research in 2013 found that only 5 per cent of complainants had escalated their complaint to OS:E.[73] The research identified six reasons why complaints were not escalated, which included lack of awareness of OS:E; poor experience with companies' handling

[69] See M Doyle, V Bondy and C Hirst, 'The Use of Informal Resolution Approaches by Ombudsmen in the UK and Ireland: A Mapping Study' (Ombudsman Research, 2014), available at: ombudsmanresearch.files.wordpress.com/2014/10/the-use-of-informal-resolution-approaches-by-ombudsmen-in-the-uk-and-ireland-a-mapping-study-1.pdf.

[70] The ADR Entity reports from 2016–19 report an average of 33.75 days.

[71] See: www.ofgem.gov.uk/system/files/docs/2017/07/memorandum_of_understanding_-_between_ofgem_ombudsman_-_signed_copy_da.pdf.

[72] There is limited information available publicly about the performance of OS:E.

[73] GfK, 'Complaints to Ombudsman Services Energy' (n 61).

of the complaint; and lack of information provided by the companies. On this last point, the most recent research done for Ofgem concluded that complainants were given very little information about third-party solutions and alternative redress.[74] Another way of thinking about this issue is in Table 13.3 below, which shows the number of complaints to four large energy companies in 2019, the number of complaints resolved and those resolved within eight weeks, after which a complainant may go to OS:E The difference between the number of complaints and those two categories gives an indication of the number of complaints eligible for OS:E, between around 167,000 and 213,000. These numbers are an underestimate because two of the largest six suppliers have been excluded and the six largest suppliers only have a combined market share of around 70 per cent.

Table 13.3 Energy company complaints received and resolution

Complaints received	Complaints resolved	Complaints resolved within 8 weeks
2,116,872	1,949,289	1,903,169

Source: Company complaints data 2019. Four companies are used: British Gas, E.ON, Scottish Power and SSE. Npower was excluded because it does not publish the data and EDF was excluded because data was only available for 3 of the 4 quarters

It is also evident from the table that there was a significant rise in complaints to OS:E in 2014 which appears to have been driven by Scottish Power and Npower's failure to implement a new billing system, although these numbers have not dropped subsequently.[75]

Table 13.4 Complaints to Ombudsman Services: Energy

Year	Contacts	Number of complaints resolved
2019		54,104
2018	108,349	45,667
2017	88,423	48,737
2016	88,255	41,622
April–December 2015	89,569	39,281
2014–15	140,092	46,632
2013–14	87,542	15,031
2012–13	47,477	8,768
2011–12	74,505	≈ 6,600

Source: OS:E Annual Reports.

[74] Quadrangle, 'Customer satisfaction with energy supplier complaints handling 2018' (Ofgem, 2018) 35, available at: www.ofgem.gov.uk/system/files/docs/2018/09/quadrangle_ofgemchs2018_researchreport.pdf.

[75] See Ofgem, 'Notice of decision to impose final penalty on Npower …' (Ofgem, 2016); and Ofgem, 'Notice of decision to impose final penalty on Scottish Power …' (Ofgem, 2016).

Table 13.5 Complaints outside OS:E jurisdiction

	2016	2017	2018	2019
Disputes received	103,859	83,608	97,996	114,311
Within jurisdiction	56,064	45,277	52,198	59,694
OS:E refused	20,227	17,028	21,865	31,342
Because no contact with company (%)	68	89	97	98
Discontinued	27,568	21,310	23,894	23,106
Not within rules (%)	11	19	26	13
Insufficient information (%)	88	78	67	63
Out of time (%)	33	38	38	26

Source: OS:E ADR Entity Reports: www.ombudsman-services.org/about-us/annual-reports/alternative-dispute-reso23/04/20) Numbers are not consistent with those above because of different reporting periods.

The vast majority of cases are complaints about billing.

If a case is accepted by OS:E, then consumers have a very high success rate, seen below in Table 13.6. OS:E has four categories of outcome: Upheld, not upheld, settled and maintained. Upheld and not upheld are self-explanatory. Settled cases are where an agreement is reached between the consumer and the company after the complaint came to OS:E but before the outcome of an investigation. Maintained cases are where the complaint was justified but the company had taken fair and reasonable action to resolve the issue. Most of the successful cases involve some level of financial compensation, which on average seems to be in the region of £100. OS:E does not publish any decisions.

Table 13.6 OS:E outcomes of case – %

	2016	2017	2018
Upheld	51	63	64
Not upheld	7	8	6
Settled	12	8	11
Maintained	30	21	19

Source: OS:E Annual reports.

There is limited information available about the types of people who use OS:E. Creutzfeldt's work, which dates back to 2014, suggests that people using OS:E are largely male, highly educated and either employed or retired.[76] OS:E's customer satisfaction survey suggests that its users are largely happy with the service with

[76] N Creutzfeldt, Trust in alternative dispute resolution case study: Ombudsman Services: Energy' 15–16, available at: www.law.ox.ac.uk/sites/files/oxlaw/oxford_report_os-e.pdf.

customer satisfaction at 77 per cent in 2018.[77] This is consistent with Creutzfeldt's findings, although later work by Money Saving Expert offered a more mixed picture, although there are methodological concerns with the latter work.[78]

Finally, as well as handling individual complaints, OS:E is supposed to have some role in improving standards in the energy industry, either through identifying systemic issues with individual companies or issues across the industry. In the MoU, it is stated that OS:E will bring to Ofgem's attention any trends or issues of concern that it considers are arising within the industry. It will also alert Ofgem to any problems with individual companies that it has been unable to resolve.[79] Since 2017, OS:E has been part of a tripartite group with Ofgem and Citizens Advice which involves bi-monthly meetings with the aim of, among other things, identifying emerging trends.[80] This is a relatively new role for OS:E which has arisen in part as a response to a critical report commissioned by Ofgem which found that although OS:E agreed it had a wider role than just complaint handling, it had not focused on the wider role, was unsure about it and had limited systems and processes to support it.[81]

There is, however, very limited information available on how OS:E works on wider issues. There is no publicly available documentation for the tripartite working group. As part of its obligation as a recognised ADR entity, OS:E is required as part of its annual report to identify systemic or significant problems and make recommendations as to how these might be solved in the future. These reports are very brief and serve only as a high-level identification of the issues. There is no report on whether the issues identified have been addressed. Similarly, OS:E's own annual reports mention issues on a high-level basis but with little supporting information and no details of, for example, the companies concerned.

The performance of OS:E is best described as a mixed bag. There is clearly a problem about access to it from the companies as it looks as if a significant number of eligible complaints do not reach it. There are also a large number of enquiries that are premature, or which fail because consumers have not supplied sufficient information. The consumers who enter the system seem not to be representative of the population as a whole. Once, however, a consumer successfully enters the system, they are likely to obtain some redress and the best evidence suggests a high level of satisfaction. In terms of helping to address systemic issues, it is difficult to find publicly available evidence as to OS:E's contribution. In general, there is very limited publicly available information about OS:E's workings.

[77] OS:E, *Annual Report 2018* (OS:E, 2018) 4.

[78] N Creutzfeldt, Trust in alternative dispute resolution case study: Ombudsman Services: Energy', MoneySavingExpert *Sharper teeth: The consumer need for Ombudsman Reform* (MoneySavingExpert, 2017).

[79] MoU, para 7.2.

[80] See: www.ofgem.gov.uk/publications-and-updates/tripartite-group-engagement-diagram.

[81] Lucerna Partners, *Review of Ombudsman Services: Energy* (Ofgem, 2015), available at: www.ofgem.gov.uk/sites/default/files/docs/2015/09/review_of_ombudsman_services_energy_2.pdf. See also, OS:E, 'Review of the OS response to Lucerna Report' (OS:E, 2016), available at: www.ombudsman-services.org/about-us/annual-reports.

D. What can be Done?

The evidence discussed above indicates that the energy suppliers' complaint handling procedures do not work well for consumers. Ofgem's research, now extending to a decade's worth of work, consistently shows what can be described, at best, as indifferent procedures which leave most consumers dissatisfied. Furthermore, Ofgem recognises this problem because it has taken significant levels of enforcement action against the suppliers over the same time frame. This matters because relatively few cases are escalated from the companies to OS:E. There is no indication that there will be any significant change.

OS:E is part of the problem. It is fair to say that the majority of the evidence suggests that once consumers arrive at OS:E they feel that they are well and fairly treated and are likely to obtain redress. It also seems fair to say that those who do access OS:E are better educated, better-off, older and male, which makes them not representative of the general population. OS:E has been identified by Ofgem research as being weak at identifying systemic issues in the industry or within individual companies although attempts have been made to address this. There is also an unclear relationship with the enforcement process. There has been some effort to improve performance here, but little public evidence of that.

There is therefore an access to justice problem here. There is a mismatch between consumer expectations and what the companies are delivering, as indicated by the number of complaints. The complaints process does not, however, resolve these issues, leaving the majority of consumer dissatisfied with their experience. Ofgem has been concerned with this issue for at least a decade, but there are few signs of progress and as the market has become more competitive, the issue seems to be degenerating as smaller companies are generating significant numbers of complaints to OS:E.

VI. Conclusion

Great Britain has a centralised system of energy regulation. There are structures and policies, for example on fuel poverty and vulnerability, in place to address access to energy justice issues and there appears to be some evidence that they are working, albeit imperfectly. If this interpretation is accepted, then it follows that reform should be incremental. An alternative argument is that the technocratic, centralised system has not addressed access to energy justice issues in this sector. A better alternative would be a decentralised, populist system with greater scope for those affected to have a voice in decision-making as well as a move away from market mechanisms. Underpinning this argument is a further argument about changes to the energy system in pursuit of a major policy goal of decarbonisation.

INDEX

Lightning Source UK Ltd.
Milton Keynes UK
UKHW020107101121
393688UK00003B/160

9 781509 939435